"Thomas Lickona has achieved the rare feat of combining good scholarship with helpful, practical applications. All teachers and parents will find this book exceedingly useful."
—Sidney Callahan, Ph.D.,
Professor of Psychology, Mercy College, and author of *In Good Conscience: Reason and Emotion in Moral Decision Making*

"Lickona's book provides so many examples and helpful teaching strategies that it is bound to rekindle hope and commitment."
—Lisa Kuhmerker, Ph.D.,
Publisher/Editor of *Moral Education Forum* and author of *The Kohlberg Legacy for the Helping Professions*

"*Educating for Character* is a work of scholarship and of vision . . . an enormously important resource for educators everywhere."
—Dr. Eric Schaps,
President, Developmental Studies Center

"A moral society doesn't just happen. It takes work and effort by parents, educators, church leaders, and community agencies. *Educating for Character* will be a unique resource for all those who try to carry out this awesome responsibility."
—Sister Catherine McNamee, C.S.J.,
President, National Catholic Education Association

"Professor Lickona shows teachers how to create the kind of responsibility and caring classroom community within which both academic achievement and moral development will flourish."
—Drs. Nan and Ted Graves,
Executive Editors, *Cooperative Learning Magazine*

"An extraordinarily important and useful book. It not only makes a compelling case for revitalizing education's role as a developer of character, it provides a solid means of accomplishing the task."
—Michael Josephson,
President, The Joseph and Edna Josephson Institute of Ethics

"A powerful statement of the need for values education in the nation's schools, and a detailed roadmap of how to go about teaching moral values."
—The Journal of Moral Education

ALSO BY THOMAS LICKONA:
Raising Good Children

Educating
for
Character

HOW OUR SCHOOLS CAN TEACH
RESPECT AND RESPONSIBILITY

Thomas Lickona

BANTAM BOOKS

NEW YORK · TORONTO · LONDON · SYDNEY · AUCKLAND

EDUCATING FOR CHARACTER:
HOW OUR SCHOOLS CAN TEACH
RESPECT AND RESPONSIBILITY
A Bantam Book
PUBLISHING HISTORY
Bantam hardcover edition published November 1991
Bantam trade paperback edition/October 1992

Bantam Books are published by Bantam Books, a division of Bantam Doubleday Dell Publishing Group, Inc. Its trademark, consisting of the words "Bantam Books" and the portrayal of a rooster, is Registered in U.S. Patent and Trademark Office and in other countries. Marca Registrada. Bantam Books, 1540 Broadway, New York, New York 10036.

PRINTED IN THE UNITED STATES OF AMERICA

BVG 0 9 8 7 6 5 4

for God

Acknowledgments

I would like to express heartfelt thanks:

To all the teachers I have been privileged to learn from during the past 20 years—teachers in my graduate courses, teachers whose classrooms I've observed, teachers I've interviewed—whose practical wisdom and examples of values education fill the pages of this book.

To my wife Judith for being a true partner on this book—for reading every line of every draft and serving as my first editor; for dozens of suggestions that improved the shape and substance of chapters; for a continuing conversation about the problems children face today and what they need from adults to grow into good people; and for shoring up my faith when discouragement was at the door.

To my father and mother, Edward and Winifred Lickona, and to my father-in-law Tom Barker, for their steadfast love and encouragement; to Sweetheart, who I know helps me still; and to my sons Mark and Matthew, for the love and laughter they bring to my life and for all the times they asked, "How's the book going, Dad?"

To Toni Burbank, my editor at Bantam, for many things: her commitment to the subject of the book; her unerring ability to pinpoint where a change was needed in content, length, or handling of material; her suggestion of the book's title; and her taking every possible step—from guidance in the early stages to selection of the copy editor—to enhance the appeal of the book and help it reach its intended audience. I feel blessed to have an editor with her sensitivity, skill, and caring.

To Robin Straus, my agent, for handling with her consummate professionalism all the steps from submitting the book proposal to placing pre-publication excerpts; for her wonderful, uplifting letters along the way; and for patience when progress was slow.

To William D. Drennan and Nancy Scott, Bantam's copy editors for the book, for their sensitive suggestions for improving the manuscript; to Charlie Trantino for her conscientious work on the index; and to Linda Gross at Bantam, for her hard work on the many details involved in bringing the book to completion.

To the college where I teach, the State University of New York at Cortland, for supporting my research with a 1985 fall sabbatical that enabled me to visit U.S. and Canadian schools known for their programs in values education.

To Eric Schaps and his Developmental Studies Center for generously subsidizing the travel involved in my sabbatical research; to Marilyn Watson, Jacques Benninga, Ed Wynne, Howard Radest, Mary Ellen Flaherty, and Steve Barrs for helping to arrange school visits and taking me into their homes during my sabbatical travels; and to all the teachers, administrators, parents, and students at the schools I visited for assisting me in learning about their schools' efforts to teach good values.

To Suzanne Brisk and Tina Metzcus for helpful materials on sex education, and Ted Graves for suggestions on Chapters 10 and 15.

To all the people who have kept me in their prayers, especially my dear neighbor Elizabeth Dwyer.

In his book *The Road Less Traveled,* psychiatrist Scott Peck writes about "amazing grace"—all the times in our lives when we feel helped in ways that do not seem attributable to natural causes. For religious believers, such graced moments are experienced as the loving action of a God who holds each of us in His awareness. As a personal example, Peck tells of unexpectedly receiving, from a person who previously had been quite unfriendly to him, the kind offer of a book that provided the ideal resolution of a problem Peck was just then struggling with in his writing. I have often had the same sort of experience as I worked on this book. Instances, for example, when exactly the right piece of information or conversation came my way, without my seeking it, as I began to work on a particular section of the manuscript.

For me, such moments call to mind a statement by St. Thomas Aquinas: All truth comes from the Holy Spirit. For the errors in this book, I take responsibility. For whatever truth it contains, I would like to thank the source.

Tom Lickona
Cortland, New York
April, 1991

Note to the Reader

There is a story that Haim Ginott used to tell about a teacher who was honored by her community as the "teacher of the year." The day after receiving this award, on the way home from school, she spied two boys writing in the wet cement in front of her house. As she drew closer, she saw that they were writing uncomplimentary inscriptions about her. So she went up to the boys and beat them up.

The next morning, a shocked school principal summoned the teacher to his office. "Mrs. Smith," he said, "I hardly know where to begin. You, the teacher of the year, a person to whom we all look as a model, someone who *loves* children, have just gone and beaten two of them up!"

Mrs. Smith looked down, paused, and said, "Well, I love them in the abstract but not in the concrete."

Good education is easier to espouse in the abstract than to provide in the concrete. So in writing this book, which I hope will be a practical resource, I have tried to be as concrete as possible.

Part 1 of the book establishes the theoretical framework for values education: why schools should do it, the values schools may legitimately teach in a democratic society, and the sort of character they ought to try to develop around those values. Parts Two and Three of the book describe practice—how to implement a comprehensive, twelve-component approach to values education. In illustrating each of the twelve components, I tell stories of what good teachers and schools are doing all across the United States and Canada to help students become honest, caring, responsible people.

I feel a great debt to the educators who are the source of these examples of good practice. Whenever possible, I have acknowledged teachers, administrators, and schools by name. I am no less grateful to those persons who remain anonymous because I did not have their names.

Sometimes the text will tell you where to get more information about a particular values education program or practice. Where the text doesn't provide that information, a footnote will. Please note, however, that a particular classroom or school may have changed since the time I learned of its work, and that a given teacher, principal, or program may no longer be there.

Finally, a word about terminology. Throughout the book, I have used "values education" and "moral education" interchangeably—and both as shorthand for "moral values education." The book's focus is not values in general (which include such things as one's choice of career) but rather *moral* values such as respect and responsibility—those values that are a matter of moral obligation, not mere preference, and around which good character is formed.

Contents

PART ONE

Educating for Values and Character

1. The Case for Values Education   3
2. Educating for Character—and Why Schools Need Help
   from Home   23
3. What Values Should Schools Teach?   37
4. What Is Good Character?   49

PART TWO

Classroom Strategies for Teaching Respect and Responsibility

Introduction to Parts Two and Three:
Teaching Respect and Responsibility: The Big Ideas   67

5. The Teacher as Caregiver, Model, and Mentor   71
6. Creating a Moral Community in the Classroom   89
7. Moral Discipline   109
8. Creating a Democratic Classroom Environment:
   The Class Meeting   135
9. Teaching Values Through the Curriculum   161
10. Cooperative Learning   185

11. The Conscience of Craft   208
12. Encouraging Moral Reflection   228
13. Raising the Level of Moral Discussion   249
14. Teaching Controversial Issues   268
15. Teaching Children to Solve Conflicts   286

PART THREE

Schoolwide Strategies for Teaching Respect and Responsibility

16. Caring Beyond the Classroom   303
17. Creating a Positive Moral Culture in the School   323
18. Sex Education   348
19. Drugs and Alcohol   375
20. Schools, Parents, and Communities Working Together 395

Appendix A: Getting Started and Maintaining
Momentum   421

Notes   425

Index   457

It was the deep belief of the founders that the republic could succeed only with virtuous citizens. Only if there was a moral law within would citizens be able to maintain a free government.

—ROBERT BELLAH, Bicentennial
Lectures, Cornell University

As Aristotle taught, people do not naturally or spontaneously grow up to be morally excellent or practically wise. They become so, if at all, only as the result of a lifelong personal and community effort.

—JON MOLINE, "Classical Ideas
About Moral Education," in
*Character Policy: An Emerging
Issue*

PART ONE

EDUCATING FOR VALUES AND CHARACTER

CHAPTER 1

The Case for Values Education

> To *educate a person in mind and not in morals is to educate a menace to society.*
>
> —THEODORE ROOSEVELT

> *The pendulum is swinging back from the romantic idea that all societal values are oppressive. But educators went along with all this craziness, so we've ended up with students who are ethically illiterate.*[1]
>
> —BILL HONIG, Superintendent of Public Instruction, California

S hould the schools teach values?

Just a few years ago, if you put that question to a group of people, it was sure to start an argument. If anyone said yes, schools should teach children values, somebody else would immediately retort, "*Whose values?*" In a society where people held different values, it seemed impossible to get agreement on which ones should be taught in our public schools. Pluralism produced paralysis; schools for the most part ended up trying to stay officially neutral on the subject of values.

With remarkable swiftness, that has changed. Escalating moral problems in society—ranging from greed and dishonesty to violent crime to self-destructive behaviors such as drug abuse and suicide—are bringing about a new consensus. Now, from all across the country, from private citizens and public organizations, from liberals and conservatives alike, comes a summons to the schools: Take up the role of moral teachers of our children.

Of all the moral problems that have fueled this concern, none has been more disturbing than rising youth violence. From 1978 to 1988, according to FBI statistics, rape arrests for 13- and 14-year-old males nearly doubled.[2] Over a 20-year period (1968 to 1988), there was a 53 percent increase in all violent crime—murder, rape, robbery, and assault—for males and females seventeen or under.[3] Moreover, juvenile crimes of violence, often carried out by kid-next-door teenagers, have of late combined new lows in brutality with a seeming total lack of conscience or remorse.

- In Brooklyn, three teenage boys, described by neighbors as "nice kids," were arrested for dousing sleeping homeless men with gasoline and setting fire to them. As the youths were booked at the police station, one of them said, "We just like to harass the bums."[4]

- Five teenagers in affluent Glen Ridge, New Jersey—including two brothers who were cocaptains of the high school football team—were arrested and charged with sexually assaulting a 17-year-old mentally retarded girl in the basement of the brothers' home. Eight other teenagers watched.[5]

There is today a widespread, deeply unsettling sense that children are changing—in ways that tell us much about ourselves as a society. And these changes are reflected not just in the violent extremes of teenage behavior but in the everyday speech and actions of younger children as well. In New Orleans, a boy in first grade shaves chalk and passes it around the classroom, pretending it is cocaine.[6] In a small-town school in upstate New York, a first-grade boy leans over and asks the girl in the next row, "Are you a virgin?" A *Newsweek* story titled "So Long Wonder Years" reports the findings of a new Carnegie Corporation study: One quarter of all junior high school students are involved in some *combination* of smoking, drinking, drug use, and sex; fully half are involved in at least one of these activities.[7]

Children with the most glaring deficiencies in moral values almost always come, their teachers say, from troubled families. Indeed, poor parenting looms as one of the major reasons why schools now feel compelled to get involved in values education. Another part of the problem is the mass media and the prominent place it occupies in the lives of children. The typical elementary school child spends 30 hours a week in front of the television set. By age 16, the average child will have witnessed an estimated 200,000 acts of violence[8] and by age 18, approximately 40,000 sexually titillating scenes.[9] Episodes of sexualized violence are increasingly common.

Not surprisingly, many young people growing up in this kind of media culture are stunted in their moral judgment. Large numbers, for example, don't even know that rape is wrong. In a 1988 survey conducted by the Rhode Island Rape Crisis Center, 1,700 sixth- to ninth-graders were asked, "Is it acceptable for a man to force a woman to have sex if he has spent money on her?" A total of 24 percent of the boys and 16 percent of the girls in grades seven through nine said yes. When asked, "Is it acceptable for a man to force a woman to have sex if they have been dating for more than six months?," 65 percent of the boys said yes. So did 47 percent of the girls.[10]

Simultaneously, a wave of greed and materialism threatens to engulf us. Money increasingly drives our society and shapes the values and goals of our youth. Making money becomes the justification for breaking rules. In a recent survey, two thirds of U.S. high school seniors said they would lie to achieve a business objective.[11]

The most basic kinds of moral knowledge, moreover, seem to be disappearing from our common culture. Baltimore school official James Sarnecki says that he used to bring up the Golden Rule when he talked to students about a discipline problem. But he finally decided to drop the reference when students started to respond with blank stares.[12] Educators began to speak of the "ethical illiteracy" they saw among young people.

To be sure, even in the face of problems like these, considerable controversy still surrounds the proposition that schools should teach morality. Values education is the hottest topic in education today. Some groups, on both the political right and left, are deeply suspicious about any kind of values teaching in the schools. But beneath the battles is a steadily growing conviction: Schools cannot be ethical bystanders at a time when our society is in deep moral trouble. Rather, schools must do what they can to contribute to the character of the young and the moral health of the nation.

SMART AND GOOD: THE TWO GREAT GOALS OF EDUCATION

Moral education is not a new idea. It is, in fact, as old as education itself. Down through history, in countries all over the world, education has had two great goals: to help young people become smart and to help them become good.

We know that smart and good are not the same. Not long ago, in an upstate New York community, four suburban teenagers—three girls and a boy—broke into their high school at night, emptied several jugs of gasoline, and ignited a fire that did $500,000 worth of damage before it was brought under control. The oldest member of the group was an honor student; the other three were described in press reports as "bright students." The only discernible motive was that one member of the group was upset because he had missed a French class and had been disciplined.

Realizing that smart and good are not the same, wise societies since the time of Plato have made moral education a deliberate aim of schooling. They have educated for character as well as intellect, decency as well as literacy, virtue as well as knowledge. They have tried to form citizens who will use their intelligence to benefit others as well as themselves, who will try to build a better world.

At the beginning of our country, we had this ancient wisdom about the purposes of schooling. Let's look at those beginnings, at the forces that drove moral education out of the schools, and at those that are bringing it back.

EDUCATION FOR VIRTUE: THE FOUNDATION OF DEMOCRACY

Moral education, the founders of our democracy asserted, is essential for the success of a democratic society.

Their reasoning went like this: Democracy is government by the people; the people themselves are responsible for ensuring a free and just society. That means the people must, at least in some minimal sense, be good. They must understand and be committed to the moral foundations of democracy: respect for the rights of individuals, regard for law, voluntary participation in public life, and concern for the common good. Loyalty to these democratic virtues, Thomas Jefferson argued, must be instilled at an early age.

Energized by that belief, schools in the early days of the republic tackled character education head on. Through discipline, the teacher's good example, and the curriculum, schools sought to instruct children in the virtues of patriotism, hard work, honesty, thriftiness, altruism, and courage.

When children practiced their reading, for example, they typically did so through *McGuffey Reader* tales of heroism and virtue. The tales might seem corny to modern readers, but they captured the imagination of an earlier age. By 1919 the *McGuffey Reader* had the largest circulation of any book in the world next to the Bible. Better than anything else, *McGuffey Reader* stories expressed the confidence of an age that knew what it thought about virtue and how to go about instilling it in children.

That same age, of course, was far from perfectly virtuous. Economic exploitation and racial, ethnic, and sexual discrimination were well-entrenched parts of society—and issues not likely to be addressed in the *McGuffey Reader*. But moral education, however limited, was very much a part of the public school agenda.

WHY MORAL EDUCATION DECLINED

With time, the confident consensus supporting old-fashioned character education began to crumble. It did so under the hammer blows of several powerful forces. Darwinism said that biological life was the product of evolution; that view led people to see other things, including morality, as evolving rather than fixed and certain.[13] Einstein's theory of relativity, though intended to explain only the behavior of physical matter, affected thinking about moral behavior as well. When it comes to right and wrong, many people began to think, "It's all relative to your point of view."

Empirical psychology also struck at the conceptual underpinnings of character education. In the late 1920s, Yale University psychologists Hugh Hartshorne and Mark May studied the behavior of some 10,000 children who were given opportunities to lie, cheat, or steal in activities as varied as classroom work, home duties, party games, and athletic contests.[14] The inconsistency of children was striking; it was very difficult to predict, for example, whether a child who cheated on the playing field would also cheat in the classroom, or vice versa.

That finding led Hartshorne and May to propound the "doctrine of specificity": Honest or dishonest behavior by a person is highly variable and determined by the specific situation (such as the degree of risk involved), not by some consistent internal state that one could call "character." If character didn't exist, how could one educate for it? Later analyses of Hartshorne and May's data by other researchers did find some evidence of character; some children were in fact more "integrated" (either consistently honest or consistently dishonest) than other children.[15] But when the original study was released, it was the seemingly situation-specific nature of moral behavior that got the headlines—and that weakened support for traditional character education.

Meanwhile, in both American and European universities, a new philosophy was gaining a foothold. "Logical positivism" introduced a fundamental distinction between "fact" and "value." It held that the only real facts or truths were ones that could be scientifically demonstrated (e.g., "A steel ball when dropped will fall to the ground"). Moral or value statements, by contrast, were considered "emotive"—expressions of feeling rather than fact. Even a statement such as "Rape is wrong" was judged to be personal sentiment rather than objective truth.

In everyday conversations among people who never heard of "logical positivism," the fallout from this philosophy fell like a cold ash on moral dialogue. If you did happen to express a moral viewpoint, it was common for someone to wag a finger and object, "That's a value judgment!" A value judgment was automatically dismissed as "just your personal opinion" rather than as a rational, objective claim about what's good or bad, better or worse. Morality was "privatized"—made to seem purely a matter of private choice, not a matter for public debate and certainly not for public transmission through the schools.

When much of society came to think of morality as being in flux, relative to the individual, situationally variable, and essentially private, public schools retreated from their once central role as moral educators. "In our district," says a retired elementary school teacher, "it happened in the mid-1950s. The word came down from the administration that we were no longer to teach values; we were to stick to academics." She comments:

> I think the average classroom teacher wanted to go on teaching values. I remember getting into arguments, though, with some of my younger colleagues who'd say, "My values aren't the same as your values." I'd say, "Well, what about values like honesty, kindness, and responsibility—can't we teach those?" But I didn't get far; there was this new feeling that if we taught any kind of morality, we'd be "imposing our values" on the children.

"Somewhere between Sputnik and computers," observes a veteran fifth-grade teacher, "morality got lost." That's not entirely true, because to some extent schools can't avoid doing moral education. As social institutions, they must regulate moral behavior: They require students to obey their teachers, forbid them to fight, punish them for cheating, and so on. They also provide, through the visible actions of teachers and other adults, examples of fairness or unfairness, respect or disrespect, caring attention or the lack of it. But when schools got the idea that they shouldn't "impose" any one set of values, values education, if not actively discouraged, became at best unplanned and unreflective, part of the unexamined curriculum. It was left to the discretion of the individual teacher, without benefit of discussion of which values should be taught and how.[16]

THE 1960s AND 1970s: THE RISE OF "PERSONALISM"

Social change had been building slowly in the first half of the twentieth century. In the 1960s it accelerated dramatically.

The 1960s saw a worldwide surge of "personalism." Personalism celebrated the worth, dignity, and autonomy of the individual person, including the subjective self or inner life of the person. It emphasized rights more than responsibility, freedom more than commitment. It led people to focus on expressing and fulfilling themselves as free individuals rather than on fulfilling their obligations as members of groups such as family, church, community, or country.[17]

All through the turbulent 1960s and into the 1970s, personalism held high the banner of human freedom and the value of the individual person. From this new focus came many good things, such as the civil rights movement, a concern for the rights of women, and a new respect for the child as a person. But along with these advances came problems. People began to regard any kind of constraint on their personal freedom as an intolerable restriction of their individuality. The emphasis on individual freedom fostered general rebellion against authority, and, in many cases, a reluctance on the part of authority figures (including teachers and parents) to exercise their legitimate authority. In the United States, the abuses of power represented by Vietnam and Watergate hastened the general erosion of respect for authority, but the same erosion was occurring in countries around the world.

Personalism spawned a new selfishness. Books with titles such as *Looking Out for Number 1* became best-sellers. Slogans such as "Get all you can" and "You can have it all" guided popular thinking about the pursuit of happiness. Polls revealed the emergence of a "new breed" of parents, ones who considered self-fulfillment more important than the old parental ethic of self-denial and sacrifice for one's children.[18] The sexual revolution, which elevated short-term gratification above values of restraint and long-term commitment, was another socially destabilizing manifestation of the new ethic of self-fulfillment.

VALUES CLARIFICATION: PERSONALISM GOES TO SCHOOL

How did the personalism of the 1960s and 1970s affect moral education in the schools?

It gave birth to "values clarification." This new approach to values in the schools made its debut in 1966 with the publication of *Values and Teaching* by New York University Professor Louis Raths.[19] What did values clarification tell teachers to do? Not to try to teach values at all. Instead, the teacher's job was to help students learn how to "clarify" their own values. The idea that adults should directly instruct children in right and wrong, or even try to influence students' "value positions," was explicitly rejected.

Values clarification caught on in part because it seemed so simple to use. It called for no special training. It offered teachers literally dozens of activities, laid out in cookbook fashion, that could be plugged into any available slot in the day. Here are just two of 79 activities described in *Values Clarification: A Handbook of Practical Strategies for Teachers and Students,*[20] a 1972 paperback that could soon be found on teachers' desks all over the country:

VALUES WHIP

The teacher or student poses a question to the class and provides a few moments for the members to think about their answers. Then the teacher whips around the room calling upon students to give their answers. Sample questions:

- What is something you are proud of?
- What is some issue about which you have taken a public stand recently?
- What is something you really believe in strongly?

VALUES VOTING

The teacher reads aloud, one by one, questions which begin, "How many of you . . . ?" Then the class votes with a show of hands. Sample questions:

_____ think there are times when cheating is justified?

_____ like to read the comics first thing in the Sunday paper?

_____ would like to own a sailboat?

_____ think capital punishment should be abolished?

_____ approve of premarital sex?

In practice, teachers often weren't sure what to do after students had clarified their values. A ninth-grade English teacher, for example, told of the following experience: As part of a "values voting" exercise, she asked her students, "How many of you have ever shoplifted?" Most raised their hands.

"Don't you think shoplifting is wrong?" the teacher asked (slipping momentarily from the prescribed neutrality). "We have a right to the material things in life," answered a student. Others nodded their agreement. "At that point I thought," the teacher says, " 'Good grief, where do I go from here?' Thank God the bell rang."

At its best, values clarification raised some important value issues for students to think about and encouraged them to close the gap between a value they professed (e.g., "Pollution is bad") and personal action ("What are you doing about it?"). Certain values clarification techniques, as we'll see in later chapters, can be effectively integrated into a broader approach to moral education. At its worst, however, values clarification mixed up trivial questions ("Do you like to read the comics?") with important ethical issues ("Should capital punishment be abolished?"). Most seriously, it took the shallow moral relativism loose in the land and brought it into the schools.

Values clarification discussions made no distinction between what you might *want* to do (such as shoplift) and what you *ought* to do (respect the property rights of others). There was no requirement to evaluate one's values against a standard, no suggestion that some values might be better or worse than others.[21] As one critic observed, "There's a big problem with any approach that doesn't distinguish between Mother Teresa and the Happy Hooker."

In the end, values clarification made the mistake of treating kids like grown-ups who only needed to clarify values that were already sound. It forgot that children, and a lot of adults who are still moral children, need a good deal of help in developing sound values in the first place.

During the 1970s, values clarification got some competition from other approaches to moral education—such as Lawrence Kohlberg's "moral dilemma discussions" and an approach called "rational decision-making" that was developed by moral philosophers. These approaches (described more fully in Chapters 12 and 13) rejected values clarification's moral relativism and attempted to help students develop ethically valid ways of reasoning about moral issues. But their focus was still on "process"—thinking skills—rather than moral content. Teachers still didn't see it as their role to teach or foster particular values.

SIGNS OF A MORAL DECLINE

Meanwhile, as society celebrated the individual and schools stayed neutral on values, clouds appeared on the moral horizon. There was accumulating evidence of a moral decline, first in society at large and then among the young.

For a while it seemed as if "the establishment" was the source of all evil. Institutional scandals broke with numbing regularity. By the late 1970s, the media reported that more than a hundred American companies had admitted to paying large sums to buy special treatment from U.S. politicians and foreign government officials. The companies' justification: Everyone was doing it.

The 1980s brought more of the same and then some. *Yale Alumni Magazine,* in an article titled "Ethics in the Boesky Era," noted tersely: "Perhaps more than at any time in recent American history, high-level greed and deceit are being seen as business as usual." [22]

But the moral slippage wasn't limited to high-level wheelers and dealers. For many ordinary people, personalism's emphasis on the individual had made selfishness a respectable life style. Lots of people also got to thinking, "Everybody else is ripping the system off—I'd be a fool not to."

As evidence that more people are joining in the rule-breaking, Dr. Jerald Jellison, a University of Southern California psychologist who specializes in moral trends, cites rising employee theft (which as of 1984 cost department stores and specialty chains $16 million a day) and increasing misrepresentation of job qualifications (e.g., submitting a phony résumé). Discouraging data on the state of personal ethics also came from a *Psychology Today* survey in the early 1980s. [23] More than 24,000 readers completed the 49-item questionnaire, titled "Making Ethical Choices." Respondents ranged in age from 13 to 81, but a majority—67 percent—were young adults, in their twenties or thirties. The average level of education of respondents was unusually high; 48 percent of those over 24 had attended graduate school (compared to 7 percent in the general population). Here are some of the moral behaviors that this relatively youthful, highly educated group of persons reported:

- 41 percent had driven while drunk or under the influence of drugs.

- 33 percent had deceived their best friend about something important in the past year.

- 38 percent had cheated on their tax returns.

- 45 percent of the respondents—including 49 percent of the men and 44 percent of the women—had cheated on their marriage partners (compared to 38 percent of all respondents in a 1969 *Psychology Today* survey of sexual behavior).[24]

When *Psychology Today* broke its respondents down into subgroups, two additional findings emerged: The more religious people were, the *less* likely they were to engage in morally questionable acts; and the younger they were, the *more* likely they were to engage in such behaviors. For the younger respondents, or at least a sizable percentage of them, the old rules had clearly given way to a "new morality."

TROUBLING YOUTH TRENDS

Certainly, not all young people have adopted shoddy moral standards; indeed, many demonstrate a higher moral consciousness—commitment to human rights, concern about the environment, global awareness—than most of their elders or previous generations. But the general youth trends present a darker picture. Consider the following ten indicators that we are, to a significant degree, failing as a society to provide for the moral development of the young:

1. **Violence and vandalism.** Among leading industrial nations, the United States has by far the highest murder rate for 15- to 24-year-old males—seven times higher than Canada's and 40 times higher than Japan's.[25] From 1965 to 1975, the murder rate for American youths under 18 doubled. It stabilized for a decade, then rose an alarming 48 percent between 1985 and 1988.[26]

Males are seven times more likely than females to engage in juvenile violent crime.[27] But girls are not exempt: From 1965 to 1988, arrests of under-18 girls for aggravated assault more than tripled.[28] Rising youth violence also cuts across race: Both white and nonwhite youths showed large increases in criminal violence during the past two and a half decades.[29]

The statistics are even more appalling when you consider the absolute numbers of violent criminal acts carried out each year by children. In 1985, according to the National Center for Juvenile Justice, children *11 years old or younger* were responsible for 21 killings, 3,434 assaults, 1,735 robberies, and 435 rapes.[30]

Youth crimes are also increasingly vicious. "Thieves used to mug a person and run off," says a Sacramento psychologist. "Now they beat their victims."[31]

Sometimes youth violence feeds on the twisted values of Satanic cults. Police report increasing instances of youth crimes where Satanism appears to be involved. Father Joseph Brennan, author of *Kingdom of Darkness* and a priest who counsels victims of ritual abuse and Satanic cults, estimates conservatively that there are 8,000 Satanic cults in the United States with 100,000 members nationwide.[32]

If young people do violence to other human beings, it's hardly surprising that they do the same to property. In a small upstate New York community, two boys, ages 7 and 8, and three girls, ages 5, 6, and 7, recently broke into their school, overturned desks and cabinets, destroyed hanging plants, and smashed two computers and a movie projector. Nationwide, the annual bill for school vandalism runs into the hundreds of millions of dollars.

2. **Stealing.** In 1981 the National Organization to Prevent Shoplifting surveyed 100,000 young people aged 9 to 21. Half of those surveyed said they had shoplifted at least once; most who had, said they would do it again. Colleges across the country face a rash of library theft; students often razor out assigned articles or book chapters from library materials and take them home for their private use.

3. **Cheating.** In October 1990 the Josephson Institute of Ethics issued a report *The Ethics of American Youth* documenting, among other moral problems, widespread cheating by young people.[33] In one national survey of more than 6,000 college freshmen and sophomores, 76 percent admitted to cheating in high school.[34]

Even more disturbing is students' acceptance of such dishonesty as normal, even necessary, behavior. A series of studies of Georgia high schools asked students to agree or disagree with the statement "sometimes it is necessary to cheat." In 1969 only one of three students agreed. Ten years later nearly two of three students (65 percent) agreed.[35]

Cheating used to become a problem in junior high school; now it is a concern of teachers in the elementary grades as well. One sixth-grade teacher, a student in my graduate course in moral education, surveyed her students (11- to 12-year-olds) and found that 48 percent admitted to having cheated. Most said they would do so again.

4. **Disrespect for authority.** Students' respect for authority varies widely from school to school, but overall, teachers say, there is a serious problem: Large numbers of children show attitudes of disrespect and defiance that make them resistant to control and basic socialization.

Says a fifth-grade male teacher with 16 years of experience in a suburban school: "You can say to kids, 'Don't do that' and they turn right around and do it. On the playground I find kids more hostile to adult intervention. If you try to break up a fight, they argue with you and then throw another punch as they walk away. *That* didn't used to happen."

5. **Peer cruelty.** Says a widely respected elementary school teacher: "The change in kids over the past 10 years has been incredible. . . . It's not only . . . disrespect for me, and I find a lot of that. Students also show a lot of cruelty toward one another. They insult, they hurt, they pick on the weakest member of the group, they bully, they push, they solve their problems through physical violence."

Another teacher, working in a different school district, echoes those observations: "I've started subbing after being away for eight years. I can't believe how cruel kids are with each other. If it's not physical, it's verbal. It's constant, and it's intense. It's worst in fourth through sixth grades, but it's all the way down in the younger grades, too."

6. **Bigotry.** After the civil rights movements of the 1960s, we assumed that the battle against bigotry as accepted social behavior had been won. Now it's painfully clear that that moral victory will have to be won again with a new generation. On college campuses all across the country, noted a *Time* report titled "Bigotry in the Ivory Tower," "bigotry and prejudice are making a comeback."[36]

According to the National Institute Against Prejudice and Hostility, incidents of racial violence or hostility have been reported at more than 300 U.S. colleges and universities over the past five years. In the fall of 1988, the first black fraternity house at the University of Mississippi was torched before its members had even moved in. At Yale, a swastika and the words WHITE POWER! were painted on the university's Afro-American Cultural Center.[37]

There is a hopeful countertrend: The numbers of American college freshmen stating that it is "essential" or "very important" for them to "help promote racial understanding" reached an all-time high of 38 percent in 1990.[38] But the fact that so many college students are now concerned about racial prejudice indicates just how serious the problem is. Most worrisome, the resurgence of prejudice on the part of many youths is occurring at the very time that greater tolerance is needed. Young people growing up today will have to function in an increasingly multicultural society—one in which a third of all Americans will be members of nonwhite racial or ethnic groups by the year 2000.

7. **Bad language.** Language is an index of civilization; changes in language are socially significant. If you ask teachers how children have changed, one of the first things they mention is their language.

Says a fifth-grade teacher in a Westchester County, New York, suburb: "Kids' language these days is appalling. If someone is playing a game and misses a shot, a four-letter word is the standard reaction. It's how casual they are about it that disturbs me the most." Adds a high school counselor: "We have kids who will shout to their friends in the hall, 'Hey, what the f—— are you doin' after school?' They are totally egocentric—utterly oblivious to the fact that someone else might find such language offensive."

Students, moreover, get so used to using four-letter words that the same words come out in conflicts, with all the explosive impact such language has when used with hostility. "Most physical violence in my school," says an elementary school principal, "begins with foul language." Such language is directed at adults as well as at fellow students: A 1987 Harvard University study of violence in schools reported that 59 percent of teachers in urban schools and 40 percent in rural areas said they face swearing and obscene gestures from students.[39]

8. **Sexual precocity and abuse.** Children's vulgar language is often part of a larger pattern: a loss of innocence that includes sexual precocity.

A sixth-grade teacher in a central New York town comments: "These are kids who have grown up on R-rated movies, TV shows, and ads that push sex at them constantly. I've seen the influence of this in my own classroom, where the boys bring in *Playboy*, the girls wear high heels, makeup, and jewelry, and the kids write sexual notes to one another."

Each year 14,000 girls under age 14 have babies.[40] In my own small community, there is a counselor who works with a group of 11- to 13-year-old girls who have already been sexually active, some since they were 10.

All such premature sexual behavior on the part of the young should really be classified as abuse—of both self and other. But even if one looks only at what traditionally counts as abuse—acts of coercion—there is evidence of a marked increase of sexual abuse of children by other children, and at younger and younger ages. In May 1988, *The Washington Post* ran a story that began: "Two 7-year-old Washington boys recently were arrested, held for six hours, fingerprinted, and photographed after they held a 7-year-old girl to the ground [at knife-point], exposed their genitals and hers, and pressed against her."[41]

At a recent national conference in Keystone, Colorado, mental health experts and social workers testified that thousands of young Americans (usually victims of adult sex abusers) sexually abuse thousands of even younger Americans every year.[42] New York City psychiatrist Dr. Judith Becker reports: "The age of the perpetrators has been decreasing, and the age of the victims has been decreasing. When I first got involved [15 years ago], the average age of the victims was 12. Now it's 8."[43]

9. **Increasing self-centeredness and declining civic responsibility.** In a 1989 Gallup poll, young adults aged 18 to 29 made the following self-indictment: A total of 89 percent said their generation was more selfish than people their age twenty years ago, and 82 percent said they were more materialistic.[44]

Materialism rears its head as early as the elementary school grades. Says a teacher of third grade: "There's a lot more talk about money in school. I have kids who say to me, 'You can't tell me what to do—my father makes more money than you do.' "

Among college students, the preoccupation with money is starkly evident. Each fall UCLA's Higher Education Research Institute polls the country's entering college freshmen at approximately 550 colleges in a survey, *The American Freshman,* that serves as a barometer of national values. Students are asked to rate the importance of various life goals. In 1970 only 39.1 percent rated *being very well off financially* as an "essential" or "very important" life goal. By 1987 that figure had soared to a record high of 75.6 percent. (Since then it has dropped slightly—to 73.7 percent in 1990.)[45] In 1970 the most strongly endorsed goal was *developing a meaningful philosophy of life;* 82.9 percent of college freshmen rated that as essential or very important. By 1987 that number had fallen to 39.4 percent.[46]

Meanwhile, the Economic Policy Institute releases a study showing that in the past decade America's rich have significantly increased their income while the poor have grown poorer—a reversal of trends in earlier decades.[47]

It shouldn't be surprising that the quest for personal wealth has been accompanied by a lessening of civic responsibility. Young people's growing detachment from public life was the subject of an extensive study conducted by the Times Mirror Center and published in June 1990 as a report titled *The Age of Indifference*. Its major conclusion: "Today's young Americans, aged 18 to 30, know less and care less about news and public affairs than any other generation of Americans in the past 50 years."[48]

On the bright side there are some tentative signs of a recovery of social consciousness, at least about some issues. In 1990, for example, 33.9 percent of college freshmen said they considered it essential or very important to "become involved in programs to clean up the environment"—more than double the number just five years before.[49] But the overall picture still shows a weak sense of civic responsibility, especially when compared with that of previous generations.

10. **Self-destructive behavior.** As young people have become more self-centered, they have also become more self-destructive.

Premature sexual activity, already discussed, is certainly a prime example of such self-injurious behavior. According to a 1988 United Nations report, the United States now has one of the highest teenage pregnancy rates and the highest teen abortion rate in the developed world.[50] By one estimate, 1 in 7 American adolescents has a sexually transmitted disease.[51] And despite the widespread publicity about the threat of AIDS, the proportion of college freshmen who agree that "if two people really like each other, it's all right for them to have sex even if they have known each other for only a very short time" increased to 51.0 percent in 1990 (up from 46.8 percent in 1984).[52]

Drugs are a national scourge. According to the National Institute on Drug Abuse, U.S. youth still show the highest level of drug use of young people anywhere in the industrialized world.[53] By the mid-1980s, according to a University of Michigan study, 4 of every 10 Americans in their late twenties had tried cocaine.[54] Only a third of college students surveyed said they saw any risk. Meanwhile, between 1984 and 1988, cocaine-related deaths nationwide more than tripled.[55]

Increasingly, drugs are infiltrating elementary schools. In the Bronx, one 11-year-old was found with 411 vials of crack. The month before on Long Island, a 10-year-old was arrested for selling crack.

As in other problem areas, it's the attitudes toward drugs that are even more disturbing than the behavior. When Ben Johnson was found to have used steroids to win the hundred-meter race in the 1988 Summer Olympics, one of his competitors in the hundred, Horace Dove-Edwin of California, reacted with the following comment:

> Everybody uses drugs. Give me a break . . . they have got everything, human blood hormone, all kinds of drugs. Steroids is nothing anymore. It's just a little itty-bitty drug. You can get it anywhere.[56]

Alcohol abuse by the young is also epidemic. In a survey carried out by the National Institute on Alcohol Abuse and Alcoholism, 2 of 5 high school seniors said they get drunk (5 or more consecutive drinks) once or more every weekend.[57] One of 3 teens has a serious alcohol-related problem. Four of every 10 people killed in drunk-driving accidents are teenagers.[58]

Finally, the suicide rate of children in the United States has risen 300 percent during the past three decades.[59] Annually, about a half million teenagers try to kill themselves; about 6,000 succeed. In a 1988 survey by the U.S. Department of Health and Human Services, 1 in 7 teens (1 in 10 boys and 1 in 5 girls) said they have tried to commit suicide.[60]

The United States has no monopoly on these problems. Here is a Canadian magazine, arguing the case for values education in the schools: A total of 70 percent of Ontario's children in grades 7 through 13 use alcohol; 33 percent of tenth-grade boys and 25 percent of girls have had sexual intercourse, accompanied by rising rates of teen pregnancy and abortion; suicide is the second leading cause of death among teenagers.[61]

In the summer of 1987, I was in Japan for the first East–West conference on moral education. Speakers from 15 countries described the moral problems their nations faced and how they were trying to address them. The similarities were striking: Everyone is concerned about the breakdown of the family; everyone is concerned about the negative impact of television on children; everyone is concerned about the growing self-centeredness, materialism, and delinquency they see among their young.

Faced with problems like these, countries all over the world are turning to their educational systems for help. The paralyzing concern of a few years ago that teaching values might violate pluralism and upset some people is giving way to what now seems like a self-evident truth: *Not* to equip the young with a moral sense is a grave ethical failure on the part of any society.

SUMMING UP THE CASE FOR VALUES EDUCATION

As we stand on the threshold of the twenty-first century, there are at least ten good reasons why schools should be making a clearheaded and wholehearted commitment to teaching moral values and developing good character:

1. **There is a clear and urgent need.** Young people are increasingly hurting themselves and others, and decreasingly concerned about contributing to the welfare of their fellow human beings. In this they reflect the ills of societies in need of moral and spiritual renewal.

2. **Transmitting values is and always has been the work of civilization.**[62] A society needs values education both to survive and to thrive—to keep itself intact, and to keep itself growing toward conditions that support the full human development of all its members. Historically, three social institutions have shared the work of moral education: the home, the church, and the school. In taking up values education, schools are returning to their time-honored role, abandoned briefly in the middle part of this century.

3. **The school's role as moral educator becomes even more vital at a time when millions of children get little moral teaching from their parents and when value-centered influences such as church or temple are also absent from their lives.** These days, when schools don't do moral education, influences hostile to good character rush in to fill the values vacuum.

4. **There is common ethical ground even in our value-conflicted society.** Americans have intense and often angry differences over moral issues such as abortion, homosexuality, euthanasia, and capital punishment. Despite this diversity, we can identify basic, shared values that allow us to engage in public moral education in a pluralistic society. Indeed, pluralism itself is not possible without agreement on values such as justice, honesty, civility, democratic process, and a respect for truth.[63]

5. **Democracies have a special need for moral education, because democracy is government by the people themselves.** The people must care about the rights of others and the common good and be willing to assume the responsibilities of democratic citizenship.

6. **There is no such thing as value-free education.** Everything a school does teaches values—including the way teachers and other adults treat students, the way the principal treats teachers, the way the school treats parents, and the way students are allowed to treat school staff and

each other. If questions of right and wrong are never discussed in class-rooms, that, too, teaches a lesson about how much morality matters. In short, the relevant issue is never "Should schools teach values?" but rather "Which values will they teach?" and "How well will they teach them?"

7. **The great questions facing both the individual person and the human race are moral questions.** For each of us as individuals, a ques-tion of the utmost existential importance is: "How should I live my life?" For all of humanity, the two most important questions facing us as we enter the next century are: "How can we live with each other?" and "How can we live with nature?"[64]

8. **There is broad-based, growing support for values education in the schools.** It comes from the federal government, which has identified values education as essential in the fight against drugs and crime. It comes from statehouses, which have passed resolutions calling upon all school districts to teach the values necessary for good citizenship and a law-abiding society. It comes from business, which recognizes that a responsible labor force requires workers who have character traits of honesty, dependability, pride in work, and the capacity to cooperate with others.

Support also comes from reform-minded groups such as Educators for Social Responsibility, which know that progress toward social jus-tice and global peace demands morally principled citizens. It comes from groups such as the American Jewish Committee, which in 1988 reversed its long-standing caution against values education and issued a report urging schools to teach "civic virtues" such as "honesty, civil-ity, responsibility, tolerance, and loyalty. . . ."[65]

Perhaps most significantly, support for school-based values educa-tion comes from parents who are looking for help in a world where it's harder than ever to raise good children. For more than a decade, every Gallup poll that has asked parents whether schools should teach morals has come up with an unequivocal yes. Typical is the finding that 84 percent of parents with school-age children say they want the public schools to provide "instruction that would deal with morals and moral behavior."[66]

9. **An unabashed commitment to moral education is essential if we are to attract and keep good teachers.** Says a young woman preparing to enter the teaching profession:

> I am not a teacher yet, but I need a sense of hope that teachers can help
> to turn around the community-shattering values of today's society: mate-

rialism, me-first apathy, and disregard for truth and justice. Many of the teachers with whom I've spoken have been frustrated, some to the point of despair, with the deteriorating moral fiber of their students and the lack of effective methods in the schools to counter this trend. It is a hard message for me to hear as I stand on the threshold of a teaching career.

If you want to do one thing to improve the lives of teachers, says Boston University educator Kevin Ryan, make moral education—including the creation of a civil, humane community in the school—the center of school life.

10. **Values education is a doable job.** Given the enormous moral problems facing the country, their deep social roots, and the ever-increasing responsibilities that schools already shoulder, the prospect of taking on moral education can seem overwhelming. The good news, as we will see, is that values education can be done within the school day, is happening now in school systems all across the country, and is making a positive difference in the moral attitudes and behavior of students, with the result that it's easier for teachers to teach and students to learn.

Until recently, calls for school reform have focused on academic achievement. Now we know that character development is needed as well. That awareness cuts across all spheres of society; the current call for teaching values in the schools is part of an "ethics boom" that has seen more than a hundred institutionalized ethics programs—in fields as varied as journalism, medicine, law, and business—established in the United States in just the past few years.[67] We are recovering a foundational understanding: Just as character is the ultimate measure of an individual, so it is also the ultimate measure of a nation.

To develop the character of our children in a complex and changing world is no small task. But it is time to take up the challenge.

CHAPTER 2

Educating for Character— and Why Schools Need Help from Home

Schools today must lead the battle against the worst psycho-social epidemics that have ever plagued the children of our society. . . . Schools need programs to protect children against the ravages of social disorganization and family collapse.

—PERRY LONDON, Professor, Harvard Graduate School of Education[1]

The moral education thing bothers me because I feel as if I'm doing it alone. Many parents seem to enjoy their rights— having a child—but no longer seem to want the responsibilities. I get the feeling, who's helping me here?

—Elementary school teacher, central New York

In the face of a deteriorating social fabric, schools know they must do something to try to teach children good values. To take on that task, however, they need two things: hope that it can be done, and the feeling that they won't be doing it alone.

Hope that it can be done comes from examples of schools that have made a deliberate effort to teach values and are seeing results. The feeling that the school won't have to do this alone comes from another encouraging trend: schools and families working together to educate a moral child.

WHAT'S WORKING

Here, from around the country and Canada, are glimpses of what schools are doing to promote positive values and good character[2]:

• Since 1984, Atlanta high schoolers must demonstrate a spirit of citizenship by completing 75 hours of community work before graduation. At a high school in St. Louis, the principal tells students that they've taken from St. Louis for a long time; now it's their turn to give something back. Sometime during their four years, they each render community service.[3]

• In Chicago, an organization called For Character has sponsored an awards program to recognize area elementary and secondary schools that excel in fostering both student character and academic excellence. A survey of winning schools, which include some inner-city schools in poverty areas plagued by crime, finds they have many things in common: clarity of school goals, rigorous academics, consistent and fair discipline, strong leadership, the cultivation of school spirit, and a stress on conduct that is considerate of the welfare of others.[4]

The way a school is run, For Character believes, is the most important kind of character education it provides.

• Birch Meadow Elementary School in Reading, Massachusetts, believes that schools should be run with a healthy dose of democracy to teach students the skills and values of democratic citizenship. Teachers conduct daily class meetings on topics such as what to do about a complaint from the second-graders that the older kids are hogging the playground equipment during recess. Elected class representatives take concerns and proposals to the Primary Student Council (grades 1 through 3) or the Intermediate Student Council (grades 4 through 6), both of which meet weekly over lunch with the principal. The overall aim: to create the feeling that "this is everybody's school, and everybody has a responsibility to make it a good place to be and learn."[5]

• Developing students' understanding of and respect for the law is the focus of Law in a Free Society, an educational project of the California State Bar Association.[6] Says project associate Mike Leong: "Even kids in kindergarten can understand why there is a need for authority, what would happen on the playground if there were no rules, and what makes a good rule."[7] Law in a Free Society develops and disseminates classroom curricula for kindergarten through twelfth grade, explaining concepts such as authority, justice, privacy, responsibility, freedom, diversity, property, and participation.[8]

• "To strengthen self-esteem in the face of peer pressure"; "to deal with conflict in a positive, nonviolent manner"; "to develop an understanding of prejudice"; "to take responsibility for one's decisions"— these are some of the goals of PREPARE, a popular Canadian, curriculum-based citizenship program for grades 4 through 6. Developed by the Hamilton, Ontario, Board of Education with funding from the local Rotary Club, PREPARE consists of 7 curriculum units, each including a student activity book and teacher's guide focused on a particular theme. The units were developed employing a curriculum-design strategy widely used in Canada: taking a broad concept and breaking it down into 6 to 8 "key ideas." Classroom activities are then developed that help students grasp and apply each of the key ideas.

PREPARE has spread to dozens of other school systems in Ontario and elsewhere. A parallel citizenship program for teens, Preparing Adolescents for Tomorrow, features units on impaired driving, family law, making relationships work, personal safety, shoplifting, and suicide prevention.[9]

• In San Ramon, California, three elementary schools have participated in what is very likely the most ambitious, well-researched values education program in the world: the Child Development Project (CDP). Supported by a $1 million-a-year grant from the Hewlett Foundation, CDP has helped these three schools implement a values program consisting of five interlocking components: (1) cooperative learning; (2) using children's literature to develop empathy and understanding of others; (3) exposing students to a variety of prosocial examples; (4) involving students in helping relationships (e.g., cross-age tutors and buddies); and (5) developmental discipline, aimed at fostering students' moral reasoning and self-control. Besides its comprehensive school-based approach, CDP has a home program aimed at getting parents on board.

The object of hundreds of inquiries from school systems around the country, the Child Development Project has been singled out as an exemplary school program by the National School Boards Association, the National Council for the Social Studies, and the U.S. Department of Education.[10]

• Since 1979, eighth-graders in Brookline, Massachusetts, as part of their social studies curriculum, have participated in an award-winning program called Facing History and Ourselves. Devoted to the study of the Nazi Holocaust and the universal human tendency toward prejudice and scapegoating, Facing History and Ourselves poses the question "How could this happen?"

During the eight weeks of the program, students express their thoughts and feelings in journals, which become one of the most important indicators of the curriculum's impact. At the end of the eight weeks, one girl wrote:

> I'm glad this unit was taught to us, and especially to me. At the beginning, I have to admit I was prejudiced against Jews and was glad they were killed. I know this is awful, especially if that is your religion. Then you and the class discussions proved to me I was wrong! Jewish is just like me and other people.[11]

Brookline's Facing History and Ourselves Foundation offers training to school staffs that wish to implement this curriculum.[12] To date, Facing History and Ourselves has been used in more than 300 courses in 46 states and Canada.

• In 1988 Dr. James Finch, superintendent of Sweet Home School District in Amherst, New York, decided "to take values education out of the closet and make it our top district priority."[13] He wrote a letter to his entire staff and asked, "Who thinks this is important and would like to get involved?" A total of 75 people replied. He then set up a 19-member Values Education Council, chaired by teacher Sharon Banas, which challenged each school to identify its top values concerns and create strategies for addressing them. At Sweet Home Middle School, students constructed large vinyl banners that read I AM RESPONSIBLE FOR MY DAY or I WANT RESPECT AND I SHOW IT, and hung them in key spots around the school. Daily messages on respect and responsibility are included in the morning announcements and repeated on the electronic message board in the cafeteria. As part of the Positive Bus Program initiated by bus driver Mary Zimmerman, district drivers developed respect and responsibility rules to post on their buses. Drivers also hand out green ribbons for students to give to someone they see performing a caring act during the school day. At Heritage Heights Elementary School, students now have values education assemblies twice a week. At the high school, a proposal is in the works for awarding a varsity letter for community service.

"There hasn't been a single parent complaint about the school teaching values," says Dee Serrio, president of Sweet Home's PTA Council.

"Parents had input, and this whole program contains nothing more than the values parents said they wanted for their children."[14]

DOES VALUES EDUCATION MAKE A DIFFERENCE?

What is the effectiveness of these new efforts in values education? Have they improved the moral attitudes and behavior of students?

Early indicators are encouraging. My research for this book has taken me across this country and to Canada for a firsthand look at schools doing deliberate moral education, and at every school I've visited, people say that the commitment to values education has paid off.

The evidence for that claim varies. Sometimes schools can point to numbers. At San Marcos Junior High School in California, a course in responsible decision-making is now required of all seventh- and eighth-graders. Says assistant superintendent Joseph DeDiminicantanio: "Last year we had one drug incident all year, compared to about a dozen the year before" (prior to implementing the new curriculum). Student pregnancies are also down, and test scores are up.[15]

Sometimes the testimonies are subjective but nonetheless persuasive, especially when they come from the students themselves. One of the Canadian schools I visited was the Scarborough Village Public School in Ontario, recommended to me by that province's Values Education Centre.[16] I interviewed a group of fifth-graders and asked them how many had gone to schools other than this one; about half raised their hands. "How is this school different?" I asked.

A girl answered: "People don't pick on you here. At my last school, they used to flush my gloves down the toilet. They teased me. I was too short one year, too tall the next. It kept on getting worse. If I tried to do something about it, they'd do it more. Sometimes they'd punch me in the stomach. They said I was a sissy if I told."

"What did teachers do if you told them about it?"

"They said, 'There's nothing I can do.' "

"How do kids treat you here?"

"Special—like I belong."

"How do they make you feel that you belong?"

"They don't beat me up. They talk with me. They play with me. People are just nice here."

"Not that these kids are angels," a volunteer mother hastened to add afterward. But it was clear, from the interactions I observed and what adults and children said, that the fifth-grade girl's comment "People are just nice here" defined the prevailing norm.

The most severe test of a values education program is whether it can turn a bad situation around. Winkelman Elementary School, serving a diverse community north of Chicago (some children are from welfare families, others arrive in limousines), is a case in point. Several years ago, fights and put-downs among children were a serious problem at Winkelman, and children would often "smart-off" to teachers and other adults.

Resolved to make a change, Winkelman launched a project called Let's Be Courteous, Let's Be Caring. The values of courtesy and caring were stressed at every opportunity, through photo displays in the corridors, discussions in classrooms, private conversations between teachers and children, school assemblies, citizenship awards, meetings with parents, and service projects in the community.

The moral environment at Winkelman steadily improved. When I visited the school, parents said fights are now very rare; children said if they forgot their lunch, they could always count on somebody giving them some of theirs; an experienced teacher who was new to the school testified that children treat adults and each other with an impressive degree of respect; and the principal reported that a kindergartner had recently come up to her and said, "I like this school because I get to say 'please' and 'thank you' here." In recognition of its efforts and success, Winkelman was one of the schools selected for an award by the Chicago organization For Character.[17]

WHAT THE RESEARCH SHOWS

What does the formal research show? Most of the current efforts in values education have not been subjected to a controlled research evaluation. But the empirical studies that have been done are promising.[18]

For example: Students in the Holocaust curriculum Facing History and Ourselves were compared on a number of measures with a control group (like-ability eighth-grade students in the same school who did not get the Holocaust program). Facing History students were significantly superior in their understanding of how individuals' decisions are affected by their society and in the complexity of their reasoning about issues such as leadership, exclusion, and conflict resolution.[19]

By far, the most extensive evaluation of any values education program has been carried out by California's Child Development Project. Its Hewlett Foundation support has enabled CDP to employ a team of research psychologists who have amassed a mountain of data aimed at answering this question: Does a multifaceted values program, begun in kindergarten and sustained throughout a child's elementary school years, make a measurable and lasting difference in a child's moral thinking, attitudes, and behavior?

In setting up its research design, CDP asked San Ramon's 13 elementary schools, "Who would like to participate?" Six schools were eager to do so. Those six schools were then divided into two groups of three, matched for size and socioeconomic factors, and a coin was flipped to determine which three schools would be the program schools and which would be the control schools.

Five years later, in 1989, CDP's report card was positive. Results were in for children who had participated in the program from kindergarten through fourth grade. Not all of the tests and observations showed statistically significant differences between program schools and comparison schools. But significant differences emerged in four areas:

1. **Classroom behavior:** Program students showed more spontaneous acts of helping, cooperation, affection, and encouragement toward one another in the classroom.

2. **Playground behavior:** Program children showed more concern toward others on the playground—but were not less assertive than comparison children.

3. **Social problem-solving skills:** In resolving hypothetical conflicts, program students paid more attention to the needs of all parties, were less likely to propose aggressive solutions, and came up with more alternative plans.

4. **Commitment to democratic values:** Program children were more committed to democratic values such as the belief that all members of a group have a right to participate in the group's decisions and activities.[20]

What's more, these gains have been achieved without any sacrifice in academic achievement—crucial results in an age of high-pressure academic accountability. CDP children scored as well as their comparison school counterparts on California's standardized measures of school success.

CDP's grant has been extended for several more years so that additional questions can be investigated: Will the positive program effects persist now that students have moved on to junior high school, where there is no special values program? Will CDP students be less likely to be represented among teen pregnancies and students who get involved in substance abuse? And will the CDP program work in a less affluent, more ethnically heterogeneous school district such as Hayward, California (where implementation of CDP is now under way)?

WHAT IS THE FAMILY'S ROLE?

There is growing evidence that schools can make a difference in the character development of the young. But can they do the whole job? What is the role of the family?

Common sense tells us that the family is the primary moral educator of the child. Parents are their children's first moral teachers. They are also the most enduring influence: Children change teachers every year but typically have at least one of the same parents all through their growing years. The parent-child relationship is also laden with special emotional significance, causing children to feel either loved and worthwhile or unloved and unimportant. Finally, parents are in a position to teach morality as part of a larger worldview that offers a vision of life's meaning and ultimate reasons for leading a moral life. All this is confirmed by a stack of studies pointing to the power of parental influence.[21]

In one study, adolescents who followed their consciences when faced with a moral dilemma had parents who took their children's moral transgressions seriously. These parents, when their youngster broke trust or hurt a third person in some way, were much more likely than parents of less morally mature children to express disappointment, show indignation, point out the unfairness of the act, appeal to the child's own sense of responsibility, and demand apologies and reparation.[22]

How well parents teach their children to respect their authority also lays the foundation for future moral growth. The parents who are most effective, the research indicates, are "authoritative"—requiring obedience from their children but providing clear reasons for their expectations, so that children eventually internalize the moral rationale and act responsibly on their own. By contrast, both "permissive" parents (who are reluctant to set rules and confront transgressions) and "authoritarian" parents (who are high on control but low on reasoning to explain rules and motivate compliance) are less successful at all age levels in raising self-controlled, socially responsible children.[23]

Love, like authority, is foundational. Eighth-graders who are relatively mature in their moral reasoning rate their fathers as more affectionate and more involved with them than do eighth-graders who are immature in their moral reasoning.[24] Young children who are most securely attached to their parents are the ones most likely to comply with family rules.[25]

Finally, the quality of parenting is the best predictor of whether a youngster gets in trouble with the law. One classic study looked at several thousand junior and senior high school teenagers. It found that the closer the mother's supervision of the child, the better the communication with his or her father, and the greater the affection between child and both parents, the less the likelihood of juvenile delinquency.[26]

CHANGES IN THE FAMILY

The family has undeniable clout as a moral socializer of children. But families are changing.

Most families have been touched, in one way or another, by the heartache of divorce. One of two U.S. marriages now ends in divorce. Our divorce rate, which has more than doubled since 1960,[27] is the highest in the world. About 60 percent of children whose parents break up will spend the rest of their childhood in a single-parent home.[28]

Nearly always, women are the ones who must shoulder the responsibility of raising their children without a helpmate and often must do so with the additional burden of poverty. By 1988, according to a National Commission on Children report, 55 percent of families headed by a single mother were poor (compared with 12 percent of two-parent families).

For the first time in history, more than half of all children under 18 have a mother who works outside the home, often out of economic necessity. Nearly half of all mothers of 1-year-olds are now in the labor force.

Families are also more mobile than ever before. Every year, one of five families in America moves—away from the people who give parents a support network and children a sense of who they are.[29]

How have all these changes in the family affected children?

It depends. Many parents, despite adverse circumstances, make raising their children a high priority, and their children manage to thrive. All too often, however, fractured families and the stress of outside commitments carry a cost that children pay. The impact of broken homes, social science is beginning to reveal, may be greater than anyone had supposed. In the early 1970s, Dr. Judith Wallerstein, psychologist and senior lecturer at the University of California at Berkeley, embarked on what she thought would be a one-year study of middle-class families that had just been through a divorce. Her thesis was that "normal, healthy people would be able to work out their problems following divorce in about one year's time." Instead, she ended up doing a 10-year study documenting just how wrong her original assumption was. In her best-selling book *Second Chances: Men, Women, and Children a Decade After Divorce,* she writes:

> When we conducted follow-up interviews one year to 18 months later, we found most families still in crisis. Their wounds were wide open. Turmoil and distress had not noticeably subsided. Many adults still felt angry, humiliated, and rejected, and most had not gotten their lives back together. An unexpectedly large number of children were on a downward course. Their symptoms were worse than before.[30]

Many children, Wallerstein says, realize the finality of the situation only with the passage of time. Hence the "sleeper effect": At the five-year mark, straight-A students began to have problems at school, and quiet, well-behaved boys became hyperactive bullies. At both the five- and ten-year marks, more than a third of the children were suffering from either drug and alcohol addiction, depression, or sexual promiscuity.

Even before the scientific evidence began to come in, teachers and principals could testify to the pain in children's lives caused by ruptured family relationships. Here is Fred Gula, who has logged more than two decades as principal of a small elementary school in the town of Scotia, New York:

> The biggest change I've seen has been the increase in the number of single-parent families. This morning I had a fourth-grader in my office who is home at night by himself. His mom is a waitress. No father. He takes care of his 5-year-old sister. There's a boyfriend who is sometimes in the home; he is abusive toward the boy. There's no family structure. And then we demand that the child perform at school. I think most behavior problems we see today can be traced to home situations.

Many single parents, it's important to recognize, make conscientious efforts to meet their children's needs; they set aside time to play with them, have private talks with them, help them with their homework, keep track of their lives, and try to teach good values.[31] By comparison, some two-parent families make their children less of a priority.

In the United States there are now more than 8 million latchkey children.[32] A fourth-grade teacher in central New York comments:

The changes we're seeing in kids, such as the increase in meanness, reflect changes in families. A lot of these kids are coming home to empty houses. They open the door, open a can of Spaghetti-O's, do their own laundry, take the same clothes, and put them back on. These kids have a lot of responsibility, but only for themselves. They develop a hard shell. That's why so many of them are coming up cruel.

Often, family relationships are the casualties of life in the fast lane. Many parents overschedule themselves and their children to the point where parent-child face-to-face communication nearly disappears. A Baltimore County, Maryland, public school survey found that parents spent an average of two minutes a day in "meaningful dialogue" with their children.

WHEN CHILDREN AND PARENTS DON'T HAVE A CLOSE RELATIONSHIP

When children don't have a close relationship with their parents and an identification with family values, they are more vulnerable to peer pressure. Says an elementary teacher:

We're seeing peer pressure at an earlier age. It used to be in the teens. Now it's strong even by fourth grade. Kids don't seem to be able to resist the group. They don't seem to have the strong foundation at home that would enable them to resist.

Add to this heightened susceptibility to peer pressure the reduced supervision by parents, and you have the recipe for the kind of self-destructive behavior that is jeopardizing many young people's lives. I spoke with a junior high school teacher whose 24-year-old daughter is a church youth worker in an affluent New Jersey suburb. This teacher said:

My daughter says she can see a change in the six years since she graduated from high school. She says the kids she works with party every weekend, and it's beer, cocaine, and sex. They can usually find a house where the parents are gone for the weekend. The parents have no idea what their kids are doing; one of the leaders is the minister's son. These are people who live in beautiful homes on acre lots. On the outside, they're superstar families.

Finally, for several reasons—confusion about their own values, the seeming laxness of other parents, the fear that their children won't accept their advice or controls—many parents have lost a crucial commodity in child-rearing: confidence in their own authority. Comments a Wisconsin superintendent: "Parents ask us questions like, 'I don't want my daughter to go out on school nights, but what do I say when she says other parents let *their* kids go out during the week?' Many of these parents are bright and successful at their jobs but are not grounded in a clear sense of their own values. That gets in the way of their offering moral counsel to their children or taking stands that require moral courage."

THE PLIGHT OF SCHOOLS: A BIGGER JOB WITH LESS SUPPORT

How have the changes in families affected the school's job as moral educator? They've made it harder in several ways.

When families don't meet the basic physical and emotional needs of children, children are not prepared to function in school mentally *or* morally. Increasingly, children come to school without breakfast, without enough sleep, without their homework done, and without the feeling that anybody really cares about them. Learning difficulties and' behavior problems are often the result.

When parents don't develop a close relationship with their children and use that relationship to teach them right conduct, schools have to start from scratch. Says a fifth-grade teacher in a Boston suburb:

About ten years ago I showed my class some moral dilemma filmstrips. I found they knew right from wrong, even if they didn't always practice it. Now I find more and more of them don't know. They don't think it's wrong to pick up another person's property without their permission or to go into somebody else's desk. They barge between two adults when they're talking and seem to lack manners in general. You want to ask them, "Didn't your mother ever teach you that?"

Moreover, when families are overstressed or undercommitted to their children, they give teachers little help when their child is a problem in school. Says a first-grade teacher: "I have children who steal, fight, and use bad language—and when I talk to their parents, they are frequently apathetic or haven't any idea what to do about the problem."

Some parents even espouse values that are the direct opposite of what the school is trying to teach—as in the case of the second-grader who reported that his mother told him, "It's okay if you steal. You're not 16 yet, so they can't put you in jail."

Often the subversion of the school's values is less direct but no less detrimental. Says an assistant headmaster at an elite northeastern private high school: "When you catch kids cheating on a test or plagiarizing on a paper and their parents come in to defend them, you feel undermined—how can you hope to get the student to take standards of honesty seriously?"

"It used to be," observes a Kansas City principal, "that if you were in trouble at school, you were in double trouble at home. Parents and teachers closed ranks. Now the parent is likely to be on the phone carrying on about their child's 'rights.' "

In short, schools are being asked to carry more and more of the burden of moral education with less support. They can no longer assume, as they once generally could, a strong, cohesive family that supports and teaches the value norms of the school.[33]

SCHOOLS AND FAMILIES: ESSENTIAL PARTNERS

Even if schools can improve students' conduct while they are in school—and the evidence shows that they can indeed do that—the likelihood of lasting impact on the character of a child is diminished if the school's values aren't supported at home. For that reason, schools and families must come together in common cause. Working together, these two formative social institutions have real power to raise up moral human beings and to elevate the moral life of the nation.

In that hope, many schools are already recruiting parents as partners in moral education. One approach is to propose to parents the moral values the school wants to teach, get their input, and then get a commitment to common goals. Says the assistant headmaster who was upset by families defending children caught cheating: "We have suffered in the past from not having an explicit compact with our parents."

Another approach begins by recognizing that many parents are isolated from each other, don't know the parents of their children's friends, aren't sure what limits are appropriate for children of different ages, and so have trouble exercising parental authority. To help with that situation, one K–12 school in Washington, D.C., has formed "parent peer groups," which meet periodically (once a month, for example), sometimes at school, sometimes in a parent's home.

A teacher or the principal participates in each group. Each meeting begins with parents introducing themselves, giving their children's names, and suggesting one or two topics they would like to address. In the lower school (prekindergarten to grade 4), typical questions are, "How do you get your kids to help around the house?" and "What TV programs are right for young children?"

Middle school parents ask questions such as, "What would you do if your sixth-grader got invited to a birthday party where the entertainment was going to be an R-rated movie?" High school parents ask each other, "What do you do when your child gets invited to an open party and doesn't know whether the parents are going to be there or whether there'll be drinking?" "What rules do you have about using the car?"[34]

Schools that have sponsored parent support groups like these report that participating parents work together more to plan events for the school and community and feel helped in their parenting by being able to share values and get support from other parents. These schools are restoring what has been recently missing: *a moral community around the school* that provides the support system schools need to do effective character education.[35]

There are other reasons for optimism that families and schools can function as allies. Recall the large majority of parents who tell the public opinion polls that they want schools to "teach morals." Not all of them are passing the buck. Many are saying, "We're willing to do our part, but we need help."

Some parents, to be sure, will remain apathetic or hostile toward the school's efforts in the area of values. But it doesn't take everybody to make an idea work; it takes only a critical mass. Committed schools are already showing that there are many parents willing to join forces to help children grow into good and decent people. That alliance is an important part of the new character education.

CHAPTER 3

What Values Should Schools Teach?

A lot of teachers are scared of this area. They're afraid of tak-ing on vested interest groups. They worry about the legal aspects. Can somebody take them to court if they don't like the way the teacher is teaching values? Whose values should they teach? And where does God come in? Will you have some people on your neck if you mention God and other people on your neck if you don't?

—ALAN PARDOEN, Dean, State
University of New York
at Potsdam

E ven though polls show broad public support for the general idea of moral education—and growing numbers of schools are success-fully doing it—other schools hesitate. Says one superintendent: "We're dealing with so many different cultures and family situations that teaching values may be easier said than done."[1] Teachers worry about the flak they may get from some parents if they begin to teach values in a deliberate and systematic way.

Schools also wonder, "Should we *teach* values, in the sense of trying to get kids to adopt certain values, or should we just teach *about* val-ues?" Some educators argue that promoting the adoption of certain values is a form of indoctrination and that schools should restrict themselves to encouraging critical thinking about values. Others challenge that position, arguing, "Would we be satisfied to produce students who can think critically about a value such as honesty but nevertheless choose, in their own lives, to lie, cheat, and steal?"

Schools wishing to do values education, I believe, need to be confident that: (1) There are objectively worthwhile, universally agreed-upon values that schools can and should teach in a pluralistic society; and (2) schools should not only expose students to these values but also help them to *understand, internalize, and act upon* such values. To be confident about those two propositions, schools need first to get clear about the nature of values.

WHAT IS A "MORAL VALUE"?

Values are of two kinds: *moral* and *nonmoral*. Moral values such as honesty, responsibility, and fairness carry obligation. We feel obligated to keep a promise, pay our bills, care for our children, and be fair in our dealings with others. Moral values tell us what we *ought* to do. We must abide by them even when we'd rather not.

Nonmoral values carry no such obligation. They express what we want or like to do. I might personally value listening to classical music, for example, or reading a good novel. But clearly I am not obliged to do so.

Moral (obligatory) values can be further broken down into two categories: *universal* and *nonuniversal*. Universal moral values—such as treating all people justly and respecting their lives, liberty, and equality—bind all persons everywhere because they affirm our fundamental human worth and dignity. We have a right and even a duty to insist that all people behave in accordance with these universal moral values.

In 1948 the United Nations recognized the universal validity of these basic moral values by adopting the Universal Declaration of Human Rights. This landmark document asserts that *every* citizen of *every* nation has the right to: life, liberty, and freedom from personal attack; freedom from slavery; recognition before the law and the presumption of innocence until proven guilty; freedom from torture; freedom of conscience and religion; freedom of expression; privacy, family, and correspondence; freedom to participate freely in community life; education; and a standard of living adequate for maintaining health and well-being. True, not all nations consistently respect these rights in the actual way they treat their citizens. But these failures to live up to the Universal Declaration of Human Rights in no way deny the universal validity of the moral values underlying the document.

*Non*universal moral values, by contrast, do not carry a universal moral obligation. These are values—such as duties specific to one's religion (e.g., worshiping, fasting, observing holy days)—toward which I as an individual may feel a serious personal obligation. But I may not impose these personally felt obligations on others.

WHAT IS THE RELATIONSHIP BETWEEN MORALITY AND RELIGION?

We live in a religiously diverse society founded on the First Amendment principle that the government "shall make no law respecting an establishment of religion, or prohibiting the free exercise thereof." The fact that our society includes people of different religious beliefs, as well as people of no religious belief, is for some educators an obstacle to moral education. They think, "Doesn't morality get you into religion, and how can schools get into that without violating the First Amendment?"

For this reason it's important to clarify the relationship between morality and religion. Several points are relevant:

1. Most people in our country profess some kind of religious belief or identity. In a March 27, 1989, *Newsweek* poll, for example, 94 percent of Americans said they believe in a Supreme Being. In a 1981 national poll carried out by Research and Forecasts, Inc., three quarters of the American public said they considered themselves "religious."[2] For many people, their first and foremost guide to moral decisions is their religion.[3]

2. Religion is for many a central motive for leading a moral life. Although religions may differ on what we must do to gain salvation, they agree that our actions in this life, including our moral choices, affect our fate in the hereafter.

3. Within a religious worldview, God is seen as giving us the essential help, the grace, that we need to achieve the goodness commanded by God. Veteran educator Barbara Jones observes: "The moral decline in this country began when religious institutions started to lose their influence, and morality became divorced from the power to act morally. We are trying to do good without the empowering of God's help."[4]

4. The founders of our country saw an intimate connection between religion and our human rights and democratic government. The Declaration of Independence, which provides the moral framework for the

U.S. Constitution, asserts that the state cannot take away our rights because they come from God ("We hold these truths to be self-evident, that all Men are created equal, that they are endowed by their Creator with certain unalienable Rights, that among these are Life, Liberty, and the pursuit of Happiness . . .").

In his farewell presidential address in 1796, George Washington warned the nation against severing the connection between morality and religion. "Both reason and experience," he said, "forbid us to expect that national morality can prevail in exclusion of religious principle." As the first vice president under the new Constitution, John Adams expressed the consensus of his time when he wrote: "We have no government armed with power capable of contending with human passions unbridled by morality and religion. Our Constitution was made only for a moral and religious people."[5]

Religion has continued to be a significant moral force in American life. Leaders of social reform movements ranging from the abolition of slavery to the twentieth-century struggle for civil rights have been motivated by a deep religious belief: We are all equal in the sight of God, children of a common Creator who calls us to live in equality, harmony, and justice. This religious vision is not diminished by those who have betrayed it—persons who profess to believe in a God of love but practice intolerance and hatred.

5. Most students today are ignorant of the role of religion in our moral beginnings and development as a nation. One reason is that since the 1960s, the story of religion in American history has shrunk to nearly nothing in public school textbooks.[6] In 1986 New York University professor Paul Vitz published his much-discussed book *Censorship: Evidence of Bias in Our Textbooks,* reporting example after example of how the portrayal of religion had been systematically excluded from school texts.

One elementary social studies book, for instance, contained some 30 pages on the Pilgrims, including the first Thanksgiving, but not a single word or image that referred to religion as even a part of the Pilgrims' life. In another book cited by Vitz, a story by Nobel Laureate Jewish writer Isaac Bashevis Singer was altered: In the original, the main character, a boy, prayed "to God" and later remarked "Thank God"; in the edited school-text version, the words "to God" were taken out and the expression "Thank God" was changed to "Thank goodness."[7]

Recently, politically liberal groups such as People for the American Way and Americans United for the Separation of Church and State have joined other critics in calling for a restoration of religion to its proper place in American history and culture.[8] Schools, moreover, should encourage students to make use of *all* their intellectual and cultural resources—including their religious beliefs and values—when they consider social issues[9] (e.g., "What is our obligation to the poor?") and make personal moral decisions (e.g., "Is it right to have sex before marriage?").

6. There are many people, however, in whose lives religion does not play a significant role. There are others who, for one or another reason, have a negative attitude toward religion. They do not want their children being taught that being a moral person requires being religious. And they would be correct in pointing out that while public schools may teach *about* religion (showing its role in our culture and history), they may not, under the Constitution as presently interpreted, *promote* religion as good or true. That means that public schools have a twofold task: They should accurately portray the role of religion in history and encourage students to consider what their religion has to say about moral questions; but they must also find a basis for defining and teaching morality that compels rational assent without requiring religious belief.

7. The way to define morality in rational terms acceptable to all is suggested by an old theological principle—the idea of a "natural moral law"—confirmed by some recent psychological research. The research was a series of studies investigating children's moral reasoning, carried out by University of Illinois psychologist Larry Nucci. He asked several hundred Jewish, Catholic, and fundamentalist Protestant children questions about acts such as hitting, stealing, and damaging somebody's reputation. Would these things be wrong even if God had not given us a law prohibiting them?

Nearly all of the children of all faiths said *yes*, such actions would still be wrong. Moreover, 100 percent of the reasons children gave for this view had to do with the fact that such actions are unfair or harmful to others.[10]

In subsequent studies, Nucci asked children how they know that what God commands is right, and whether a hypothetical command by God could make morally right something they perceive to be wrong. Here is one such interview with a 10-year-old Jewish boy, Michael (a pseudonym):

INTERVIEWER: Michael, how do we know that what is written in the Torah is really the right thing to do?

MICHAEL: He doesn't harm us, do bad for us. We believe in God. We think that God wrote the Torah, and we think that God likes us if we do those things, and we think we are giving presents to God by praying, by following his rules.

INTERVIEWER: Okay, but how can we be sure that what God is telling us is really the right thing?

MICHAEL: We've tried it. We tried every rule in the Torah, and we know.

INTERVIEWER: Let's suppose that God had written in the Torah that Jews should steal. Would it then be right for Jews to steal?

MICHAEL: No.

INTERVIEWER: Why not?

MICHAEL: Even if God says it, we know he can't mean it, because it's a very bad thing to steal. Maybe it's a test, but we just know that he can't mean it.

INTERVIEWER: Why wouldn't God mean it?

MICHAEL: Because we think of God as very good—as an absolutely perfect person.

INTERVIEWER: And because he's perfect he wouldn't say to steal? Why not?

MICHAEL: Well, because we people are not perfect, but we still understand. We are not dumb. We still understand that stealing is a bad thing.[11]

Michael's responses to these questions, Nucci reports, are typical, paralleled by those given by children of other faiths. What these children are saying is that a good God can't command a bad thing like stealing—and that even a kid, using his intelligence, can figure out that something like stealing is bad because it hurts other people.

This research provides new support for what many theologians and philosophers have long held: There is a natural moral law that prohibits injustice to others and that can be arrived at through the use of human reason. This natural moral law is consistent with revealed religious principles (such as "Love your neighbor" and "Thou shalt not steal") but has its own independent logic that even children can grasp. The educational implication of this universal natural law is very important: It gives public schools the objective moral content—"Be just and caring toward others"—that they may legitimately teach in a religiously diverse society.

TWO GREAT MORAL VALUES:
RESPECT AND RESPONSIBILITY

The natural moral law defining the public school's moral agenda can be expressed in terms of two great values: *respect* and *responsibility*. These values constitute the core of a universal, public morality. They have objective, demonstrable worth in that they promote the good of the individual and the good of the whole community. These values of respect and responsibility are necessary for:

- Healthy personal development

- Caring interpersonal relationships

- A humane and democratic society

- A just and peaceful world

Respect and responsibility are the "fourth and fifth R's" that schools not only may but also must teach if they are to develop ethically literate persons who can take their place as responsible citizens of society. What are the concrete moral meanings of these foundational values?

Respect. Respect means showing regard for the worth of someone or something. It takes three major forms: respect for oneself, respect for other people, and respect for all forms of life and the environment that sustains them.

Respect for self requires us to treat our own life and person as having inherent value. That's why it's wrong to engage in self-destructive behavior such as drug or alcohol abuse. Respect for others requires us to treat all other human beings—even those we dislike—as having dignity and rights equal to our own. That's the heart of the Golden Rule ("Do unto others as you would have them do unto you"). Respect for the whole complex web of life prohibits cruelty to animals and calls us to act with care toward the natural environment, the fragile ecosystem on which all life depends.

Other forms of respect derive from these. Respect for property, for example, comes from understanding that property is an extension of a person or a community of persons. Respect for authority comes from understanding that legitimate authority figures are entrusted with the care of others. Without somebody in charge, you can't run a family, a school, or a country. When people don't respect authority, things don't work very well and everybody suffers.

"Common courtesy" also derives from a basic respect for persons. I once spent time in the classroom of Molly Angelini, a gentle fifth-grade teacher in Moravia, New York, who made courtesy-as-respect a high priority. If a student banged a desk top shut, Mrs. Angelini paused to allow the student to say "Excuse me" to the class (they had discussed the fact that loud noises were an interruption if someone was speaking or a distraction if people were trying to think). Children were expected to apologize if they called someone a name. They were taught to say "Pardon me?" instead of "What?" when they wished something repeated. They were taught to say "Thank you" to the cafeteria workers who served them as they went through the lunch line. And they were taught that all of these behaviors were not mechanical gestures but meaningful ways of respecting other people.

Finally, just as the value of respect is involved in the smallest everyday interactions, it also underlies the major organizing principles of a democracy. It's respect for persons that leads people to create constitutions that require the government to protect, not violate, the rights of the governed.

The first moral mission of our schools is to teach this fundamental value of respect for self, others, and the environment.

Responsibility. Responsibility is an extension of respect. If we respect other people, we value them. If we value them, we feel a measure of responsibility for their welfare.

Responsibility literally means "ability to respond."[12] It means orienting toward others, paying attention to them, actively responding to their needs. Responsibility emphasizes our positive obligations to care for each other.

Respect, by comparison, emphasizes our negative obligations. It tells us for the most part what *not* to do. This is sometimes called a "prohibitive morality." Lest we underestimate the "power of negative thinking," philosopher Jon Moline points out the importance of these moral prohibitions: They tell us our duty exactly.[13] "Thou shalt not murder" has a precision that "Love your neighbor" does not.

A list of moral don'ts, however, is not enough. A responsibility ethic supplies the vital giving side of morality. Where respect says "Don't hurt," responsibility says "Do help." It's true that the call to "love your neighbor" and "think of others" is open-ended; it doesn't tell us how much we should sacrifice for our families, give to charitable causes, work for our communities, or be there for those who need us. But a morality of responsibility does point us in the right direction. Over the long haul it calls us to try, in whatever way we can, to nurture and support each other, alleviate suffering, and make the world a better place for all.

What else does responsibility mean? It means being dependable, not letting others down. We help people by keeping our commitments, and we create problems for them when we don't. "I'm distressed," says a high school band instructor, "by the tendency I see in kids to think they can quit at any time." Responsibility means carrying out any job or duty—in the family, at school, in the workplace—to the best of our ability. In recent years there has been no more disturbing index of declining work responsibility than reports that large numbers of adults use drugs on the job—even as they provide hospital care, build cars, operate trains, and repair nuclear reactors.

Finally, an emphasis on responsibility is especially important today as a corrective for the modern preoccupation with "rights." In the not too distant past, British essayist Christopher Derrick notes, when people thought about morality, they were likely to ask: "Am I fulfilling all my obligations?" If the answer was partly negative, their grievance was *against themselves;* they had to strive to do better.

Today when people think about morality, they are more likely to ask: "Am I getting all my rights?" When the answer is partly negative (as it invariably is, life being imperfect), people have a sense of grievance *against others,* either other individuals or society at large. "The seeds of contention and violence," Derrick observes, are thereby sown.[14]

Obviously, rights are an indispensable part of morality. But one of the moral challenges of our time is to balance rights and responsibilities and to raise young people who have a strong sense of both.

OTHER MORAL VALUES SCHOOLS SHOULD TEACH

Respect and responsibility are the two foundational moral values that schools should teach. Are there others?

There are—such as honesty, fairness, tolerance, prudence, self-discipline, helpfulness, compassion, cooperation, courage, and a host of democratic values. These specific values are forms of respect and/or responsibility or aids to acting respectfully and responsibly.

Honesty is one such value. Dealing honestly with people—not deceiving them, cheating them, or stealing from them—is one basic way of respecting them. So is fairness, which requires us to treat people impartially and not play favorites.

Tolerance, too, expresses respect. Although tolerance can dissolve into a neutral relativism that seeks to escape ethical judgment, tolerance in its root meaning is one of the hallmarks of civilization.[15] Tolerance is a fair and objective attitude toward those whose ideas, race, or creed are different from our own. Tolerance is what makes the world safe for diversity.

Other values help us respect ourselves. Prudence, for example, tells us not to put ourselves in physical or moral danger (the old idea of "avoiding the occasion of sin"). Self-discipline tells us not to indulge in self-demeaning or self-destructive pleasures but to pursue what is good for us—and to pursue healthy pleasures in moderation. Self-discipline also enables us to delay gratification, develop our talents, work toward distant goals, and make something of our lives. These are all forms of self-respect.

In a similar way, values such as helpfulness, compassion, and cooperation aid us in carrying out the broad ethic of responsibility. A helpful spirit takes pleasure in doing a kindness. Compassion (meaning "suffering with") helps us not only know our responsibility but also feel it. Cooperation recognizes that "no man is an island"[16] and that, in an increasingly interdependent world, we must work together toward goals as basic as human survival.

Some qualities, such as moral courage, are an aid to both respect and responsibility. Courage helps young people respect themselves by resisting peer pressure to do things that are harmful to their own welfare. Courage helps all of us respect the rights of others when we face pressure to join the crowd in perpetrating an injustice. Courage also enables us to take bold, positive action on behalf of others.

What about democratic values? It's easy to see how they help to create a society based on respect and responsibility. Rule of law, equality of opportunity, due process, reasoned argument, representative government, checks and balances, democratic decision-making—all these are "procedural values" that, taken together, define democracy.

Democracy, in turn, is the best way we know of securing our individual rights (respecting persons) and promoting the general welfare (acting responsibly for the good of all). Teaching an understanding and appreciation of these democratic values—and how they are made realities through the laws of the land—is a central part of the school's moral charge. These values also help us define the kind of "patriotism" that schools should teach. In a democracy, patriotism doesn't mean

"My country, right or wrong"; it means loyalty to the great democratic values on which the country was founded.

DEVELOPING A LIST OF TARGET VALUES

Even if a school begins with respect and responsibility—which I think are helpful starting points—and ends up with most or all of the values I've discussed, it's still important for people to go through the process of working up their own list of values they want to teach. (See Chapter 20 for examples of ways schools have gone about doing that.) That process is a chance to bring together—or at least survey for their input—teachers, administrators, other school staff, parents, students, and community representatives—to get broad-scale support. Moreover, the actual list that a school or district comes up with in this way is likely to bear its own special stamp and distinctive priorities.

It's instructive—a way to identify our moral blind spots—to compare lists drawn up by different groups, especially groups in countries other than our own. For example, when the Ontario, Canada, Ministry of Education identified twenty values for schools to teach, its list included moderation, patience, and peace[17]—three values less likely to show up on U.S. lists but obviously important for the well-being of both the individual and society.

Getting agreement about shared values does not, of course, guarantee that people will agree about how to *apply* those values in every situation. It's at the point of applying values, especially when values conflict, that differences of moral judgment or emphasis often arise. For example, what weight should be given to "respect for life" and "freedom of choice" in the abortion debate? What does "patriotism" mean in time of war?

However, disagreement at the level of application must not obscure agreement about the values (e.g., respect for life, liberty, responsible citizenship) themselves—or the fact that most of the time we do agree about how to translate moral values into social living. For example, our civil laws, defining our rights and obligations as citizens, represent literally hundreds of ways we have agreed to put our shared values into action. And when it comes to the moral values we want our children to have, we can readily agree on the basics. We don't want them to lie, cheat on tests, take what's not theirs, call names, hit each other, or be cruel to animals; we do want them to tell the truth, play fair, be polite, respect their parents and teachers, do their schoolwork, and be kind to others.

In short, even in a society where values often clash, respect, responsibility, and their everyday manifestations are common moral ground. Recognizing that common ground is the essential first step in doing values education in our schools.

CHAPTER 4

What Is Good Character?

Strong personal character should manifest itself in service to organizations and communities and in courage in public life. The moral crisis of our time means more and more people lack the liberating self-mastery that allows them to commit and serve with an independence and integrity befitting a free people.

—WALTER NICGORSKI, "The Moral Crisis"[1]

Character is destiny.

—HERACLITUS

Respect and responsibility—and all the other values that derive from them—give schools the moral content they can and should teach in a democracy. But schools need more than a list of values. They need a concept of character—and a commitment to developing it in their students.

One of the most significant ethical developments during the past two decades has been a deepening concern for character.[2] We are rediscovering the link between private character and public life. We are coming to see that our societal moral problems reflect, in no small measure, our personal vices. Scholarly discussion, media analysis, and everyday conversation have all focused attention on the character of our elected leaders, our fellow citizens, and our children.

I encounter this concern wherever I go. Recently I was asked to speak to school parents in an affluent community in the Northeast. One of the mothers met me at the airport. She said, "I worry about the effects of all the material affluence that surrounds our kids. Will they come to value it above everything else?" The eighth-grade daughter of the family I stayed with that night told of a classmate whose parents offered to pay her $100 for every A and $75 for every B she got on her report card. For a C or lower, she had money taken away. Other parents in this community have offered their kids $10,000 if they don't smoke before they graduate. (When kids break the deal, as they often do, parents feel they have no card left to play.)

Traditional wisdom and the lessons of history teach us that riches tend to corrupt. But today, as educational writer James Stenson observes, *most* of us are rich when measured by the standards of the past. We enjoy a level of prosperity—an abundance of food, drink, amusements, clothing, conveniences, and the like—unprecedented in human history. And yet, as Stenson points out, our children are not happier. On the contrary, as young adults they are often "weighed down with skepticism, despair, self-centeredness and loneliness."[3] A great many are soft and undisciplined, put off by hard work and drawn to the easy pleasures of sex, drugs, drinking, material consumption, and absorption in the electronic media. They lack strong personal character.

WHAT IS CHARACTER?

Good character is what we want for our children. Of what does it consist?

The Greek philosopher Aristotle defined good character as the life of right conduct—right conduct in relation to other persons and in relation to oneself.[4] Aristotle reminds us of what, in modern times, we are prone to forget: The virtuous life includes self-oriented virtues (such as self-control and moderation) as well as other-oriented virtues (such as generosity and compassion), and the two kinds of virtue are connected. We need to be in control of ourselves—our appetites, our passions—to do right by others.

Character, observes contemporary philosopher Michael Novak, is "a compatible mix of all those virtues identified by religious traditions, literary stories, the sages, and persons of common sense down through history."[5] No one, as Novak points out, has all the virtues, and everyone has some weaknesses. Persons of much-admired character may differ considerably from one another.

Building on these classic understandings, I would like to offer a way of thinking about character that is appropriate for values education: Character consists of *operative values,* values in action. We progress in our character as a value becomes a virtue, a reliable inner disposition to respond to situations in a morally good way.

Character so conceived has three interrelated parts: moral knowing, moral feeling, and moral behavior. *Good character consists of knowing the good, desiring the good, and doing the good*—habits of the mind, habits of the heart, and habits of action. All three are necessary for leading a moral life; all three make up moral maturity. When we think about the kind of character we want for our children, it's clear that we want them to be able to judge what is right, care deeply about what is right, and then do what they believe to be right—even in the face of pressure from without and temptation from within.

AN EXAMPLE OF GOOD CHARACTER

We have no trouble recognizing good character when we see it. To illustrate how character involves moral knowing, feeling, and acting, let me share with you a story that a father told me about his 19-year-old son.[6]

Andy was a bright boy with a special talent for music, but he was going through a difficult time. He didn't know what he wanted to do with his life, or what to do until he decided. Without a direction, he wasn't motivated to go to college, and he didn't have his heart in the odd jobs he picked up. He was living with his parents, but his general unhappiness often made for strained relations with them.

Then Andy got a job that made use of his musical abilities and his particular skill at the organ. He worked as an assistant to a man in his late twenties who tuned organs and pianos in a large city. The man did an especially good business in organs, since there were many churches in the city that needed this service. For the first time in his life, Andy was making good money at a job he enjoyed.

About three weeks later, however, Andy went to his father and said that something was really bothering him. The man he worked for, he had discovered, was running a crooked business. "He's ripping off these churches," Andy explained. "He tells them they need to have their organs tuned four times a year, which isn't true. I've watched him—he'll come in and play the organ for half an hour and make like he's adjusting it, but he really doesn't do anything. I don't think I can go on working for this guy."

A couple of days later, Andy quit the job and went to a priest he knew at one of the churches to advise him to get another tuner. Andy's father, in telling this story, said: "He gave up good money, but for a good reason. I told him I was proud of what he had done."

Andy's decision clearly involved all three parts of character: moral knowing (judging his boss's behavior to be wrong); moral feeling (being upset about the churches' getting charged for phony service, and disturbed to be part of a dishonest business); and moral action (quitting the job and notifying at least one church about the problem). In this case, moral judgment gave rise to strong feelings, and both judgment and feelings motivated moral action.

The accompanying diagram identifies the particular moral qualities—the character traits—that make up moral knowing, moral feeling, and moral action.[7] These, I believe, are the specific qualities we should try to help our children develop, for their sake and for the sake of society.

The arrows linking each domain of character with the other two are meant to emphasize their interrelationship. Moral knowing, feeling, and acting do not function as separate spheres but interpenetrate and influence each other in all sorts of ways.

Moral judgment can give rise to moral feeling, but moral emotion can also influence thinking. In her illuminating book, *In Good Conscience: Reason and Emotion in Moral Decision Making,* Mercy College psychologist Sidney Callahan points out that much of our creative moral thinking arises from emotionally laden experience. Important moral revolutions have been initiated by empathy felt for previously excluded groups (slaves, women, workers, children, the handicapped, and so on).

Moral judgment and moral feelings quite obviously affect our moral behavior, especially when they work together. But here, too, the influence is reciprocal: How we behave also influences how we think and feel (e.g., when we forgive and act kindly toward someone with whom we had been angry, we commonly find that our thoughts and feelings regarding that person become more positive).

Let's look now at each domain of character and its constituent components. Keep in mind that in the lived moral life, these various components of character typically work together in complex, simultaneous ways of which we may not even be aware.

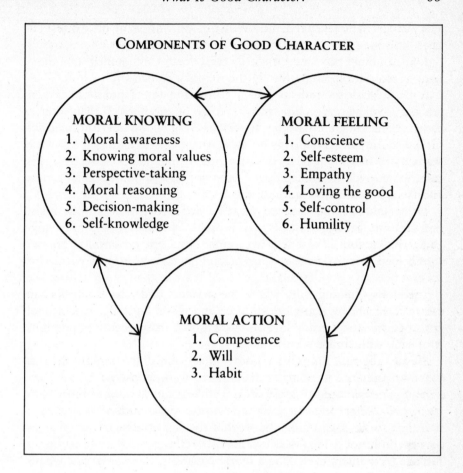

COMPONENTS OF GOOD CHARACTER

MORAL KNOWING
1. Moral awareness
2. Knowing moral values
3. Perspective-taking
4. Moral reasoning
5. Decision-making
6. Self-knowledge

MORAL FEELING
1. Conscience
2. Self-esteem
3. Empathy
4. Loving the good
5. Self-control
6. Humility

MORAL ACTION
1. Competence
2. Will
3. Habit

MORAL KNOWING

There are many different kinds of moral knowing we need to draw on as we deal with life's moral challenges. The following six stand out as desirable goals of character education.

1. **Moral awareness.** A common moral failing in people of all ages is moral blindness; we simply don't see the ways that the situation at hand involves a moral issue and calls for moral judgment. Young people are especially prone to this failing—to act without asking "Is this right?"

Even if the general question "What's right?" does cross a person's mind, he or she may fail utterly to see the specific moral issues in a situation. A father offered the following illustration involving his 15-year-old son.

John, an intelligent and ordinarily trustworthy boy, joined four classmates on a dinner outing during the school's French Club trip to Quebec. Because these students had a reputation for responsibility, their teacher gave them special permission to go off alone. With their dinner, the students ordered a bottle of wine. Doing so violated the school's "No drinking on school trips" policy, which was well known to all the students. When the teacher later learned of the violation, she felt personally betrayed by the students' behavior. Upon the students' return to school, the principal gave all five a day of in-school suspension.

When John's father learned what he had done, he was quite upset and sat him down to discuss it. John said, "I honestly didn't see anything wrong with it—I knew we weren't going to get drunk." His father helped John to see that what he and his friends did was wrong for several reasons: It violated the personal trust of their teacher; it broke the school's drinking rule, which the students understood and had in effect agreed to by going on the trip; and it endangered future school trips, which were already known to be in jeopardy because of previous problems with student drinking.

"I was amazed," the father said, "that John didn't see any of this when he and the others made the decision to order the wine."

Young people need to know that their first moral responsibility is to *use their intelligence to see when a situation requires moral judgment*— and then to think carefully about what the right course of action is.

A second aspect of moral awareness is taking the trouble to be informed. Very often, in making a moral judgment, we can't decide what's right until we know what's true. If we don't have the foggiest idea what's going on internationally, we certainly can't make a sound moral judgment about our country's foreign policy. If we're not aware that there is poverty in our midst or torture in many countries or hunger in most of the world, we can't support social policies or groups that help to alleviate such problems.

Responsible citizenship demands this effort to be informed. Values education can teach that lesson by involving students in the hard work of trying to determine the facts before making a moral judgment.

2. **Knowing moral values.** Moral values such as respect for life and liberty, responsibility toward others, honesty, fairness, tolerance, courtesy, self-discipline, integrity, kindness, compassion, and courage define all the many ways of being a good person. Taken together, they are

the moral heritage one generation passes on to the next. Ethical literacy requires knowing these values.

Knowing a value also means understanding how to apply it in various situations. What does "responsibility" mean when you see somebody defacing school property or taking something that isn't theirs? What does "respect" tell you to do when someone passes on information that is damaging to another person's reputation? When students, both boys and girls, say on questionnaires that it's okay for a man to force sex on a woman if he's spent money on her, that should tell us that much of the work of moral education is "translation"—helping young people translate the abstract values of respect and responsibility into concrete moral behavior in their personal relationships.

3. **Perspective-taking.** Perspective-taking is the ability to take the viewpoint of other people, see a situation as they see it, imagine how they might think, react, and feel. It's a prerequisite for moral judgment: We can't very well respect people and act justly toward their needs if we don't understand them. A fundamental goal of moral education must be to help students to experience the world from the point of view of others, especially those who are different from themselves.

4. **Moral reasoning.** Moral reasoning involves understanding what it means to be moral and *why* we should be moral. Why is it important to keep a promise? Do my best work? Share what I have with others in need? Moral reasoning has been the focus of most of this century's psychological research on moral development, beginning with Jean Piaget's 1932 book *The Moral Judgment of the Child* and continuing with the research of Lawrence Kohlberg, Carol Gilligan, William Damon, Nancy Eisenberg, James Rest, Mary Brabeck, and others.[8]

As children develop moral reasoning—and the research tells us that growth is gradual[9]—they learn what counts as a good moral reason for doing something and what doesn't count. At its higher levels, moral reasoning also includes an understanding of classic moral principles: "Respect the intrinsic worth of every individual"; "Act to achieve the greatest good for the greatest number"; and "Act as you would have all others act under similar circumstances." Such principles guide moral action in many different situations.

5. **Decision-making.** Asked to describe a real-life dilemma he was experiencing, a 13-year-old wrote:

> There is one kid in school who isn't as smart as most kids but is in some regular classes. He used to be one of my friends when I was younger,

but then he started slowing down. Now some of my friends make fun of him, but I don't say anything to them.

Not at peace with this acquiescence in his peers' cruelty to his former friend, this teenager needs to make a moral decision. He can do so thoughtfully by asking: What are my options? What are the probable consequences of different courses of action for the people who will be affected by my decision? What course of action would most likely maximize the good consequences and be faithful to the important values at stake?

Being able to think one's way through a moral problem in this manner is the skill of reflective decision-making. A what-are-my-choices, what-are-the-consequences approach to making moral decisions has been taught even to preschoolers.[10]

6. **Self-knowledge.** Knowing ourselves is the hardest kind of moral knowledge to obtain, but it is necessary for character development. Becoming a moral person requires the ability to review our own behavior and critically evaluate it.

Developing moral self-knowledge includes becoming aware of the strengths and weaknesses of our individual characters and how to compensate for our weaknesses, among them, the nearly universal human tendency of doing what we want and then justifying it after the fact. Some teachers try to help students develop this self-knowledge by having them keep "ethics journals"—noting moral events in their lives, how they responded to them, and whether their response was as ethically responsible as it might have been.

Moral awareness, knowing moral values, perspective-taking, moral reasoning, decision-making, and self-knowledge—these are the qualities of mind that make up moral knowing. All make an important contribution to the cognitive side of character.

MORAL FEELING

The emotional side of character has been vastly neglected in discussions of moral education, but it is profoundly important. Simply knowing what is right is no guarantee of right conduct. People can be very smart about matters of right and wrong and still choose the wrong.

John Dean, after being sentenced to jail for his role in the Watergate scandal, was asked by an interviewer: "Do you think the outcome of your career might have been different had law school focused to a greater extent on questions of professional responsibility?" Dean answered:

> No, I don't think so. I must say that I knew the things I was doing were wrong; one learns the difference between right and wrong long before entering law school. A course in legal ethics wouldn't have changed anything.[11]

A few years ago, *The New York Times* carried a story that provides another example of the difference between knowing what's right and doing it. According to the *Times* report, Random House had announced that it would not go ahead with plans to publish a book titled *Telling Right from Wrong*, dealing with moral philosophy applied to everyday life. This was most regrettable, said Random House's editor, because the book was "absolutely brilliant" in its treatment of ethics and a "terribly important" work.

The reason for halting publication: The author of this insightful book about ethics had sent Random House a letter that praised his book highly and was ostensibly written by Professor Robert Nozick, chairman of Harvard University's Philosophy Department. In fact, the laudatory letter had been forged by the author himself. When the author's deception came to light, he made no apology; instead, he defended his forged letter as "vigorous gamesmanship."

How much we *care* about being honest, fair, and decent toward others clearly influences whether our moral knowledge leads to moral behavior. This emotional side of character, like the intellectual side, is open to development by schools and families. The following aspects of emotional moral life warrant our attention as we try to educate for good character.

1. **Conscience.** Conscience has two sides: a cognitive side—knowing what's right—and an emotional side—feeling obligated to do what's right. Lots of people know what's right but feel little obligation to act accordingly.

Three colleagues and I recently completed a study of cheating at our college that sheds light on the cognitive and emotional aspects of conscience.[12] We gave a several-page "Questionnaire on Academic Attitudes and Behavior" to a random sample of over 300 graduate and undergraduate students from all departments on campus.[13] The questionnaire asked, "Do you consider the following behavior wrong?" and listed seven behaviors, such as using crib notes on a test, copying another student's assignment, submitting another's report or paper as one's own, and copying word for word from a book without crediting the author. Students could respond, "Yes," "No," or "It depends."

To our surprise, we got relatively few "It depends" (under 10 percent of the responses). Instead, the overwhelming majority of students judged the various kinds of academic dishonesty to be wrong. For several of the behaviors, the disapproval rate was more than 90 percent.

Then we listed the same behaviors and asked a different question: "Would you ever do the following if you were certain you would not get caught?" Now the percentages shifted, sometimes dramatically. More than half said yes, they would cheat on a test if they could get away with it; more than half said they would copy another person's assignment; nearly half said they would help another student on an exam in a way not permitted by the instructor.

The meaning of these results is clear: While nearly all students judged the various forms of cheating to be wrong, significantly fewer were sufficiently *committed* to the value of academic honesty to refrain from cheating when they could get away with it. Large numbers of students lacked a fully developed conscience in that they didn't feel obligated to avoid the behavior they judged to be wrong.

A mature conscience includes, besides a sense of moral obligation, the capacity for constructive guilt. If you feel obligated in conscience to behave in a certain way, you will feel guilty when you don't. This is different from destructive guilt, which causes someone to think, "I'm a bad person." Constructive guilt says, "I didn't live up to my own standards. I feel bad about that, but I'm going to do better." The capacity for constructive guilt also helps us resist temptation.

For people of conscience, morality matters. They are committed to living out their moral values because those values are deeply rooted in a moral self. Such persons can't lie and cheat and walk away from it because they identify with their moral actions; they feel "out of character" when they go against their values. Becoming personally committed to moral values is a developmental process, and helping students in that process is one of our most important challenges as moral educators.

2. **Self-esteem.** When we have a healthy measure of self-esteem, we value ourselves. When we value ourselves, we respect ourselves. We're less likely to abuse our bodies or minds or allow others to abuse us.

When we have self-esteem, we're less dependent on the approval of others. Studies show that children with high self-esteem are more resistant to peer pressure and better able to follow their own judgment than those with low self-esteem.[14]

When we have positive regard for ourselves, we're more likely to treat others in positive ways. If we have little or no self-respect, it's hard to extend respect to other people.[15]

Teachers know the importance of self-esteem. "I see more and more children coming to school with poor self-concepts," says a third-grade teacher. "These tend to be the same children who are out for themselves."

High self-esteem by itself doesn't assure good character. It's obviously possible to have self-esteem based on things that have nothing to do with good character—such as possessions, good looks, popularity, or power. Part of our challenge as educators is helping young people develop positive self-regard based on values such as responsibility, honesty, and kindness and on faith in their own capacity for goodness.

3. **Empathy.** Empathy is identification with, or vicarious experience of, the state of another person. Empathy enables us to climb out of our own skin and into another's. It's the emotional side of perspective-taking.

Differences in empathy appear at an early age. In one study, toddlers between ages one and two responded very differently to another child in distress. Some showed concern and offered comfort or help. Others, however, were simply curious. Still others withdrew in response to the other's distress, and some children even became aggressive, scolding or hitting the complaining victim.[16] The fact that children are so different in their natural inclination to empathize suggests that parents and teachers will need to work harder with some children to help them understand and be sympathetic toward the feelings of others.

In our society today we may be witnessing a decline in empathy. Increasingly, youth crime has included brutal acts that reveal a complete detachment from the suffering of the victim. The perpetrators often turn out to be young people that family and neighbors describe as "good kids." They may be capable of empathy toward those they know and care about, but they show an utter lack of empathic feeling for the victims of their violence. One of our tasks as moral educators is developing a *generalized* empathy, the kind that sees beneath differences and responds to our common humanity.

4. **Loving the good.** The highest form of character includes being genuinely attracted to the good.

Says Kevin Ryan, director of Boston University's Center for the Advancement of Ethics and Character: "As a parent, I want my children to develop an emotional attachment to being a good person. When I think of their moral education in school, my question is: What is happening there that will help them fall in love with the good?". Writes Boston College psychologist Kirk Kilpatrick: "In education for virtue, the heart is trained as well as the mind. The virtuous person learns not only to distinguish between good and evil but to love the one and hate the other." [17] That's why teachers have traditionally looked to literature as a way of instilling a felt sense of right and wrong. When children encounter villains and heroes in the pages of a good book, they feel repelled by the evil and drawn, irresistibly, to the good.

When people love the good, they take pleasure in doing good. They have a morality of desire, not just a morality of duty. This capacity to find fulfillment in service is not limited to saints; it's part of the moral potential of ordinary people, even children. That potential is being developed, through programs like peer tutoring and community service, in schools all across the country.

5. **Self-control.** In 1978 Ronald Trowbridge was an English professor at a large university when his institution was struck for two weeks. When Trowbridge crossed the picket line, he found people he had considered close colleagues and even friends screaming "scab" and X-rated expletives at him. He wondered, "How can someone listen to Mozart, read Jane Austen, speak French, attend teas, and then degenerate into a mobster?"

Emotion can overwhelm reason. That's one reason why self-control is a necessary moral virtue.

A fourth-grade teacher reprimanded two girls who were insulting each other during ethics class. "Don't you know," one of the girls protested, "that we can't be ethical all the time! We don't *want* to be ethical all the time—sometimes we're mean to someone because we *want* to hurt them." She's right, of course; we don't want to be ethical all the time. Self-control helps us be ethical even when we don't want to be.

Self-control is also necessary to curb self-indulgence. If one looks for the roots of the present moral disorder, writes University of Notre Dame Program of Liberal Studies professor Walter Nicgorski, "one finds it in self-indulgence, in the pursuit of pleasure that leads so many to absorb themselves totally in the pursuit of financial gain. High ideals fall in the face of this pattern." [18] And unless self-control becomes a greater part of the character of young people, problems such as teen substance abuse and premature sexual activity will not be significantly reduced.

6. **Humility.** Humility is a neglected moral virtue but an essential part of good character. Humility is the affective side of self-knowledge. It is both genuine openness to the truth and a willingness to act to correct our failings.

Humility also helps us overcome pride. The great Christian writer C. S. Lewis called pride "the worst vice, a spiritual cancer." [19] Pride is the source of arrogance, prejudice, looking down on others. Wounded pride feeds anger and blocks forgiveness.

Finally, humility is the best safeguard against doing evil. The French scientist and philosopher Blaise Pascal observed that "Evil is never done so thoroughly or so well as when it is done with a good conscience." The ultimate sin of pride is self-deception, doing evil and calling it good. In his provocative book *People of the Lie: The Hope for Healing Human Evil,* psychiatrist Scott Peck argues that self-righteous people are capable of great evil because they are incapable of self-criticism. They tell themselves the lie that they are not capable of doing wrong. [20] Believing that, they are able to commit any evil, even genocide.

Conscience, self-esteem, empathy, loving the good, self-control, and humility—these make up the emotional side of our moral selves. These feelings about self, others, and goodness itself combine with moral knowing to form the source of our moral motivation; they help us cross the bridge from knowing what's right to doing it. The presence or absence of these moral feelings explains in large part why some people practice their moral principles and others do not. For this reason, values education that is merely intellectual—that touches the mind but not the heart—misses a crucial part of character.

MORAL ACTION

Moral action is, to a large extent, the outcome of the other two parts of character. If people have the moral qualities of intellect and emotion we have just examined, they are likely to do what they know and feel to be right.

There are times, however, when we may know what we should do, feel we should do it, but still fail to translate thought and feeling into action. To understand fully what moves a person to act morally—or keeps a person from doing so—we need to look at three more aspects of character: competence, will, and habit.

1. **Competence.** Moral competence is having the ability to turn moral judgment and feeling into effective moral action. To solve a conflict

fairly, for example, we need practical skills: listening, communicating our viewpoint without denigrating the other, and working out a mutually acceptable solution. When I was a marriage and family counselor, most of the people I saw did not have these skills.

Competence comes into play in other moral situations as well. To aid a person in distress, we must be able to conceive and execute a plan of action. That's easier to do if we've had previous experience helping people under unusual circumstances. For example: Psychologist Ervin Staub found that children who had had guided experience in role-playing a series of distress situations in which one child helped another were subsequently more likely (compared to children without such practice at helping) to investigate the sound of a child crying in a nearby room.[21] A recent study of 400 people who helped Jews escape the Nazis finds that these rescuers had, in addition to compassionate values, a strong sense of personal competence.[22]

2. **Will.** The right choice in a moral situation is usually the hard one. Being good frequently requires a real act of will, a mobilizing of moral energy to do what we think we should.

It takes will to keep emotion under the control of reason. It takes will to see and think through all the moral dimensions of a situation. It takes will to put duty before pleasure. It takes will to resist temptation, stand up to peer pressure, and buck the tide. Will is at the core of moral courage.

3. **Habit.** In a great many situations, moral conduct benefits from habit. People who have good character, as William Bennett has pointed out, "act truthfully, loyally, bravely, kindly, and fairly without being much tempted by the opposite course."[23] Often they don't even think consciously about "the right choice." They do the right thing by force of habit.

For this reason, children need, as part of their moral education, lots of opportunities to *develop* good habits, plenty of practice at being good persons. That means repeated experiences in doing what's helpful and honest and courteous and fair. The good habits thereby formed will serve them well even when the going is tough.

In a person of good character, moral knowing, feeling, and acting generally work together to support each other. Not always, of course; even exceptionally good people often fall short of their best moral selves. But as we develop character—a lifelong process—the moral life we lead increasingly integrates judgment, feeling, and patterns of right conduct.

CHARACTER AND THE MORAL ENVIRONMENT

Character doesn't function in a vacuum; it functions in a social environment. Often that environment suppresses moral concerns. Sometimes it is such that many or even most people feel foolish doing the "moral thing." Here, for example, is the response of a 10-year-old girl from the Bronx who was asked, as part of an IQ test, "What are you supposed to do if you find someone's wallet or pocketbook in a store?" She answered:

> I know what you're *supposed* to do—take it to the police station. But you don't do this in New York. Just take the money and throw the rest away . . . You're supposed to find out whose it is, but you have to be out of your mind to do this in New York.[24]

Dr. Paul Mok, a psychologist who has conducted seminars on values for large corporations, describes the corrosive effects of a company environment that tolerates shoddy ethics:

> If employees see a frequent pattern of billing customers for false charges, padding expense accounts, or altering time records, they can become desensitized to their own values and accept what goes on around them as "the way things are." If you don't spend some time in a company on ethics, then ethics will take a remote back seat in people's consciousness.[25]

A psychology of character, to understand how people go morally awry and how to help them be good, has to pay attention to the impact of environment. So do schools if they wish to develop character. They must provide a moral environment that accents good values and keeps them in the forefront of everyone's consciousness. It takes a long time for a value to become a virtue—to develop from mere intellectual awareness into personal habits of thinking, feeling, and acting that make it a functioning priority. The whole school environment, the moral culture of the school, has to support that growth.

Respect, responsibility, and their derivatives are the *values* that schools may legitimately teach. Moral knowing, feeling, and action in their many manifestations are the *qualities of character* that make moral values a lived reality. The next question, and what the rest of this book attempts to answer, is: What are all the ways that schools can teach these values and develop these qualities of character in our children?

PART TWO

CLASSROOM STRATEGIES FOR TEACHING RESPECT AND RESPONSIBILITY

Teaching Respect and Responsibility: the Big Ideas

Parts 2 and 3 of this book present a comprehensive approach to values education aimed at teaching respect and responsibility and developing the kind of character that puts those values into practice. These are the "big ideas" that define this approach:

1. Down through history and all over the world, education has had two great goals: to help people become smart and to help them become good.

2. "Good" can be defined in terms of moral values that have objective worth—values that affirm our human dignity and promote the good of the individual and society.

3. Two universal moral values form the core of a public, teachable morality: respect and responsibility.

4. *Respect* means showing regard for the worth of someone or something. It includes respect for self, respect for the rights and dignity of all persons, and respect for the environment that sustains all life. Respect is the restraining side of morality; it keeps us from hurting what we ought to value.

Responsibility is the active side of morality. It includes taking care of self and others, fulfilling our obligations, contributing to our communities, alleviating suffering, and building a better world.

5. To educate for respect and responsibility—to make them operative values in the lives of students—is to educate for *character*. Character consists of:
   - *moral knowing* (moral awareness, knowing moral values, perspective-taking, moral reasoning, decision-making, and self-knowledge)
   - *moral feeling* (conscience, self-esteem, empathy, loving the good, self-control, and humility)
   - *moral action* (competence, will, and habit)

6. Faced with a deteriorating social fabric, schools that hope to build character must take a *comprehensive, all-embracing approach to values education* that uses all phases of school life to foster character development. This comprehensive approach includes 12 classroom and schoolwide strategies (each explained and illustrated in the chapters that follow) aimed at making respect and responsibility living values in the character of the young.

Within the classroom, a comprehensive approach calls upon *the teacher* to:

1. **Act as caregiver, model, and mentor,** treating students with love and respect, setting a good example, supporting prosocial behavior, and correcting hurtful actions.

2. **Create a moral community in the classroom,** helping students know each other, respect and care about each other, and feel valued membership in the group.

3. **Practice moral discipline,** using the creation and enforcement of rules as opportunities to foster moral reasoning, self-control, and a generalized respect for others.

4. **Create a democratic classroom environment,** involving students in decision-making and shared responsibility for making the classroom a good place to be and to learn.

5. **Teach values through the curriculum,** using academic subjects as a vehicle for examining ethical issues. (This is simultaneously a schoolwide strategy when the curriculum addresses cross-grade concerns such as sex, drug, and alcohol education.)

A Comprehensive Approach to Values and Character Education

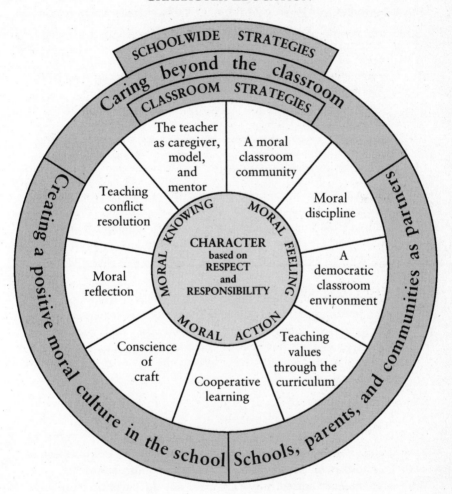

6. **Use cooperative learning** to teach children the disposition and skills of helping each other and working together.

7. **Develop the "conscience of craft"** by fostering students' academic responsibility and their regard for the value of learning and work.

8. **Encourage moral reflection** through reading, writing, discussion, decision-making exercises, and debate.

9. **Teach conflict resolution** so that students have the capacity and commitment to solve conflicts in fair, nonviolent ways.

A comprehensive approach calls upon *the school* to:

10. **Foster caring beyond the classroom,** using inspiring role models and opportunities for school and community service to help students learn to care by giving care.

11. **Create a positive moral culture in the school,** developing a total school environment (through the leadership of the principal, schoolwide discipline, a schoolwide sense of community, democratic student government, a moral community among adults, and time for addressing moral concerns) that supports and amplifies the values taught in classrooms.

12. **Recruit parents and the community as partners in values education,** supporting parents as the child's first moral teacher; encouraging parents to support the school in its efforts to foster good values; and seeking the help of the community (e.g., churches, business, and the media) in reinforcing the values the school is trying to teach.

Schools inevitably teach good or bad values in everything they do. Every interaction, whether part of the academic curriculum or the human curriculum of rules, roles, and relationships, has the potential to affect a child's values and character for good or for ill. The question is not whether to do values education but whether to do it well.

With that understanding, how can we make all parts of school life work together for the moral growth of our children?

CHAPTER 5

The Teacher as Caregiver, Model, and Mentor

I have come to a frightening conclusion that I am the decisive element in the classroom . . . As a teacher, I possess tremendous power to make a child's life miserable or joyous. I can be a tool of torture or an instrument of inspiration. I can humiliate or humor, hurt or heal. In all situations, it is my response that decides whether a crisis will be escalated or de-escalated, and a child humanized or dehumanized.

—Haim Ginott[1]

We teach who we are.

—Sign at a teachers' conference

M orality deals in large part with relationships—with the way people treat each other. In the small society of the classroom, students have two kinds of relationships: their relationship with the teacher and their relationships with each other. Both have great potential for positive or negative impact on a young person's character development. This chapter looks at the moral importance of the relationship between teacher and student.

Teachers have the power to affect the values and character of the young in at least three ways:

1. Teachers can serve as effective caregivers—loving and respecting their students, helping them succeed in school, building their self-esteem, and enabling them to experience what morality is by having the teacher treat them in a moral way.

2. Teachers can serve as models—ethical persons who demonstrate a high level of respect and responsibility both inside and outside the classroom. Teachers can also model moral concern and moral reasoning by their reactions to morally significant events in the life of the school and in the world at large.

3. Teachers can serve as ethical mentors—providing moral instruction and guidance through explanation, classroom discussion, storytelling, personal encouragement, and corrective feedback when students hurt others or themselves.

Not all teachers, of course, use their moral influence in these positive ways. Some treat students in ways that damage their self-esteem. One woman, now a teacher herself, remembers the painful humiliation she felt as a second-grader when the teacher made her sit under her desk for being bad.

Other teachers err through neglect. They simply don't see themselves as moral educators. Consequently, they don't take time to try to foster moral values through their interactions with the whole class or with individual students.

A great many teachers, however, do relate to students in ways that model and nurture character. What is it that effective teachers do? How do they develop teacher-student relationships that foster moral values and good character?

THE TEACHER AS CAREGIVER: TREATING STUDENTS WITH RESPECT AND LOVE

The most basic form of moral education is the treatment we receive. British moral educator Peter McPhail states it well: "Children take pleasure in being treated with care and warmth; their prime source of happiness is being treated in this way. Further, when children are supported by such treatment, they enjoy treating people, animals, and even inanimate objects in the same way."[2]

Bill Rose teaches a tenth-grade class in government in racially mixed Upper Dublin High School, Fort Washington, Pennsylvania. Because of his ability to establish rapport with students and motivate them to learn, his classroom was selected for inclusion in a "great teachers" videocassette series.[3] School counselors send Bill Rose the students with a long history of school failure. Here is how he describes them:

> A lot of our students are battered students as far as failure is concerned. They have such a fear of failure that they don't want to try again. If you climbed a mountain and every time you got half way up, you fell and broke a leg, after 12 or 13 years of climbing you'd give up. Some of our students have given up the climb.[4]

Knowing his students' fear of failure, Bill Rose starts the year by "plugging in some quick successes." He tells his class he's been studying memory techniques for the past eight years and he's going to teach them to use these techniques to learn about their government. To the students' amazement, they learn all the amendments to the Constitution—and their dates—in two periods.

"Once they have a success," teacher Rose says, "they want another one. And because they're feeling good about themselves, they want to come to this happy spot. They think, 'This is a good place. I can do well here.' "[5]

At the beginning of the year, he says, a lot of students come to school on drugs. They say they need to be high "to deal with school." He tells them they need to be straight to deal with his class.

Bill Rose's students know that he cares about them because he works hard to help them succeed. Helping students succeed at the work of school is one of the most important ways teachers show they care about their students. Mr. Rose also tries to treat his students fairly, with respect. He tells them: "If at any time in class you feel you're being abused by me, or I'm embarrassing you in front of the whole class, you have to let me know. I don't know how everybody feels."[6]

Bill Rose's classroom is testimony to the power of treating students with love and respect. His students talk of how the class is "a family," how they don't come late, how they have straightened themselves out and gotten their grades up, and how they work hard for Mr. Rose because he cares about them and they don't want to let him down. They are learning about the meaning of respect and love by experiencing them firsthand.

WHEN KIDS DON'T KNOW THE ANSWER

Much of what happens in a classroom consists of the teacher asking questions and students attempting to answer them. How teachers handle these interactions, which can number in the thousands by the time a student finishes schooling, can affect a student's self-esteem and teach important lessons about respect.

I tell the student teachers I work with that what they say when a child gives a wrong answer is likely to influence that child's confidence and willingness to venture a response again. I encourage them to try to find something in a child's response that they can affirm ("That's part of the answer but not the whole answer," "You're on the right track," or "Why do you think that? I'm interested in your reasoning").

How can the teacher respect and support a child when that student is struggling with a problem in front of the class?

In a combined first- and second-grade classroom in Scarborough, Ontario, it was Jimmy's turn to read his *All About Me* book to his classmates. He got stuck. His teacher did not say, "Do you need someone to help you?" (in which case another child usually takes over). Instead she said: "Jimmy, would you like Sam to sit with you so you can work it out together?" Jimmy accepted this without embarrassment, since he was a collaborator with Sam rather than a passive recipient of help. His dignity was intact.

RESPECTING THE CONCERNS OF CHILDREN

Teachers convey and model respect by speaking the language of respect in their interactions with children. They also teach respect by taking children's thoughts and feelings seriously.

At Barry Elementary School in Cortland, New York, two kindergarten boys found a toad on a brick wall outside their classroom as they were coming into school. They gave it to their teacher, Tracy Mahoney, who showed it to the other children. The class decided to keep it in a jar with a piece of screen over the top.

Shortly thereafter, however, another boy, Stephen, approached the teacher. "Miss Mahoney," he said, "I don't think it's fair to keep the toad in the jar. He doesn't have his freedom."

Teacher Mahoney called the children together on the rug and invited Stephen to share his concern with his classmates. He did, and they discussed whether to keep the toad or let it go. They voted to keep it for a little while and then set it free.

Small incidents like these make up the moral life of the classroom. By providing a class forum for Stephen's concern, teacher Mahoney showed respect for his feelings as well as for the life of the toad. Valuing children's concerns in this way contributes importantly to a relationship of mutual respect between teacher and students.

BUILDING RAPPORT BY BEING HUMAN

To have rapport with a class is to have the kind of warm, human, and appropriately personal relationship with students that makes it easier for them to talk about problems and be receptive to moral guidance. Without rapport a teacher's moral influence is greatly diminished. Moreover, research suggests that warm and supportive adult-child relationships are central to a child's development of concern for others.[7]

As a beginning second-grade teacher in Belle Sherman Elementary School in Ithaca, New York, Linda Nickels found that disclosing personal things about herself created a warm, open relationship with her children. She says:

> I try to come down to their level a lot. I brought in a story I wrote as a second-grader. They could see all the misspellings and how my teacher wrote, "This should be neater." I also brought in my personal scrapbook.
>
> This year I had a really good friend who died of cancer. I was in tears one day, so I told them about it. They said, "It's okay that you're crying."
>
> After a while, kids open up to you. Some take longer than others. It's taken one little girl until now, nearly the end of the year, to do that. I sensed something was wrong at home and suspected some kind of abuse. I said to her, "Carla, if you tell me what's wrong, I can help to make it stop." It turned out she had three older brothers who were sexually abusing her. I reported it to the principal, and the school was able to get this family some help.

Kim McConnell is a sixth-grade teacher at Walt Disney Elementary School in San Ramon, California. On the first day of the school year, she invites the class to interview her and take notes on her answers. Based on this interview, they write her biography as their first homework assignment. Teacher McConnell knows that many students will share the assignment with their parents. In this way, not only they but also many of their parents will get to know something about her.

COMBINING GOOD EXAMPLE AND DIRECT TEACHING

When students feel successful, respected, and secure in the classroom, and when they feel a personal connection with their teacher, they're more likely to be receptive to their teacher's moral teaching and guidance.

When our younger son Matthew was in fourth grade, he'd come home with stories of what his favorite teacher, Mr. Passalugo, had talked about in social studies that day. There was the day Mr. Passalugo told about how his bike was stolen when he was a boy. That brought forth stories from several class members of how their bikes also had been stolen, and a discussion of how it feels when somebody steals something from you.

There was the day Mr. Passalugo said, "Put away your books, we're going to talk about shoplifting." He explained that shoplifting could not only get you arrested—that had just happened to two local teenagers—but also causes higher prices for everybody and a special hardship for old people on fixed incomes.

There was the day when a boy beat up a girl on the playground and Mr. Passalugo was really upset. He talked about husbands who physically abuse their wives and said that if you go around punching out girls now, you may grow up to be the kind of man who beats his wife. Mr. Passalugo said that it's a sign of weakness, not manhood, to use your superior strength to bully a girl or woman.

These discussions made a deep impression on Matthew. And he listened intently to them—and the moral lessons they conveyed—because he loved Mr. Passalugo as a teacher. That emotional bond gave Mr. Passalugo his moral clout.

It's frequently said that "values are caught, not taught." That's a half-truth. The whole truth is that values are caught (through good example) *and* taught (through direct explanation). Mr. Passalugo was certainly a good model, but he was also a moral teacher in the classic sense. He explained to his students why behaviors such as stealing bikes, shoplifting from stores, and bullying others are wrong. In the classroom as in the family, adults have their greatest moral impact when they provide, in the context of a caring relationship, *both* a good example and reasoned advocacy of good values.[8]

HELPING STUDENTS THINK CLEARLY ABOUT CHEATING

Unfortunately, many teachers are hesitant to give students direct moral guidance, even on matters as basic as cheating and theft. One English teacher in an elite private high school says she is distressed by the increasingly blatant forms of academic dishonesty she sees, such as students breaking into teachers' briefcases to steal exams. But her own approach to addressing this moral problem is quite indirect. "I don't give sermons," she says; "it's not my style. When I raise the issue of cheating in my classes, I ask them questions, ask them how they think about it."

She remembers with great fondness, however, a teacher she had in high school who "talked to us in a highly moralistic way about the importance of being honest, about how she *knew* she could walk out of the room during any test and trust each of us to behave honorably. I didn't mind her preaching; I took it as a form of love. It worked then, but I could never do that now."

We need to re-create a moral environment in which teachers are comfortable, as they once were, speaking to their students in a straightforward way about right and wrong. The indirect approach can be a valuable form of moral education (as we'll see in Chapters 12 through 14), but at some point in the discussion, young people benefit by hearing directly, from adults they respect, why a moral value such as academic honesty is important. Indeed, if there is a good teacher-student relationship, students will *want* to know what their teacher thinks.

With respect to honesty, teachers should be able to say to students—or guide them through discussion to the realization—that cheating is wrong for several reasons:

1. It will ultimately lower your self-respect, because you can never be proud of anything you got by cheating.

2. Cheating is a lie, because it deceives other people into thinking you know more than you do.

3. Cheating violates the teacher's trust that you will do your own work. Furthermore, it undermines the whole trust relationship between a teacher and his or her class.

4. Cheating is unfair to all the people who aren't cheating.

5. If you cheat in school now, you'll find it easier to cheat in other situations later in life—perhaps even in your closest personal relationships.

For those students struggling to resist the considerable pressures to cheat, moral clarity about why they shouldn't will be an important support. For kids who cheat without a second thought, it may cause them to think twice the next time. For all students, it leaves no doubt about where the teacher stands and why.

Teachers may wonder, "What if my students ask me if *I* ever cheated in school?" For some teachers, the fact that they did cheat is an impediment to bringing up this issue for class discussion. They'd rather just go ahead with a policy of giving zeroes when they catch somebody cheating. But that doesn't teach students to be more honest, only more careful. One way to handle the "What if they ask me if I did it?" problem (in any context) is to say something like this:

> Whether or not I did it is irrelevant to whether it's right or wrong. Like most people, I made my share of mistakes when I was young. You should think carefully about what's right—what's respectful of yourself and others—and base your behavior on that.

A final point about cheating: Wise teachers also try to uncover the causes of students' cheating. Says one third-grade teacher: "I've got several children who feel terrific pressure from home to get A's. Their parents don't care if they forget what they learned two weeks later as long as they bring home those A's on tests and quizzes." A class meeting (see Chapter 8) and individual conferences can help a teacher identify all the factors that lead kids to cheat. Once the reasons are identified, the teacher and the class (or individual student) can devise positive, academically honest approaches to dealing with those problems.

TEACHING STUDENTS TO CARE ABOUT MORAL VALUES

Talking to students in a clear and direct way about a matter such as cheating will help them understand what honesty is and why it's important. But getting them to value honesty or any other moral quality personally is a bigger challenge. As we saw in our examination of character in Chapter 4, lots of people know what's right but don't care enough to act accordingly.

One of the ways teachers can foster caring about what's right is to show how deeply *they* care. They can do that by the way they react to violations of moral values.

Recent childrearing research finds that children who are the most empathic and altruistic have parents who react strongly to their children's offenses ("You *hurt* Amy—pulling hair hurts! Don't *ever* pull hair!).[9] It's the combination of the parents' moral reasoning and moral feeling that appears to motivate children to take seriously what they have done and become sensitive to the feelings of others.

If this is true in parent-child relationships, it's reasonable to believe that it's true for teacher-student relationships as well. When teachers take students' moral transgressions seriously, it's more likely that students will come to take them seriously, too.

A case in point: Professor Herbert Kramer was a first-year English teacher at Harvard University. Among the first batch of essays handed in by one of his freshman classes was a paper by a female student that was unquestionably plagiarized.

Says Professor Kramer:

> I walked into my next meeting with this class in a cold sweat. I was full of anger and disappointment. I handed back all the papers. I said, "One of you has plagiarized. You know who you are. Put the paper in my mailbox within 15 minutes and I will consider the matter closed."
>
> I said there would be no class today, and walked out of the room.
>
> Fifteen minutes later, I went to my mailbox, and the paper was there. The student said nothing to me about it, and I probably didn't say more than three words to her during the rest of the semester.

Ten years later, Professor Kramer says, when he was at a conference for college English teachers, a young woman came up to him. It was his former student who had plagiarized, now an English professor herself. She said to him:

> When I turned in that plagiarized paper, you taught me a lesson that I never forgot. You didn't teach me honesty; I already knew that cheating was wrong. But by letting me see your hurt and anger, you showed how much you cared about that value. Now I know, of course, that you can't be a scholar without integrity.

Morality won't be important to young people if it isn't important to adults. A high school teacher puts it this way: "We have to share ourselves, not just our subject matter."

STORYTELLING AS MORAL TEACHING

Other forms of moral teaching are less direct but no less important. Storytelling is a classic example.

Stories, read or told, have always been among the favorite teaching instruments of the world's great moral educators. Stories teach by attraction rather than compulsion; they invite rather than impose.[10] They capture the imagination and touch the heart. All of us have experienced the power of a good story to stir strong feelings. That's why

THE TEACHER AS CAREGIVER, MODEL, AND MENTOR

Teachers can serve as caregivers, moral models, and ethical mentors if they:

1. Avoid favoritism, sarcasm, embarrassing students, or any other behavior which undermines a student's dignity and self-esteem.

2. Treat their students with respect and love by:
   - Developing the kind of rapport that leads students to be open to the teacher's positive influence.
   - Helping them succeed at the work of school.
   - Being fair.
   - Responding to wrong or incomplete answers in a way that affirms whatever is good about a student's response and reduces fear of making mistakes.
   - Valuing the views of students by providing a forum for their thoughts and concerns.

3. Combine good example and direct moral teaching by:
   - Giving moral issues importance by taking class time to discuss them when they arise.
   - Offering personal moral commentary that helps students understand why behaviors such as cheating, stealing, bullying, and name-calling are hurtful and wrong.
   - Teaching students to care deeply about moral values such as honesty and respect by showing the depth of one's own feelings when those values are violated.
   - Storytelling that teaches good values.

4. Mentor one-on-one by:
   - Trying to discover, affirm, and develop each child's special talents and strengths.
   - Complimenting students through written notes; having students keep journals and writing comments in response to their entries as a way to make a personal connection with every student, build self-esteem, and offer advice on dealing with social-moral problems.
   - Using personal conferences to give students corrective feedback when they need that.

storytelling is such a natural way to engage and develop the emotional side of a child's character. (For psychological theory pointing to the human hunger for morally compelling narratives, see the article "The Use of Stories in Moral Development" by New York University's Paul Vitz in the June 1990 *American Psychologist*.)

Some teachers tell a story on the first day of the school year. They find it captivates a class and creates an immediate rapport.

Tim Kent, who teaches sixth grade in Dry Creek Elementary School in Clovis, California, says he learned storytelling in a course at Fresno State from Arne Nixon, whom he calls "the greatest storyteller I ever met." Now Tim Kent considers storytelling one of his most important teaching tools.

When I walked into his classroom, he was sitting on the edge of his desk, telling his students about a man who invented a rain-making machine to help people sleep. Then he told a story about W. C. Fields:

> When W. C. Fields was dying, he was very uncomfortable. He couldn't sleep; he hadn't slept for nights. His wife knew he loved to go to sleep to the sound of rain falling on the roof. So one night she stood outside for a long time, spraying water on the roof with a hose to make the sound of rain. She loved him so much that she did that. He fell asleep, and that night he died in his sleep.

The children were obviously taken with this story; they were pensive as they filed out for lunch. "I like to tell stories like that," Tim Kent said. "I plug them in whenever I've got a few minutes. To me, it's teaching values. That story about W. C. Fields teaches the value of love."

The week before, he said, he told his kids the story of Sean Marsee, a boy who began using snuff at age 12 and got oral cancer at age 18. It was based on an article in *Reader's Digest*. "I didn't read the article to them," he explained; "I paraphrased it from memory. That's what makes it storytelling. I find they prefer it that way."

Before he told them the story, he asked them if they knew what smokeless tobacco was. Most knew. He asked how many people had tried it; two boys were honest enough to raise their hands. He asked what their reaction was; they said they got sick. After the class talked for a little while about ads for snuff they'd seen on TV, he told them the story of Sean Marsee.

> Sean Marsee was a superb athlete. He was voted the most outstanding athlete in his high school. He won 28 medals as a member of the track

team. He always took excellent care of his body. He watched his diet; he lifted weights; he ran 5 miles a day. He didn't smoke or drink.

He was also the kind of person you'd like for a friend or brother. He was the oldest of five children. He once saved his sister Marian from drowning when she fell through the ice. His sister Melissa considered him the model of an ideal husband. He taught his younger brothers Shannon and Jason to hunt, fish, and trap.

But Sean had a habit of dipping snuff. He started when he was 12. It was popular among high school athletes who didn't want to break training. He didn't think smokeless tobacco could hurt him.

When Sean was 18, he developed a bad sore on his tongue. It was malignant. The doctor had to take out part of his tongue. But after the operation, the cancer spread to his neck. They had to operate on that, too.

The cancer spread again. This time his jawbone had to be removed. Then more lumps formed on his neck. On February 24, less than a year after they discovered the cancer, Sean Marsee died.

Sean's mother, Betty Marsee, recently testified at a Massachusetts Public Health Hearing on whether to label snuff a hazardous substance. She told Sean's story. Scientists at the hearing explained that oral cancer is caused by nitrosamines. Nitrosamines are chemical compounds, one of which forms in the mouth when tobacco and saliva combine. They said that one dip of snuff delivers the same amount of nicotine as a cigarette— but *ten times* the nitrosamines.

Since that hearing, Massachusetts and eight other states require warning labels on snuff cans. The Federal Trade Commission has asked the surgeon general to review the evidence concerning snuff.

Shortly before he died, when he could no longer talk, Sean Marsee wrote two brief messages for John O'Dell, a former football player who came to visit him from the local Fellowship of Christian Athletes. One message was a simple statement of his Christian faith. The other was a plea to young athletes: "Don't dip snuff!" [11]

"When I finished the story," Tim Kent said, "there was complete quiet in the room. You could see that it had moved them. I began the discussion by asking, 'What good do you think came out of Sean Marsee's death?'

"They said his mother was able to get the warning labels on the snuff cans. I said, 'What about the tobacco companies' argument that snuff isn't dangerous?' They said the scientists showed that snuff releases ten times as much nitrosamines as cigarettes—that's dangerous enough.

"We talked some more about the advertising for snuff, how they've got chewing gum and candy packaged like snuff, how they're getting you ready for it. Then I asked them, 'How many of you think you'll try snuff sometime in the future?' Nobody raised a hand. I asked, 'What might tempt you to try it?'

" 'Peer pressure,' they said. I said, 'How are you going to handle that? Think about it. You have a warning that Sean Marsee didn't have.'

"I stopped it there. I didn't want to turn it into a lecture; I wanted them to think. That was last Friday. I had at least six kids go home and find the *Reader's Digest* article and read the whole thing. Three brought it into class. And I had more positive feedback from parents on this than anything I've done in a while. They said how glad they were that I had told the kids this story."

Educators debate the best way to do drug education. Nearly all agree that simple scare tactics don't work. Many are also coming to agree that drug education, to be effective, must be part of a broader program of values education that helps students value themselves, aspire to worthwhile goals, and reject all forms of self-damaging behavior.

If Tim Kent succeeded in reaching his sixth-graders about the dangers of snuff, it wasn't just because he had a convincing story. It was because *he* told the story; it came *through* him to his students. That made it personal, a gift from him to them. That is the special beauty of storytelling. And the gift of Tim Kent's stories come in the context of a strong positive relationship with his class, in which values such as respect and caring are taught, in spoken and unspoken ways, daily.

Convinced of the power of storytelling as a tool for moral education, some school systems have brought in professional storytellers to teach their art to faculty. The Ferguson-Florissant School District in Ferguson, Missouri, is one example. They have engaged storytellers from their region to demonstrate storytelling with student groups, videotape stories, and do workshops for classroom teachers on the storytelling process.

MENTORING ONE-ON-ONE

Dr. Harvey Greenberg, professor of adolescent psychiatry at Albert Einstein College of Medicine, says that young people today "face a garbage culture with no values to latch on to, and so they're preoccupied with themselves. Kids need mentors. Teachers used to do this, but they do it less now because they're angry or just worn down." [12]

So far we've talked about how a teacher can build a relationship with the whole class and use that as an avenue of moral influence. But individual interactions and relationships with students are just as important, sometimes more so. Schools must encourage teachers in this role and try to minimize those aspects of school life that keep teachers from giving unhurried attention to students as individuals.

When I was visiting a Catholic elementary school in Thunder Bay, Ontario, I observed a sixth-grade teacher who took pains to get to know her students in a personal way. "I'm especially concerned about bringing out the shy child," she said, "because I myself was a painfully shy child."

While I was in the classroom, the teacher had her students write an essay on the topic "What are my special talents? How do I plan to use them in my development as a person?" When the children had finished their essays, she asked for volunteers to read theirs to the class. Almost all the hands went straining upward.

One boy read a confident essay about his athletic skills; he planned to be a hockey star. A girl spoke about her equally strong desire to be a singer but added that most other people didn't think she could sing very well and she wasn't sure either, but she really, really *hoped* she would be a good singer someday. A third student, a rather small boy, said he had many dreams of what he'd like to be, but he didn't think any of them would come true.

The teacher learned a lot about these children from this simple exercise. She gained information she could follow up on. She would make a special effort, she told me, to build up the confidence of the little boy with big dreams but no hopes. "He's very good at the computer," she said; "I'd like to have him teach that to Robert, who is a stronger student overall but knows very little about computers." By giving the shy child the chance to teach something he could do well, she would be boosting his self-esteem.

Some teachers who highly value personal contact with children have found new ways to achieve it. For example: Irene Bourne, a second-grade teacher at Birch Meadow Elementary School in Reading, Massachusetts, recently began having lunch in her classroom every Wednesday with just two of her children. She comments:

> I find out what makes them angry, what worries them, what happens on the long bus ride to school. They learn about my own children, what I like to do, how I feel about some of the topics we talk about in class. They say they like this time to talk to me without any interruptions. I think it makes them feel important.

With difficult children, a personal relationship between teacher and child can make all the difference in the teacher's ability to have a positive influence. Louise Lotz has taught elementary school for 23 years and is now a third-grade teacher at San Ramon's Walt Disney Elementary School. She remembers one boy "who was practically a juvenile delinquent by the time he came to third grade." She describes his background and behavior and how she approached him:

> Ryan's mother openly told me that she did not like him. Ryan's father beat the mother. Ryan beat up other kids on the playground. He was violent with adults who tried to intervene.
>
> My strategy with kids like Ryan is to love them to death. They fight authority, so you're not going to win them that way.
>
> I knew that Ryan liked baseball, so I had my brother, who is a baseball player, write to him and send him stuff. He liked that. Then we'd work on one thing each day—staying in his seat, for example. Every time he was doing it, I'd look him in the eye and give him a warm smile that said, "You're staying on track—keep it up!"

First you reach 'em, then you teach 'em.

GIVING STUDENTS INDIVIDUAL GUIDANCE

Some of the most important moral education that teachers do occurs when they quietly take a student aside and give corrective feedback.

Seven-year-old Bret had a negative self-image, problems getting along with other kids, and a habit of taking their things. "His pockets are full every afternoon," his teacher said. "Little things. A pencil. An eraser. A hot wheels car. Anything he doesn't have."

> I had a talk with him. I said, "Bret, how do you think others feel when they find their things are gone?" He shrugged his shoulders.
>
> I said, "You really like that beautiful green monster you bring to school. How would you like it if Joey took that?" "I wouldn't," he said.
>
> "Well, then, do you think it's fair for you to take other kids' stuff?" "No," he said. "Is there anything you need to give me today before you go home?" "Just one thing," he said.
>
> I know it won't be an overnight change with Bret. But he knows I care about him, and we continue to talk about this. A week after our first serious talk, he's still taking things, but now he returns them on his own.

To maximize chances that this kind of individual moral counseling will have a positive effect on a child, the teacher-child conference should:

1. Take place privately and at a time when the teacher and student can discuss the problem thoughtfully.

2. Help the child understand the hurtful consequences of his or her behavior, both for self and others.

3. Be followed by other teacher-student conversations that monitor the problem and affirm the student for whatever improvement has been made.

Teachers can usually see whether a child stops a particular problem behavior in their classroom, but they usually don't know their long-range effect on a child's moral development. Years later, however, many people remember the influence of a teacher who took seriously a misdeed they committed.

REACHING STUDENTS THROUGH WRITTEN COMMUNICATION

Sometimes a written note from teacher to student can be a very effective way to get a moral message across. For example, a child's self-esteem can get a big boost from a simple note from the teacher. One student teacher noticed that many of her sixth-grade students had negative views of themselves. So she wrote a note to each child stating one of the child's characteristics that she admired. She also asked students to write back to her what they liked about themselves.

The student teacher comments:

They were so excited about these notes that we discussed them at our "Ups and Downs" circle time. Subsequently I observed that many students were more likely to display in their behavior the positive characteristics that had been identified through our note exchange and group sharing.

Many teachers have students keep a journal and write in it every day. Some teachers don't structure the writing; others give students sentence starters such as "My best friend . . . ," "I'm good at . . . ," "When I'm on the playground . . . ," "I wish my teacher would . . . ," "I learn best when . . . ," or "A problem I'm having in school this year . . ."

Teachers typically collect the journals and write comments in them—over the weekend, for example.

Says a fifth-grade teacher: "Commenting on my kids' journal entries gives me a running conversation with each of them. And they treasure their journals. They take very good care of them, and several years later, when they come back to visit, they still talk about their journals."

Sometimes students use their journal to talk about a moral problem they might not otherwise disclose. Comments an eighth-grade teacher, who says that the journal "is just between me and the student":

> I have a girl who is interested in a boy in this class. She wrote in her journal that she's upset because her father said they couldn't go out. She doesn't want to sneak. We talked after school about how she could try to talk to her parents about this. I complimented her for not sneaking and for wanting to keep their trust.

THE LIMITS ON WHAT A TEACHER CAN DO

In pointing out all the ways teachers can have moral influence on students, I want to recognize that there are limits on what a teacher can do. Without help from the home, one teacher may not be able to turn around the growing number of difficult or disturbed children with whom a teacher has to deal. But even a child who shows little immediate improvement is certainly better off for having a teacher who's giving love and moral guidance—if only for the reason that things would most likely be worse without the teacher's efforts. And we know that in moral development as in intellectual development, there is sometimes a "sleeper effect": The effects of a teacher's intervention may not show up until years later.[13]

However unseen and uncertain the fruits of a teacher's labors, values education in the classroom necessarily begins with the relationship between the teacher and child. That is the foundation for everything else. If students do not experience the teacher as a person who respects and cares about them, they are not likely to be open to anything else that teacher might wish to teach them about values.

Realizing the importance of this teacher-student relationship requires that a teacher have moral vision. To be a moral educator requires seeing the moral significance of social interactions and even small events, imagining the long-range effects of children's experience at school on their values and character and the kind of society they will someday help to create, seeing teaching as it was once seen—as a special calling, a "moral craft."[14]

This is a role, I believe, that large numbers of teachers are naturally attracted to. A great many already function as models and mentors, though they might not call it that. Many went into teaching in the first place not just because they liked kids but also because they wanted to make a difference in students' lives, teach them good values as well as reading and math, affect the kind of human beings they would become.

Happily, that is a goal still within the reach of a teacher who makes it a priority.

For an excellent example of how a schoolwide advisory system can be used to provide mentoring for every student, write for Shoreham-Wading River Middle School's publication One on One: A Middle School Advisory System *and its advisory handbook (Shoreham-Wading River Middle School, Randall Road, Shoreham, NY 11786; tel. 516-929-8500.)*

CHAPTER 6

―――――

Creating a Moral Community in the Classroom

The best and the deepest moral training is that which one gets by having to enter into proper relations with others. . . . Present educational systems, so far as they destroy or neglect this unity, render it difficult or impossible to get any genuine, regular moral training.

―JOHN DEWEY [1]

Sticks and stones may break our bones, but words will break our hearts.

―ROBERT FULGHUM [2]

A teacher in an affluent, suburban school system describes her fifth-grade class:

There's a lot of name-calling. Boys who aren't tough or athletic get called "fags." The name-calling has been hardest of all on the three Chinese children, who get called "egg roll," "wonton soup," and other such names. Boys also call girls names—"fat," "pancake face," and the like. They don't do it when I'm around, only when I'm not.

And here is a kindergarten teacher in a rural community:

I started teaching a few years ago. I was amazed at what these 5-year-olds call each other—"dummy," "stupid," "queer," "homo." They quarrel, bicker, can't play together. "She took my marker!" "He pushed me!" Today I had a girl hit in the head by a swing because another child pushed her.

A great many teachers take pains to form a relationship with their students that is based on respect and caring. Teachers are often at a loss, however, as to how to foster a similar level of respect and caring among their students. They are distressed by what they see as an increasing tendency among students of all ages to be egocentric, callous, and abusive in their treatment of schoolmates. Teachers sense correctly that much of what they are doing to try to build students' respect for self and others can be eroded by peer cruelty.

Left to its own devices, the peer group often ends up being ruled by the worst tendencies in children. Domination, exclusion, and put-downs become the prevailing social norms. A preoccupation with "the right clothes" is now part of that problem; the *Los Angeles Times* recently carried a story with reports from around the country of how elementary school children are taunted by peers if they don't have the latest brand-name clothes. The article quoted parent after parent saying that their children are in emotional knots before school worrying about what they should wear.[3]

Education fails, John Dewey asserted, when it neglects school as a form of community life.[4] To succeed in teaching respect and responsibility, teachers must make the development of a classroom moral community a central educational objective.

Children learn morality by living it. They need to *be* a community—to interact, form relationships, work out problems, grow as a group, and learn directly, from their first-hand social experience, lessons about fair play, cooperation, forgiveness, and respect for the worth and dignity of every individual.

The need for this kind of positive social interaction in school is greater than ever because so many children aren't getting it outside of school. Observes middle school teacher Phyllis Smith-Hansen of Lansing, New York: "A lot of the kids we're seeing now aren't immoral; they're amoral. They just haven't learned. Their biggest source of interaction has been with something you plug in and turn on."

Finally, for all students, there is a better atmosphere for academic learning when they're not preoccupied by worries about peer rejection and abuse.

What creates a moral community in the classroom? Three conditions are basic:

1. Students know each other.

2. Students respect, affirm, and care about each other.

3. Students feel membership in, and responsibility to, the group.

HELPING STUDENTS GET TO KNOW EACH OTHER

Helping students get to know each other is the first step in building a moral community. That's because it's easier to value others and feel an attachment to them if we know something about them.

Building bonds starts on the first day of school, an important time to begin to create a feeling of friendliness in the classroom. One way to do that is to give students a nonthreatening task to do with one other person or a small group. This approach is used by Kristen Field and Virginia Holmes, who team-teach in a combined third and fourth grade at Pierce Elementary School in Brookline, Massachusetts.

Partners. These teachers pair their students with someone they don't already know and give them about 10 minutes to complete a sheet titled "Partners" (see the accompanying box). After the children have completed their sheets, they are invited to come together in a circle and share their lists with the group.

This activity accomplishes several things: Partners learn quite a bit about each other; each class member learns about the others through the whole-group sharing; and the activity shows that people are both similar and different, laying the groundwork for a classroom community that values individuality and diversity as well as unity.[5]

People hunt. Another first-day activity that works well with students of different ages is the "people hunt." I observed Ruby Tellsworth, a second-grade teacher at Rancho Romero Elementary School in San Ramon, California, use this with her class. She gave each of her students a list of 20 items and instructed them to fill in people's names for as many items as they could by going around the room and talking to classmates. Sample items:

1. A person who can whistle_____.

2. Likes pizza_____.

3. Enjoys reading_____.

PARTNERS

Name _____   Name _____

Ways We Are Alike	*Ways We Are Different*

Some questions you can ask each other:

1. What is your favorite food?
2. What are two things you like to do?
3. What's your favorite color?
4. Do you have any brothers or sisters?
5. What is your favorite subject or activity in school?
6. What is something you learned to do during the last year?

---

4. Likes to fish_____.

5. Is new in our school_____.

6. Has a great-grandfather_____.

7. Can ride a horse_____.

Snapshots. Another teacher takes individual snapshots of all his students on the first day. He mounts these on the bulletin board, with each child's name printed clearly beneath his or her picture.

Class directory. Substitute teachers say they can go into a classroom near the end of the school year and find many children who still don't know the names of all their classmates. Learning names and developing friendships can both be facilitated by a class directory.

At Lawrence Elementary School in Brookline, Massachusetts, during the first week of school, our son Matthew's kindergarten teacher had each of the children draw a picture of himself or herself on the top half of a ditto master. Beneath this self-portrait were three sentences, which the child completed (with the teacher's help if necessary): "My name is _____"; "I like to _____ and _____"; and "My phone number is _____ ."

Mrs. Watts then made an *Our Class* booklet for the children. Matthew had written that he liked to swim and draw. The day the booklets were passed out, he was excited to get two phone calls when he got home. One was from Jason, who liked to swim; Matthew and Jason became swimming buddies. The other call was from Yoshi, a shy Japanese boy who liked to draw; subsequently, Matthew and Yoshi spent many happy hours quietly drawing together. If Matthew's experience was any indication, there was very likely a whole network of new friendships in Mrs. Watts's room and the beginnings of a cohesive classroom community.

Teachers of older grades have adapted the class directory idea by having students interview each other, take notes, and then write biographical sketches, which the teacher then duplicates to make a directory.

The treasure bag. Sherry Chappelle is a fourth-grade teacher at Rippowam-Cisqua School in Bedford, New York. One of her favorite community-building activities is "treasure bag," which she does during the second week of school. She directs her students to "bring in a bag containing five things that tell something about you." Together they brainstorm the sorts of things people might include in their bags that would reveal something about them. Comments teacher Chappelle:

> We'll take a bag without knowing the owner and try to guess whose it is. Then we ask, "Will the real owner of the bag please stand up?" This activity also helps self-worth. One boy, when we were discussing his bag, said, "I'm not good at anything." Other kids said, "Yes, you are!" and pointed out things they *knew* he was good at, such as drawing.

Class pen pals. Two sixth-grade teachers in different cities decided to have their classes write to each other. Each student got a pen pal in the other class. Comments one of the teachers:

> Each time we wrote, I had all of my students read their letters out loud to the rest of the class. . . . A girl with one eye wrote to her pen pal about that. When she read her letter to the class, the reaction was, "Wow, she's not afraid to tell people about that." They admired her for this and became more comfortable with her handicap once they knew she accepted it in this matter-of-fact way.

"As we continued writing to our pen pal class," the teacher reports, "my students would say, 'They're just like us' and 'They're different from us.' There was an appreciation of both. And there was an increase in school spirit, because they wanted to show off the best of the school. The whole experience made us a closer group."

COMBATING SOCIAL CLIQUES

One of the paradoxes of moral development is that children's moral behavior sometimes seems to regress, even though their moral thinking is advancing. For example: Fifth- and sixth-graders can give more sophisticated verbal responses to moral dilemmas but are often crueler to each other in their everyday interactions than they were when they were younger. They tend to form exclusive cliques, which meet the need for social membership of the kids who are "in" but at the expense of those who are "out." Such cliques can spell death for an overall sense of community in the classroom.

The seat lottery. Janet Fagal faced this problem repeatedly with her fifth-grade class at State Street Elementary School in Skaneateles, New York. So one year she introduced a seat lottery. She rearranged the desks into a large rectangle and gave each desk a number. The last thing every Friday afternoon, each student went to the center of the room and drew from a fishbowl a number that designated his or her desk for the next week.

The seat lottery came to be eagerly anticipated. A new desk almost always meant two new neighbors. That year there were more friendships in the room than ever before, and the social groups that did form were more open and less antagonistic.

BUILDING COMMUNITY WITH OLDER STUDENTS

Teachers of higher grades—seventh and eighth, for example—also see a lot of interpersonal hostility among their students. At this age it's fed by rising self-consciousness and anxiety about being accepted by peers. And precisely because of their self-consciousness, students this age tend to say, "That's dumb!" to community-building activities that younger students more readily go along with.

One way to cope with that is to anticipate it. A junior high teacher can say, by way of introducing a community-building activity: "Some of you may think this is really dumb, and that's okay, but I'd like you to do it anyway. The way I run my class, it's important for people to know and respect each other." Or it can help to make an "academic" justification: "The subject matter of this class will require a lot of discussion, so I want you to feel comfortable speaking out and reacting to each other's ideas."

IMPROVING THE QUALITY OF GROUP INTERACTION

Many secondary-level teachers are discouraged by the low quality of discussion in their classrooms. It's a common pattern for only a very few students to contribute while others remain passive.

This pattern is a problem from a moral as well as an academic perspective. Creating a moral community must include creating a *learning community* where students actively and willingly participate in the learning process and where they share responsibility for making the class a good one.

Good feelings/bad feelings. One way a teacher can lay the groundwork for better participation in discussion is to start the year with an exercise that helps students become comfortable with each other and gets them thinking about their responsibilities as class members. Students are asked to write "two things other people can do that give you good feelings in a group discussion" and "two things people sometimes do that give you bad feelings in a group discussion."[6]

Then students, in groups of three, share their lists. Following that, the class forms a circle and does a "circle whip," each person telling one of his or her positives, and then, another time around, each telling one of his or her negatives. Everyone keeps a running list of what is mentioned and at the end chooses one thing to try to get better at as a member of group discussion.

This procedure won't eliminate all problems—follow-up is needed—but it's a good consciousness-raiser about what makes for productive discussion. Typically, many students say it makes them feel good when somebody really listens to them, and nearly always some students mention that they don't like it when somebody monopolizes discussion or when other people never say anything at all.

Coat of arms. Secondary teachers have also used a variety of self-reflective values activities to break the ice and help students feel at ease in the group. "Coat of arms" is a common example. In this activity, students draw a shield on poster board, divide it into six parts, then enter into each space responses to questions such as "What are three things you're good at?" "What is one thing others can do to make you happy?" "What is one thing you are striving to attain?"

Values clarification handbooks, which are generally *not* adequate guides to discussing moral issues (see Chapter 12), are good sources of activities like this that lead students to think about themselves and share personally significant information with each other.[7]

TEACHING STUDENTS TO RESPECT, AFFIRM, AND CARE ABOUT EACH OTHER

When students know something about each other, it's easier for a teacher to develop the second aspect of moral community: students' respecting, affirming, and caring about each other.

Sometimes this is a matter of developing their empathy, which in turn is a matter of providing certain information. When Barb Butler taught fourth grade in Dryden, New York, she had a boy whose parents were going through a difficult divorce and who was "being a real bother to the other kids." One day, when this child was absent, teacher Butler asked her class, "How many of you have had the experience of having to live with just one of your parents?"

About half the children raised their hands. "How many of you have felt upset about that?" Lots of hands again. "Well, that's what's happening with Stephen. And he's still dealing with it—he hasn't worked through it yet. So you need to help him, be patient with him." Once the children had this understanding, their behavior toward Stephen became noticeably more tolerant and supportive.

STOPPING CRUELTY TO A CHILD WHO'S "DIFFERENT"

Most teachers are especially concerned to promote peer acceptance of children who are "different." Teachers know that these children have a tough enough road in life without abuse and ostracism from other kids. And teachers judge, correctly, that intolerance of differences is a serious moral deficiency that underlies much of the prejudice, hatred, and violence that plague society and the world.

Rhonda was a visibly different child. She was 10 years old, two years older and physically bigger than the other kids in her third-grade class. Her family lived in a shack in the country, and she usually came to school shabbily dressed. Classmates made fun of the holes in her clothes. She was sloppy in her personal conduct, and kids made jokes about that. She also had a learning disability, and classmates teased her when she had to go to the resource room for special help. Even ordinarily friendly children joined in the taunting.

Many children also seemed to be using Rhonda as a scapegoat. Moreover, no one in the class would sit with her at lunch or play with her at recess. Even Paul, her only friend, deserted her.

Rhonda's response was slowly to withdraw into herself and to show increasingly immature behavior. More and more, she used "baby talk." She also began to insist that she couldn't do simple things for herself.

I know this story because I was the college supervisor for the class's student teacher, Ro Tilkin. She was very distressed by the persecution of Rhonda and determined to do something about it. She spoke with the regular teacher, who was also dismayed by the children's treatment of Rhonda but said she didn't know how to change it. So the student teacher tried to rectify the situation on her own, through speeches ("Everybody has a right to be treated with respect"), reasoned appeals ("Come on, she's like everybody else—ease up a little"), "guilt trips" ("You've ruined her whole day"), role-taking ("How would you like it if I said you have an ugly red shirt on?"), asking certain children why they were teasing Rhonda, and even punishment. Nothing worked.

Finally, at the student teacher's request, the resource room teacher, Laura LoParco, came into the class to speak directly with the children.

She used a very calm approach, saying that she was there not as a punisher but as a "mediator." To explain, she drew a circle standing for Rhonda on one side of the board, a lot of circles standing for Rhonda's classmates on the other side of the board, and a circle in the middle—containing a large "M"—representing herself as the mediator, the one "in the middle." By being in the middle, she said, she might be able to understand both sides and help solve the problem.

Next she asked, "Do you know what a learning disability is?" They didn't. She gave examples of the different kinds of learning disabilities experienced by the children she taught in the resource room. She made it clear that it was harder for these children to do things like reading and math, not because they were stupid but because their brains worked differently. "But," she said, "they're really not different from you in most ways—they have feelings just like you, and they need friends."

Then she said, "I want to know your feelings about Rhonda. I'm not going to punish you for anything you say, and I won't tell Rhonda what you've said." Several students then said what annoyed them about Rhonda. "I felt it was important," teacher LoParco later commented, "to let them express this before trying to get them to consider Rhonda's feelings."

Next she asked them to stand in Rhonda's place. "How," she asked, "do you suppose Rhonda feels?" There was quiet. Gradually, kids spoke up to say how Rhonda probably felt in response to the teasing and to being shunned by all the other kids.

Teacher LoParco then tried to help the children understand how their behavior was affecting Rhonda:

> What you are doing is hurting Rhonda here [pointing to her own head], in her mind. You can't see it; it's invisible, but it's very real. . . . You can make her think that she is stupid and the kind of person that nobody likes. That may stay in her mind for a very long time, even years. It can affect her ability to learn and her ability to make friends with other peo- ple.

She gave the children one more insight: "Do you realize that you often use Rhonda to take out your own feelings?" She asked them to think of some times when that might be true.

Then she said to the class: "You have a decision to make. Do you want to continue doing this?"

The children said they did not.

After this discussion, there was a great change in the class's treat- ment of Rhonda. Says the student teacher:

> Kids went overboard at first—wrote Rhonda cards, asked her if she'd like to color with them or sit by them, that sort of thing. Now it's more normal. . . . Every now and then I'll have to do follow-up with individ- ual kids, but in general, there's no longer a problem.

I think there are at least three lessons to be learned from this story:

1. **Don't give up, even if a group seems to be resistant to corrective influence.** Through the persistence of the student teacher and the skilled intervention of the resource room teacher, a group of children who had been merciless in their ostracism of a classmate stopped their cruelty and began to behave decently toward her. Children have the capacity for both kind and hurtful behavior; it's the task of the moral educator to call forth the kindness.

2. **Children's moral behavior can be changed by appealing to their minds and their hearts.** Teacher LoParco was able to do this success- fully because she enlarged the children's moral understanding and ap- pealed to their sense of compassion and responsibility in a systematic, in-depth manner.

3. **Prevention is preferable to cure.** Although some instances of peer mistreatment will occur even when teachers have tried to build com-

munity, extreme cruelty of the kind inflicted on Rhonda is a sign that there is not much of a moral community in the classroom. Building a classroom community around group norms of respect and kindness is the best way to forestall peer cruelty before it gets a foothold.

TEACHING KIDS TO AFFIRM EACH OTHER

One way to prevent peer abuse, establish norms of respect and kindness, and build self-esteem among students is to help them develop habits of affirming each other. Initially, that requires providing structured activities that make it "safe" for students to say publicly something positive about a peer.

Appreciation time. Debbie Wilcox, who has been a fifth-grade teacher in Johnson City, New York, fosters peer affirmation through a classroom tradition she calls "appreciation time." Three times a week, she gathers her students into a circle and invites them to "tell something that someone else did that you appreciated."

At one meeting, for example, one girl said: "I'd like to appreciate Julie for giving me some paper when I forgot mine. All I did was tell Donna that I forgot my paper, and there was Julie standing there offering me some of hers." (At this, Julie beamed.) Another girl said: "I'd like to appreciate Laurie for helping me with my spelling this week. That was the first time this year that I ever got a hundred!" Teacher Wilcox says, " 'Appreciation time' has become the single most popular thing we do."

An activity like appreciation time transforms social relations in two ways: It provides opportunities for peer affirmation, and it promotes further acts of helpfulness and caring.

Good deeds tree. A Canadian sixth-grade teacher achieved similar results through a "good deeds tree." Twice a week early in the school year he asked his students, "What's a good deed that someone did for you, or that you saw someone do for another person?"

On one of the class bulletin boards, he had done a large drawing of a tree with bare branches; next to that was a box of "leaves" he had cut out from green construction paper. For each good deed reported, he took a leaf, wrote on it the name of the student who had done the good deed, and affixed it to a branch on the tree. Gradually, the tree leafed out and became a visible symbol of the children's growing kindnesses toward each other.

Positive word power. "Positive word power"[8] can be a very effective antidote to put-downs. I used it once in a fifth-grade class where the

---

CREATING A MORAL COMMUNITY IN THE CLASSROOM

1. Help students *know each other* through activities such as:
   - Partners
   - Class directory
   - The treasure bag
   - Pen pals with another class
   - Seat lottery (to reduce the influence of cliques)
   - Good feelings/bad feelings (to improve discussion)
   - Coat of arms (to share achievements, aspirations, etc.)

2. Teach students to *respect, affirm, and care about each other.*
   - Develop empathy by providing information about others.
   - Stop cruelty to children who are different.
   - Do activities such as "appreciation time," "good deeds tree," "positive word power," and "hugs for health" that enable students to develop habits of affirming each other and that promote norms of positive regard and helpfulness.

3. Help students develop *a feeling of membership in and responsibility to and for the group.*
   - Develop class cohesion and identity through traditions and symbols.
   - Develop each student's feeling of being a unique and valued member of the class community; intervene to help the ostracized child gain peer acceptance.
   - Create accountability to group rules.
   - Foster an ethic of interdependence ("Who has a problem the rest of us can help to solve?").

---

teacher said that the name-calling and disrespect among his students were the worst he'd ever seen.

After arranging students' desks in a horseshoe, I asked, "What kinds of words can we say that give people positive feelings?" The class gave examples. Then I asked, "What kinds of words do people sometimes say that give others bad feelings?" There was a flurry of responses to that.

"So words have power," I said. "They have the power to make another person feel good or bad. I'd like to do something now that gives you a chance to exercise *positive* word power." I wrote "POSITIVE WORD POWER" on the board and explained how the activity worked:

"You'll be given a stack of blank slips of paper, one for each member of the class. We'll go around the circle, focusing on one person at a time. You'll have one minute to write down, on a slip of paper, that person's first name, and something you like, admire, or appreciate about that person.

"Don't sign your name.

"When you've finished writing about a particular person, just turn that slip upside down, and your teacher will collect it. The slips written to you will be placed upside down on your desk. When we've done everybody, you'll be able to turn over your slips and read them."

As the teacher collected the slips, he monitored their content, returning ones that were inappropriate with a private word of explanation. When all class members had been written to—including the teacher—I gave the signal for them to turn over their stack of slips and read them.

For several minutes there was complete quiet. Then the class erupted into an excited buzz as kids went around showing their friends what people had said about them. One boy said, beaming, "Somebody complimented me on my big vocabulary—wow, I didn't think anybody would admire me for that!"

Then the teacher quieted the class and asked, "When do you feel better—when you're a giver of positive words or a giver of negative words?"

The students responded as one that they felt *much* better when they were givers of positive words. The teacher said: "But doesn't it also feel good to put somebody down?" Students said yes, but it doesn't last, and the person usually gets you back.

"Why is it so hard to say something nice to somebody?" the teacher asked.

"You feel embarrassed," a boy said.

"You feel vulnerable, don't you?" the teacher said. "You don't know whether they're going to say something nice back." Children nodded their agreement.

Activities like positive word power help remove that vulnerability.

Parents also attest to the power of peer affirmation. Says one mother: "The three times Andrew got most excited about the values program were when the class talked about his assets and he had to talk about the assets of others. He told me about this as he came through the door, which is very unusual for him."

Hugs for health.[9] Affirmation doesn't always have to be verbal. Says Dee Bent, a kindergarten teacher in Emily Carr Elementary School in Scarborough, Ontario:

We love each other a lot in this classroom. I hug the kids, and they hug each other. At circle, sometimes I'll begin by asking, "Is anybody feeling a little lonely this morning?" Usually somebody will say, "I am." I'll say, "Well, come on up and get a hug." Then somebody else will say, "I'm feeling lonely, too." Then the child who just got a hug from me gives one to that child.

I find that kids will start interacting and playing together much more quickly if I do this than if I don't. And they'll also respond to me better if there's that bond.

DEVELOPING A FEELING OF MEMBERSHIP

A feeling of membership in the group is the third basic aspect of moral community in the classroom. Three things contribute to this aspect of moral community: (1) The class has a group identity; (2) each individual student feels that he or she is a valued member of the group; and (3) individuals feel responsible to and for the group.

DEVELOPING A GROUP IDENTITY

How can a teacher develop a group identity? Rituals and traditions are one way. Anthropologist Herve Varenne observes that rituals and traditions occupy a less central place in schools and society today than in the past because we have become a more private and individualistic people.[10] We have lost touch with the fact that rituals and traditions are ways in which we celebrate and nurture our existence as a community.

Classroom rituals or traditions are effective in creating group identity because they are repeated, tangible expressions of the group's communal life. Some teachers begin the day with a song, one of the oldest rituals for creating a feeling of unity. (An excellent source of songs that both foster community and stimulate thinking about values is the tape "Walk a Mile," available from Lovable Creature Music, 105 King St., Ithaca, NY 14850.)

The class meeting is another tradition that many teachers use to start the day. For example: Joline Mallan, a second-grade teacher at St. Patrick's Elementary School in Burlington, Ontario, holds a 10- to 15-minute class meeting the first thing each morning. She compliments the class on good things that happened the day before, reviews "classroom helper" responsibilities for the day, and provides an overview of the day's schedule and any special events.

Then she asks the children, "Who has some news to share?" At a meeting I observed, one child told of how his dad had won $25, another child of how his sister was sick, another of how her cat had had kittens. The teacher wrote a sentence about each incident on lined paper on an easel, and after five or six news items the class read these sentences aloud together.

The teacher comments: "It's hard to say who benefits more from our meeting—the kids or me. It gives me time to get a reading on the children, to know where they are. I hate to do without it." Besides giving the teacher a chance to tune into the moods and needs of the children, the daily class meeting helps the children concretely experience their identity not just as individuals but also as members of something larger than themselves—their class.

Many secondary-level teachers do something similar: At the start of the period, they'll ask who has some good news to share, or they'll comment on the success of a class member in some school or community event.

Class symbols. Many teachers use symbols to represent visibly both students' individuality and their membership in the group. A third-grade teacher, for example, had her 24 children each make a link out of colored construction paper and write their name on the link they had made. Then she stapled all the links together to make one circular chain, which she hung in the classroom—symbolizing the class as a whole and each child's role in it. She made the point that a chain is only as strong as its weakest link—and that this applied to the class, too.

DEVELOPING EACH STUDENT'S FEELING OF BEING A VALUED GROUP MEMBER

In addition to helping the group as a whole develop a strong sense of unity, how can a teacher help each individual student feel like a valued member of the group?

I'm important. Karen Walters, a kindergarten teacher in Weedsport Elementary School, Weedsport, New York, does a number of activities that pay attention to children as individuals and the distinct contributions they make to the group. For example, she holds a circle meeting in which children take turns completing the sentence "I am important to this class because . . ." (Prior to the meeting, she helps each child think of something.) In one of these sharing circles, one child said, "Because I can write people's names in cursive." Another said, "Because I can help Pete with his work when he doesn't know what to do." After the circle meeting she gives each child an "I'm important" badge to wear for the rest of the day.

Class applause. Teacher Walters also has a tradition of class applause—for a child's success on a mastery test or any other kind of accomplishment. In this way she encourages the children to take pride in the successes of every class member.

Student of the week. A popular classroom tradition that helps each child feel known and valued by the whole group is "student of the week." The featured student, randomly selected, is in the limelight for the whole week: He or she gets to take class attendance, act as host or hostess for the class in the event of visitors, lead the Pledge of Allegiance, lead all lines, run errands for the teacher, and bring in something from home each day—such as a toy, book, hobby, or family photo album—to share with the class.

The teacher also asks every other student to write anonymously on a slip of paper "one nice thing" about this person. All the slips are mounted around a picture of the student of the week on a poster, which is then hung outside the classroom. At the end of the week the student takes the poster home.[11]

Teacher intervention. Teachers often have at least one child who is not readily accepted by peers. The community-building strategies we've discussed may help to integrate that child, but a teacher may have to make additional efforts.

Peggy Doyle, recently retired from Groton Elementary School in Groton, New York, was the kind of teacher who looked for opportunities to help an individual child break into the group. She remembers a fifth-grade boy who had been excluded by his classmates:

> Shawn was overweight, and the other boys wouldn't let him play kickball because they said he ran too slow. He used to just stand and watch. Well, one day the field was wet and slippery, and they all had to run slow to avoid slipping. So when I said, "Come on, Shawn, why don't you get in the game?" they let him in. He did fine, and after that they let him play. He started to feel a lot better about himself in the class.

DEVELOPING RESPONSIBILITY TO AND FOR THE GROUP

The third aspect of group membership is a sense of responsibility to and for the group. This is ordinarily a by-product of the feeling of class unity and of being a valued member of the group, but there are also direct approaches to developing it.

Goals and rules. Setting goals and rules together makes explicit everyone's responsibility to act in a way that considers the good of all. Students are helped to think, "How do my actions affect other kids and the class as a whole?" This approach is discussed in greater detail in Chapter 7, "Moral Discipline," but I mention it here because it's part of what fosters responsibility to the group.

An ethic of interdependence. Developing the responsibility dimension of moral community also means fostering an ethic of interdependence—the feeling that one person's problem is everybody's problem. This is a time-honored moral value that gains expression in the belief that we are all in the same boat, and, since we share the same vulnerable human condition, we bear a measure of responsibility for each other's welfare.

Translated into the life of the classroom, this means that if one person loses something, others help to look for it. If some children in the class are new to the school, the teacher and the other class members take it upon themselves to ask, "How can we make our new class members feel at home here?"

Kindergarten teacher Nell Woodmancy of Syracuse, New York, found that her children, normally squirmy in circle meetings, were surprisingly attentive when she posed the question "Who has a problem they would like other people to help them solve?" First-grade teacher Kathy Kittle turned to this kind of real-life problem-solving after her children complained that class meetings were "too boring." She found they enjoyed tackling each other's problems. She shares this example:

TEACHER: Who has a problem we might be able to help with?

MARK: My problem is I don't have anyplace to park my bike because the bike rack is full.

TEACHER: The rack is full when you get to school?

MARK: Yeah, and Mr. Bashaw [the principal] will take your bike away if you leave it on the grass.

TEACHER: Well, we certainly don't want to lose our bikes. How can we help solve Mark's problem?

KEVIN: Let's build another bike rack.

TEACHER: Could we do that?

ANDREA: No, it's made of metal. But maybe my father [the school custodian] could build one.

ERIN: Yeah, or we could give each kid a name where his bike goes.

JEFF: Maybe we should talk to Mr. Bashaw.

ROBBIE: All you have to do, Mark, is get to school earlier!

TROY: I know, Mark, you could move somebody else's bike and put yours there [laughing]!

TEACHER: What do you think of that idea?

SEVERAL: It wouldn't be fair.

TEACHER: Why not?

TROY: [Now seriously] 'Cause if everyone moved someone else's bike, no one would be able to find their own bike.

JEFF: I still think we should go talk to Mr. Bashaw [followed by general agreement].

The children went to Mr. Bashaw. He checked with the high school, found that they had an extra bike rack, and requested that it be moved to the elementary school. Mark's problem was thereby solved.

Some teachers, sensitive to the fact that shyness may inhibit a child from speaking up at circle time, have their students write out their problem on a slip of paper (they don't have to sign it) and put it in a box. Other teachers promote peer helpfulness in a less formal way: If they notice that a child lacks companions or seems to be down, they say to other kids, "How can you help so-and-so have a better day?"

Claire Betinas, a second-grade teacher at Birch Meadow Elementary School in Reading, Massachusetts, gives an example of how children can help each other deal with feelings such as normal childhood fears. She had invited her children to talk about their New Year's resolutions. One little girl, Lindsey, said she resolved to try to stay in her own bed all through the night; she had been getting up and going to sleep with her 3-year-old sister because she was afraid.

The teacher comments: "The other kids were full of suggestions, things that helped them when they couldn't sleep. The amount of caring in the group was very touching. I think they also felt relieved that Lindsey would talk about this, because a lot of them were still struggling with it, too."

When students are enabled to care for each other in this way, they are learning an important lesson about human interdependence: They can give help when others come to them with a problem, and can go to others when they have a problem of their own. If children experience this kind of support system throughout their elementary school years, they may be less likely as adolescents to keep inside the kind of problems that lead many young people to take their own lives.

Coping with a crisis. Social problems in the classroom don't disappear, of course, even when there is a high level of moral community.

But that sense of community provides the cohesion and caring needed to deal with the crises that may occur.

A teacher at a conference on moral education told a story about a year when she taught a combined second and third grade and for the first time made a systematic and ongoing effort to build community. A strong class spirit developed, and behavior problems were far fewer than they had been during the previous year.

Then one day, toward the end of the school year, a project that several students had worked on and left displayed in the back of the room was found badly damaged. The teacher stopped all activity and called an emergency class meeting.

"We have good times together, and we have problems," she said. "Something very serious has happened. We cannot continue our work until we find out who is responsible and the damage is somehow repaired. This is a chance to show if we really care about each other."

There was a tense silence. Then one student spoke up: "Come on— whoever did it, tell. It's okay, we'll forgive you!" A chorus of similar appeals went up from the children.

Finally, two boys stood up and admitted that they had accidentally knocked the project over when they were fooling around in the back of the room. The other children, the teacher says, jumped to their feet and hugged the two culprits in celebration of their confession. There was a spirited discussion about how they could work together to restore the damaged project. The teacher said she was sure this crisis could not have been resolved in this way had it not been for the strong sense of community the class had built up all through the school year.

Ultimately we want to send forth young people from our schools who will develop what Michael Walzer has called "communities of character"—communities in which men and women share "some special commitment to one another and some special sense of their common life." [12] One of the major moral problems of modern societies is the lack of the sense of community. Individualism, in the view of Robert Bellah in his best-selling book *Habits of the Heart,* "may have grown cancerous," may be destroying our ability to participate in public life and even in intimate relationships, such as marriage and family, that require a significant giving of self. [13]

To educate people who value community and who see their individuality as developed by rather than threatened by responsibility and commitment to others, we need to provide a positive experience of community as an integral part of schooling. Children spend more than

12,000 hours in classrooms before they graduate from high school. If even a significant portion of that time were spent in truly moral communities, that social experience would surely leave its mark on their developing characters and on the way they participate in human communities throughout their lives.

CHAPTER 7

Moral Discipline

Discipline is not a simple device for securing superficial peace in the classroom; it is the morality of the classroom as a small society.

—Emile Durkheim [1]

Fewer students today come to school with an attitude of respect toward adults; many are astonishingly bold in their disrespect for teachers and other authority figures. Children's disrespectful behavior at school all too often reflects the miseducation, neglect, or outright abuse they have received at home.

A student teacher I recently worked with was struggling to keep her head above water in a small-town, third-grade classroom that had lots of discipline problems. Of her 22 students, she learned, only six came from intact families. The boy who was her most severe discipline problem had had four "fathers" in the past year.

Teachers, and even older students, comment on the amount of anger today's children bring to school. Seniors in a New Hampshire high school went into fifth-grade classrooms to lead discussions of feelings, peer pressure, and self-esteem. Later they commented, "These kids are angrier than we've ever been in our lives!" Sometimes the anger is more than a child can contain. In the third-grade classroom mentioned above, a boy named Billy came to school one Monday with a knife and announced seriously that he was going to "kill the music teacher." Over the weekend, he later disclosed, his stepfather had gotten mad at the dog and made Billy watch as he took the dog into the backyard and shot its tail off.

It is not a kinder and gentler world for millions of children. And so it is a more difficult world for their teachers. Trouble with discipline is one of the leading sources of teacher stress and burnout.

Discipline, however, is not just a problem; it is also, fortunately, a moral education opportunity. As the French sociologist Emile Durkheim observed, discipline provides the moral code that makes it possible for the small society of the classroom to function.

A moral education approach to discipline (or "moral discipline," as my college students have shortened it) uses discipline as a tool for teaching the values of respect and responsibility. This approach holds that the ultimate goal of discipline is self-discipline—the kind of self-control that underlies voluntary compliance with just rules and laws, that is a mark of mature character, and that a civilized society expects of its citizens. Discipline without moral education is merely crowd control—managing behavior without teaching morality.

Teachers who rely on largely external methods of control may succeed in getting students to toe the line under their supervision. But what happens when they're not around? Says a teacher who uses "assertive discipline"[2] (where the teacher lays down the law and punishes every infraction, with little attention to developing generalized self-control): "My children are very good for me, but they can be holy terrors for a teacher who doesn't use this approach." Research points to the same conclusion: Children subjected extensively to discipline based on external controls develop low internal commitment to good behavior.[3]

Moral discipline, by contrast, has the long-range goal of helping young people to behave responsibly in any situation, not just when they're under the control of a particular adult. Moral discipline seeks to develop students' reasoned respect for rules, the rights of others, and the teacher's legitimate authority; students' sense of responsibility for their own behavior; and their responsibility to the moral community of the classroom.

Teachers who practice moral discipline do four things:

1. They project a clear sense of their moral authority—their right and duty to teach students respect and responsibility and to hold them accountable to those standards of behavior.

2. They approach discipline, including rule-setting, as part of a larger, ongoing effort to develop a good moral community in the classroom.

3. They establish and enforce consequences in an educational way—one that helps students appreciate a rule's purpose, make amends for wrongdoing, and take responsibility for improving their behavior.

4. They convey caring and respect for the individual student by trying to find the cause of a discipline problem and a solution that helps that student become a successful, responsible member of the classroom community.

Let's look at each of these four features of moral discipline.

EXERCISING MORAL AUTHORITY IN THE CLASSROOM

Says an elementary school teacher who has taught for 17 years and is now regarded as a master teacher:

> My first year of teaching was a total shock to me. I was too open in the beginning. I had to come to terms with the fact that there has to be a central authority in the classroom and that structure is something that kids need.

The teacher is the central moral authority in the classroom. That authority is based, first of all, on the fact that the school has given the teacher the responsibility of creating a good moral and learning environment and of looking after students' safety and general welfare. That responsibility gives the teacher the right to tell students to follow directions, do their work, obey the classroom rules, and stop any behavior the teacher considers contrary to the best interests of an individual or the group.

In the course of managing the classroom, the teacher also functions as a moral mentor—instructing children in why it's not polite to interrupt, not fair to cut in line, not kind to call names, not respectful to "borrow" somebody's property without asking, and so on.

Exercising authority, however, doesn't mean being authoritarian. Authority works best when it's infused with respect and love. Says a fifth- and sixth-grade teacher:

> I spend a lot of time talking with my children, listening to their feelings and what's important in their lives. When a child knows I really care about what happens in his or her life, then my expectation that they obey

the rules in my class has a power I can't get by whip-cracking and yelling. They care about disappointing me. They want my positive regard.

A COOPERATIVE APPROACH TO RULE-SETTING

Rules imposed by external constraint remain external to the child's spirit. Rules due to mutual respect and cooperation take root inside the child's mind.

—JEAN PIAGET[4]

The first way to involve students in sharing responsibility for good classroom discipline is cooperative rule-setting.

When the teacher and students formulate rules together, rule-making becomes one of the first acts of cooperation and mutual respect in the development of their moral community.

Lisa is a third-grader whose class makes the rules with the teacher. "Does that work?" I asked Lisa. "Oh, yes," she said. "If just the teacher makes them, you might not want to follow them. But if you help make them, you do."

Here is how different teachers do collaborative rule-setting:

Kim McConnell teaches sixth grade at Walt Disney Elementary School in San Ramon, California, one of the schools participating in the nationally recognized Child Development Project (see Chapter 2). She develops rules with her students on the second day of school.

She puts her students four to a table. They stay in those groups for a month; she believes it's important for students to have a support group. Then she asks each small group to brainstorm rules that will help them:

1. Get our work done.

2. Feel safe.

3. Be glad we're in school.

Each small group writes its rules on butcher paper and tapes the list on the blackboard. Teacher McConnell comments: "I add a list that I've made up in advance, and the kids are interested to see how similar my rules are to theirs. Drawing from all the lists, we come up with one that will serve as our class rules."

Teacher McConnell's strategy has two noteworthy advantages: (1) It combines rule-making and community-building (kids getting to know each other in their support groups); and (2) it gets every member of the class actively involved in talking and thinking about the rules they should have.

Gayla Miller teaches fourth grade at the Middle School in Trumansburg, New York. She begins the year with an approach she has used with children as young as first grade: talking about the U.S. Constitution and relating it to the idea of a Class Constitution. She then asks the children to form small groups and develop a list of rules that the class needs "in order for people to learn and be safe."

When they get back together, they list all the rules on the board and star the five most important. These become their Class Constitution. If the class doesn't come up with a rule Mrs. Miller needs, she'll say so ("There's a rule I need because . . .") and add it to the list. (Some teachers prefer to begin by stating one or two personally important rules and then invite students to add to them.) (For an approach that elaborates on how to use the U.S. Constitution as a basis for classroom rules, see *Judicious Discipline* by Forrest Gathercoal[5] and *Practicing Judicious Discipline: An Educator's Guide to a Democratic Classroom* by Barbara McEwan.[6])

Amy Bennett teaches second grade at Burton Street Elementary School in Cazenovia, New York. I invite her to speak in my undergraduate course on classroom discipline because she demonstrates how the teacher's questioning is instrumental in helping young children think about rules and their necessity both inside and outside the classroom.

> The first thing we do on the first day of school is to sit in a circle on the floor and have a class meeting. After introductions, I ask the children: Are rules good or bad? . . . What would it be like if we didn't have any rules? Think of what it would be like if you could come in and do whatever you wanted. If you wanted to do the work, that would be okay; if you didn't want to do it, that would be okay, too. If someone hit you, you could hit them back. Basically, you could do whatever you wanted in school.

The prospect of having no rules stirs a lot of discussion. At first there are always children who say, "Boy, that'd be great!" or "I'd like that!" But the more the class talks about it, the more they come to see that a classroom without rules wouldn't be a very good idea. "People would fight," they say. "People wouldn't get along." "And that's what I want them to understand," teacher Bennett says, "that we have rules so we can get our work done and have our classroom be a happy place."

Then she broadens the discussion: "Do we have rules in life? How about at home? What about on the road when we drive a car? We talk about how if their parents speed, they might get a ticket. I want them to see that we have rules for our whole life, and these are called laws." That sets the stage for the concluding part of the discussion: "Then I say that our classroom is like that: We're a community, we're like a family, we need rules, too. What rules would help us get along and have a happy classroom?"

These last two approaches—linking classroom rules to the U.S. Constitution and other laws of our society—lend an additional seriousness of purpose to the process of classroom rule-setting. They make explicit an important connection between school and the wider world: Just as societies have laws, so classrooms have rules; just as lawmakers discuss and debate what are good laws, so teachers and students discuss and debate what are good rules; and just as adults are citizens with responsibilities to society, so students are citizens of the classroom and the school.

Note that in all of the above approaches, the teacher structures the discussion to make it clear that rules are not a "wish list"; rather, rules are needed to achieve a goal (have a classroom that is safe, happy, productive, etc.).

After the rules are set together, maintenance is needed—sitting down periodically to evaluate the rules. How are they working? Do any need changing? Are new rules needed? This kind of discussion can lead to improvement in a class's rules and a deepening of students' commitment to following them.

Will this kind of cooperative approach work in, say, a tough urban school?

Beecher Elementary School in Elmira, New York, is a good example. Nearly half the children come from families on welfare. Many are no strangers to violence; some have seen murders in the street, some in their own homes. Discipline used to be a big problem in the school, but over the past several years, behavior problems have been reduced to a low level. One reason: Every classroom now has clear rules, consistently enforced, shared with parents, and developed *with* the children during the first week of school. At the high school level, the cooperative, "just community" approach has been successful in the South Bronx (see Chapter 17) in a difficult urban school.

BENEFITS OF COOPERATIVE RULE-SETTING

Involving students in setting classroom rules and in taking personal and group responsibility for following them benefits students in these ways:

1. It reaches out to the class to form a partnership, working together to create rules that serve the good of the classroom community.

2. It fosters students' feeling of ownership of the classroom rules and a moral obligation to follow them.

3. It treats the child as a moral thinker and invests time in helping students develop better moral reasoning.

4. It helps students to see the values (e.g., respect and responsibility) that lie behind rules and to generalize responsible rule-following beyond the classroom.

5. It helps students learn to think critically about rules and to develop competence at making good rules themselves.

6. It emphasizes internal rather than external control and so fosters *voluntary* compliance with rules and laws.

RULE-SETTING IN SECONDARY-LEVEL CLASSROOMS

Some secondary-level teachers point out what they see as a problem with involving their students in setting rules: "As a junior high or high school teacher, you have many different classes. If every class were to be involved in drawing up the rules, you'd end up with five or six different sets of rules." Other secondary teachers point out that older students may have already been through the activity of developing classroom rules in the younger grades; it may seem childish to them to repeat this process in the upper grades.

Secondary teachers who want to avoid these problems but still use a moral discipline approach have several options. One is to seek input from all of their classes, then develop a single set of rules from the pooled suggestions. Another is to use cooperative rule-setting only with those classes (e.g., an immature or unruly group) that, in the teacher's judgment, most need the benefit of extended discussion of behavior. Another option is for the teacher simply to present a list of behavioral expectations on day one, discuss it briefly, and then involve students more actively at a later point in developing rules to deal with a particular problem that arises.

With adolescents, this much is essential: that they be required to think about what is respectful and responsible behavior in the classroom and to commit themselves to practicing it. Many secondary students behave in rude, egocentric, and disruptive ways in classrooms because the teacher hasn't related rules to values of respect and responsibility and hasn't sought a commitment to developing a good classroom community. So the challenge for the secondary teacher is to avoid talking down to students while at the same time delivering a message about rules that sets a high moral standard and invites students on board.

Many secondary teachers are able to do that without necessarily involving students in coming up with the rules. For example: John Perricone is a respected and popular teacher of a high school health education course at Maine-Endwell High School in Endwell, New York. He spends the first day of class getting to know his students and talking about his love of teaching and his philosophy of education. ("Teaching is like a dance," he says. "I come in here all ready to dance, but if you don't want to dance [and here he slouches in a chair with a totally bored expression], what can I do?" This gets a laugh from the class.) He does this as he goes over a course handout that includes the following section on student behavior:

> Please remember that this is your room and your class. The behavior and participation of each person will shape the type of learning that will occur. Since one person's behavior affects everyone else, I request that everyone in the class be responsible for classroom management.
>
> To ensure that *our* rights are protected and upheld, the following laws have been established for this classroom:
>
> *The Law: To Be Followed Without Exception*
>
> 1. Be on time, prepared, and ready to work at the beginning of class.
> 2. Please raise your hand when you wish to speak, and wait to be called upon.
> 3. Please listen with all your heart and soul.
> 4. Please treat others as you would like to be treated.
>
> I very much enjoy relating to people on a mutual respect level. It has been my experience that human interaction can be tremendously rewarding when such respect exists. I will always extend this consideration to you, and ask only that you return this in kind. Thank you.

In Mr. Perricone's written and oral explication of "the law," there's a lot of moral education going on. Despite his personable manner and sense of humor, it's clear he's dead serious about his rules. He relates these rules to a moral purpose: the protection of his right to teach and his students' right to learn. He asks everybody to share the responsibility for creating an optimal learning environment. He models courtesy in his language. And he makes a strong moral appeal to the norm of reciprocity, promising to extend respect and asking students to return it.

Even if students don't help to make the rules, they can be invited to reflect on, and commit themselves to, behavioral guidelines whose importance for the classroom community the teacher makes clear.

ESTABLISHING AND ENFORCING CONSEQUENCES

When rules are established, whether by the teacher or by the teacher and class together, it's natural for kids to wonder, "What happens if you break the rules?" Obviously, if nothing happens when someone breaks a rule, students learn not to take the rule seriously.

In moral discipline the general principle is to use consequences, like rule-setting, as an opportunity for moral education. The relevant question is: How do you help the student understand the rule and be motivated to follow it out of a sense of responsibility to self and others?

Enforcement as a teachable moment. One helpful practice is to treat rule enforcement as a teachable moment. One elementary school teacher, instead of just giving a child a warning for a first offense, often goes over to the child's desk and privately asks: "Do you know what rule you just broke? Why did the class agree that that was a good rule?"

Children are sensitive to differences in the way teachers respond to rule violations. In one study, children rated highest those teachers who responded to moral transgressions with statements focusing on the effects of the student's act (e.g., "Joe, that really hurt Mike"). Children gave lower ratings to teachers who responded with unelaborated statements of school rules or expectations ("That's not the way for a Hawthorne student to act"). Rated lowest of all were teachers who used simple commands ("Stop it!" or "Don't hit"!).[7]

Setting consequences with group involvement. How should the teacher set up consequences in the first place? One method is to involve students in formulating appropriate consequences ("What do you think is a fair consequence for breaking this rule?") as a direct extension of cooperative rule-setting.

Many elementary school students will propose outlandishly harsh punishments. These are natural responses at early stages of moral development—and another opportunity for the teacher to develop moral reasoning. The teacher who has involved children in thinking critically about what makes a good rule can continue the same critical thinking process with regard to consequences. By discussing what are fair and effective consequences, the teacher can help students understand that the purpose of a consequence is not to make them suffer but to help them improve their behavior.

Involving students in coming up with fair consequences has another advantage: Rule enforcement then has the collective consent of the group behind it. Confronting a rule-breaker, the teacher can say: "What did we agree was the consequence for breaking that rule?" Often, when kids are punished by a teacher or parent for breaking a rule, they become angry at the punishing adult rather than sorry for their misdeed. But if they have consented in advance to the consequences, it's easier to get them to look at what they did and take responsibility for their behavior.

The teacher sets the consequences. Some teachers, however, prefer to set the consequences themselves, at least for some of the rules. Says one fourth-grade teacher: "I think I'm in a better position to know what consequences are going to work. For example, when we make the rules together, one of the rules I always contribute is that homework has to be in on time. I want to control the consequences for that: The first time homework isn't in, they get a warning; the second time, the person does it during recess; the third time, I call the parent." Teachers who set the consequences themselves can change them quickly if they're not working.

A middle course. Kathy Long, who teaches second grade at West Frankfort Elementary School in Frankfort, New York, follows a middle path. She has two sets of rules: "Teacher Rules," which she makes (e.g., "Raise your hand to speak" and "Follow directions the first time"); and "Kids' Rules," which she asks students to make "to help you get along with each other" (sample Kids' Rules: "No fighting," "No calling names," and "Share"). She sets the consequences for Teacher Rules but allows the children, with her guidance, to set the consequences for Kids' Rules.

What's most important from a moral education standpoint is that there be a *spirit* of shared responsibility for an orderly classroom. What is common to different approaches to achieving that spirit is spending enough time discussing the rules and consequences so that students understand their fairness and how they help to create a good classroom community.

SHOULD THE CONSEQUENCES BE FIXED OR VARIABLE?

Teachers face another practical issue as they develop their discipline plans: Should the consequences for rule-breaking be fixed, or should they vary with the rule, the cause of the misbehavior, and other relevant factors?

"Assertive discipline" is a fixed system; it uses the same consequences for all different kinds of rule violations.[8] Regardless of whether you talk out of turn, don't get your math book out when told to, or call the kid in the next row a "retard," the sequence of consequences is the same (e.g., a warning for the first offense; write the rule 25 times for the second offense; lose 15 minutes of recess for the third offense, etc.). The punishment doesn't necessarily fit the crime.

Moral discipline, by contrast, favors logical consequences, which can serve as a moral teacher. For example, with a rule such as "No put-downs," logical consequences should involve some sort of reparation, as in the following:

- *First offense:* Explain to the teacher the reason for the "No put-downs" rule and then sincerely apologize to the person you offended (saying *why* you're sorry).

- *Second offense:* Meet with the teacher to discuss the reason for the continued problem; write a letter of apology to the offended person.

- *Third offense:* Make a public apology, pay the victim five compliments, and write out a plan for avoiding put-downs in the future.

A logical link between the offense and the consequence helps teach the student *why* the behavior was wrong and how to make up for it.

Deciding consequences case by case. Teachers can try to make consequences logical while reserving the freedom to decide the particular consequence case by case. They may wish to make greater allowances, say, for a child who's having a bad day because he's not feeling well or because his parents are going through a divorce. They might impose a stricter consequence, skipping the warning, with a student they think needs to be jolted into taking the rules seriously. A junior high school teacher explains his rationale for taking this flexible approach:

I see all my students as individuals, so I treat them that way. Consequences for misbehavior are individualized.

If a student keeps acting up after one warning, I'll give the class some work to do and take the disruptive person out into the hall. This way the rest of the class can't interfere, and I can assign a consequence tailored to the needs of this student. My consistency lies in the fact that students know they will receive fair consequences.

WINNING OVER THE HOSTILE STUDENT

For students who come to the classroom with a hostile attitude toward authority, a flexible approach can make the difference between reaching them and not reaching them.

For example: Gary Robinson, when he taught fourth grade in Skaneateles, New York, had a student named Eric, large for his age, who had the reputation of being a wise guy and a show-off. On the first day of the school year he told Mr. Robinson that he wasn't afraid of him or the principal—only his father could tell him what to do.

Mr. Robinson just smiled and said he hoped they would have a good year. He told the class as a whole that he had just one rule: the Golden Rule. "What do you think the Golden Rule is?" he asked. "Write it down." They spent some time talking about how to apply the Golden Rule in different situations.

During the first week, when Eric was disruptive the teacher avoided a public confrontation but instead told him privately what behavior he expected from him and why. He spent time at recess playing games with him and other students who were interested. Some days, after school, they played Ping-Pong together and talked about what they liked to do outside of school.

As the year went on, Mr. Robinson and Eric developed a very positive relationship, to the point where Eric would work diligently for Mr. Robinson to earn his approval. All this was possible, the teacher felt, because his flexible system of discipline gave him the option of quietly talking to Eric about his expectations for behavior, avoiding a contest of wills, and winning him over through informal contact outside the classroom.

I am not suggesting, however, that a teacher be lenient with a difficult child and ignore inappropriate behavior. Teachers who have good classroom control, whether they have preannounced consequences or not, have at least one thing in common: They start out firm and nip problems in the bud. Comments one teacher: "The first month sets the tone for the whole year."

If a teacher does have a system of predetermined and announced consequences, being firm means following through and not hesitating in the application of those consequences. If a teacher doesn't have predetermined consequences, being firm means reacting to student misconduct in some way (e.g., "Bob, I'd like to talk to you at the end of the period") that lets the student know that the disruptive behavior won't be tolerated—and why.

THE TIME-OUT AND THE INDIVIDUAL CONFERENCE

Two moral discipline consequences designed to promote rule-following and moral growth are the time-out (temporary separation from the group) and the individual conference.

THE TIME-OUT

Why is a time-out or separation from the group (such as sending the student to a table in the back) a logical and educational consequence?

A time-out says to a student: "If you want to be part of the group, you have to follow the rules of the group. Your disruptive behavior is interfering with other people's right to learn."

There are two kinds of time-outs. The first is the fixed-interval time-out: a specified length of time (5, 10, or 15 minutes) when the student is away from the group. The second is the conditional time-out: The student may return to the group when he thinks he's ready to follow the rules or when he's satisfied some other condition (such as talking with the teacher).

Sometimes kids will come back before they're in control of their behavior, and in a minute they're into trouble again. A way to deal with that is to have a two-step system: With the first time-out, you can come back when you're ready; but if you repeat the offense within the next 30 minutes, you're out for a fixed length of time. It's also good to help prepare kids for reentry by asking, "Are you ready to go back? What do you have to do to go back?" ["Follow the rules."].[9]

What if a student refuses to go for a time-out? The teacher can assign the group something to do and take the student aside to try to find out the source of the resistance. If the student continues to resist, the teacher can say: "Let's think about this. Why do we have a classroom rule about time-out? Why am I asking you to take a time-out now?"

If the student still refuses to cooperate, the teacher can calmly offer a choice: "Sally, your actions require a time-out. Can you follow our rule about time-out now, or do we need to talk about this during recess [or after school, or with your parents]?"

The goal is to cool down rather than heat up the confrontation, get the student to think, yet maintain an insistence on a fair consequence. Generally, if the time-out procedure has been discussed in advance with students and explained as something that's meant to help them regain control of their behavior, they will accept it as a consequence in the discipline situation.

THE INDIVIDUAL CONFERENCE

The time-out is most effective when followed by at least a short teacher-student conference. Students who seem impervious to the teacher's influence when they're part of the group can often be reached through a personal conference.

The personal conference enables a teacher to individualize discipline, much in the way that good teachers try, when possible, to individualize instruction to meet the needs of different learners. The individual conference allows the teacher and student to explore the problem out of the limelight and enables the teacher to try to get at the cause of the problem.

The conference also allows the teacher to explain why the disruptive behavior is not acceptable. Finally, it enables the teacher and the student to develop a plan, based on an understanding of the problem, to prevent its recurrence.

It is usually wise—with some students, it's essential—to put the behavior improvement plan *in writing* and have the students sign it to indicate their commitment to making it work.

Sixth-graders Kevin and Dan were best buddies and always sat next to each other. This became a problem when Kevin began talking to Dan and distracting him from his work. Student teacher Christine Peredo spoke to Kevin in class about this problem, but it persisted.

So the student teacher asked Kevin to see her after class. "Do you know why I want to talk to you?" she began. He did. "I know that you and Dan are very good friends," she said. "But when you talk in class, is it helping you or Dan to get your work done?" Kevin acknowledged that it wasn't.

"What do you think would make the situation better?" Miss Peredo asked. Kevin said that when they had individual work to do, he could sit at another desk away from Dan. With the student teacher's help, he wrote out this plan:

Kevin's Plan

1. I'll sit away from Dan when we have individual work to do.

2. If we each get our individual assignments in on time, we can work together on the group project at the end of the week.

3. At the end of the week, I'll meet with Ms. Peredo to discuss how this plan is working.

Signature: *Kevin*

Date: *October 3*

The goal of this problem-solving approach—"What can we do to make the situation better?"—is to put the teacher and the student on the same side, working toward a shared goal: solving the problem in a way that is in everyone's best interest. One junior high teacher says she finds it helpful to begin a conference by asking, "If you were the teacher and had this problem, how would you handle it?"

SITUATIONAL SUPPORTS FOR SELF-CONTROL

Effective individual behavior plans often also include a "situational support"—something that helps the student control his or her behavior.

Ruby Tellsworth, who teaches second grade at Rancho Romero Elementary School in San Ramon, California, says she once had a boy "who had a great deal of trouble sitting still. We talked about it and decided that when he felt he couldn't sit still, he'd give me a signal. I'd then let him go out and run around the playground for a few minutes [within my view]. After that, he'd be able to sit down and work."

Won't other children consider it unfair if one child gets that kind of special treatment? Not if the teacher has developed in the classroom a good sense of community that includes acceptance of individual differences. In that atmosphere, the teacher can casually mention the plan that she and the child in question have worked out to help him solve his problem. In most cases other students will be glad the teacher has found a way to reduce a classmate's disruptive behavior.

WHEN SHOULD A PERSONAL PLAN INCLUDE A NEGATIVE CONSEQUENCE?

Sometimes an individual plan needs to include a negative incentive that will motivate the student to change for the better.

For example: Pam, a fifth-grader, fooled around during morning math instead of getting her math problems done. The teacher talked with her and listened to her feelings about not liking math. The teacher gave Pam some new strategies for concentrating and for doing the problems and reduced somewhat the number of problems she had to do during math time.

But still Pam failed to make a serious effort. So the teacher and Pam met again and agreed that if she didn't get her math work done during the allotted time, she would have to finish it before going to lunch. Pam's math work improved.

Says one elementary school teacher: "I want to make sure the child sees this connection between the consequence and the goal of self-control. So when I'm considering a particular consequence, I'll check with the child by asking, 'Do you think this will help you control your behavior?' If the child doesn't think it will help, then we try to come up with a consequence that will."

SELF-CONTROL THROUGH SELF-AWARENESS

A lot of children who act up simply aren't very aware of their behavior. Having them keep track of their own behavior can have the effect of increasing their awareness and their self-control.

"Counting and charting" is one such control-through-awareness technique. Developed by psychologist Ogden Lindsley, this method has the teacher and the student keep count of the number of times a problem behavior (e.g., hitting or talking out of turn) occurs during the day. At the end of the day (or half-day), the teacher and student meet, tally the total, and enter it on a graph (kept private unless the student wishes to reveal it).

The graph makes even small improvements in behavior visible to the teacher and the student. Sometimes this precise feedback is enough in itself to motivate a student's continued effort to improve. And the graph supplies an attainable goal: to show some decrease in the problem be-

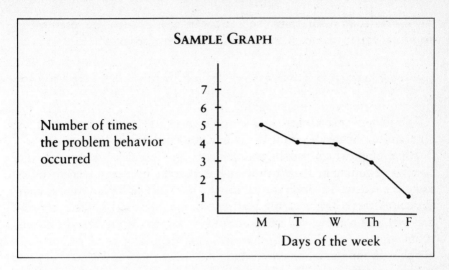

SAMPLE GRAPH

Number of times
the problem behavior
occurred

7
6
5
4
3
2
1

M   T   W   Th   F

Days of the week

havior from the beginning of the week to the end. Some teachers add a reward (e.g., extra time at the computer or some other favorite activity) as a further incentive for achieving this goal.

A third-grade teacher shared her system for increasing self-awareness and control. She gives all of her students a 5 x 7 card to tape on the right corner of their desktops. They put a small x on their card every time they misbehave. When 4 x's are on the card, they write a letter to the teacher about why they have misbehaved.

The teacher decides what consequences students will receive for their misbehavior. She comments: "This works great for me. Children really seem to understand and accept it."

EXPERIMENTING TO FIND WHAT WORKS

Sometimes a teacher has to experiment to find what works. Linda Nickels describes how she did this when she taught second grade in Ithaca, New York:

I had a very needy little boy from a poor family. One day Joey stood up, after I told him to do something, and said, "You're a butt-hole. I'm gonna sue you. I'm gonna get you fired. My father has a lot of money."

In fact, he didn't have any father—at least not any father he knew. He wasn't afraid of anything. The only way I could get him to stop that kind of talking was to hit the tape recorder when he started. Then he stopped.

Before his mother heard the tape, she simply didn't believe he was talking to me that way. Dealing with him took a lot of trial and error.

Turning Joey around involved carrot as well as stick. Teacher Nickels had a male student, Mark, from Ithaca College come into the classroom to work with Joey as his "buddy." Joey understood that he had to be good to have this privilege; otherwise the teacher would have Mark work with someone else. Joey hated to lose Mark's companionship, so he improved his behavior.

The general class rules and consequences are usually sufficient to regulate the behavior of all but a few students. For those few, the individual plan (which usually supplements the class plan) is not only the best way to manage their behavior but also the best way to help them mature morally. Through the personal conference and plan, the teacher communicates a lot of caring and respect for the student as an individual person—helping the student find a way to overcome whatever problem is keeping him or her from participating as a responsible member of the classroom community.

One qualification: There are times when rational discussion alone doesn't get through to a child—and when getting indignant is a moral, human, and effective thing for the teacher to do. Says a second-grade teacher:

> I have a boy this year whose behavior has been terrible. I had many conversations with him, used time-outs, made plans; he showed no improvement. Finally I lost my patience. I said, "Okay, I've had enough! We've got rules, mister, and you're going to follow them!" After that he was much better.

With children like this, a strong assertion of authority lets them know the teacher means business. "First you have to get their attention," is the way one teacher puts it; "then you can reason with them."

Boys represent a disproportionate number of the serious behavior problems, but growing numbers of girls also present a real challenge for the teacher. The accompanying box tells the story of Andrea and the persistent, sensitive efforts of her kindergarten teacher to help her curb her destructive behavior and find a place in the group. The variety of things this teacher did—getting more information about Andrea's background, teaching her how to make friends, finding a positive outlet for her stress—reminds us of an important principle: seeing the child as a whole person, not just a "behavior problem," and searching for a holistic, growth-supporting solution.

ANDREA
A KINDERGARTEN CHILD WITH RELATIONSHIP PROBLEMS

Andrea had many social problems in and out of the classroom. She was verbally abusive to the other children; she would deliberately try to hurt their feelings; she would often become physical with them. The children who were shy, she would try to overpower and manipulate.

I became frustrated in my attempts to help her change; nothing seemed to work. Then I found out some background information. Andrea is repeating kindergarten this year, so I spoke with last year's teacher. She said Andrea has a very negative home life. This helped me understand why she was lashing out at other children.

I decided that Andrea needed to be dealt with very delicately. I have found that she responds well to praise and lots of encouragement. To help her curb her abusive behavior toward other children, I have had a lot of talks with her on being a good friend. I've also worked with the whole class a lot on being good friends.

Now, when Andrea comes to school, if I detect a lot of anxiety, I ask her to draw a picture of how she feels. I allow her time to talk to me or to a friend about her picture. I have realized that if I give her a way to release some of the stress she experiences, it doesn't spill over into the classroom.

So far this has worked for her. She has developed a more positive self-concept and now has many new friends.

—Jill Myers, kindergarten teacher

USING POSITIVE INCENTIVES

Positive incentives are an important part of a behavior improvement plan for some students.

First-grade teacher Colleen Megan of Winkelman Elementary School north of Chicago offers an illustration. At the beginning of the year, she says, Jeremy's language was "unbelievable." He got suspended for pulling down his pants on the playground—and then did it again. He frequently punched other children. Punishment didn't make a dent in his behavior.

I took a positive approach with him. If he was good in the morning, he got to choose a sticker before lunch. If he was good for the afternoon, he got another one at the end of the day. If he was extra good, he got a

"Scratch 'n' Sniff" sticker. And if he had a good week, he got a SuperKid emblem pinned on him on Friday. I also sent home positive notes to Mom at the end of a good day. He turned right around.

Many teachers also use group incentives to motivate good behavior. Group incentives foster class solidarity by providing a group goal to work for.

For example: A sixth-grade teacher takes his class out for a 15-minute extra recess at the end of the day if there have been no more than three rule violations all day long. He finds that his students tend to police themselves so they can earn this special time.

From a moral education perspective, for rewards to work, teachers have to get across the message "I expect you to follow the rules *because that's the right thing to do,* because the rules are there to help everybody. And if you do an especially good job of that, I'd like to do this nice thing for you to show my appreciation." In this way the teacher creates the context that determines the moral meaning rewards have for children.

To guard against kids' seeing rewards as the primary or only reason for being good, a teacher can do any or all of the following:

1. Introduce rewards as an additional motivator only *after* rules have been discussed and established as necessary for the functioning of the classroom community.

2. Use a reward system every so often rather than constantly, to avoid dependence on the external motivators.

3. Make it clear to students, through ongoing class discussion and one-to-one contact, that the most important reason for following the rules is that doing so shows respect for others and makes the classroom a good place to be.

4. Have a system wherein the reward for being good is another opportunity to be good—such as doing an errand for the teacher or tutoring another student.

INVOLVING PARENTS

To recruit parents as partners in moral education, it makes sense to start with discipline. There are several ways a teacher can try to get help from home in this area.

1. **Send parents a copy of the classroom discipline plan.** At the be-

ginning of the year, many teachers send home a copy of the class's discipline plan stating classroom rules and the consequences of breaking them. Some teachers send two copies: one for the parent to keep; another to sign and return, with a space for comments, suggestions, and any information about the child that the parent would like the teacher to know.

Sharing the discipline plan with parents lets them know what behavior the teacher expects, and they can discuss this with their child. They also know what will happen if their child does not follow the classroom rules. And if the teacher has a set hierarchy of discipline consequences that includes parent involvement, the parent will know that in advance. Parent involvement, for example, is called for at three points in the following consequences plan of a first-grade teacher in an inner-city parochial school in Chicago (there is no carryover from day to day; the child starts each day with a clean slate):

First offense: The teacher will remind you of the rule.
Second offense: The teacher will talk with you outside the room.
Third offense: A note goes home to your parents.
Fourth offense: Your parent comes to the school to talk with the teacher.
Fifth offense: Your parent, the teacher, and the principal will have a conference.

A third benefit of sending the discipline plan home is that it gives teachers a chance to explain to parents what values they are trying to teach, not only through their discipline policy but in other ways as well. A second-grade teacher in Quebec writes a letter to parents explaining how she uses the class meeting not only to set up the rules with the children but also to address problems that arise during the year. She adds, "If your child is having any sort of a problem—for example, if he or she is ever the victim of unkind behavior by other children—please let me know and we will find a way to address this constructively through our class meeting." Parents, this teacher reports, say they are grateful for this channel of communication, and nearly every year at least one parent has let the teacher know about a problem his or her child is having.

2. **Establish a positive connection with the parent through a good news message early in the year.** It's also a wise practice to try to contact parents, by phone or note, with a good news message about their child early in the school year. Says one fifth-grade teacher in Liverpool, New York: "I make it a goal to phone every parent by the end of

September with some sort of good news. It might be the fact that their child did his best yet on a math quiz, wrote a really creative story, or did a nice thing for a new kid in school. I've found that when I've made this kind of positive contact first, it makes a tremendous difference in the response I get when I have to call home about a problem."

3. **Notify parents of a discipline problem when help is truly needed and do so in a positive rather than a punitive manner.** Says one mother who is also an elementary school teacher: "I believe teachers should be able to handle the run-of-the-mill discipline problems without involving parents. As a parent, I don't want to get a call because my child has talked out of turn three times that day. But if there is a more serious problem—fighting, for example, or some recurring misbehavior—then I do want to know about it."

A junior high school teacher comments: "A lot of parents are already frustrated and overstressed; it's not fair to put an extra burden on them. If their child is a discipline problem in school, chances are the parents can't handle the kid either. I call parents with good news, but if possible I would rather handle problems myself."

If a teacher does decide to call a child's home, it should be done in a positive, not punitive, way. Says an eighth-grade teacher: "If I've tried a number of things to help a student who's having a behavior problem and the problem persists, that's when I call home. When I call the parent, I look at it as soliciting an alliance to help solve a problem rather than as a punishment for the guilty student. There might be something happening in the student's life that I don't know about."

4. **Meet face-to-face with the parent, rather than calling about a problem, if you think there's a danger the parent will react abusively to a call.** As families become less stable and child abuse more prevalent, teachers have necessarily become more cautious about calling home with bad news. Says one elementary school teacher: "My first year teaching I made a terrible mistake: I called a student's home and left a message on the answering machine that he had behaved badly that day. Later I learned that the father became violent with the boy when he got the message."

If teachers have reasonable grounds to suspect child abuse, they are legally obligated to report it to the designated school authority. But when the teacher has no way of knowing how a particular parent will handle a bad news call, it's prudent to make an appointment to sit down with the parent. Begin by identifying the child's strengths; then present the problem as an area for growth; agree on a plan for helping

ELEMENTS OF MORAL DISCIPLINE

Moral discipline, which uses discipline as a tool for moral growth, has these elements:

1. The teacher's role as the central moral authority of the classroom.

2. Cooperative rule-setting, or discussing with students how the classroom rules express mutual respect and serve the good of the classroom community.

3. An educational approach to consequences, using the occasion of rule-enforcement to help students understand and voluntarily follow the rules.

4. Logical consequences for rule infractions to help students gain self-control, understand why their behavior was inappropriate, and make reparation.

5. Where appropriate, deciding consequences on a case-by-case basis.

6. Individual conferences to promote teacher-student understanding, uncover the cause of a problem, and work out an agreed-upon plan for correcting it.

7. Providing situational supports for self-control, including methods that help students gain control through self-awareness.

8. Including positive and/or negative incentives as part of individual behavior improvement plans where such incentives are needed for motivation.

9. Taking care to use group and individual incentives in a way that supports rather than undermines the moral foundation of classroom rules.

10. Taking a holistic approach that sees students as persons and searches for solutions that help them succeed as members of the classroom community.

11. Involving parents—e.g., by sending home the classroom discipline plan, contacting them about positive as well as negative behavior, and recruiting their cooperation in dealing with problems.

the child improve; and agree to talk by phone a week later to assess how the plan is working.

5. When desirable, implement a cooperative home-school plan for improving a child's behavior. When the teacher's normal disciplinary efforts aren't bringing about the hoped-for results, a home-school behavior improvement plan may achieve a breakthrough, as with this third-grader:

> Travis wasn't responding to the rules and consequences we agreed on as a class, or to my individual conversations with him, so I decided to try a different tack. At the start of each day, I gave him a three-by-five index card with 15 gold stars on it. Every time I had to speak to him about his behavior, he lost a gold star. One immediate effect of this was to help him become more aware of his behavior.
>
> During the first week of this plan, if he had 10 gold stars left at the end of the day, his parents would give him a small reward that night at home— a special dessert, staying up 15 minutes later than usual, playing a board game with his father, and so on. After the first week, we raised the standard; he had to have 12 stars left to earn the reward. He responded well to this approach.

The daily report card is another cooperative home-school approach—one that has proven to be successful with difficult students in kindergarten through high school.[10] The teacher meets with the parents, then with the student, to set up the system: The teacher sends home a report each day that rates the student's behavior and effort (e.g., "good," "satisfactory," "needs improvement") in each school subject. Through academic and behavioral improvement the student earns points at home toward some kind of reward. The teacher calls the parents at the end of the week to see how the system is working and makes modifications as needed.

As the student improves, the daily reporting is phased out by using a weekly, then a monthly, report card. As a result of this process, there is improved communication between the parents and school and also between the parents and child. Parents become more invested in their child's education, and, over time, so does their child.

Given that a child's problems in school often stem from problems at home, it may be tempting to write off parents as a resource for dealing with discipline problems. But home-school cooperation, even in cases where we might think the parent "doesn't care," is the ideal we need to strive for. In their moral and academic development, children are best served when schools and families support each other.

PROFILE OF A MORAL DISCIPLINE TEACHER

Pat Grant is a friendly and enthusiastic teacher who teaches life sciences to seventh-graders at Dryden High School in Dryden, New York. She is widely respected as someone who motivates her students to learn and has good classroom control.

"I don't have any serious discipline problems," she says. "I make a real effort to treat students fairly." She finds that good organization—effective planning so that students are always busy—prevents most problems. She comments: "I plan by the week and post the plans in the front of the room so students are aware of them. I know what I want to accomplish on a particular day, and it's clear to them as well."

She makes her students responsible for the rules. "The first day they come in, we discuss rules. Then they come up with the rules themselves. I write them on the blackboard, and they copy them down in their notebooks. In this way they take ownership."

Student ownership of the rules helps with enforcement. In one class a boy began to disrupt a discussion. Teacher Grant said in a friendly but business-like tone, "Dan, do we need to go over the rules again?" "No," Dan said, and was quiet.

At another point, as Mrs. Grant was answering a student's question, two girls began whispering. While continuing to answer the student's question, Mrs. Grant walked over to the girls and gave a gentle hand signal alerting them to pay attention. During lab time, if students are becoming excited and loud, Mrs. Grant simply holds up an orange tray— a signal that they need to quiet down. One by one, students see the tray and tell one another to be quiet.

If a student continues to misbehave despite verbal or nonverbal reminders, Mrs. Grant will ask him to come in after school to talk things over. Together, she and the student discuss the problem and decide on a solution that is fair both to herself and to the student. If students continue to misbehave even after they have had this after-school conference, then Mrs. Grant contacts the parents and asks for their help in solving the problem.

Teacher Grant also prevents problems by having students change seats every five weeks. She pairs up students she knows can work well together. Moving to new seats is refreshing, she finds, and helps to diminish problems that arise from boredom or lack of cooperation between desk partners.

—from a report by Yvette de Boer, graduate student in classroom discipline, SUNY, Cortland

Discipline in the classroom clearly affects many things: how students view themselves; how they treat each other; how they act toward the teacher; and, to no small degree, how they behave outside the classroom. A teacher's discipline policy also affects the classroom climate, the development of the classroom moral community, the moral growth of the individual members of that community, and the relationship between school and home. For all these reasons, the teacher's development of a discipline plan, from a values education standpoint, is one of the most important things a teacher does.

Moral discipline knows that external controls of some kind are needed to help students learn to regulate their behavior. But it also knows that external control is a starting point, not an end point. And it believes that the way to foster the character trait of self-control is to use the whole process of discipline as a tool for moral growth—one that blends authoritative control with appeals to students' capacity for reason and cooperation.

That balanced approach, I believe, stands the best chance of both creating classroom order and helping students develop good character.

An excellent new classroom management program for the primary grades is Free to Learn, Free to Teach *by JoAnn Shaheen and Lisa Kuhmerker. For information, write: The MASTER Teacher, Inc., Leadership Lane, P.O. Box 1207, Manhattan, KS 66502 (1-800-669-9633).*

CHAPTER 8

Creating a Democratic Classroom Environment: The Class Meeting

How are we to bring children to the spirit of citizenship and humanity which is postulated by democratic societies? By the actual practice of democracy at school. It is unbelievable that at a time when democratic ideas enter into every phase of life, they should have been so little utilized as instruments of education.

—JEAN PIAGET[1]

I like class meetings because you get to talk about things instead of just leaving things the way they already are.

—STACEY SAUNDERS, fifth-grade
student, State Street Elementary
School, Skaneateles, New York

Carl Fospero was a 20-year-old graduate student working on his secondary teaching certification when he got a call to take over a tenth-grade Spanish class at the local high school. A month before, the regular teacher had unexpectedly taken a leave of absence to go into the hospital. A week later, she was dead of cancer.

135

In the month that followed, the Spanish class—a low-achieving group with a history of behavior problems—became virtually uncontrollable, going through four substitute teachers in four weeks. Then the principal called in Carl Fospero, who had done some subbing in this school before.

I tell this story to my teacher education students and ask them, "What would you do as the teacher in this situation, faced with a hostile group of adolescents who have just chewed up four other subs?"

The first thing Carl Fospero did was to ask every student to take out a piece of paper and write him a letter. What were their feelings about the class? How could it be improved? What personal problems were they having with the course? Students wrote that other substitute teachers had been "throwing worksheets" at them; they couldn't keep up with the material; they didn't understand or like Spanish; and so on.

Carl Fospero read portions of the students' letters aloud to the class, using them as a springboard for an open discussion on how to improve the course. The class decided to slow down the pace of instruction to make sure people weren't getting lost. They decided to make time during each class for cooperative learning—such as conversational Spanish between partners—as well as teacher-led instruction. Teacher Fospero said he wanted to try some things they hadn't done before—like writing a play in Spanish and performing and videotaping it. The class also started to write and publish a class newspaper—all in Spanish.

Class morale and learning improved dramatically, as did student behavior. Students respected and liked their teacher and worked well together. Carl Fospero became known as "the miracle sub," and the principal offered him a regular position.

Carl Fospero achieved a remarkable success, but his approach and experience are not unique. Consider a second story, about a substitute teacher who faced a very similar situation at the elementary level.

"MISS WILCOX, THIS IS THE BAD CLASS OF THE SCHOOL"

It was mid-November when Debbie Wilcox got a call from the principal of Harding Elementary School[2] asking her to take over a third-grade class of 26 children for six weeks. The regular teacher, the principal said, found them the worst she'd ever dealt with, was close to a nervous breakdown, and had requested a six-week mental health leave.

A year out of college, Debbie Wilcox had earned a reputation as an effective substitute. But this would be a challenge: When she arrived at the classroom she was to have for six weeks, a student greeted her at the door with the announcement, "Miss Wilcox, this is the bad class of the school."

She began, as was her normal procedure, with a class meeting. She elicited ground rules for discussion, asking children to give a reason for each rule they suggested. Then the discussion turned to rules for the whole classroom. Most students, she found, proposed rules in negative terms: "Don't push," "Don't punch," "Don't tear up somebody's homework." "What does it mean," she asked, "when we push or punch someone?" One student answered, "That we don't care about them."

"What can we do, then, to make this a better class?" teacher Wilcox asked. "Care for each other," a student said. The teacher printed CARE FOR EACH OTHER in large block letters on a piece of butcher paper and hung it above the blackboard. That became their primary rule.

In the weeks that followed, the teacher began each day with a class meeting. As the meetings continued, more class members participated, and students listened more quietly when someone else was speaking.

During the rest of the school day, teacher Wilcox observed that "small changes in behavior began to appear; children stopped running to me with every problem, and instead often decided among themselves what was wrong and what to do about it." Sharing behavior began to replace the constant "Give it to me, it's mine" exchanges. Students' schoolwork also showed an improvement, and many began to express a liking for school.

"Emergency" class meetings were sometimes required. Teacher Wilcox would ask: "What are people doing? What rule did we agree to?" However, serious behavior problems, she says, "became almost non-existent."

She attributed that change primarily to the daily class meetings and the resulting feeling of accountability to class rules. But the meetings also "gave each child," the teacher says, "a group of people who felt that he or she was worth listening to. The changes I observed in children convince me all the more that children develop respect for others when they begin to respect themselves."

At the end of the six weeks, when the regular teacher was about to return, two of the children came to Debbie Wilcox and said: "Miss Wilcox, we don't want to lose our class meetings. Will you teach Mrs. Blodgett[3] how to do them?" Miss Wilcox said she would see what she could do.

Mrs. Blodgett listened politely to Debbie Wilcox's account of the class meetings but did not continue them. Two months later, teacher Wilcox was called to the same school to substitute-teach in another classroom. She happened to pass by the room where she had spent those six weeks. The children were behaving badly, and the teacher was screaming at them. Other faculty commented that this third-grade class was once again the "bad class" of the school.

THE CLASS MEETING AS A VEHICLE FOR CHARACTER DEVELOPMENT

What can be learned from the experiences of Carl Fospero and Debbie Wilcox? Both succeeded in creating a good moral environment and in getting students to learn by applying a widely known but much-neglected educational principle: Involve students in making decisions about the life of the classroom.

Both teachers did this through the class meeting. The class meeting provides an experience in democracy, making students full partners in creating the best possible classroom. It changes the dynamics and deepens the bond between teacher and class, enhancing the teacher's influence as model and mentor at the same time that it enlarges the role and responsibilities of students. In the process, it fosters the moral growth of the group and its individual members.

Why, in the case of Debbie Wilcox, did the children regress when the regular teacher returned? That was no doubt due to a combination of factors, but it's reasonable to think that the loss of the class meetings played a significant role. Morality, in the words of one teacher, "takes a lot of slow to grow." While it is growing, it is fragile, very much in need of support structures that hold it together.

The moral community of the classroom is one such support structure. The class meeting, because it regularly calls the group together as a conscious, decision-making community, is the single most important support system for eliciting and strengthening students' best values and behavior. Because the class meeting is a master strategy in values education, this chapter examines its structure, goals, and many uses in the classroom.

GOALS AND VARIETIES OF CLASS MEETINGS

What exactly is a class meeting? It is:

- A meeting of the whole class, emphasizing *interactive* discussion among class members.

- Led by the teacher, a student, or the teacher and a student together.

- Whenever possible, conducted in a circle to allow eye contact among participants.

- Held at regularly scheduled times (e.g., the first thing every morning, every Wednesday after recess, every Monday and Friday at the end of the day) and in response to special needs.

- Usually 10 to 30 minutes long, depending on the age of the students, the complexity of the topic, and the interest level during the meeting.

The character development goals of the class meeting are to:

1. Improve, through regular, face-to-face communication, students' ability to listen respectfully to others and understand their perspectives.

2. Provide a forum where students' thoughts are valued and where they can gain the self-esteem that comes from learning to express themselves in a group.

3. Foster all three parts of character—habits of moral judgment, feeling, and behavior—through the continuing challenge of putting respect and responsibility into practice in everyday classroom life.

4. Create a moral community as a support structure to nurture and hold in place the qualities of good character that students are developing.

5. Develop the attitudes and skills needed to take part in democratic group decision-making and become participating citizens of a democracy.

This last goal has special significance in a democratic society. "Democracy," John Dewey wrote,

is much broader than a method of conducting government. *It is a way of life.* Its foundation is faith in human intelligence . . . faith that each individual has something to contribute, whose value can be assessed only as it enters into the pooled intelligence constituted by the contributions of all [emphasis added].[4]

The interactive participation of all individuals, Dewey asserted, is "the keynote of democracy as a way of life."[5]

The class meeting enables children to learn democracy by experiencing it. Through the class meeting they are able to participate in a form of the democratic process that is a suitable match for the collective life of the classroom. Although teachers are still in charge, bearing ultimate responsibility for students' safety, welfare, and learning, they can, through the class meeting, give students an important educational experience of democracy in the broad sense that Dewey spoke about—solving problems through the pooled intelligence of all.

There is, unfortunately, plenty of evidence that large numbers of citizens don't value their opportunity to participate in the democratic process. In the United States, only half those eligible to vote currently do so in presidential elections. A 1990 survey revealed vast ignorance on the part of U.S. students regarding the democratic society they live in: Only half of eighth-graders even knew that we have a representative democracy, and only 38 percent were aware that Congress makes the laws.[6]

But by itself textbook knowledge of democracy is unlikely to raise levels of participation. Students need to be empowered through education that leads them to *value* participation. The opportunities to do that through class meetings are many and varied. The boxed material on the following pages presents some of them.

COMMUNITY-BUILDING THROUGH CLASS MEETINGS

In the early stages of developing the meeting, topics that help students get to know each other are good choices. Claire Betinas, a teacher at Birch Meadow Elementary School in Reading, Massachusetts, talks about how she uses class meetings to build community among her second-graders:

> Every day we begin with some kind of circle meeting. On Monday I'll ask, "What did you do over the weekend?" That topic is also good for memory skills—at first, many children have a hard time remembering what they did over the weekend.
>
> After a while, we begin compliment time. We take one student a day and tell that student the abilities and qualities of character he or she has that we admire.
>
> The circle helps kids get to know each other better, but it also helps me get to know them. I might learn something about a child's grandparents or the names of brothers and sisters. This makes the child feel more at home in the room, and it makes it easier for me to talk to the child.

TWENTY KINDS OF CLASS MEETINGS

1. *Good news meeting:* "Who has some good news to share?"

2. *Circle whip:* Go around the circle; everyone can either complete the "sentence-starter" or choose to pass. After everyone has had a turn, the teacher can use individual students' responses as a springboard for interactive discussion. Some sample sentence-starters are:
   - "Something I like about this class . . ."
   - "Something I think would make our class better . . ."
   - "A decision I think we should make . . ."
   - "I'm wondering why . . ."
   - "Something that bothers me . . ."
   - "I wish . . ."

3. *Appreciation time:* "Who would you like to appreciate?"

4. *Compliment time:* One or two children are chosen; taking one child at a time, the teacher invites classmates to say something they like or admire about that person.

5. *Goal-setting meeting:* Discuss the goals for the morning, the day, the week, a curriculum unit, the academic year.

6. *Rule-setting meeting:* "What rules do we need for our classroom?" "For going to gym?" "For the upcoming field trip?"

7. *Rule-evaluating meeting:* Have students write about, then discuss the following questions: "What are the school rules? Why do we have them? Are they good rules? If you could change one rule, what would it be?[7] . . . Do any of our classroom rules need changing to make them work better?"

8. *Stage-setting meeting:* For example, before a small-group activity: "What can you do to make things go smoothly in your group?"

9. *Feedback and evaluation:* "How well did you work together?" "How could you make it go better the next time?" "What was good about today?" "How can we make tomorrow a better day?"

10. *Reflections on learnings:* "What did you learn from this activity (unit, project, book)?" "One new idea or understanding?"

11. *Student presentation:* One or two students present a piece of their work, such as a project or story; other class members ask questions and offer appreciative comments.

12. *Problem-solving meetings:*
    - *Individual problem:* "Who's having a problem that we might be able to help solve?"
    - *Group problem:* "What's a class problem we should talk about?"
    - *Complaints and recommendations:* Ground rule: You can make a complaint about a problem, but you have to offer a recommendation for correcting it.[8]
    - *Fairness meeting:* "How can we solve this conflict (e.g., cutting in line, disputes over materials or equipment, arguments over cleanup) in a way that's fair to everybody?"

13. *Academic issues:* "Why do we have to study this?" "What would help you do a better job on homework?" "On the next test?" "How could the last test have been improved?"

14. *Classroom improvement meeting:* "What changes would make our classroom better?" Possibilities: changing the physical arrangement of the classroom, new ways of working together, new learning games, ideas for class-created bulletin boards, etc.

15. *Follow-up meeting:* "How is the solution/change we agreed upon working? Can we make it work better?"

16. *Planning meeting:* "What group projects would you like to do?" "What topics to study?" "What field trips to take?" "What would be fun to do differently next week in spelling, math, or science?" "What would be the most exciting way to study this next topic?"

17. *Concept meeting:* "What is a friend? How do you make one?" "What is a conscience? How does it help you?" "What is a lie? Is it ever right to tell one?" "What is trust? Why is it important?" "What is courage? How do people show it?"

18. *Sticky situations:*[9] "What should you/would you do if: You find a wallet on the sidewalk with $20 in it?" . . . "You find just a $20 bill?" . . . "You see a kid stealing something from somebody else's locker?" . . . "There's a new kid that you'd like to be nice to but your friends think she/he is weird?" . . . "A friend asks to copy your homework?" . . . "A friend you're with shoplifts a CD?" . . . "Two kids on the bus are picking on a little kid and making him cry?"

19. *Suggestion box/class business box:* Any appropriate item students have submitted for discussion.

20. *Meeting on meetings:* "What have you liked about our class meetings? What haven't you liked? What have we accomplished? How can we improve our meetings?"[10]

An eighth-grade teacher uses homeroom at the beginning of the day to hold a class meeting. One of her standard topics is "Something New and Good." Students share something new in their lives, inside or outside of school, that they're feeling good about.

PROBLEM-SOLVING THROUGH CLASS MEETINGS

At all developmental levels, the class meeting can be used for problem-solving in ways that foster higher levels of respect and responsibility.

HIGH SCHOOL LEVEL

Hassles over Homework

Student teachers, like substitutes, often have the most difficulty with classroom control. The class meeting is a way for the student teacher to head off potential problems and deal positively with ones that arise. Martha Bigelow found that out when she student-taught English to several classes of tenth-graders. She began her student-teaching experience by holding a class meeting in all of her classes. She and the students discussed, agreed upon, and signed a contract for classroom behavior.

However, as she progressed through her first unit—on the play *A Raisin in the Sun*—one of her expectations in the contract, "Come prepared to class," was not being upheld. She was assigning homework three to four nights a week and finding that in two of her classes, half to two-thirds of the students were not doing it.

She reports:

> I immediately held another class meeting concerning this specific problem. I stated the numbers of people not finishing their homework and the importance of finishing the homework in order to have a good discussion of the play in class. I explained that it was very disappointing and frustrating for me to be spending several hours preparing for class while so many students were coming unprepared. Finally, I said that it seemed to me that they were apathetic and didn't care about school.

That last statement touched a nerve. Most students insisted that they *did* care. "If we didn't care," some said, "we wouldn't be here!" Then they talked about why they didn't get the reading and related questions done. Teacher Bigelow suggested ways in which they could manage their time more efficiently. She worked out an agreed-upon system for grading homework that would reward timely completion and penalize noncompletion. She spent more time explaining assignments. And a week later she held a follow-up meeting.

Although a few students continued to be lax about homework, the performance of most improved considerably. "The idea of class meetings," teacher Bigelow comments, "was the most important thing I learned this semester."

MIDDLE SCHOOL LEVEL

Trouble with Talking

Because the class meeting recruits the group as a problem-solving ally, it often succeeds where the teacher's single-handed efforts fail.

Seventh-grade students are notoriously "squirrelly," and one seventh-grade math teacher was getting worn down by this problem. Becoming upset, making speeches about the importance of courtesy and attentive behavior, and sending students to detention had not helped.

One day he held a class meeting, told students he was tired of getting on their case about talking, and discovered that they didn't like it either. Some students said they were tired of the issue taking up so much class time.

The teacher asked for their suggestions in writing. Then he asked for five volunteers to stay after school to go over all the suggestions and come up with a proposal to present to the class the next day. When the five-person committee presented its plan, the class voted to adopt it with minor modifications. The teacher comments:

> Their system was to have a list of all the students' names at the front of the room. If a student broke the rule about talking, he'd have to come up and put a check by his name. If he talked out of turn again in the same period, he'd get a detention. This warning and detention system was actually quite similar to what I had been using without success, but when it was the students' own plan, it worked much better.

Fury over Fanny-Grabbing

A seventh-grade teacher in Montreal, Canada, finds a suggestion box a good source of meeting topics, including issues students would be too embarrassed to bring up themselves at a meeting.

For example: One year several girls put angry notes in the suggestion box about "fanny-grabbing." Apparently a number of boys had been doing this to the girls.

The teacher read the complaints at a class meeting. How did other girls feel about this? she asked. To a person, they said it made them *furious* when boys did this. The boys appeared genuinely shocked that girls felt this way. They were just fooling around, they said; they really liked the girls. Well, that was no way to show it, the girls replied.

After this class meeting, the fanny-grabbing stopped.

ELEMENTARY SCHOOL LEVEL

At the elementary school level, teachers have used class meetings as a problem-solving vehicle in many different ways.

On-the-spot meetings are one example. Linda Nickels often used those as a first-year teacher of second-graders at Belle Sherman Elementary School in Ithaca, New York. She says: "If we were having trouble about something, I'd get the kids together and deal with it right then. Sometimes I would have a circle meeting at the end of the afternoon and say, 'Today was a lousy day. What can we do to make tomorrow better?' It helped."

"We have something called the class business box," says Marie Adams, a second-grade teacher at Country Club Elementary School in San Ramon, California. "Kids can put in anything they would like brought up at our Wednesday class meeting."

Phyllis Smith-Hansen, when she was a third-grade teacher at Lansing Elementary School in Lansing, New York, kept a chart at the front of the room with the incomplete sentence "This was the week when . . ." During the week, both she and her students could enter incidents they wanted to discuss at their Friday morning meeting. Having the problems posted ahead of time, the teacher says, gave both her and the students time to think about the problems before they sat down to try to solve them.

Chaos in the Coat Closet

The class meeting allows a teacher and a class to put their heads together to work out management problems that, left unsolved, can undermine feelings of community in the classroom.

Patti Brody, when she was a parochial school teacher in Syracuse, New York, faced one such management problem with her second-graders. She explains:

> Ever since the snow arrived, and with it all the extra clothing the kids wore to school every day, our coat closet had been a disaster area. There was very little space for all the coats, boots, mittens, and so on. The kids were getting their boots mixed up, and some were even missing the bus

because it took them so long to find their things. And when it came time to get ready to go, they completely forgot about being kind and loving— it was every person for himself!

In their class meeting, the children brainstormed possible solutions, the teacher wrote each idea on the board, and they voted to adopt the following plan: "Everyone will be assigned a hook in the closet, with his or her name under it; you are responsible for putting your coat and hat on your own hook, and your boots underneath it."

"How are we going to be sure everyone does this?" the teacher asked. A girl responded: "If someone doesn't put their things where they belong, they should have to keep them at their desk for a day and see how uncomfortable that is!" The class agreed that that was a fair consequence.

Teacher Brody took one further step: She asked each child to make a *personal commitment* to abide by the group's decision.

I wrote the agreement on a large sheet of paper and drew 34 smiling faces. Each child signed his or her name after one of the faces. The contract is on the coat room doors, where everyone can see it. We marked each hook in the closet; each person has a spot.

Since we adopted this plan, not a single person has missed the bus.

Dealing with Aggression

Kindergarten teacher Marcia Helbig of Cazenovia, New York, held her first class meeting when aggression became a problem in her room. She showed the class a large photograph of two hands and asked, "What should we do when someone brings their hurting hands to school instead of their helping hands?"

After a lively discussion, the group settled on one child's suggestion to have a "thinking chair." The aggressor would go there to sit and think about what he should have done instead of hitting. When that person has thought of another way he could have solved his problem, he would tell the teacher, apologize to the child he hit, and then reenter the group.

Dealing with Stealing

Donna Matthewson teaches 30 first-graders in a low-income section of Syracuse, New York. She held her first class meeting on stealing, which had become a serious problem in the classroom. She began the meeting by reviewing all the things that had turned up missing in recent weeks. Then she asked two very good questions: (1) "I want you to think of a time when something of yours was taken. . . . How did you feel?" Children spoke freely about that; they said they felt angry and sad—and very happy if they were fortunate enough to get the missing possession back. (2) "How do you feel when *you* take something that isn't yours?" There was silence. Finally one boy spoke up: "I don't feel so good when I take something." Other children made similar admissions.

Teacher Matthewson accomplished at least two things: sensitizing children to how others felt when they had something taken, and sensitizing them to the fact that they didn't feel very good about themselves when they took something. After the meeting, to encourage honesty further, she decided to have a lost-and-found box instead of asking children to bring "found" objects to her desk. Soon all sorts of lost things began turning up in the box, and the frequency of missing items sharply declined. The teacher comments:

> It's become accepted behavior in our room to be honest—something I did not expect. If children find something that doesn't belong to them, they put it in the box, and they go to find their own things there. If someone does slip and keep something that isn't theirs, it's the kids who pitch in and find it, not me. . . . I've been using other class meetings to reinforce this honest and thoughtful behavior. The class is very proud of its progress, and so am I.

Sometimes moral attitudes and behaviors are difficult to change, rooted as they are in children's developmental immaturity or in values learned outside school. But time and again, teachers are surprised at their ability to influence group norms positively through the class meeting, and at the power of these class norms to influence individual students' behavior.

EXPANDING STUDENTS' ROLE IN DECISION-MAKING

The class meeting can also be used in other ways to bring students into a broader decision-making role. The suggestion box can be adapted for this purpose. Says Patti Brody of her second-grade class:

> Children can write down any suggestion they have for helping themselves do better (they might want to change their seat, for example), for improving our class, or for something I might do better as a teacher. I try

to respond in one way or another to all of their suggestions, and I select those I think are appropriate for whole-group discussion at class meeting.

Some teachers use class meetings to involve children in planning. Students might help to plan a special class project such as a field trip or a class play. And one fifth-grade teacher says that when her language arts lessons are getting stale, she'll ask students for their thoughts about something different they'd like to do in spelling or writing—and she always gets good ideas. Richard Lauricella, an award-winning[11] fifth-grade teacher at Lakeland Elementary School in Solvay, New York, says:

> I've been teaching for more than 30 years, and I would have been burned out long ago but for the fact that I involve my kids in designing the curriculum. I'll say to them, "What's the *most* exciting way we could study this next unit?" If we decide that their first suggestion isn't feasible, I'll say, "Okay, what's the *next* most exciting way we could study this?" They always come up with good proposals, they're motivated because I'm using their ideas, and I never do the unit in the same way twice.

Brookline, Massachusetts, teachers Kristen Field and Virginia Holmes enable their combined third- and fourth-grade class to participate in a variety of decisions that affect their learning. A math group, for example, can decide if they are ready to move on to division or if they need more time on multiplication. The class can decide if they would rather demonstrate their understanding of a just-completed unit on ancient culture by writing stories or by drawing a sequence of pictures. These teachers comment:

> We don't relinquish control of the decision-making responsibility; we structure options clearly. Our children gain a greater sense of worth when they become active decision-makers. They show more zest for their studies and are more invested in their products as something *they* value rather than something they do for us.

At the junior high and senior high levels, a workable way to get student input is through the feedback form shown in the accompanying box. Two or three times a semester, the teacher can set aside 15 minutes of class time for students to complete this short questionnaire about the course.

The teacher can take the completed forms home, read the students' comments, group them according to theme, note students she wishes

FEEDBACK FORM

1. How satisfied are you with the course this quarter (semester)?

1	2	3	4	5
Not at all				Very
Satisfied				Satisfied

2. What about the class have you liked or found helpful?

3. What would make classes more valuable for you?

4. What problems are you having in the course that you'd like help with?

5. What can you do to help yourself do better in the course?

Name (optional) [12]

to see individually about problems, and consider any course adjustments she'd like to make based on the feedback. The teacher can then read aloud to the class various student comments concerning positive features of the course, summarize student suggestions, and tell the class which suggestions she'd like to try.

The benefits of this exercise are several: The teacher gets to hear what students like about her class as well as what problems they may be having; students feel respected because the instructor has cared enough to ask for their feedback; the teacher almost always gets some practical student suggestions that can be incorporated; and the students come to feel a greater ownership of and commitment to the class.

Some secondary-level teachers also use the last 15 minutes or so of the last period of the week for a "class council." This can be structured around particular questions or may be "open frame," where the teacher and students can bring up any issue, question, or concern. Other secondary-level teachers sometimes use the last 5 to 10 minutes of a period for a class meeting on a specific question. Comments Itzick Vatnick, a central New York science teacher:

> I used a class meeting to solicit responses to the format of the last exam they took. I got excellent responses from the students for the construction of the next exam. The meeting also helped to dispel the feeling some students had that the exam was constructed purposefully to be too difficult.

DEVELOPING A SUCCESSFUL CLASS MEETING

These success stories may make it sound as if class meetings are easy. They're not. The fruits of the class meeting—the growth of the group as a moral community and the social-moral development of individual children—come slowly. They require patience and persistence on the part of the teacher.

Beginnings are likely to be bumpy. Says Nell Woodmancy, a former Syracuse, New York, kindergarten teacher:

> When we tried to talk about problems in our class meeting, the children with short attention spans became disruptive. Some children would try to engage in serious discussion, but the attitude of their classmates was, "Come on, it's my turn to talk!" The attitudes of caring and helpfulness were not strong enough.
>
> When I tried to have them think about rules for good listening, their "listening" was the worst yet. I felt very ineffective as a facilitator. As the confusion mounted and children called out horrible punishments that should be meted out to nonlisteners, it took great self-discipline to not just say, "We'll do it *this* way."

The challenge is to keep trying. Teacher Woodmancy, for example, did get her kindergartners to make and regularly review rules for classroom behavior, including circle time. That gradually led to better listening. She also found that meetings had greater cohesion when she began by having the children cross arms, join hands, and sing the song "The More We Get Together . . . the Happier We'll Be."

She experimented with the way she posed questions, and found that that made a considerable difference in how the children responded. For example: Instead of saying to the whole group, "Is there anything that's upsetting or bothering you?" and ending up with a list of class complaints, she asked: "Who has a problem they'd like us to help them

TEN STEPS IN A CLASS MEETING

1. *Circle up:* Form a good circle and call the meeting to order.

2. *Set the agenda:* State the purpose and goals of the meeting.

3. *Set the rules:* Establish or review rules for "good talking and listening."

4. *Identify partners:* Pair up students who will discuss the problem or topic under consideration.

5. *Pose the problem or question:* For example, "Several people have said there's a lot of name-calling on the playground lately. What can we do to solve this problem?"

6. *Personal thinking time:* Give students a silent minute to think about the question individually.

7. *Signal for quiet:* Establish a signal (e.g., flick of the lights) for stopping partner talk in order to begin whole-group discussion.

8. *Partner talk:* Have partners (in place) share thoughts with each other (3 to 5 minutes); circulate to help those who may be slow to interact.

9. *Whole-group discussion:* Invite several pairs of students to share their ideas with the group; invite reactions to these ideas; pose follow-up questions; if appropriate, reach and record agreement on action to be taken and plan implementation, and set a time for a follow-up meeting.

10. *Close the meeting:* See the accompanying box "Various Ways to Close a Class Meeting."

with?" The latter question, she says, focused the attention of the class on helping to resolve each other's problems.

One strategy for increasing the chances of a good meeting is to hand out to students (if they can read) a sheet showing the steps of the class meeting that you intend to follow. There are various meeting formats, but I recommend the sequence set forth in the accompanying box "Ten Steps in a Class Meeting" as a well-structured way to begin.

The most crucial step is to establish rules that will lead to an orderly discussion. I have observed class meetings where children repeatedly interrupted each other, talked to their neighbors, paid no attention to

---

VARIOUS WAYS TO CLOSE A CLASS MEETING

1. *Review:* If the meeting produced an agreement, review it.

2. *'Round the horn:* "Let's go around for final, brief comments; you may pass if you wish."

3. *Remembering:* "What's something somebody said that you thought was a good point, even if you didn't agree with it? Take a moment to think . . . then share."

4. *Learning:* "Think of something you learned from today's meeting . . ." Then go around, or ask for volunteers.

5. *Questions:* "What's a question that's still on your mind?"

6. *Complete the sentence:* Invite all to complete a sentence starter (e.g., "At the end of this meeting, I think . . ." or, "I feel . . ." or, "I hope . . .").

7. *Partners:* Students respond to any of the above, then share it with their class meeting partner (or change partners).

8. *Future topics:* "Suggested topics for our next meeting?"

9. *Silence:* "Take a minute to think about today's meeting . . . a new idea you got . . . something you'll do differently as a result of our discussion. . . . Write it down or just keep it in mind."

10. *Evaluation:* "What did you like about today's meeting? What made it a good discussion? What could we do better or differently next time?"

---

the speaker—and where the teacher vacillated between trying to ignore these behaviors and reprimanding the offenders. Teachers are demoralized because they feel the contradiction: They're trying to have a meeting about a moral issue such as how to get along better, and the meeting itself is an exercise in mutual disrespect. To avoid this situation, teachers need a careful plan for developing and maintaining order in the meeting.

Teachers find that students of all ages, when asked, can generate rules that will facilitate good discussion. Here, for example, are the rules that one fourth-grade class agreed on:

1. No talking out—raise your hand if you want to speak.

2. Keep hands down until the speaker is finished.

3. Don't whisper to a friend.

4. Stick to the subject.

5. No put-downs.

6. Don't laugh if a person is saying something serious; do laugh if the person *is* trying to make a joke.

WHAT HAPPENS IF STUDENTS BREAK THE CLASS MEETING RULES?

Simply making discussion rules, even with democratic participation, doesn't ensure that all class members will follow them.

Gloria Cox knew that. When she held class meetings as a kindergarten teacher in Ithaca, New York, she used her first meeting of the year to read and discuss a story and compliment children on good listening; her second meeting to establish rules for talking and listening; and her third meeting to discuss consequences of rule-breaking. In the third meeting, there were almost always some children who broke the rules they had just agreed on the day before.

For example: In the third class meeting of one year, two boys talked out of turn, played with blocks, and generally disturbed those around them. Teacher Cox immediately engaged the group in problem-solving. She said, "Yesterday, we agreed on a list of rules to help us have good discussions. Today we have some people who are not following our rules. How can we, together, solve this problem?"

The class decided that they should add another rule to their list: "A person will be asked to leave the group if, after one reminder, that person continues not to follow the rules." They agreed that the "reminder" could be delivered by either the teacher or another child, and that those who were asked to leave the group should go to a desk or table and do a quiet activity there.

At the next class meeting, the two boys were still disruptive and had to leave the group. "But after a couple of days of leaving the meeting," teacher Cox reports, "they joined the group successfully." Later the class agreed that students not able to follow the rules on a particular day would leave the circle on their own.

DEVELOPING STUDENTS' PARTICIPATION SKILLS

Besides the basic step of setting and enforcing rules for discussion, how else can teachers develop students' class meeting participation skills? Here are 18 suggestions drawn from the experience of teachers who have used class meetings:

1. **A good circle.** Make sure there's a good circle. (Getting the chairs into a circle can be done with surprising efficiency if the teacher and the class work out a plan for doing so.) Teachers who try the circle format for the first time are often surprised at the difference this face-to-face arrangement makes in the amount and quality of discussion. "I had more kids talking than usual," comments a ninth-grade social studies teacher, "and some students who almost never speak in class contributed frequently."

   Chairs in a circle work better than desks in a circle because the desk can be a subtle barrier between the individual and the group. One teacher who had started a values discussion program with her sixth-graders initially had them sitting at desks in a circle and was disappointed that they didn't talk very much. When she had them sit in chairs without their desks, participation improved considerably.

2. **Nonverbal signals.** Use nonverbal reminders of the discussion rules. One second-grade teacher gives a ticket with a sad face on it to anyone who interrupts (two sad faces and you have to leave the meeting).

3. **Talk ticket.** Use a talk ticket (a 5 x 8 index card is a good size). When someone has it, it's his or her turn to talk. When the student is finished, he or she passes it around or across the circle to the next person who wishes to speak. As an alternative, some teachers use a yarn ball, which can be tossed (underhanded) to the next speaker.

4. **Model good listening.** Teach the difference between good and bad listening. One kindergarten teacher, for example, had her 5-year-olds role-play good and bad listening, two at a time, in the center of their circle. ("Could I have two volunteers to show me what good listening is? . . . Okay, Billy, you tell Sara something you like to do after school. Sara, you show us how to be a good listener. . . . Now can I have two people to show me what *bad* listening is? . . .")

5. **Reinforce good listening.** Compliment individual students and the group as a whole on good listening.

6. **Invite student paraphrasing.** To motivate good listening, call on students sometimes to restate in their own words what the last speaker said. If students don't seem really to be hearing the other side's arguments, ask two students with opposing viewpoints to paraphrase each other's views until both feel understood.

7. **Remembering.** Do "remembering" at the end of the meeting. Announce at the start, "At the end of today's class meeting, I'll ask you to try to remember something that somebody else said that you thought was a good point—something that made you think even if you didn't agree with it. Listen carefully so you'll be able to remember."

8. **Encourage interaction.** Encourage students to *respond* to each other's contributions. Ask interaction questions such as "Can we have a reaction to Mary's idea?," "Who would like to add to what Bill just said?," or "Who has a point of view that's similar to or different from Tim's?"

9. **Verbal structures.** Teach students the verbal structures that enable them to agree or disagree with each other respectfully. For example: Ron Fuller, a fifth-grade teacher at Heath Elementary School in Brookline, Massachusetts, taught his students to say, "I'd like to support what _____ said . . ." if they wanted to agree with somebody; "I'd like to challenge what _____ said . . ." if they wished to disagree; and "I'd like to support and challenge _____ " if they wanted to both agree and disagree.

10. **Encourage everyone to participate.** Encourage quiet members of the group to talk by saying, "For the next five minutes I'd like to hear from people who haven't had a chance to contribute yet." Or at the start of the meeting say, "Today I'd like to encourage everyone to contribute at least once. So if you notice that there are some members of the group who haven't spoken yet and you've already spoken two or three times, you can encourage them to share their thoughts by not taking another turn yourself." Or invite quiet persons to contribute in a way that leaves them the option to "pass": "Sue, what are your thoughts about this?" (pause) "Do you want to think about it and I'll come back to you later?"

11. **Sentence-starters.** Create a nonthreatening way for everyone to speak by supplying a "sentence-starter" and giving students a

minute or so to write a completion. Sample starters: "I feel good when . . . ," "I feel bad when . . . ," "I am proud of . . . ," "I wish . . . ," and "When I see a kid being mean to somebody else . . ." Then go around the circle, asking each person to give his or her completion of the sentence. (See the box "Twenty Kinds of Class Meetings" on pages 141 and 142 for other sentence-starters.)

Use a sentence starter as a springboard for more interactive, open-ended discussion (e.g.,"What is the best thing to do when you see someone being mean to someone else? Why?").

12. **Partner buzz.** To maximize participation at the start of a meeting or revive it if it's lagging, assign partners, pose a question (e.g., "What are two things we can do tomorrow to make this a better classroom?"), and give partners two minutes to come up with an answer together. Then ask them to report to the group as a team. Children who are shy about speaking alone are more likely to talk when they're part of a twosome.

13. **Meeting buddies.** Assign each child a regular "class meeting buddy" for two to three weeks. Buddies are responsible for reminding each other to follow the meeting rules.

14. **Kids call on kids.** To encourage class participation, have the person who speaks call on the next person who wishes to speak. Stipulations: (1) The speaker must select "someone who was doing a good job of listening"; (2) a boy must choose a girl (if one wishes to speak) and a girl a boy (to avoid same-sex selection); and (3) the facilitator of the meeting (whether a teacher or a student) may interject a question or refocusing comment at any time.

15. **Assign roles.** Assign students special roles that increase their responsibility for the meeting. A committee of students can be in charge of preparing the agenda, soliciting input from the teacher and the class. Anne Roubos, when she taught first grade at Homer Elementary School in Homer, New York, rotated responsibility for "leading" the meeting. The student leader was called the V.I.P. (Very Important Person), sat on a high stool, started the meeting by shaking a maraca and saying "Class meeting come to order!," called on people to speak, and closed the meeting by shaking the maraca again and saying "Class meeting adjourned!"

Older students can take on more sophisticated responsibilities. A teacher of grades 5 through 8, for example, assigns students the roles of facilitator, assistant, hand-caller, and process observer. The facilitator starts the meeting, states the problem, and keeps the focus. The teacher comments: "I will model this role first, then describe to the student what I did, then let the student try it, then model it again. The first time the student tries it, the discussion is pretty wild, but by the third time the student leads a discussion, it's quite orderly."

The assistant writes issues, points, and decisions on the board or an easel. The hand-caller writes on the board the names of the people who have raised their hands to speak, and calls on them in the order that they raised them. The process observer makes notes about the process of the meeting (how well people listen, participate, and follow the rules), gives the group feedback at the end, and asks the facilitator, "What do you feel worked for you as leader? What could have made things go better? What could the rest of us have done to make the meeting go better?"

16. **Record ideas.** Record students' ideas (on a pad or the board) as they express them, and read them back, giving students credit by name, when the brainstorming part of the meeting is done. This shows that you take their ideas seriously, encourages thoughtful proposals, and inspires good attending. The role of writing down and reading back ideas can also be delegated to a student recorder.

17. **Evaluate meetings.** Periodically have each student rate the class meetings on a scale of 1 to 5, where 1 is poor and 5 is excellent (see the accompanying box "Class Meeting Evaluation"); then have a class meeting where people share their ratings and discuss constructive proposals for making meetings better. As an aid to evaluation, audiotape or videotape a meeting; have the students listen to or view the tape and then complete this sentence: "We could improve our class meeting by . . ."

18. **Demonstration meeting.** Encourage pride in the class meeting and progress in communication skills by having the class work toward doing a demonstration meeting—for the principal, superintendent, parents, or School Board.

THE ROLE OF THE CLASS MEETING IN THE LIFE OF THE CLASSROOM

The role that the class meeting plays in the life of the classroom will evolve if the teacher lets it.

CLASS MEETING EVALUATION[13]

1. Circle the number that best describes this class meeting:

5	4	3	2	1
Excellent	Very good	Good	Fair	Poor

2. Circle the word that describes what you think of this meeting:

Wow   So-so   Yuk

3. Complete these sentences:

This class meeting was _____

_____.

In our meeting we decided _____

_____.

I helped this meeting by _____

_____.

I think the class meetings have helped _____

_____.

Since we have class meetings, people have _____

_____.

Our class meetings would be better if _____

_____.

Janet Clauson, a first-grade teacher in central New York, says she began by holding her class meeting twice a week after recess. "But as we continued with the meetings," she says, "the children displayed a great enough interest and response that we began to meet each day."

Topics expanded to include classroom management problems, moral dilemmas (Should a boy who needs money to go on a trip with his friends return the $10 an old man has accidentally overpaid him for a delivery?), and friendship themes (How do you make a friend? Keep a friend? Know when a friend is really a friend?).

They established a set routine: Children were instructed to go directly to the bathroom and to get a drink following recess, then set up the circle for the meeting—a responsibility they were excited about and handled surprisingly well. "The children learned that I could not carry a class discussion by myself," the teacher says. "They were just as important to the discussion as I was. In the beginning it was often necessary to prod many students to get them to respond. By the end of the year almost all of the children were responding freely and frequently."

Finally, teacher Clauson says, the class meeting had unexpected benefits for her overall teaching: "I feel my teaching is more effective now because I am better able to teach on the child's level. . . . [The class meeting] has helped me to treat each child as an individual."[14]

SUPPORTING GOOD VALUES

The class meeting is a practical tool for setting up rules and maintaining good discipline, makes the classroom a more interesting and enjoyable place for all, and helps the teacher get to know each student, and students to know and care about each other. It also gives young people firsthand lessons in the benefits of democracy.

For many teachers, the class meeting has also been an affirmation of their faith in children's potential for goodness. One such teacher is Muriel Rossi, who works with a multiaged group of second-graders at Charlotte Kenyon Elementary School in Chenango Forks, New York. Some have special learning problems and stay with teacher Rossi for more than a year.

She tells of a class meeting she had at the beginning of one year. The topic "bad words" was raised by a child who had been in the class the year before, when they had decided not to use certain words in school. On this day, a child new to the group had used one of those words.

Soon into the meeting, one girl said, "My mother lets me say some bad words. Like I can say [here she used a particularly offensive racial slur]."

Teacher Rossi paused, then said to the children, "What are your thoughts about that?"

"I don't think that's a good idea," a boy said. "People don't like to be called that name. We're all the same even if our skin is different." Others agreed.

The teacher comments:

I find that there are always children—even in groups with a lot of problems—who will come forth with the high-level values. And the others respond. It's almost as if children *want* to have good values. But so often they're not getting support for that from their environment.

The class meeting provides that support.

CHAPTER 9

Teaching Values Through the Curriculum

S ixth-grade teacher Bill Elasky was feeling burned out at 37 and thinking of leaving the profession when he took a sabbatical. That year he studied with George Wood at Ohio University's Institute for Democracy in Education.[1]

"The fundamental reason for public schooling," Wood taught, "is democracy. Education for democratic citizenship should be active, engaging children in real tasks, often of their choosing, from which they learn a variety of skills."[2]

Elasky returned to his sixth-grade classroom in Amesville, Ohio, with a new sense of education's potential to prepare students for life in a democratic society. He started the school year with a "reading web" that dealt with nature and ecology.

Not long afterward, a local fuel oil company accidentally dumped solvent into Amesville's Federal Creek, which flowed near the school and right by several students' houses and farms. The Environmental Protection Agency came in to clean up, but, Elasky says, "we were skeptical."

Elasky's class decided to do its own investigation. Calling themselves the "Amesville Sixth-Grade Water Chemists," they made plans to test water samples from 11 different places on Federal Creek.

Students then called Ohio University, local and state EPA offices, and the State Health Department to get information on water test kits. In class meetings, Elasky and his students decided that student groups should investigate sources and effects of the pollutants they were testing for and present their findings to the class; interview people who know about water pollution and creek ecology; develop one big chart on which to tabulate test results; and launch an ad campaign to sell their testing service to individuals in the community (revenue would offset classroom expenses).

"We spend a lot of time discussing how things are going to happen," Elasky says, "but it's not dead time. It creates understanding of democratic processes and a lot of opportunity to develop critical thinking and discussion skills."[3]

During the ensuing months, students interviewed experts at Ohio University about pollutants; talked to officials at the local water and sewage plant; traced their area's history; kept journals; used computers to chart pollutants; drew maps; took and printed their own photographs; wrote to government officials; and tested wells, cisterns, and waterways in Amesville. At the end of the school year they proudly described their project at an Ohio University conference on public education in a democratic society. Here is how they spoke about their experience:

> Learning without textbooks is more fun than spending the whole day long in them. We learned to cooperate with each other. We think this kind of project is important because we are learning many things, including responsibility. It is also helping us in our science, health, English, spelling, writing, and reading.
>
> We also enjoy this because it is fun, and we feel we are mature enough to work with chemicals and be in charge. Another reason is we think it is important to know what you're drinking every day.[4]

THE CURRICULUM AS MORAL EDUCATOR

Bill Elasky and his sixth-graders are part of an emerging trend: to teach values such as concern for the environment while also teaching the academic skills and content that are the main agenda of school. There is a new awareness that the academic curriculum has been a sleeping giant in values education.

Other important methods of values education—the teacher's role as model and mentor, building a moral community, and the class meeting—make respect and responsibility living values in the classroom. But the academic curriculum is the chief business of schooling. We would be wasting a great opportunity if we failed to use that curriculum as a vehicle for developing values and ethical awareness.

State textbook policies reflect this new attention to the value dimension of the school curriculum. In states such as California, textbook guidelines now require discussion of ethical issues in science.[5] And as awareness grows that our survival in the next century will depend on our ability to live with nature, teachers are finding new ways to help students develop respect and responsibility toward the environment. In *Connect,* a newsletter for K–8 teachers, Rhode Island educator Lorraine Keeney reports: "Teachers and students are proving that environmental projects not only lead to solid scientific learning but also dispel attitudes of hopelessness and despair about the environment, develop citizenship skills, and instill self-esteem."[6]

Comments Sally Aberth, science teacher at Fieldston Lower School in Riverdale, New York: "Even young children watch the news and hear all the bad things that are happening. It's very important for kids to have some sense of control over making the planet better."[7]

Sixth-graders in Warwick, Rhode Island, were concerned about the thinning of the Earth's ozone layer and lobbied local businesses to reduce ozone-damaging practices. Says their teacher, Lois Morris:

> All the kids I've had since I've been doing ecology issues are so tuned in—they have become staunch protectors of the Earth. They don't drop wrappers on the ground; they put them in their pockets. They are going to be the generation that will take care of the Earth.
>
> This year they went down to the beach and cleaned up. They were disgusted. They said they would never think of bringing this or that to the beach and dropping it.
>
> It's had an influence on their families as well. Several helped clean up after the Newport oil spill.[8]

For examples of many kinds of environmental projects carried out by children, see the April 1990 issue of *Sojourner,* "Children and Mother Earth."

TEACHING RESPECT AND RESPONSIBILITY TOWARD ANIMALS

A natural extension of concern for the environment is concern for animals. This is a good values topic because it fits in with science; nearly all children have a natural empathy for animals; and, sadly, animal neglect and abuse are on the rise.

One seventh-grade teacher read his students news clippings describing recent cases of animal abuse in their community. The director of the local Animal Welfare League was quoted as saying, "I get 200 or more calls a week about cruelty to animals, including farm animals, not just pets." She attributed the increase in cases both to better reporting and to increased drug and alcohol abuse.

After discussing why people mistreat animals, the seventh-graders considered ways in which they might help to reduce animal abuse in their community.

Schools can also take advantage of community groups, such as the Society for the Prevention of Cruelty to Animals, that help children learn to treat animals kindly. *The New York Times* ran a feature story[9] on the SPCA's expanded education program and its popularity with New York City schools.[10] Students from second grade all the way up through high school come to the SPCA's headquarters to participate in a 90-minute class touching on animal-related careers, humane issues, and pet care and responsibility.

Teacher Joe Binenbaum brought his ninth-grade science class from the East Harlem Maritime School to the SPCA. After staffer Maureen Martin's presentation, talk turned to pets. "All of these kids have some kind of pet," teacher Binenbaum says, "and I want them to understand that they are responsible for them. When they get tired of them, they just can't dump them on the street."[11]

Back at Maritime School, Mr. Binenbaum and his students operate a "minizoo." They adopt some animals from the SPCA and some from private pet owners, whose donations have included a 16-foot python, boa constrictors, turtles, ring-necked doves, ferrets, and an iguana. The private pet owners say that if the school had not taken the pets, they would have been destroyed.

"So the kids really feel they've saved these animals," Mr. Binenbaum says. They learn to handle and care for them. They hold snack sales to pay for feed for the zoo animals, and over the holidays, when school was out, they visited the zoo every day. Students who had previously been truant have come back to school to work with the zoo.

What students have learned from the SPCA and the minizoo program, Joe Binenbaum reports, they have generalized to concern about strays in their neighborhood. They often bring the strays to the school grounds to be fed.[12]

Through this program—combining adult models who care deeply about animals, solid information, and the opportunity for students to care for animals themselves—children's capacity for kindness is being tapped and developed.

FROM ANIMAL CARE TO ANIMAL RIGHTS

Schools also must deal with controversial issues of animal rights.

When it came time to dissect animals in her tenth-grade biology class at Woodstown High School, New Jersey, Maggie McCool refused. "It goes against my ethical beliefs," she explained. "I just don't think it's right to kill animals, especially if it's not necessary."[13]

Complete the lab work or you'll fail the course, the school said. But Maggie and her parents challenged the school in court—and won. In her New Jersey school district, students with strong beliefs against dissecting and handling dead animals must now be provided with alternatives.

Students refusing to dissect animals, as *Teacher* magazine points out, is only one facet of a growing animal rights movement that is making its way into the classroom—and the values education curriculum. Teachers who are animal rights activists have been in the forefront of getting schools to look at the attitudes toward animals that they consciously or unconsciously teach.

Larry Brown, a special-education teacher in Bradford, Ohio, argues that most schools' curricula and materials are biased against animal rights. "Far from being value-free," Brown says, "schools promote, if not actively, at least in subtle ways, the following beliefs: Animals are ours to use as we see fit; their suffering is inconsequential; our benefit is the primary criterion governing their use; animals are simply a collection of muscles, bones, nerves, and tissues; and the use of animals is not an issue to be seriously discussed."[14]

Loretta Gray finds that animal rights education has a special value for the inner-city children she teaches at Washington, D.C.'s, Winston Educational Center:

> These children have been abused and neglected. We're finding that children are guiding themselves through television, learning what's on television, and incorporating that kind of life-style into their own. That frequently includes sexual promiscuity, no respect for life, and violence. They accept that as a way of life, and they bring it into the classroom with them. It has a profound effect on the learning process.[15]

Teacher Gray says that discussing animal rights with these children gets them thinking about their relationships with and responsibilities to other creatures. It can be a real breakthrough—their first step toward developing a positive value system.

SCHOOLWIDE APPROACHES TO A VALUE-CENTERED CURRICULUM

Environmental education and animal welfare issues are timely, high-interest topics that offer entry points into a value-centered curriculum. How can a school go beyond these special-focus issues to a broader use of the curriculum as a tool for teaching values?

Portland, Maine, offers one way. In the early 1980s, the Portland school district launched a values education program centered on six noncontroversial values: *respect, courage, honesty, justice, willingness to work,* and *self-discipline.* The charge to individual schools was to infuse these values in every way possible throughout the curriculum and school day.

Moreover, during each school year one of the six values would be spotlighted as the "Value of the Year." During "The Year of Self-Discipline," for example, a leadership committee provided teachers with suggestions relevant to all academic subjects:

- *Science* and *math* teachers can focus attention on the lives of prominent men and women in either field. In addition, the highly structured, disciplined methodology found in both courses of study can be stressed.

- *English* teachers can draw models of self-discipline from the study of literature. Students can also be asked to write compositions dealing with this important character trait.

- *History* teachers can direct attention to specific moments in history when great men and women exhibited self-discipline.

- *Art* and *music* instructors can examine the lives of great artists and composers as models of self-discipline.

- *Home economics* and *industrial arts* teachers can stress the role of self-discipline in designing and creating in wood, metal, clothing, and so on.

• *Physical education* and *health* teachers can show students that one must maintain a certain degree of self-control to maintain a healthy body.[16]

One classroom activity used by some teachers was "Quote of the Day." The teacher writes on the board a quotable quote that pertains to the Value of the Year. When it was self-discipline, quotes included:

• "No person has a right to do as he pleases, except when he pleases to do right."

• "Where there's a will, there's a way."

• "The hardest victory is the victory over self."

Students were asked to copy the quote for the day into their notebooks and then to respond in ways appropriate to their development level (younger students drew a picture illustrating the meaning of the quote; older students wrote an essay on its meaning and relevance to their lives).

"WHAT ARE THE ETHICAL ISSUES AND VALUES IN THE SUBJECT I TEACH?"

Mining the school curriculum for its ethical potential requires teachers to look at their grade-level curriculum and ask, "What are the ethical issues and values in the subject I teach? How can I make those issues and values more salient to my students?"

Carol Nylen taught fifth grade at Portland, Maine's, Nathan Clifford Elementary School. The school district asked her to take on a special assignment: Go through the fifth-grade American history curriculum and pinpoint opportunities to explore the district's six target values (courage, honesty, respect, justice, willingness to work, and self-discipline).

First she formulated a table with the six values listed across the top and with five time periods ("Before 1600" through "1900s") as the vertical column. The accompanying table "Ethical Values in American History," an abbreviated version of hers, lists four values and three time periods.

Then she went through the school's fifth-grade American history textbook page by page and asked this question: "For each time period,

ETHICAL VALUES IN AMERICAN HISTORY*

	Courage	Honesty
1700s	• Participants in Boston Tea Party • Soldiers in Revolutionary War (both sides) • Daniel Boone and pioneers	• Freedom of the press—1734—printing the truth • Our cotton mill was not invented here but was a result of stolen plans from England in 1789
1800s	• Lewis and Clark explorers • Harriet Tubman, workers on Underground Railroad • Slaves fighting against Confederacy • Freed blacks trying to build new life • Immigrants coming to build new life	• "Honest Abe" • Fugitive Slave Law—slave hunters could claim *any* black man as a runaway; were they always honest?
1900s	• Wilbur and Orville Wright • Women working on campaign for right to vote • Charles Lindbergh • Migrants • FDR • Soldiers, WWI, WWII • Martin Luther King, Jr., and civil rights movement	• Factory owners recruit immigrants with false promises • Muckrakers • "Separate but equal"—were Americans lying to themselves?

* Adapted from Carol Nylen, "Integrating Ethics into History," *Ethics in Education,* 3 (March, 1984), pp. 2–3.

what topics do I deal with that could be used to discuss courage, honesty, respect, justice, willingness to work, or self-discipline?"

She entered her notes on each topic in the appropriate sections of the table, and these served as her point of departure for planning specific lessons.

During the 1800s, for example, she notes that:

Respect	Justice

• Loyalists' continued respect for England
• U.S. Constitution's laws demonstrate respect for individual rights
• Farmers left land when it lost richness; does this show respect for the land?
	• Injustices:
	  · Treatment of Indians and slaves
	  · Women, slaves, and Indians not allowed vote
	  · Taxation without representation
	  · Laws passed forbidding people to teach slaves to read or write

• Blacks not considered citizens even when "free"
• Annihilation of the buffalo (respect?)
• Difference between Indians' respect for land and that of pioneers, colonists
	• Injustices:
	  · Railroads built over Indians', farmers' lands
	  · Child labor (working from sunrise to sunset)
	  · Kidnapping blacks for use as slaves, splitting up slave families
	• Justice: Emancipation Proclamation

• Babe Ruth earned respect—set records that still stand • FDR—helping the nation out of a crisis • Pollution (air, land, water); have we respected our environment as a nation? • Discrimination against non-whites—respect?	• Strikes by labor unions—just or unjust? • Muckrakers get laws passed to protect city dwellers • Farmers let food go, kill surplus livestock while others starve in 1920 • Internment camps for Japanese • Civil rights movement seeks justice

- *Courage* can be discussed with reference to: great explorers such as Lewis and Clark; Harriet Tubman and workers on the Underground Railroad; slaves fighting against the Confederacy; freed blacks trying to build a new life; and immigrants coming to build a new life.

- *Justice* can be taught through the study of various examples of injustice—railroads built over Indians' and farmers' lands; child labor;

kidnapping blacks for use as slaves and splitting up slave families—and through the positive example of justice provided by the Emancipation Proclamation.[17]

SELECTING GOOD MATERIALS

Once a teacher has identified an opening in the curriculum for exploring a moral value, the next step is to plan an effective lesson or unit around that value. That means selecting good materials.

Alan Lockwood (a specialist in moral education at the University of Wisconsin at Madison) and David Harris (a social studies teacher with the Pontiac, Michigan, schools) knew that teachers, especially at the secondary level, feel pressured to cover the curriculum. Teachers who want to engage their students in moral discussion must build it into the required curriculum.

So Lockwood and Harris took a social studies curriculum and found the most dramatic moments of moral conflict embedded in American history. Each such moral dilemma became a case study in their two-book series *Reasoning with Democratic Values: Ethical Problems in United States History*. Their "Letter to Students" explains:

> We have written true stories showing people making difficult decisions. These decisions involved such basic values as authority, equality, liberty, life, loyalty, promise-keeping, property, and truth. We invite you to follow the stories of these decisions and make judgments about them.
>
> For example, you will observe as Illinois Governor John Peter Altgeld struggles with the case of the Haymarket anarchists. . . . You will accompany Jewish refugees from Nazi Germany seeking admission into the United States. . . . You will follow Marie Ragghianti as she decides whether or not to expose government corruption in Tennessee. You will trace Jimmy Carter's long ordeal over American hostages in Iran. You will watch officials of the University of California defend their affirmative action plan for minority medical students.[18]

To give you the flavor of this material, here (in much-abbreviated form) is one of the authors' 49 ethical episodes:

The United States was moving toward involvement in the First World War. In February 1917, Germany launched unrestricted submarine warfare against all shipping. Soon a German sub sank a U.S. ship, killing Americans, and the United States declared war on Germany.

President Woodrow Wilson called on all Americans to support the war effort. He said, "No government can afford to tolerate open dissent in wartime." On June 15, 1917, Congress passed the Espionage Act, making it a crime to speak against the war. All over the country, citizens who openly opposed the war were imprisoned.

Eugene Debs, the Socialist Party's nominee for president, challenged the Espionage Act publicly: How could a country fighting a war "to make the world safe for democracy" deny the right of democratic freedom of speech to its own citizens? On June 16, 1918, Debs addressed the Ohio convention of the Socialist Party and condemned the war with these words: "The master class has always declared the wars; the subject class has always fought the battles. The master class has had all to gain and nothing to lose while the subject class has had nothing to gain and all to lose—especially their lives."

Two weeks later, Eugene Debs was arrested for violating the Espionage Act. The jury found him guilty; the judge sentenced him to 10 years in prison, a conviction upheld by the U.S. Supreme Court.

World War I ended in November 1918. Public sentiment grew for a release of those who were in prison because they opposed the war. A group appealed to President Wilson for the release of Debs, who was 64 by then and in failing health. Wilson read the appeal and replied:

> I will never consent to the pardon of this man. While the flower of American youth was pouring out its blood, this man, Debs, stood behind the lines, sniping, attacking, and denouncing them. Before the war, he had a perfect right to exercise his freedom of speech, but once the Congress of the United States declared war, silence on his part would have been the proper course. This man was a traitor to his country.[19]

How does the teacher get students to engage such material thoughtfully? Following each case study, Lockwood and Harris provide questions to help students review the facts of the case, analyze the ethical issues involved, and formulate their best moral reasoning.

For example, questions about the Debs case include:

1. Should Debs have made his Canton, Ohio, speech opposing U.S. involvement in World War I? Why or why not?

2. The First Amendment to the U.S. Constitution guarantees citizens the right to freedom of speech. Throughout the nation's history there has been debate over the limits of free speech. Do you think a citizen should have the right to:

- criticize a public official?
- make false statements that harm someone's reputation?
- make true statements that damage someone's reputation?
- falsely yell "fire" in a crowded theater?
- use obscene language?
- urge someone to act violently?
- reveal the name of an American secret agent?
- encourage someone to break a law?

3. Should President Wilson have pardoned Debs when World War I ended? Why or why not?

The Lockwood and Harris case studies are valuable for another reason: They include stories, like the one about Eugene Debs, of people who stood up for their moral convictions, often at great personal cost.

Another such source of "profiles of courage" is the book *The Courage of Their Convictions* by Peter Irons. Appropriate for students in junior high and up, *The Courage of Their Convictions* tells the stories of moral and legal conflicts that reached all the way to the U.S. Supreme Court. In the telling, the author allows the leading participants to speak for themselves. Those who read this book, writes columnist Nat Hentoff, will never again be able to see the U.S. Constitution as an abstract document.[20]

CHOOSING AN EFFECTIVE TEACHING STRATEGY

Even with good materials, a lesson can fizzle. A teacher also needs an effective teaching strategy that stimulates students to engage the material and think about it seriously.

Tom Ladenburg is a master teacher of American history at Brookline High School in Brookline, Massachusetts. His "moral dilemma units" have earned him recognition as an instructor who can motivate students to enter deeply into an ethical issue.

Here's how students learn history à la Ladenburg:

1. First they study an issue—slavery, for example—in its historical context.

2. Then they debate and resolve it—without knowing the actual outcome at that juncture of history.

3. Only after they reach their own resolutions do they look at the decisions of the historical figures involved and compare the merits of the two sets of resolutions.

For example: In the unit on the U.S. Constitution, students are given detailed historical biographies of the most influential delegates at the 1787 Constitutional Convention. Then they are asked to debate and decide on several thorny issues before the convention: states' rights, the definition of democracy, rights to be guaranteed to the people, and slavery. Ladenburg supplies excerpts from James Madison's convention notes; these provide further insight into the Founding Fathers' thinking so the students are able to frame arguments and counterarguments on the various points of contention.

After resolving each issue in this mock convention, students read the U.S. Constitution—and discover how these issues were really settled over two centuries ago. Finally, they consider what the historical resolutions reveal about the ideals and values of the framers.[21]

Originally designed for tenth-graders, Ladenburg's mock Constitutional Convention has been successfully enacted by fifth-graders as well. With a little imagination, a curriculum activity for one grade level can usually be adapted up or down.

MAKING ETHICS THE UNIFYING THEME OF THE ACADEMIC CURRICULUM

Fieldston Lower School, a private elementary school in Riverdale, New York, is one of the Ethical Culture Schools.[22] From the standpoint of values education, Fieldston is noteworthy for two reasons.

First, it has a schoolwide philosophy that integrates ethical and intellectual development and provides a unifying theme for the school's entire curriculum. That philosophy is expressed in the school's goals:

1. To help children learn about the interdependence of all living things (not just humans)

2. To help children identify with, and hence deeply value, other people and the world around them

3. To help children develop, through their learning, a sense of obligation to nurture, protect, and respect all life.

Second, Fieldston is noteworthy because of the creative and varied ways that individual teachers foster ethical growth. In their classrooms you can see the stamp of the school's general philosophy—the emphasis on interdependence, for example. But in the implementation of that unifying theme, the accent is on diversity. That includes an open and responsive teaching style that allows the curriculum to evolve continually as teachers work to wrest the moral meanings from their individual subject areas.

Let me offer some images of what these teachers do, drawing from my observations at Fieldston and from teachers' own accounts of their work in a special issue of Lisa Kuhmerker's journal (which I recommend to values educators), *Moral Education Forum*.[23]

LITERATURE AS THE STAPLE OF THE ETHICS CLASS

Should morality be taught as a separate subject or integrated throughout the curriculum?

Fieldston Lower School does both. Besides a curriculumwide emphasis on values, the school offers a 45-minute, three-times-a-week ethics class taught by Elizabeth Saenger. Children in grades 2 through 6 go to her special ethics class the same way that kids in most schools leave their regular classroom to go to music, art, and gym. In teaching her ethics class, Elizabeth Saenger says she relies upon children's literature as her principal tool.

At all educational levels, literature is gaining renewed attention for its power as a moral teacher. At the college and advanced high school levels, Susan Resneck Parr's fine book *The Moral of the Story* shows teachers how to sensitize students to the ethical questions and concerns raised by particular novels.[24] In their article "Moral Development and Literature," Andrew Garrod and Guy Bramble illustrate how the novels *Huckleberry Finn* and *A Separate Peace* can be used with high school students to promote critical thinking and moral reasoning.[25] California's Child Development Project (see Chapter 2) identifies outstanding value-laden children's books and develops, for each book, a teacher's guide that includes discussion questions, classroom activities, and related questions for parents and children to talk about at home.[26]

Elizabeth Saenger explains why literature is her most valuable resource in her ethics classes for children:

> I've found that children this age need the sustained narrative of a story in order to have it resonate with their own lives and ethical problems. By

comparison, the characters in a hypothetical moral dilemma—"Should Heinz steal the drug to save his dying wife?"—are removed from any experiential context. In a book, the characters come alive. Children get emotionally involved with them. Of all the things I've tried, children's literature works the best.

Elizabeth Saenger says she reads over 50 children's books for every one she finds that she thinks will work well at a particular grade level. Through that sifting and winnowing she has produced an excellent bibliography of children's literature (available on request[27]) organized by grades (2 through 6) and including her own analysis of each book and suggested questions for classroom discussion.

A typical ethics class revolves around Saenger's reading aloud a children's book or story. She reads until she hits a passage that raises a moral issue. She stops there and poses a question for discussion. After discussing the moral issue—usually for no more than 5 or 10 minutes (the children usually let her know when they want to move on)—she resumes reading.

On the day that I observed, teacher Saenger read to a group of twelve third-graders from the book *Ramona the Pest* by Beverly Cleary.[28] Ramona and her classmate Sandra have a running feud. Ms. Saenger stopped reading at the point where Sandra once again insults Ramona by calling her "Ramona the pest." Previously, Ramona has responded to this taunting by pulling Sandra's long curls. Teacher Saenger asks, "What do you think Ramona should do when Sandra insults her?" Opinion is divided:

HEATHER: She should say, "Call me this, call me that, call yourself a dirty rat."

MARCIA: She *shouldn't* say, "Please stop . . ." [this in a mocking, sing-song voice]. She's *mad*!

DEBBY: But talking is better. If you *fight* back, you get hurt. If you talk back, you don't.

MARCIA: It depends on who's tougher.

PHILIP: I think Ramona and Sandra have irreconcilable differences. [This display of vocabulary power draws looks from all and produces an outburst of everyone talking at the same time.]

TEACHER: One at a time, please!

MARCIA: I have a friend I like to make mad. She annoys me sometimes. It's hard to control yourself when someone annoys
you! So I make her angry and then pretend I didn't do
anything. But she annoys me so much that I *have* to annoy
her!

TEACHER: Do you think it's ever *really* true that you can't control
yourself?

MARCIA: Yes!

AARON: I think Ramona has just as much right to pull Sandra's
hair as Sandra does to call Ramona a pest.

TOM: But that'll just start it all over!

DEBBY: Ramona doesn't have a *right* to be mean to Sandra, and
Sandra doesn't have a *right* to be mean to Ramona.

AARON: Yeah, but if Sandra *is* mean, then Ramona has a right to
get back at her.

SEVERAL: Could we read now?

Teacher Saenger resumes reading. As the story continues, Ramona,
true to form, retaliates by pulling Sandra's curls. Miss Binny, the teacher,
confronts Ramona and tells her she'll have to leave the class if she can't
control her hair-pulling. Ramona says she just can't stop herself. "Very
well, Ramona," Miss Binny says, "you will have to go home until you
can make up your mind not to pull Sandra's hair." Teacher Saenger
stops reading and asks, "Do you think Miss Binny did the right thing?,"
and another discussion is off and running.

Self-control in the face of provocation—the moral problem raised by
this part of the novel—is also an issue for adults. Teacher Saenger
brought that out before reading *Ramona* by calling attention to a photograph from a magazine commemorating Martin Luther King, Jr.'s,
birthday. It showed civil rights protesters sitting at the lunch counter
of a segregated restaurant, silently enduring the indignity of whites
standing behind them pouring beer on their heads. This gave rise to
the following exchange in the class:

AMY: Why don't they *do* something?

MARK: If they fight back, they're not fighting for their *rights;* they're
just fighting. The only real way to fight for your rights is to
be nonviolent.

Mark's insight, remarkable for an 8 1/2-year-old, is the sort of statement that allows the teacher to try to get other children to respond to

high-level moral reasoning expressed by a peer. It also allows the teacher to make an explicit connection between the issue of self-control as it arises in *Ramona the Pest* and the importance of self-control in response to provocation in the nonviolent civil rights movement. Whenever possible, good teachers make these connections between school and society, learning and life.

THE MIDDLE AGES AS MORAL CURRICULUM

Gloria Frey, a fifth-grade social studies teacher at Fieldston Lower School, takes the Middle Ages as the core of her value-centered curriculum.

When I entered her classroom, children were making elaborate, medieval-style banners depicting their family names as the teacher read to them from a novel set in the Middle Ages. On the walls were posters, drawings, and photos of castles and cathedrals from around the world. On the windows was stained-glass art done by children. On the back tables were books such as *Legends of the Saints*.[29]

Teacher Frey explains why this historical period is an ideal developmental match for children aged 10 to 11. Their day-to-day concerns, she says, parallel medieval themes: (1) the struggle for power, yet the need for protection (corresponding to the social system of feudalism); (2) the guidelines for permissible aggression (the rules of chivalry); (3) the need for standards of good and evil (the rules of the Church); and (4) the issue of fairness, whether individual or social.[30]

To help children understand that justice is seldom a simple matter, they study historical events from divergent viewpoints. In their unit on the Norman Conquest, for example, the class hears different accounts, one written by Normans, another by Saxons.

To help children enter into the life and work of a monk, the classroom becomes a scriptorium. Students look up examples of initial letters, Gothic alphabets, and marginal decorations. They learn calligraphy and the use of gold leaf. The manuscripts they painstakingly produce give them "a great sense of achievement and appreciation of the artist-monk."[31]

The history of the period is also personalized by reading aloud fine historical fiction. The book that makes the deepest impact on her fifth-graders, teacher Frey says, is Barbara Leonie Picard's *One Is One*.[32] The protagonist, a boy reared to regard knighthood as the only admirable life for a man, finds himself drawn instead to the peace of the monastery and the beauty of art. Mocked by his brothers, however, he reluctantly becomes a knight. He becomes accomplished at the skills of combat through the training of a good and valiant mentor, who urges him to be true to himself:

> Listen to me, Stephen, this is important. . . . Be yourself; and whatever you want to do, do it with all your heart and soul. . . . We are each of us as God made us; and if God has seen fit to make you in an uncommon mold, be brave enough to be different.[33]

By the end of the story, Stephen, who has been drawn into the bloody conflicts that rage across England, is appalled by the brutality of battle and the horrible aftermath of war. He rejects the life of a knight and returns to the monastery to become a creative artist. *One Is One,* says the teacher, stimulates much discussion of moral choices—and the difference between physical and moral courage.

CHILDREN AS ORAL HISTORIANS

The experience of immigrants in the United States is a major theme of sixth grade at Fieldston. One year sixth-grade teacher Peter Sommer trained his students to function as oral historians. Together he and the class developed a total of 60 questions covering three categories—"Life in the Old Country," "The Journey Over," and "Life in the United States"—and went to the nearby Hebrew Home for the Aged to interview its residents.

To break the ice, the residents and the children sat together in a large circle, with the residents asking the children questions about their school activities and interests. After they were comfortable with each other, students and residents were paired up for the interviews.

Back in the classroom, children compared their preconceptions of the elderly with their newfound knowledge. Much of what they had learned was not in their textbooks.

Through the children's interviews, Sommer says, they encountered flesh-and-blood persons who were different from the conventional stereotypes of the immigrant elderly: "The residents were not ignorant—they all knew several languages and were well-read, besides having learned well from experience. They were not weak—they had lived through and triumphed over the traumas of immigration, culture shock, the Depression, the deaths (sometimes murders) of their families, poverty, anti-Semitism, and more."[34]

The isolation of the young from other generations is an oft-noted deficiency of modern society. Sommer's project brings young and old together in a way that enhances children's understanding of history and their respect for the elderly as individuals who helped to make that history.

The varied efforts of Fieldston teachers show that in designing value-centered curricula it's desirable to let a hundred flowers bloom. It's also important to validate these individual teacher efforts with a school philosophy, like Fieldston's, that elevates the importance of ethics throughout a child's schooling.

GUEST SPEAKERS

A teacher can highlight a particular value by bringing in a guest speaker. This strategy can be especially effective at the secondary level, where teachers often ask, "How do you discuss values with kids who have become cynical about everything?"

For example: Ron Schuck, a junior high school science teacher in King Ferry, New York, had been frustrated by his inability to get students to take seriously ecological disasters such as the destruction of the tropical rain forests (disappearing, according to a 1990 World Resources Institute report, at the rate of an acre and a half a second[35]). Then, as part of the unit on respect for plants, he decided to invite a guest speaker. Katsi Cook-Barriero, a Mohawk, talked to the class about nature from the perspective of her people.

She spoke of the deep reverence all Native American tribes have for nature. She said that in the Mohawk tradition virtually every plant has a use and all plants are considered sacred. She demonstrated a prayer of thanks that all Mohawks say each time they take a plant from the Earth. She discussed the importance of not just taking plants, but always being sure that one gives back to the Earth so plants can continue to grow. Finally, drawing on her knowledge as a registered nurse, she explained that plants are still the source of many modern medicines.

Students were completely attentive during Katsi Cook-Barriero's presentation and had many questions when she finished. The next day, teacher Schuck began a discussion of the worldwide destruction of the rain forests and the threat of extinction to rare species of plants within them. He put students in groups of four and asked them to generate reasons why they thought it was important to respect and take care of plants.

"This group of students was much more receptive to this task than students have been in previous years," teacher Schuck comments. "I

STRATEGIES FOR TEACHING VALUES THROUGH THE CURRICULUM

1. Engage students in projects which foster an active concern for the protection of the natural environment.

2. Teach children respect and responsibility toward animals.

3. Analyze each subject (e.g., social studies, science, literature) asking the question, "What are the values and ethical issues in the material I teach?"

4. Identify schoolwide target values; take one at a time and make it the "Value of the Year."

5. Find or develop good teaching materials.

6. Design an effective teaching methodology.

7. Develop an ethical theme (e.g., the interdependence of all living things) that unifies the school's curriculum; encourage teachers to pursue that theme in diverse ways.

8. Bring in a guest speaker to highlight a particular value.

9. Do multicultural education to develop children's understanding of and respect for people of different cultures.

10. Take advantage of published value-centered curricula.

---

attribute that difference in attitude directly to the impact of our guest speaker."

MULTICULTURAL EDUCATION

Teacher Schuck's use of a Native American guest speaker illustrates another use of the values curriculum: helping students develop knowledge of and respect for diverse cultural heritages.

In our increasingly diverse society, multicultural education is more important than ever. One American in four already defines himself or herself as Hispanic or nonwhite. By the year 2000, that figure will be one in three. By the year 2056, because of projected higher nonwhite birth rates and immigration, whites may very well be a minority group.[36] The development of a positive appreciation of cultural differences is all the more urgent in view of the recent national upsurge in racial and ethnic bigotry and violence.

Some schools do multicultural education through special schoolwide events. At the elementary level some have done a "We Are the World" assembly in which students sing and dance in costumes of their countries of origin. Others have sponsored a "culture night" in which students and their families participate in celebrating the variety of ethnic backgrounds within the school.

In the hands of a sensitive teacher, multicultural learning can be used in the individual classroom to develop a community that includes genuine cross-cultural integration among students.

During a year when she taught fourth grade, Sister Paul Barno—a Catholic nun who has taught in parochial schools in upstate New York— had a boy, Eddie, of Mexican descent who was not well accepted by the other children. That fall, every classroom was invited to contribute to the school's multicultural project, "Festival of Many Lands." Sister Paul chose Mexico as their class's contribution. She explains:

> To increase chances that Eddie would participate actively, I used a cooperative learning approach. He became a member of one of several small groups which worked on maps, charts, and displays of people, places, and things in Mexico. I chose Mexico as our topic because Eddie's mother is a Mexican. With encouragement, Eddie was able to instruct the whole class on life in Mexico, since he had visited there. His class participation and interaction with other students continued to grow.
>
> On the final day of the project, many parents joined us as we discussed our learnings, danced, ate tacos, and broke *piñatas*. Eddie's family came in with Mexican gems and silver, and Eddie proudly wore a toreador's costume made by his mother's hand.

PUBLISHED PROGRAMS

Schools can also profit from assorted published curricula, many of which are well designed and available at a modest cost.

In the field of multicultural education, for example, there is a promising new elementary-level curriculum known as Heartwood. Developed by Patricia Flach, a former elementary school teacher, and three other practitioners, Heartwood aims to "help students develop ethical standards based on multicultural understandings of the human condition and those values which nurture the growth of human beings and cultures."[37] Heartwood fosters seven values it views as universal: hope, loyalty, justice, courage, respect, honesty, and love. It does so through interdisciplinary activities based on folk tales, biographies, hero stories, legends, and contemporary tales drawn from Greece, India, China, Zimbabwe, and the United States. Heartwood has been field-tested in a number of schools, including the Pittsburgh system, and has met with enthusiastic teacher response.

There are also good published programs whose purpose is to help students understand, respect, and feel comfortable with persons who are handicapped or "physically challenged." This objective has gained new importance since mainstreaming brought physically challenged youngsters into the regular classroom.

A first-rate resource in this area is a curriculum called Understanding Handicaps.[38] It sensitizes children to particular disabilities: blindness, hearing impairments, physical disabilities, mental retardation, and special medical problems. First implemented in the Newton, Massachusetts, school system and now used in more than two dozen schools, the program takes 20 hours to teach (two hours every other week for each of five units).

What's unique about Understanding Handicaps is that it's designed and taught entirely by parent volunteers—and was started by five parents of handicapped children. Trina Schickel, now of Dryden, New York, was one of the five founding parents. She explains: "As it happened, all five of us had retarded kids. We could remember how retarded kids were treated in school when we were children, and we didn't want that for our children."

The process these enterprising parents devised for teaching each unit combines clear information about the handicap in question; simulations that give the children some idea of what it's like to have the disability; and, last, a guest speaker who actually has the handicap.

The parent instructor leaves books in the classroom about handicapped people, and many children take them home. Students exposed to Understanding Handicaps have volunteered to work with the physically challenged children in their school. Schools implementing the program report a generalized spin-off effect: Kids are nicer to all their peers.

There are lots of other special-focus values curricula. In Chapter 2, for example, I called attention to California's Law in a Free Society project, to the Holocaust curriculum Facing History and Ourselves, and to the Ontario program PREPARE. In Alberta, Canada, the Ministry of Education has produced and field-tested its Grade 8 Ethics Course, a curriculum aimed at helping young adolescents reflect and act on nine ethical values (respect, responsibility, fairness, tolerance, honesty, kindness, forgiveness, commitment to democratic ideals, and loyalty).[39] In the area of responsible citizenship, the Thomas Jefferson Research Center disseminates a variety of materials, used nationwide by hundreds of schools, including a new high school social studies unit titled Living the Constitution.[40] Educators for Social Responsibility, based in Cambridge, Massachusetts, publishes thoughtful materials such as *Taking Part,* an elementary-level sourcebook in its *Participation Series.*[41]

Philosophy for Children, a program of the Institute for the Advancement of Philosophy for Children, is unique in that it promotes ethical thinking as part of a broader effort to develop philosophical reasoning. Its materials, spanning early childhood through high school, take the form of children's novels in which children grapple with challenging ethical issues. For example, in *Lisa* (grades 7 to 8), children puzzle over questions such as: Can we both love animals and eat them? In judging lying and stealing, is it appropriate to take circumstances into account?

Philosophy for Children aims "not to indoctrinate children with a specific set of moral values but to provide children with the tools of inquiry so that they can become, on their own, more thoughtful, considerate, and reasonable human beings." The Educational Testing Service, in its evaluation of Philosophy for Children, has found significant gains in reasoning ability and in reading and mathematics skills, favoring students who get the program.[42] Philosophy for Children also publishes its own magazine, *Thinking,* and offers a variety of staff development workshops.[43]

Teachers are often discouraged by the spontaneous moral discussions they have with students. A tenth-grade biology teacher told of a student who brought in a bag of 30 pencils because the class was short of pencils and cheerfully announced he had shoplifted them from the K-Mart where he worked. His classmates who spoke up thought this was perfectly okay, especially since the student said his boss "was a jerk" who wouldn't give him a raise he had asked for. In situations like this, teachers often find themselves a lonely ethical voice, arguing with little apparent effect against a low-level peer-group culture.

Moral discussions anchored in the academic curriculum are one answer to this problem. The curriculum creates a planned context for moral discussion, requiring students to gather and absorb information about a value issue. It poses the moral questions students should consider, and it structures their learning to bring out the desirability of the moral value (honesty, kindness, respect for the environment) under consideration. It uses different realms of knowledge and experience to show the recurring validity of a moral truth or theme, such as the interrelatedness of all life. In all these ways it stacks the deck in favor of a thoughtful and mature student response.

A value-centered curriculum mainstreams moral education, moving it to the very center of teaching and learning. In so doing, it gives ethical concerns the status they deserve in the scheme of schooling and, one hopes, in the minds of teachers and students.

A new and outstanding curriculum resource for teaching the value of tolerance is the magazine Teaching Tolerance. *It and a civil rights teaching kit are available free to schools by writing Sara Bullard, Editor,* Teaching Tolerance, *400 Washington Avenue, Montgomery, AL 36104.*

A new curriculum for teaching kindness, compassion, and respect is Kindness is Contagious . . . Catch It! *For information, write: STOP Violence Coalition, 8340 Mission Road, Suite 207, Shawnee Mission, KS 66207.*

CHAPTER 10

Cooperative Learning

Cooperation, not conflict, has been the most valuable form of behavior for humans taken at any stage of their evolutionary history.

—ASHLEY MONTAGU

If there's a single bet we've missed over the years, it's making kids sit quietly at their desks instead of letting them work with each other.

—JOEL THORNLEY, Superintendent,
Hayward Schools, California

In a sixth-grade classroom in Montreal, Quebec, a teacher faced the most divisive group she had ever taught. The class was torn apart by racial conflict; blacks and whites exchanged insults and physically assaulted each other during recess and after school. The school psychologist observed the class and recommended that the teacher set up cooperative learning groups. Put together children who have trouble getting along, he said. Give them joint assignments and projects. Monitor them closely. Most important, *stick with the groups* even if they don't seem to be working in the beginning.

The teacher started having students work together—usually in threes or fours—in all subjects for part of every day. They worked on math problems in groups, researched social studies questions in groups, practiced reading to each other in groups, and so on.

"It took them two months to make this really work," the teacher says, "but they finally got it together. What's more, their test scores went up." Another teacher, who had seen them in September when they were at each other's throats, said she couldn't believe it was the same class.

At Emily Carr School in Scarborough, Ontario, second-grade teacher Karen Smith does reading partners at the start of every day. The night before, each child gets a book ready that he or she would like to read to a classmate. In the morning at circle time, the children choose partners based on the books they are interested in hearing, go off in pairs, and read aloud to each other.

The teacher comments: "I started this because I know that children learn to read by reading, and I can't listen to 27 kids read at once. They love to read to each other, and they are more confident reading with expression to one person than they are in front of the class."

In Greenwich, Connecticut, a high school English teacher says: "Cooperative learning helped the greasers, preppies, freaks, and jocks—who all sat in different corners on the first day of class—come to be on close speaking terms by the end of the year."[1] Lazett Gyant, a recent graduate of Mount Hebron High School in Ellicott City, Maryland, comments about her cooperative learning course: "I loved that class. The students would help each other, and you didn't have to be ashamed to ask. We were like a team."[2]

THE BENEFITS OF COOPERATIVE LEARNING

Cooperative learning is one of the fastest growing movements in education today. It has its own society, The International Association for the Study of Cooperation in Education. It has its own, practitioner-oriented magazine, *Cooperative Learning,* an excellent resource featuring accounts of classroom applications as well as the latest research.[3] Dozens of how-to books on cooperative learning are now available, as well as an array of videos on implementing cooperative learning in the classroom (for the most comprehensive annotated bibliography, see the September 1990 resource guide issue of *Cooperative Learning*). Cooperative learning has hundreds of studies demonstrating its effectiveness and applicability at all levels.[4]

Like curriculum-based values education, cooperative learning teaches values and academics in a single stroke. Whereas curriculum-based values education does that through the subject matter content, cooperative learning does it through the *instructional process.* It says to the teacher: "Take what you would normally teach, teach it through cooperative learning for at least part of the day or period, and you'll be teaching values and academics at the same time."

The specific benefits are these:

1. **Cooperative learning teaches the value of cooperation.** It teaches students that it's a good thing to help each other. In a review of research, psychologist Marilyn Watson finds that "the opportunity to be a contributing member of a just and benevolent peer group is conducive to caring about fellow group members, to developing more altruistic attitudes, and to a greater tendency to engage in spontaneous prosocial behaviors."[5]

2. **Cooperative learning builds community in the classroom.** It helps students get to know and care about each other and feel membership in small social units as well as in the whole group. It reduces interpersonal conflicts.

   In other studies, cooperative learning has been found to foster greater acceptance of classmates who are handicapped or from different ethnic or racial backgrounds.[6] Whereas multiethnic texts, minority history, and classroom discussion of race relations have been found to have little effect on students' racial attitudes and behavior, cooperative interracial groups have succeeded in improving race relations—often fostering crossracial friendships—to a significant degree.[7]

3. **Cooperative learning teaches basic life skills.** The skills developed by cooperative learning—among the most important in life—include listening, taking the viewpoint of others, communicating effectively, solving conflicts, and working together to achieve a common goal. Studies show that students given regular practice in cooperative learning do indeed get better at these interpersonal moral skills.[8]

4. **Cooperative learning improves academic achievement, self-esteem, and attitude toward school.** Both high- and low-ability students benefit from cooperative learning groups;[9] several studies indicate especially large gains for low-ability students.[10] Positive results have been found for all subjects and at all grade levels.

   Cooperative learning improves students' self-esteem and attitude toward school.[11] In a review of 15 classroom-based experiments, cooperative learning was found to have positive effects on self-esteem in nearly three-quarters of the studies.[12]

5. **Cooperative learning offers an alternative to tracking.** In 1985 educational researcher Jeanie Oakes published *Keeping Track: How Schools Structure Inequality;* she drew on extensive observational data from 25 junior and senior high schools to show how tracking by ability deprives many students, especially those of low socioeconomic status or minority background, of an equal education.[13] Tracking, the research consistently shows, decreases the achievement of students in the lower tracks rather than helping them achieve their full potential.

Moreover, the academic caste system that tracking creates can have corrosive moral effects on the higher-tracked students. Says a central New York high school teacher: "This fall I heard a bright freshman boy [tracking began that year for him] comment to his friends, 'Now we don't have to deal with the scum anymore.'"

Cooperative learning, Oakes argues, offers one of the best ways to avoid the negative effects of tracking and achieve educational equity. Everyone benefits from working together in mixed-ability groups, including the academically more able students. They learn to work with and care about people different from themselves, and they master the subject matter at a deeper level because they are helping to teach it to someone else.

6. **Cooperative learning has the potential to temper the negative aspects of competition.** Currently it's competition, not cooperation, that dominates our national character. We know all too well the destructive effects of unrestrained competition: In the economic arena, the dog-eat-dog pursuit of success leads businesses to do anything—never mind the effects on people—to maximize profits. In the personal realm, many people have sacrificed their marriages, family life, and ultimately their own happiness in the all-consuming competitive drive for individual success.

Competition in America has deep cultural roots. But cooperative interaction, experienced regularly in some form over the full course of children's schooling, at least holds out the hope of tempering the worst aspects of the competitive ethic that now bedevils our culture.[14]

Japan presents an interesting study in contrast. There is, on the one hand, intense competition: Japanese children take tests to compete for entrance into the best junior high schools; later they take more competitive tests to get into the best high schools; then they compete again for the relatively few spots in the most prestigious colleges and universities. One negative effect of all this competitive pressure has been a high youth suicide rate (now declining as it becomes more socially acceptable to go to trade schools instead of universities). But the intense competition never turns into the step-on-the-other-guy individualism we see in our own society, where, for example, medical students will sabotage each other's lab work in the drive for top grades. A cooperative spirit is what is most salient about Japanese people.

I asked two Japanese graduate students about this seeming cultural contradiction.

"We don't like to hurt people," one explained. The other elaborated: "If we try hard to get into the best university, that's a personal thing. We don't really see ourselves as competing with each other. We are just trying to do our best." And, they pointed out, cooperative group work is very common in both elementary and junior high schools. In junior high, for example, students are in groups of five to six; they study all their subjects in groups.

Individualistic learning (where students work independently, one person's success having no effect on another's) and competitive learning (where students compete for highest honors) each have their own value in developing a student's individual potential and pursuit of excellence. But cooperative learning should get at least equal time. Most important, an overall spirit of cooperation and sense of classroom community should pervade the moral atmosphere in which all forms of learning occur.

EIGHT KINDS OF COOPERATIVE LEARNING

Mention cooperative learning and many people conjure up an image of three or four kids working together on some kind of project for which they'll get a group grade. But many teachers avoid group grading of projects because of the fairness issue: Why should the grade of a student who has worked hard be pulled down because one or more group members did less than their best? Students doing group projects can get other kinds of evaluative feedback from the teacher, their group members, and the rest of the class.

To maximize the impact of cooperative learning on both character development and academic achievement, a teacher should make use of varied cooperative formats. Let's look at eight.

1. **Learning partners.** Paired learning, for both teachers and students, is the simplest and least threatening way to begin cooperative learning. It's a building block for other, more complex forms of cooperation.

One elementary school teacher assigns every student a learning partner (third-grade teacher Cathy Mercovitch of Spencer, New York, calls them "knee-to-knee partners"). Partners sit across from each other in traditional rows and move their desks together once or twice a day to work jointly on a task. The task might be to do a work sheet of math problems—first individually, then comparing answers and talking out those on which they disagree ("Here's how I got 42"). Or if the work involves memory practice such as learning vocabulary or times tables, partners drill each other with flash cards.

Every two to three weeks, students' names go in a jar and everybody draws a new learning partner. Over the course of the school year children get to be learning partners with more than half their classmates.

Frank Lyman of the Southern Teacher Education Center in Columbia, Maryland, recommends a cooperative discussion cycle called "think-pair-share." Students listen as the teacher poses a question, then pair briefly with a partner to discuss their responses, then share their responses with the whole group.

Partner activities like these are straightforward ways to encourage positive student interactions, enable students to help each other learn, and increase student attention span.

2. **Cluster group seating.** Central New York teacher Elaine Huebner has her second-graders sit and work in groups of three. They check each other's work before turning it in; each assignment must be initialed by two seatmates to show that they've checked it. She comments: "I find that there's more accountability with threes than with twos. When I had them working in pairs, one would sometimes say to the other, 'Don't tell her I didn't do it, okay?'"

Former classroom teacher Marilyn Burns, author of *The I Hate Mathematics! Book*, recommends a form of grouping that maximizes peer helpfulness. On day one, she would randomly assign students to groups of four and teach them three rules:

- You have final responsibility for your own work and behavior.

- You must be willing to help anyone in your group who asks.

- You may not ask the teacher for help *unless all four of you have the same question.*

This last rule, Burns says, "is pure gold." At first students need frequent reminders to follow it. But soon they learn to seek help from groupmates first, and realize that the teacher will answer a question *only* when all four members of a group have their hands raised.[15]

3. **Student team learning.** This approach, one of the most extensively researched, was developed by Dr. Robert Slavin, Director of the Center for Research on Elementary and Middle Schools at The Johns Hopkins University. Team learning can be readily used at any grade level from two to twelve and in any subject area in which there are single right answers. There are six steps: [16]

- The teacher assigns students to four-member teams mixed in ability, sex, and ethnic background. (Every five to six weeks, teams are changed.)

- The teacher presents a lesson to the whole class.

- In their teams, students work in pairs on teacher-prepared work sheets; they question each other, check responses against an answer sheet, and explain missed questions to each other. Their assigned goal: "to help all your teammates get 100 percent on the quiz."

- Moving desks apart, students take the quiz *individually*.

- Team scores are computed by adding up the improvement points earned by each team member; that total is divided by the number of team members who took the quiz.

  Students earn improvement points based on how their individual quiz scores compare to their own previous average in the subject. The more they exceed their past average, the more improvement points they get. For example:

Student's Quiz Score	Improvement Points Earned
1–10 points below own average	10
Average score to 10 points above own average	20
More than 10 points above average	30
Perfect score (regardless of one's average)	30

- Team awards are given to *all* teams that get a certain average improvement score or above. To add interest, a teacher can have two levels of awards. For example:

Criterion (Average Team Score)	Award
18–22 improvement points	Great Team certificate
23 or more improvement points	Super Team certificate

Teams winning one or another of these certificates may be rewarded in other ways as well: bonus points added to every team member's quiz score, extra recess time, or recognition in a class or school newsletter.

Why has student team learning produced such large and consistent student achievement gains as shown in cooperative-learning research? Because of several built-in motivational features:

• Every team can win by earning enough improvement points.

• Students are concerned about the learning of *every* member of the group, since group success depends on total group points.

• No group member gets a free ride, since quizzes must be taken individually.

• The normally low-achieving student is not a handicap to the group because group scores are based on improvement; if a low-average student comes through with a big improvement on a given quiz, he or she can actually be the star of the team.

Student team learning develops both group responsibility for the individual and individual responsibility to the group.

4. **Jigsaw learning.** Jigsaw learning was first developed by psychologist Elliott Aronson to help Austin, Texas, school officials deal with problems caused by school desegregation.[17] Minority students there, as in many communities moving toward integration, found themselves in tension-filled classrooms. Aronson proposed the following "jigsawing" of study materials on particular topics so that white, black, and Chicano children would be obliged to study interdependently:

• A given lesson is divided into subtopics. For example, a social studies lesson about Brazil might be divided into five parts concerning that country's form of government, topography and climate, history, industry, and agriculture.

• The class is divided into home teams of five students mixed in ability and ethnic and racial background. Within home groups *each* student is assigned the job of becoming an "expert" on *one* subtopic.

- The "experts" read and study material on their respective subtopics. Then all the experts from the different teams come together in expert groups to pool their knowledge. (All the experts on Brazil's government meet, all the experts on Brazil's history, and so on.)

- Experts then return to their home teams and take turns teaching their group members what they have learned about their subtopics.

- Finally, home team members are quizzed individually *on all of the subtopics* to determine a personal grade. If the teacher wishes, team scores can also be computed and team recognition given.

Jigsaw learning equalizes participation and builds in interdependence *by giving every student an active, essential role in two groups:* the home team and the expert group. Experts are motivated to learn their subtopic well because they're responsible for teaching it to their fellow home team members; nobody else can do that. Home team members are motivated to listen well to the experts' reports, because they know that the upcoming test will cover all of the subtopics.

The results of Aronson's project for the Austin schools were impressive: Jigsaw groups, compared with control groups, demonstrated greatly improved working relationships and friendships that crossed racial and ethnic lines. Moreover, minority students demonstrated marked gains in achievement and self-esteem.[18] Aronson's book *The Jigsaw Classroom* shows how any teacher can use this strategy to promote student learning and cooperation.[19]

5. **Team testing.** In student team learning and jigsaw learning, students take quizzes individually after their group work. By contrast, team testing has students study for a test together and take it together.

Cathy Wilson teaches third grade at the Ina E. Driscoll School in Wilton, Connecticut. When she gives a spelling test, she has the children sit facing each other in groups of three. Each group has a large sheet of paper. As the teacher reads the spelling list, group members write their answers on the sheet and discuss them. When they reach unanimous agreement on how all the words should be spelled, they submit their list for grading.[20]

Ed Carlone, who teaches eighth- and ninth-grade science at Cortland Junior-Senior High School in Cortland, New York, says that about once every three weeks or so he gives his students a partner quiz. These are his rules:

- You can work with any person you want.

- Do all the questions on your own first. [Students each have their own test paper; this allows the teacher to see how each student did *before* they worked together.]

- Compare answers, decide on the right answer together, and enter that answer on a third test sheet. Put both of your names on *this* copy; it will count as the grade for both of you.

- You may talk as much as you like about the answers but in nothing louder than a whisper.

Says teacher Carlone: "Kids say they love taking a test this way. It's a great stress-reducer. I like to walk around and listen to the discussions about which answer is right. It lets me hear how they're thinking—what they understand and what they don't."

6. **Small-group projects.** An important form of cooperative learning is one that has students work together to produce a single product. Here the emphasis is on cooperative processes such as group problem-solving, creativity, and team research rather than on learning material for a test. Some examples of small-group work:

Working in fours, students in a fourth-grade class were assigned to invent and construct a game, then teach the whole class how to play it.

In a fifth-grade class, groups of three were given a map outline of the world with nothing on it. Their geographic challenge was to label oceans and continents, put in major rivers, draw the equator, and so on.

Sixth-graders working in teams of four did research on and made models of ancient cities such as Athens and Sparta. Each group presented its project to the whole class.

In a seventh-grade English class, groups of students wrote and performed skits depicting an event in a famous person's life. The teacher videotaped their performances. Says Bill Lee, the originator of this project and a teacher at Cortland Junior-Senior High School: "This activity is a real self-esteem-builder."

Giving groups time to develop. During one school year central New York kindergarten teacher Judith Kur was struggling with the problem of four impulsive and aggressive children who had not responded to normal disciplinary efforts. She was about to try individual behavior modification contracts with each of them when she took a course that included cooperative learning. Although she had often permitted children to work together if they so chose, she realized that she had seldom structured a situation where they *had* to work together to produce one thing.

Teacher Kur began by putting the students in groups of four. She gave them craft sticks, glue, and cardboard, and instructed them to build a structure—*one* structure—of their choice. To her surprise, she found that although some groups floundered for a while, children had fewer arguments working together on this single task than they typically had when they worked side by side on individual activities.

Over the next few weeks, as the groups undertook different projects, teacher Kur observed a progression in their ability to work together in an egalitarian way. In the beginning, dominant children tended to boss others, while less confident children hung back. Gradually, however, the teacher says, "leaders became less important, shy children began to contribute more, and decision-making became a shared responsibility.

"My children are kinder people now," teacher Kur says, "more attentive to each other's needs." A little girl who had been one of the four recalcitrant behavior problems before the cooperative projects took the lead in befriending a newcomer to the class. "And cleanup time," the teacher reports, "has been cut in half since the projects began."

From her experience, teacher Kur learned a lesson of general importance: Groups, like individuals, take time to develop. With cooperative groups, as with class meetings and other moral education strategies, teachers must respect the gradual growth of children—and give them the time and practice they need to master the requisite participation skills.

Group appreciation. Many teachers who do small-group cooperative projects conclude by having each group present the product of its labors to the entire class. Prior to the presentations, I think it's helpful to give students in the class a sheet with questions such as:

- "What is something valuable that you learned from this presentation?" (Students should be given examples that help them pick out important learnings rather than minor details.)

- "What did this group do a good job on?"

Following the presentation, the teacher can ask all students to write responses to the work sheet questions or, if they're too young to write, to come up with answers in their heads. Time for reflecting will increase the quality of students' comments. Then several students can be invited to share their comments. Finally, the presenting group should get a round of applause as they return to their seats.

I've seen classrooms where the presenting children got only perfunctory feedback from the teacher and none at all from their classmates. They shuffled back to their desks, eyes down. That hardly builds self-esteem or a sense of community.

7. **Team competition.** Competition by itself can create hostility among groups. But if it takes place in a classroom with a strong sense of community governed by an overall ethic of cooperation, competition among groups can be both motivating and fun.

At the teacher's discretion, intergroup competition can be added to several of the cooperative strategies described above. For example, with student team learning, in addition to recognizing all teams that reach a certain improvement score, some special recognition or award may be given to the team with the highest score. Similarly, with jigsaw learning, bonus test points can be awarded to members of the team with the highest average test score.

In a fifth-grade class I observed at Country Club Elementary School in San Ramon, California, teacher Lincoln Olbrycht has his five-person cooperative groups take turns playing volleyball against each other during recess. The groups (which change every three to four weeks) are mixed in sex and athletic ability, so their volleyball competition is fairly even. The students greatly enjoy their tournaments, which build team spirit, and they calculate their win-loss percentages as part of math lessons. The teams work and learn together in the classroom as well as compete against each other in volleyball, so the overall level of classroom community is high.

A caveat: Competition should be introduced cautiously, after cooperative attitudes and skills are well established. Even then, a teacher should observe whether competition is eroding a cooperative spirit. Continuing to give awards to *all* groups that reach a certain performance level, as well as special recognition to the best group, is one way to prevent that.

8. **Whole-class projects.** A teacher also does well to tap the power of whole-class projects to generate a pervasive spirit of cooperation.

A class newspaper is a good example. In Lincoln Olbrycht's fifth-grade room, students put out *The Class Times*. The spring issue I saw was an impressive 12-page affair, complete with photos, with all copy neatly typed in two columns. That issue reported on a wide variety of classroom activities such as their photography projects, weather station, "spelling football," and tutoring of younger children by class members. Students' collective pride in *The Class Times*—and in the many cooperative activities it reports—is reflected in a statement under this masthead: "We hope that by reading this newspaper, you will see that we are a 'classy' group."

Fay Jeys, a sixth-grade social studies teacher at Rippowam-Cisqua School in Bedford, New York, believes that putting on a class play, better than anything else, teaches her students the importance of working together. "They can see that if they don't do their part—don't learn their lines and moves—it affects everyone else. The result is that they really pull together. And plays are wonderful for bringing out the kids who hardly say anything in class—and then get up onstage and shine."

A class can do small-group projects that fit together to make one big class project. In one fourth grade, each small group constructed a model of a different section of their town, then combined their separate efforts to make the complete town.

Whole-class projects are a lot of work, but the rewards are great: high class morale and a group spirit and energy that carry over into other cooperative activities.

HOW TO MAXIMIZE SUCCESS IN COOPERATIVE LEARNING

Cooperative learning clearly has the potential to make classrooms exciting and productive places where students learn to cooperate and cooperate to learn.[21] How can a teacher maximize the chances of success and deal constructively with the inevitable problems that occur when people work together? Here are some guidelines (see the December 1989 issue of *Educational Leadership* and the March 1990 issue of *Cooperative Learning* for other suggestions):

1. **Explain that cooperation is an important classroom goal.** To launch their combined third- and fourth-grade class, Brookline, Massachusetts, teachers Kristen Field and Virginia Holmes give their students "the speech" on the first day of school:

> We're all going to be together for 180 days. It will be much more pleasant if we get along and are able to cooperate. We don't expect you to like *everyone*. But we do expect you to respect, and take care not to hurt, every member of the class. Over the next several weeks we will help you learn the skills you need to cooperate with others and show respect for them.

COOPERATIVE LEARNING

Eight kinds of cooperative learning:

1. Learning partners
2. Cluster group seating
3. Student team learning
4. Jigsaw learning
5. Team testing
6. Small-group projects
7. Team competition
8. Whole-class projects

Nine ways to maximize the success of cooperative learning:

1. Explain that cooperation is an important classroom goal.
2. Build community.
3. Teach the specific skills needed to cooperate.
4. Establish rules for cooperation.
5. Foster the accountability of every group member to cooperate and contribute.
6. Engage students in continuing reflection on cooperation.
7. Assign roles to group members.
8. Match cooperative learning to the task.
9. Use a variety of cooperative learning strategies.

An opening statement like this sends a clear message: This is a classroom where cooperation is important. That message needs many repetitions if children are to assimilate it deeply. In the weeks that follow, teachers Field and Holmes "state and restate the primary goal of every cooperative activity we have the class do: to strengthen our ability to get along, to increase our awareness and acceptance of each other."

2. Build community. Teachers can do various community-building activities (such as those discussed in Chapter 6) to help students get to know and feel comfortable with each other. For example, if classmates are going to be learning partners or members of a learning team, it's helpful to have them first take some time to interview each other (e.g., "What are two things you're good at? Two things you like to do after school?"). Central New York teacher Mary Hogan, to help her second-graders learn more about each other, established a "hobby time" each day when children took turns teaching the whole class a hobby or skill (e.g., drawing, knot-tying, and plant-potting). Teacher Hogan says it was also "a great ego-booster for a child to be able to teach others something he or she could do."

Dr. Catherine Lewis, a research psychologist with California's Child Development Project, reports that children in Japan typically spend a much longer time in the same cooperative group than do American children. In nursery school, children might stay with the same small group for as long as two years; in elementary school, for half of the year.[22] Lewis hypothesizes that as children get to know and trust each other, they cooperate better. Moreover, she cites a study showing that their cooperative skills transfer to new groups.[23]

3. **Teach the specific skills needed to cooperate.** With many students it won't be enough to say: "Talk it over and decide as a group what kind of a project on the Egyptians you'd like to do." You have to *show* students, step by step, the process of cooperative group decision-making: going around the group giving each person a chance to state his or her ideas; having a recorder keep a list of everybody's ideas; going back through the list and crossing out the ideas that people don't agree on; and finally settling on the idea that all members like the best.

Other skills—such as dividing the labor fairly, showing somebody that you're really listening to their idea, affirming others for their contributions, reaching a compromise when there's a conflict—also need to be taught to students in a deliberate way. To keep these cooperative skills uppermost in students' minds, a teacher may wish to post a Skills for Working Together checklist in the classroom.

It helps to select one or two skills to focus on in a particular lesson. One third-grade teacher, at the start of a cooperative lesson, wrote on the board the words "SOCIAL SKILLS" (a concept she had introduced before), and underneath wrote "Taking turns" and "Using indoor (quiet) voices." She said to the class: "This morning, as you work in your groups, I'd like you to concentrate on using these two social skills. I'll be coming around to observe how you're doing."

As the teacher circulated among the groups, she made notes on children's behavior. When she gathered the class back together, she re-

---

WHAT IS COOPERATION?

CIRCLE those behaviors below that are *ways of cooperating* with members of your group.

PUT an X through those behaviors that are *not* ways of cooperating.

Insisting on having
your own way.

Helping with
the work.

Trying to use
everybody's ideas.

Being friendly toward
everyone in the group.

Making fun of
somebody else's idea.

Bossing people.

Leaving some people
out of the action.

Encouraging all
members to join in.

Compromising.

Doing your fair
share of the work.

Goofing off and letting
others do all the work.

---

ported examples of children in each group who had, she said, done an especially good job of remembering to take turns or use their indoor voices. She finds that giving this kind of positive feedback, and telling children *in advance* that she'll be doing it, motivates them to practice the group skills she wants them to work on.

4. **Establish rules for cooperation.** When students are first put in cooperative groups, they sometimes behave as if they don't have the slightest idea of what it means to cooperate. To prevent that, a teacher can hold a class meeting and give each student a copy of the accompanying "What is cooperation?" sheet.

Following a brief discussion of students' responses to this sheet, a teacher can pose this question: "What are three or four rules we need to have good cooperation?" Agreed-upon "Rules for Cooperation" can then be listed on the board (e.g., "Try to use everybody's ideas," "Make sure everybody has a job to do," "No goofing off"").

5. **Foster the accountability of every group member to cooperate and contribute.** Having cooperative learning teams evaluate how well they worked together helps increase all students' accountability to the rules

of cooperation. It's most effective to tell students *before* the activity that you'll be asking them to do this sort of evaluation.

Central New York teacher Priscilla Williams found that her fourth-graders cooperated much better when she told them that she'd be asking every group member to fill out a sheet, at the end of their group activity, answering these three questions:

1. How well did your group cooperate on this activity?

1	2	3	4	5
Not very well, many problems		So-so, need to improve		Great! Worked out any problems

2. What did *you* do to fulfill your responsibility as a member of your group?

3. What would help your group work better in tomorrow's activity?

A teacher can also promote this kind of group process evaluation by troubleshooting—circulating from group to group to spot problems and help solve them.

6. **Engage students in continuing reflection on cooperation.** Judy Clarke is coordinator of the Values Education Center with the Scarborough Board of Education in Ontario and author of *Together We Learn*, a helpful handbook for teachers on cooperative small-group learning. She writes: "One way in which cooperative learning is significantly different from other pedagogical approaches is its emphasis on regular opportunities for reflection."[24]

After each cooperative learning activity, students are asked to reflect on their learning as a way of sharpening awareness of the values and understandings they are gaining from working together. She recommends a number of questions for students to respond to—individually (e.g., in writing), in small groups, or in whole-group discussion:

• What did your group learn about helping group work go smoothly?

• What is one thing your group decided to do differently next time?

• Describe three ways in which you can help other group members feel good about belonging to your group.

- What are some ways in which you can demonstrate patience when working with others? How do you feel when others are patient with you?

- Describe something you have learned about yourself as a result of learning to cooperate with others.

- What advice would you give to a group that is having trouble staying on task? [25]

7. **Assign complementary roles to group members.** This approach was developed by David and Roger Johnson, directors of the University of Minnesota's Cooperative Learning Center. Group members are assigned specific roles so that every student has a part and knows what it is. I watched Louise Lotz, a third-grade teacher at Walt Disney Elementary School in San Ramon, California, begin a cooperative lesson by reviewing with her class the group roles of facilitator, recorder, checker, reader, and encourager.

TEACHER: What's the facilitator's job when we do cooperative learning?

STUDENT: If you need help with a word—like, you can't find it in the dictionary—they [the facilitators] can ask you [the teacher].

TEACHER: Yes, and the facilitator is the *only* one who can come to me for help. What can you do so the facilitator doesn't have to come to me?

STUDENT: Ask another person in our group.

TEACHER: Right, and remember, the facilitator is also an organizer who keeps everything going. How about the reader?

STUDENT: Reads the directions at the start and the report at the end.

TEACHER: The recorder?

STUDENT: Writes the answers down.

TEACHER: The checker?

STUDENT: Checks the paper.

TEACHER: More specifically?

STUDENT: Checks to make sure everybody agrees on the answer.

TEACHER: How about the encourager?

STUDENT: The encourager says nice things.

TEACHER: For example?

STUDENT: "That's a good idea."

STUDENT: "Good job."

TEACHER: Is any role more important than any other role?

CLASS: No.

Next teacher Lotz walked from group to group, handing out slips of paper that told children their roles for the upcoming activity. Children then set to work on their group assignment, and the teacher moved around the room, complimenting individuals on how they were carrying out their assigned roles.

Assigned roles provide a support structure that ensures the active participation of all group members. Assigned roles also increase group efficiency, since time doesn't have to be spent deciding who will do what. But these complementary roles still allow for spontaneous, free-flowing interaction, because all group members share in the thinking and work needed to complete the group's task (e.g., the recorder can volunteer ideas as well as write them down).

8. **Match cooperative learning to the task.** Use partners or groups only when the task is one in which students *benefit* by working together. I've been in classrooms where the teacher was enthusiastic about doing a particular cooperative learning exercise but the students were not—because the task wasn't right.

Comments Linda Skon, a former first-grade teacher in Minnesota: "The kids will tell you that groups are a waste of their time when worksheets are easy—when everyone can do them alone—as sometimes happens in exercises in spelling or math. But they will also tell you about the hard subjects in which it helps to talk things over with someone else. Groups are very effective in social studies and science, and wonderful in creative writing, where children can talk freely and help each other with ideas."[26]

9. **Mix cooperative learning strategies.** Mixing cooperative learning strategies yields the greatest benefits because different formats have different advantages.

Partners, triads, and groups of four each have their own interpersonal dynamics and learning patterns. Highly structured cooperative approaches aimed at learning material for individual tests (e.g., student team learning and jigsaw learning) minimize off-task behavior, facilitate evaluation of student learning (since tests are taken individually), and promote cooperation without sacrificing time on required academics.

By comparison, small-group or whole-class projects require more time and organization and are more susceptible to problems. But they afford more opportunities for group decision-making and creativity, the sense of triumph that comes from conquering a tough challenge together, and the kind of serendipitous learning that often occurs during more complex, open-ended cooperative activity.

If teachers limit themselves to a narrow range of test-oriented group strategies, they will fail to realize the full potential of cooperative learning to foster intellectual and moral development. Here is a story about a teacher whose cooperative project spanned most of a semester and is a good example of what this approach to learning can do when used in a creative and sustained manner.

A CLASSROOM FULL OF BEANS

Phyllis Smith-Hansen, recently featured in a TV special *Teaching Morality to Kids,* currently teaches two values education courses at Lansing Middle School in Lansing, New York. The first course (which she designed) is called Adolescent Issues and is taught to all fifth-graders; the second, taken by all the sixth-graders, is Quest (a nationally disseminated program jointly developed by Lions Club International and Quest International).[27]

Teacher Smith-Hansen does a lot of cooperative learning in both courses. She learned about the value of cooperative learning during a year when she taught third grade.

That year she had a high proportion of children with learning problems or emotional difficulties. She decided that these children and her class as a whole would benefit by a project that required close cooperation over a long time.

She began in February by asking them to work with a partner pursuing answers to a single question: How can you make dried beans sprout without soil? Teacher Smith-Hansen provided an assortment of dried beans, a book in which to record results, and a "garden corner" filled with various containers, wraps, paper, scales, and calipers. The children, she says, showed "a surprising lack of familiarity with the requirements for growth."

Beans were pierced, stomped, smashed, peeled, drowned, and parched. Experimentation was totally haphazard. Some teams chose to do as many as twelve experiments, covering all sorts of combinations of container, light, moisture, and bean variety, rather than pursuing a few experiments in a logical, coherent pattern. I decided to allow this scattergun approach and deal with their reasoning as a whole class.

At a class meeting, Lon and Tom reported that "small beans sprout first." "How do you know that?" the teacher asked. "Because," they said, "our lentils have already sprouted." Others then spoke up: "So has our lima!" and "So has our mung bean!" The class decided that only agreed-upon findings would be considered "real facts," and only these would be entered in a class bean book. They were learning an important lesson about the nature of science: A finding isn't a fact unless it can be replicated by somebody else.

Partners, the teacher found, also showed a good ability to divide the labor and to respect each other's abilities and preferences. Said one boy to his teammate: "You write in our record book, okay? You write neater than me. I'll empty the water 'cause I don't care if it smells."

The second phase of the project introduced "real planting," using soil. Now each team was asked to make a prediction for each experiment they chose to do, post that prediction on the wall, and report on the progress of their experiment at a class meeting. Soon the walls were dense with children's predictions. For example, "A soybean will push through a wet paper towel," and "A lima bean will push over a small stone as it sprouts."

At this point, competition and jealousy erupted. Partners, worried about the growth rate of their plants, blamed each other for over- or underwatering. Teams taunted other teams when their plants grew faster or larger. There were even some cases of sabotage: Some containers were found swamped in water, and one Monday morning the class dictionary was found placed squarely on top of a lush crop of soybean plants.

Teacher Smith-Hansen looked upon her bean project crisis as an opportunity for growth. She used their class meeting to talk about competition and jealousy, why they had those feelings, and how those feelings had led some people to perform destructive and unfair acts.

Several children said they wanted to have their own plant to care for rather than work with a partner. The teacher allowed the children to make this decision, and half the class decided to go it alone.

But not for long. During the following week, slowly but surely, partners who had gone their separate ways got back together of their own accord. One boy who had previously been unhappy with his partner explained their reunion: "I can't hold this paper [on which he had been recording the plant's growth] and mark it at the same time."

The third phase of the project began with a class visit to the greenhouse of nearby Cornell University. The teacher comments: "We learned many things—the most important being the benefits of light, heat, and moisture that a greenhouse provided. As I hoped, everyone clamored to build a greenhouse of our own, and we decided to raise flowers to beautify the school grounds." This new goal of doing something for the whole school took the project beyond classroom cooperation into the realm of altruism.

At the end of this project in May, teacher Smith-Hansen was greatly pleased by the amount of encouragement, appreciation, and sharing of ideas she had seen. She observed marked progress in children's ability to accept group goals and responsibilities. And their self-esteem, she believed, had grown by leaps and bounds because of all the positive feedback they had given each other.

It's hard to find a teacher who has seriously tried cooperative learning and is not enthusiastic about it. Says Ruby Tellsworth, a second-grade teacher at Rancho Romero School in San Ramon, California, and a participant in the Child Development Project:

> I am a *very* academic teacher, and I was leery of cooperative learning at first. But I would never dream of not teaching this way now. I've seen the results. The children get to know each other better, and I get to know them better.
>
> I had one little boy last year who at first refused to do any work, but came around because the kids in his cooperative learning group persuaded him to do his part. When my children go out of the room for science modules, other teachers tell me they help each other and argue less than most kids their age. This year it was wonderful to get children who have had cooperative learning in kindergarten, first, and second grades. They came to me knowing how to share and work together.

What do children themselves say about cooperative learning?

SECOND-GRADE BOY: I learned it can be okay to work with a girl. It's not icky; it's just like working with a boy—fun.

THIRD-GRADE GIRL: When you grow up, you have to know how to work with other people. If you don't learn to cooperate when you're young, it's harder when you're older. You might not even know what the word "cooperate" means.

SIXTH-GRADE BOY: I don't say things in front of class because I think they might be dumb. But in groups sometimes I say them as sort of a joke, and other kids think they're good ideas. It makes me feel not so dumb.

SIXTH-GRADE BOY: We all have good ideas. But when we talk about them and put them together, we get *great* ideas.

Attachment to groups, sociologist Emile Durkheim argued, helps children value other people and feel loyalty to something larger than themselves. Cooperative learning is another ally in that cause, because it teaches children that they can do more together than they can alone. That lesson in itself—given a society and world where cooperation is often in dangerously short supply—makes cooperative learning a vital part of moral education.

CHAPTER 11

The Conscience of Craft[1]

Picture students in a required academic class at a typical secondary school as a gang of street-repair workers. If they were working as hard as they do in class, half or more would be leaning on their shovels, smoking and socializing, perfectly content to let others do the work. Of those who were working, few would be working hard, and it is likely that none would be doing high-quality work.

—WILLIAM GLASSER, "The Quality
School"[2]

The man who is slothful in his work is brother to the man who is destructive.

—Proverbs 18:9

Kathy Stintson used to be a supervisor for a federally funded jobs training program for 18- to 24-year-olds. Now she is studying to be a high school counselor because she sees a problem in the values of young people.

"I was very disturbed by the moral attitudes of the trainees in our program," she says. "They felt they had a paycheck coming no matter what kind of a job they did. They felt absolutely no obligation to their employers; they would ruin materials with no thought of what it was costing the company. They typically came from blue-collar homes where the father was employed, but they themselves had no concept of what

208

it means to hold a job." Trainees, she said, would make comments such as: "I showed up 15 minutes late—so what?" and "So I wasn't here yesterday—I'm here today—what's the big deal?"

A $1 million study by a panel of corporation executives, university presidents, and various educational officials laid this kind of problem at least partly at the doorstep of schools. Titled *Investing in Our Children: Business and the Public Schools*, the report called on schools to foster good work habits and character traits of reliability, teamwork, and self-discipline. "If schools tolerate excessive absenteeism, truancy, tardiness, or misbehavior," the report said, "we cannot expect students to meet standards of minimum performance or behavior either in school or as adults."[3]

Teachers are the first to acknowledge that there has been a decline—evident as early as the elementary grades—in the work habits and motivation of students. Joanne Lott is a fifth-grade teacher with 14 years' teaching experience in small communities in upstate New York. "Each year," she says, "I see the quality of students waning. I see it in their peer relations—they have a poor self-image and are out for themselves—and in their whole attitude toward *doing*. They are constantly saying, 'Do we *have* to do this?' It makes teaching very frustrating; 90 percent of my job these days is spent motivating them."

Many teachers trace the trouble to changes in the home. "In a 16-year period," says one teacher, "I've seen parents become more concerned with themselves and less concerned with their responsibilities to their children. I have a sixth-grader this year who has not turned in a single homework assignment. During the third week of school, I sent a note home to the parents about this child's homework and received a reply that it was not their problem."

There is also peer pressure against working too hard. This problem was first observed among minority students in big-city schools, where the peer group appeared to have established an unwritten code regulating the amount of schoolwork that was "permissible." When some black parents took their children out of these schools, they gave reasons like this: "Our son John is a good boy, and he's smart. When he went to public school, he paid attention, did his homework, got good marks. Because of this, he was shut out by other kids, taunted, and even beaten up."[4]

It soon became apparent, however, that this anti-work peer ethic was not just a phenomenon of inner-city public schools. Here is a high school teacher at a largely white private school in an affluent suburb:

I discovered that private school students come to their classes without textbooks, paper, or pens; that they come to class late, with homework sloppily done or not done at all; that they talk in class and write obscenities on their test papers; and that bright private school students carefully pare down their achievements to avoid being ostracized by their friends.[5]

Another high school teacher, working in a "good" public high school, was outraged when one of his students called a classmate a "nerd" because the classmate knew the answer to a question the teacher had posed. "This pernicious attitude," the teacher wrote in a letter to *The Washington Post,* is creating an "environment of mediocrity" and "impoverished ideals and values, which cripple the minds and hearts of human beings."[6]

THE FRUITS OF APATHY

Inevitably, attitudes like these have shown up in performance.

Academic achievement by U.S. students, according to the National Assessment of Educational Progress, has declined over the last 20 years at most age levels and in most subjects.[7] In a cross-cultural study, University of Michigan psychologist Harold Stevenson compared 30 U.S. schools, including "several of undeniable quality," with 30 schools in Asia. Students from the *best* U.S. schools scored below students from *all* the Asian schools.[8] On international tests of academic achievement in 19 different subjects, U.S. students ranked dead last in seven subjects, including algebra and biology.

Fewer than half of all Americans know that the Earth moves around the Sun and takes a year to do it.[9] Scientific ignorance and apathy become all the more alarming at a time when many of the threats to human health and survival—ozone depletion, toxic and radioactive waste, acid rain—demand at least a minimal scientific awareness on the part of citizens.

Most high school seniors, on a recent nationwide geography test, couldn't locate Southeast Asia on a map. Nearly a third couldn't locate Latin America. The U.S. Department of Education, which administered the test, concluded that American students' dismal understanding of geography makes it difficult for them to get from one city to another, appreciate other cultures, and comprehend world events.[10]

WHY WORK HAS MORAL IMPORTANCE

The literature on moral education typically treats moral learning and academic learning as separate spheres. But moral education *includes* academic work, because work has moral importance.

What gives work moral meaning?

If you don't work in school, you won't learn. Ignorance, as the studies revealing scientific and geographic illiteracy point out, reduces our capacity to participate as citizens in a complex world.

Moreover, as adults we spend most of our waking lives working. Work is one of the most basic ways we affect the lives of others and contribute to the human community. When people do their jobs well—whether it's repairing cars or repairing people, growing food or growing children—all of us benefit. When people do their jobs poorly, all of us pay the price. Competent people caring enough to perform their jobs competently are a major determinant of the quality of life in any society.

Large numbers of people have lost this public sense of work as a way of contributing to the well-being of others. Many have also lost any sense of being part of a business or company. Work has become "privatized." It's what you do for personal gain—to pay your bills, buy your new stereo, finance your next vacation. When people think of work in this private, instrumental way, accountability declines. It becomes easier to do shoddy work.

Work done well is a fundamental source of our dignity and sense of worth. In school, it is exceedingly difficult for young people to feel positive self-regard when they are failing. It is also nearly impossible for students to feel good about themselves if they know they are doing much less than they are capable of. In adulthood, if we do not feel competent, productive, and needed in some sphere of life, whether at home, in the community, or in the workplace, it is very hard to maintain a positive self-image.

WORK AND THE REALITY PRINCIPLE

Behind the capacity to work is an important quality of character: the ability to delay gratification.

Well-known psychoanalyst Bruno Bettelheim points out that achievement in any domain requires this self-discipline: subordinating the *pleasure principle,* which favors immediate gratification (e.g., watching TV instead of doing homework), to the *reality principle,* which forgoes present pleasure to pursue future goals (high marks, graduation, a good job). "It is this morality alone," writes Bettelheim, "that makes possible serious and consistent learning over long periods of time."[11]

Because many young people have not learned to postpone gratification, they have a hard time meeting the school's demands for concentration, sustained effort, and sacrifice of leisure time for study. Difficulty in delaying gratification used to be considered the special handicap of children of poverty, but this problem now cuts across social classes. Says a fourth-grade teacher in an expensive private school: "In their families, these kids get what they want when they want it. In school, they can't work for long-range goals."

Many students who have trouble with long-range goals end up dropping out of school. Nationally, the dropout rate is 25 percent—a million young people each year (compared to about 10 percent in most European countries). For minorities, in some states, the rate is as high as 50 percent.

Even among students who do well enough in high school to go to the best colleges, many have trouble when the going gets tough. They turn to the easy escapes offered by drugs and alcohol. Often they carry those dependencies into later life, including the workplace.

In short, the capacity to work is a central moral competence. That competence requires developing other traits—such as self-discipline, persistence, self-evaluation, and at least a minimal sense of duty, all of which are part of good character. When people don't think work is important, don't work hard at their jobs, or don't work at all, they suffer, and so does the whole society.

THE CHALLENGE TO SCHOOLS

The chief business of schools is the work of learning. How can schools help students take that work seriously, perform it to the best of their ability, and develop the qualities of character inherent in the capacity to work well?

From the standpoint of values education, the first step for schools is to treat work as having moral importance and the work of learning as a moral activity that contributes to character development.

The second step is to realize that schools are engaging not only in bad education but also in bad *moral* education when, for whatever reason, students are not doing the work of learning. When academic expectations are low, or when the peer culture keeps students from working hard, or when students simply don't care about the quality of their work, the fundamental purpose of schooling is corrupted. In that compromised moral environment, students are learning bad moral habits—laziness, indifference to standards, evasion of responsibility—that they will likely carry over into their adult lives.

The third step is to find language that names what education should strive for in this area of character development. Moral education, I believe, should set the following objectives for students in the realm of work:

1. An attitude of *valuing* the opportunity to learn—a commitment to make the most of one's education

2. The capacity for hard work, including the ability to delay gratification in pursuit of future goals

3. Persistence in the face of discouragement or failure

4. A public sense of work as affecting the lives of others

5. A concern for excellence—what Syracuse University professor Thomas Green calls "the conscience of craft."

Let me elaborate on this last objective.

The conscience of craft, Green says, calls on us to do our jobs well, whatever they may be. To have developed the conscience of craft is to have acquired the capacity to feel satisfaction at a job well done—and to be ashamed of slovenly work. The conscience of craft motivates a mechanic to repair a car not only to our satisfaction but also to his own. It is a mark of people's character when they take care to perform their jobs and other tasks well. If people lack this kind of conscience and don't feel any obligation to do good work, something basic is missing in their moral makeup.[12]

A school that makes a commitment to developing the conscience of craft and other work values should, I believe, use extensively the co-operative learning strategies described in Chapter 10. Cooperative learning will not be a panacea for all that is deficient in students' responsibility toward their schoolwork. But it can help students develop a public sense of work as they depend on each other to do their jobs. Cooperative groups can transform an antiwork peer ethic into positive peer pressure to perform well.

A considerable body of research now makes it very clear that not all schools suffer from an environment of mediocrity. Many, even in areas where large numbers of pupils come from stressed or impoverished backgrounds, have developed academic environments that inspire responsible work attitudes and performance on the part of students. (Meredith Magnet Elementary School in Temple, Texas, is just one such example. Approximately 40 percent of its students are "disadvantaged," but by fifth grade 97 percent of them are far above the state average in reading skills.)

Effective schools—those with high student achievement and morale—create a culture of excellence. They consistently show the following characteristics:

1. Vigorous leadership: The principal works with teachers, students, parents, and community members to develop the learning environment and the school's reputation for high academic standards; incoming students know the school's reputation, and experienced students affirm the value placed on learning; faculty morale is high, and when there are openings, the principal recruits and selects teachers who share the school's goals and standards

2. A pervasive atmosphere of caring

3. Clear goals for both academic performance and classroom and school behavior

4. An emphasis on fair and consistent discipline and a safe and orderly environment

5. Teachers with the expectation that all their students can and will learn

6. Collegial interaction among teachers in support of student learning and achievement

7. High learning time

8. Regular, monitored homework

9. Frequent monitoring of students' progress in learning

10. Recognition of student achievement.[13]

Let's focus on two factors directly under the control of teachers: (1) the expectation that every student can and will learn, and how that expectation gets translated into what a teacher does; and (2) homework.

THE IMPORTANCE OF HIGH EXPECTATIONS

Ed Wynne, education professor at the University of Illinois at Chicago, wisely observes that a teacher's first obligation as a moral educator is to teach well.[14] That begins with believing that every child can learn.

As a new teacher in Nelson, California, Anne Ritter taught a class of first-graders in which 85 percent of the children came from welfare families. Her principal says she astonished fellow faculty members by getting 90 percent of her class up to grade level in reading and math. Her comment: "It's the job."

I visited Anne Ritter's current classroom, a first grade at Dry Creek Elementary School in Clovis, California. A cheerful but no-nonsense atmosphere was one of several ways she conveyed her high expectations to children. At the front of the room, writ large, was a list of "Rules for Ritter's Critters." The first rule was: "Always do your best in everything."

On the wall was a sign: A PERSON WILL SELF-DESTRUCT WITHOUT A GOAL. On the bulletin board was a display on the "value of the month." When I was there, the featured value was AMBITION, defined as "the desire to excel; hard work directed toward a worthwhile goal."

At the secondary level, good teachers make it a point to communicate high expectations when they hand out the syllabus for the course. One high school English teacher says that on the first day of class, he hands out a page with two columns: "My Responsibilities as the Teacher" and "Your Responsibilities as the Student." He comments:

> The teacher responsibilities list has up to 20 items on it. The student list is much shorter. When they see all I'm doing as the teacher, what I'm asking them to do doesn't seem so bad.

Often teachers must try to convey their high expectations in the face of students' own low expectations of themselves. Joanne Lott at Truxton Elementary School in Truxton, New York, says many of her fifth-graders initially respond to her tough standards with surprise and resistance. "Why do you expect so much of us?" they say. "We're the *low* group!"

She replies: "You've been told you can't do it, but I refuse to put you in that category. You can do it if you try!" Telling students "You can do it, and I won't settle for less than your best" is a way of saying,

"I respect your ability to learn, and I care about you too much to let you waste it."

That message gives high expectations their power. The teacher's respect and caring create a personal relationship to which the student feels accountable. Says a recent college graduate:

> During high school, if I did not have a positive relationship with a teacher, I did not perform to my fullest. My most influential teachers were those who let me know in a personal way that they expected good work from me. I wanted to learn for myself but also for them.

TEACHING SELF-EVALUATION

Good teachers don't simply impose high standards; they also help students make those standards their own.

For example: Jo Daley, a sixth-grade Catholic school teacher in Thunder Bay, Ontario, fosters the conscience of craft by teaching students strategies for self-evaluation.

When looking at a child's composition or report, she will say, "Is that your best work? How does it compare with the best work in your folder?"

Sometimes she'll have a short private conference with a student and ask, "How do you feel you could do better on this?" At other times she'll give students criteria and have them evaluate each other's work in small groups.

Cindy Christopher, a third-grade teacher-author at Tully Elementary School in Tully, New York, has her students display their work in a way that fosters both self-evaluation and self-esteem. On Friday, children select what they judge to be their best piece of writing from that week, staple it to the bottom of a personalized paper T-shirt that they have decorated, and hang it on the classroom "clothesline." "In school it's often just the brightest or most creative kids who get their work displayed," teacher Christopher comments. "I want all of my students to strive for excellence and receive recognition for what they consider their best effort." (I recommend Christopher's book *Nuts and Bolts: A Survival Guide for Teachers* as a source of creative teaching ideas.)

DEVELOPING REAL EXPERTISE

Another way to develop a commitment to standards is to give students the opportunity to develop real expertise in a given subject or skill. But most schools, caught up in the hundred-yard pedagogical dash, rush to "cover" the required curriculum. If students never have the experience of taking hold of a subject and probing it deeply, says educator Jerome Bruner, they never know the structure of a field of knowledge or the rewards of in-depth learning. And they don't develop the intellectual discipline needed to produce new knowledge.

Even if schools feel locked into broad curriculum coverage because of external guidelines, they can ensure at least some opportunities for in-depth inquiry. Fieldston Lower School, part of the Ethical Culture Schools in Riverdale, New York, is a private school with a commitment to quality learning that could be emulated by any public school. When I spent two days there, I interviewed a group of parents. One reflected the group's sentiment when she said:

> This school doesn't underestimate children. At other schools my kids have gone to, they studied birds for a week. Here, in kindergarten, they study birds for a *year*. They become experts. At six my daughter asked if we would get her the complete *Audubon Song Guide*. She really wanted the information.

Another parent commented:

> They teach kids to love to learn. When a class takes a trip to a museum, the guides can't believe how well informed the kids are. They look at a suit of armor on a knight and can tell whether it was used for jousting or some other purpose.
>
> Because they do so much drawing here, no child leaves Fieldston feeling that he or she can't draw. They come to use it as a way of taking notes, of observing the world around them. When we visited Stonehenge, our son didn't want to leave without making a sketch.

When students achieve real expertise in one area, competence becomes part of their self-image and they are more motivated to do quality work in other areas as well. Developing expertise through in-depth learning is one more way to translate high teacher expectations into children's educational experience. And one thing is clear from the research: Teachers who communicate high expectations to all their students obtain better academic performance than teachers who communicate low expectations.[15]

THE IMPORTANCE OF EARLY SUCCESS

High expectations are most effective when they are combined with high support.

Especially when children first begin school, they need a lot of support in meeting all the demands that school places on them. Teachers who help children achieve early school success help them take a big step toward long-term school achievement and responsible workmanship.

How to combine high challenge and high support is demonstrated by a program called T.I.M.E. (Tots' Intensive Multidisciplinary Environment) at Chicago's Reilly Elementary School. Team-taught by teachers Audrey Taffs and Christine Arnieri, T.I.M.E. has gained national attention for its success in helping developmentally delayed 6- and 7-year-olds learn. Some 30 children from all over Chicago come to this special classroom. Tests show that these children are so far behind in their development—many can't do things a competent 2-year-old can do—that they would almost certainly be placed in special education classes were it not for T.I.M.E.'s intervention.

Teacher Taffs describes how they work with these children:

> They become easily discouraged and throw away their work, so we use a lot of praise, stickers, and other awards to help them value what they do. If we see that they're struggling with something, we change it to help them succeed. This morning a boy was having a very hard time with his letters sheet and pushed it away. So I gave him another sheet with just two lines of writing on it and asked him if he'd try that. He said okay. When he finished that, we came back to the letters sheet.
>
> We try to make all the children feel capable and loved and to treat them with dignity. Last year we had a boy who soiled his pants almost every day. Nobody made a big deal of it; we just cleaned him up. This year he doesn't do that, and he's learning to read.

T.I.M.E also makes use of a curriculum called the I CAN COURSE. The course asks the children to set goals for each day.

On the day I was there, teacher Taffs asked the children in the group, "What is your goal for today?" One girl said, "I'm going to do all my work." A boy said, "I'm going to be good." Another said, "I'm going to do my homework tonight."

A little girl named Fiora said, "I will sing today." The teacher invited her to do so; it was their custom for someone to volunteer to sing before the group at the start of the day. Fiora came to the front and sang—shyly at first, then with greater gusto—a short song for the class. Teacher Arnieri commented to me: "Fiora barely speaks English or Spanish and said almost nothing a month ago. But now she is singing her heart out."

At the end of the two years that children typically spend in T.I.M.E., they are tested by a psychologist. By that point, fully 80 percent are able to read and do math at grade level and can be placed in regular classrooms. These children have learned that they can succeed at the work of school—and to value their schoolwork as a source of self-esteem.

CELEBRATING SUCCESS

When Fiora finished her song, her T.I.M.E. classmates responded with enthusiastic applause. In classrooms that inspire students to do their best, the celebration of effort and achievement is a regular event.

Says Mary Valentine, a third-grade teacher in Dryden, New York: "Without a good self-image, no child is ready to learn. I try to compliment children publicly as often as possible." She also encourages students to compliment each other on good work.

In a second-grade classroom, a boy described by the teacher as a low achiever correctly completed the heading on his composition paper and showed it to the teacher. She praised the paper highly and asked the boy to share it with his classmates. He walked around the room, presenting his paper to the other children, a broad smile across his face. Each child smiled in turn and offered words of praise.[16]

This teacher has created a true learning community. Learning and achieving are shared values, supported by the peer group as well as the teacher.

TEACHING TO DIFFERENT LEARNING STYLES

Translating high expectations into effective teaching also means accommodating the different learning styles that students bring to school.

Elaine Herron teaches the upper elementary grades in Columbus, Kansas. She finds helpful the theory that some students are disposed toward auditory learning, while others are disposed toward visual learning.

"Kids who are auditory will get it if you use just words," she says.

DEVELOPING THE CONSCIENCE OF CRAFT

We can help students learn to value learning and care about the quality of their work if we:

1. Set school objectives that pertain to work attitudes.

2. Use cooperative learning to develop a peer ethic that supports academic work.

3. Create a schoolwide culture of excellence consistent with what is known about effective schools.

4. Teach with the expectation that every child can learn.

5. Combine high expectations with high support.

6. Develop students' capacity for self-evaluation.

7. Foster students' love of learning and pride in knowledge by helping them develop real expertise.

8. Develop a learning community that celebrates the successes of class members.

9. Teach to different learning styles.

10. Teach to students' interests and help them discover and develop their individual talents.

11. Help students develop the discipline of doing homework.

12. Foster the virtue of hard work in the context of an engaging, meaningful curriculum, a human environment that values people, and a balanced view of work as one of several important values.

"Kids who are visual need images as well as words, and they need help with turning the images into words. They are lousy note-takers."

She finds that still other students are "haptic learners" who learn best through experience that uses their bodies. "I had a fourth-grade girl who was very frustrated because she couldn't learn to tell time. I had her use her own arms as the arms of the clock. Within half an hour she was telling time."

Another girl had not been able to learn her multiplication times tables. "I taught her to say them as she was doing jumping jacks: '3 times

2 is 6; 3 times 3 is 9 . . .' After about 10 minutes of that, I asked her to write them down. She said, 'I know some of them!' "

Students in Elaine Herron's classroom are learning an important work value: Don't quit when you get stuck. And because she helps them find their individual learning strengths, she builds their confidence and their willingness to tackle the work before them.

TEACHING TO STUDENTS' INTERESTS

Bret was a student in a ninth-grade environmental science course. Although he was, in his student teacher's words, "very bright and certainly capable of learning the material," he was in danger of failing because he refused to apply himself and complete the course assignments.

The student teacher says that she handled this problem by talking with Bret to try to find where his interests lay.

> I found that he loved deer hunting and knew a great deal about the deer's life and habitat. I was able to incorporate this interest into a class assignment, a wildlife report, to be done on any animal the student had an interest in.
>
> Bret completed a well-written, interesting report on deer and earned a grade of 95 on that assignment. After that he showed considerable improvement on other papers and ended the course with all back assignments completed and a grade well above passing.

The teacher got Bret to work by relating the subject (environmental science) to one of his interests (deer). Another teaching approach is to let students' interests *be* the subject of their investigation. Doing that maximizes their involvement and often liberates astonishing energies for work.

Early childhood specialist Ann Halpern teaches a combined first- and second-grade class at Central School in Ithaca, New York. She likes to teach thematic units that span several weeks and integrate various learnings and skills (reading, writing, science, numbers, drawing, and so on), much in the manner of the "whole language" approach to teaching language arts. Sometimes she will try to stimulate interest in a topic that she thinks has potential for a unit—but she's ready to go with the flow of what children are most eager to learn about. She says:

I have a vegetable garden that I love, so as I planned for this fall I thought we might do a unit on vegetables. As it turned out, however, my children were not much interested in vegetables. What they were interested in was *pets*. . . .

Now we're doing a unit on pets. What is a pet? What do different kinds of pets need? How do you care for a pet? How do you show you care? I'm bringing in books about pets, kids are writing stories about their pets and making graphs, charts, and drawings. We've discussed occupations that have to do with pets, the role of pets as part of a family, and the ways that pets are part of our culture and other cultures. This is a subject of intense interest to them.

Teacher Halpern points out the connection between teaching to children's interests and developing their self-esteem: "We value children by valuing what they are interested in. For me, it's one of the most authentic ways to help children value themselves."

Interest-centered teaching also elicits concentrated, sustained effort from students who might otherwise be unmotivated learners. In the process, they develop skills (reading, writing, thinking) and standards of excellence that can be transferred to other areas of their schoolwork, including those they do not freely choose.

Interest-centered projects also help students develop their unique talents (e.g., investigative research, creativity, a sense of humor). As Harvard psychologist Howard Gardner has noted, one of the most important contributions education can make to children's development is to help them toward fields where their talents best suit them, where they will be satisfied and competent.

"There are hundreds and hundreds of ways to succeed," Gardner points out, "and many, many different abilities that help you get there. We should spend less time ranking children and more time helping them to identify their natural competencies and gifts, and cultivate those."[17] Gardner's theory of multiple intelligences (as opposed to the narrow range of verbal-mathematical intelligence measured by I.Q. tests), set forth in his book *Frames of Mind,* lends support to making time in school for children to pursue seriously what interests them most.[18]

HOMEWORK

More teachers would, I believe, assign more homework if they knew what the research shows.

- When low-ability students do just one to three hours of homework a week, their grades are usually as high as those of average-ability students who do no homework.

- When average-ability students do three to five hours of homework a week, their grades usually equal those of high-ability students who do no homework.[19]

The research also shows that teachers give more homework than students complete. High school teachers say they assign about 10 hours of homework a week, but seniors report that they spend only four to five hours a week doing homework.[20] One tenth-grade English teacher voices a common complaint: "My students feel they are fulfilling their obligation if they just show up."

Fortunately, there are ways to break that pattern. Here is a baker's dozen of homework strategies that teachers have used with at least modest, and sometimes dramatic, success:

1. **The school day ends when homework is in.** A tenth-grade biology teacher says he accepts no excuses for his students not having homework; they can't leave school—or go to after-school extracurricular activities—until their homework is done. He says, "I won't let students off the hook by giving them a zero, because grades are not a motivator for a lot of kids."

2. **After-school catch-up day.** A ninth-grade English teacher whose students were not turning in homework announced this policy: Thursday would be "catch-up day." Those people who owed any homework assignments would have to stay after school with the teacher and complete them. Says this teacher: "The first week of doing this, most of the class had to stay; the second week, about half; the third week, only five students; and after four weeks, no one had to stay."

3. **Base quizzes on homework.** A student teacher found herself in a seventh-grade math class where only a handful of the 20 students were completing their homework. This student behavior was inadvertently encouraged by a school policy that prohibited teachers from grading homework, on the grounds that many students came from family situations that interfered with getting homework done.

The student teacher told the class that in the future, quizzes (given two to three times a week) would be based directly on the homework—and that they could use their completed homework as "notes" for the quizzes. When students saw how much better they did on quizzes when they had done their homework, completion of assignments improved dramatically. (Variation: Basing quizzes on the homework but not allowing students to use the homework during the test.)

4. **Discuss the assignment.** When teachers prepare written instructions and discuss an assignment with a class, research shows, students are more likely to take the homework seriously than if the assignment is simply announced.[21]

5. **Check the assignment.** For the first 10 weeks of the school year, a sixth-grade teacher trains her students in the habit of writing down homework assignments completely and accurately by initialing each student's assignment before the student leaves the room.

6. **Start the assignment.** Students are more likely to complete an outside assignment, teachers find, if they are required to begin working on it in class.

7. **Help students plan ahead.** A ninth-grade teacher posts a computer printout showing the homework assignments, and their due dates, for the next two weeks. He asks students to copy this information and decide when they need to get started on an assignment to allow enough time for their best work.

8. **Grade homework.** Most students, studies show, are more willing to do homework when the teacher evaluates it promptly and counts it as part of their grade.[22] One high school science teacher finds the following system an effective motivator: (a) Homework counts as 50 percent of a student's grade; (b) two bonus points are added to a student's final average if every assignment is handed in over a marking period; (c) students are frequently given a choice of assignments; and (d) students are allowed to come in after school to redo any assignment they are unhappy with (they try harder and often learn more, the teacher says, the second time).

9. **Graph grades.** Every Monday, one high school earth science teacher gives his students their "weekly performance grade," based on the previous week's homework and quizzes. Students then plot this grade on a personal graph that each student keeps. "Before I started doing this," the teacher says, "I'd often have kids go into a tailspin because of a problem in athletics or a breakup with a boyfriend or girlfriend. Now they see the dip in their weekly grade and are more likely to pull out of it."[23]

10. **Teach a system.** In at least some Chicago schools, beginning in the elementary grades, students are now required to keep notebooks listing assignments, due dates, and time spent completing work. In some schools, parents are also asked to initial these assignment books when

work is completed. In addition to increasing accountability, use of these books teaches students a system for keeping track of their work.

11. **Whole-class incentives.** A fourth-grade teacher who says she "was going crazy trying to get kids to turn in homework" tried a group incentive. She explains: "If *every* student got a particular assignment in, the whole class got a star. Twenty stars and we had a popcorn party. This worked amazingly well; students really got after each other."[24]

Secondary-level teachers have also found this strategy successful. In one low-achieving section of eighth-grade math, fully two thirds of the students were failing to hand in homework during a metrics unit. The teacher announced that if every student handed in every assignment on time *for the entire week,* there would be a surprise reward on Friday. To the teacher's "amazement and absolute delight," all students completed all homework on time; on Friday she brought in popcorn, and she and the class made pinwheels using metric measurements. The teacher continued this approach for the next two weeks, frequently expressing pride in the class's improvement; students maintained their new work habits and "did an excellent job on their unit test."[25]

12. **Cooperative homework groups.** Cooperative learning experts Nancy and Ted Graves explain how small groups can be used to motivate students to do homework:

- Students sit in learning teams that review homework daily. The group encourages members to get their assignments in on time.

- Within the groups, members compare answers in pairs. Then pairs share their agreed-upon answers with the whole team, which comes to an agreement on the best answer to each problem. The group submits a team answer sheet, signed by all members, reporting the agreed-upon answers. All individual homework sheets are stapled to the back of the group answer sheet.

  Grading: Each group member gets his or her own grade for the homework, *plus* bonus points if all group members turned in their homework—and additional bonus points if the group answer sheet is 100 percent correct.

13. **Class meeting on homework.** Problems with homework is a good topic for a class meeting. What are the problems from the teacher's point of view? The students' point of view? (See Chapter 8 for an example of a successful class meeting on homework at the secondary level.)

Says a small-town junior high math teacher: "I have several kids who are third- and fourth-generation welfare. Dad sits home with a can of beer and a bag of pretzels in front of the TV. That's the extent of their own ambitions. They have no interest whatever in working."

Says a high school social studies teacher: "I enjoy teaching my lower-track students more than my upper-ability class. In our school the brightest students are the laziest. I'll hear them bragging to each other in the hall about how they got a 70 on a test without even studying."

The widespread deterioration of the work ethic reflects a long cultural slide toward privatism, self-indulgence, and a get-without-giving morality. It won't be easily reversed by schools. But no matter how tough this challenge, schools clearly have no alternative but to try. They must strive to teach young people, in the words of essayist Lance Morrow, that "all life must be worked at—protected, planted, replanted, fashioned, cooked for, coaxed, diapered, formed, sustained. Work is the way we tend the world."

There are, however, three major caveats for schools as they attempt to teach students the virtue of hard work:

1. **A good educational program is essential.** Addressing the Navajo Educational Summit for the Year 2000, Rexford Brown of the Education Commission of the States offered this advice:

> Don't fall into the trap of developing the kind of mindless, fragmented, racehorse curriculum that now dominates and deadens most schools in the majority culture—the "I have to do Asia tomorrow" syndrome. The typical school curriculum is a smorgasbord. There is no unifying philosophy. It doesn't address the whole child. It is superficial and repetitive. It doesn't make sense. And it bores kids to death. Build a curriculum that has coherence and makes kids think.

That all too little thinking goes on in most schools was the conclusion of John Goodlad and colleagues in their respected book *A Place Called School*. In their observation of more than a thousand classrooms, Goodlad's research team found instruction to be amazingly similar across schools. Teachers' pedagogy was largely limited to two things: lecturing (teachers typically outtalked the entire class three to one) and monitoring seatwork. Students were passive; they rarely worked collaboratively; they weren't challenged to think; they didn't create; and evaluation of their learning typically tested only for recall. Teachers said they knew the importance of cooperative learning, inquiry methods, problem-solving approaches, experience-based projects, and the like—but didn't know how to implement them "without losing control."[26]

Motivating students to work must begin with an engaging, meaningful, well-taught curriculum. As Henry David Thoreau once said, "It is not enough to be busy. The question is, what are we busy about?"

2. **Academic achievement must not be achieved at the expense of moral education.** While academic learning has a moral dimension that makes it part of moral education, mindless academic pressures can easily become the enemy of moral education. When a narrow view of school success—higher scores on standardized tests—is in the saddle, many teachers don't feel at liberty to take the time to discuss a class problem, build moral community, experiment with cooperative learning, and so on. Teaching children to work hard and teaching them to value themselves and other people can and must proceed hand in hand.

3. **Hard work must not become workaholism.** Says Dean Richard Thain of the University of Chicago Graduate School: "There's this new workaholic concentration that has taken over. People think nothing of a 60-hour workweek." He adds: "If everybody else is working 60 hours a week, we feel guilty if we're not, as if we're not ambitious or devoted enough, as if we'll be passed over for promotions and raises."[27]

While part of the culture seems to suffer from too little of the work ethic, another part seems to suffer from too much. We want young people to grow up to be balanced adults who have other values in addition to work and achievement—who make time for friends, family, recreation, community service, and spiritual growth.

Good schools will convey a balanced message about work by creating the kind of human environment where people clearly matter. At the same time, they will be diligent in teaching students a lesson they once knew better than they do now: To succeed in life and build a better world, they need more than brains and talent; they also need the capacity for working hard. Developing that capacity must be high on the agenda of our efforts to build the character of our children.

CHAPTER 12

Encouraging Moral Reflection

Where would we have been if everyone had thought things out in those days?

—ADOLPH EICHMANN, at his trial
for Nazi war crimes[1]

I was there to follow orders, not to think.

—Defendant in the Watergate trials[2]

As part of their chick incubation project, Mrs. Williams suggested to her second-graders that they might wish to open an egg each week to monitor the embryonic development.

Later that day, in his reading group, 7-year-old Nathaniel confided to his teacher: "Mrs. Williams, I've been thinking about this for a long time—it's just too *cruel* to open an egg and kill the chick inside!" Mrs. Williams listened without comment and said she would bring it up for discussion with the whole class.

When she did, there was some agreement that Nat's point was worth considering. But many children said they were curious to see what the embryo looked like. Nat replied that being curious wasn't a good enough reason for killing a chick. "How would you like it," he said, "if somebody opened *your* sac when you were developing because they were curious to see what *you* looked like?" Anyway, he argued, the library must have pictures of chick embryos; that would be a better way of finding out what they looked like.

Some children countered that they wanted to see a *real* chick. "Is it alive?" became a question. "Not until it has hatched," some children argued. "It's alive now," others insisted, "and it *is* a chicken!"

Mrs. Williams asked the children to think about the issue overnight. By the following morning, a majority of the class had come to feel that Nat's objection should be honored: They decided not to open the eggs.

The potential moral learnings here were many: that all life, even that of a chick embryo, is to be taken seriously; that just wanting to do something isn't a good enough reason for doing it; that the reasoned dissent of even one member of the group deserves a fair hearing from the rest; that an important moral decision should not be made in haste; and that, if possible, a conflict should be resolved in a way that tries to meet the needs of all parties (the class did in fact search out pictures of chick embryos in the library). These learnings were possible because Mrs. Williams took the time to help her children think about and deal sensitively with a difficult moral dilemma arising from the real life of the classroom.

THE NEED FOR MORAL REFLECTION

History and everyday life are full of examples of small and great wrongs that occurred at least partly because people didn't stop to think, "Is this right?" Moral reflection is necessary to develop the cognitive side of character—the important part of our moral selves that enables us to make moral judgments about our own behavior and that of others. That part of character, as we saw in Chapter 4, has six facets:

1. *Being morally aware*—seeing the moral dimensions of life situations.

2. *Having an understanding of objectively worthwhile moral values* (e.g., respect and responsibility) and how to apply them in concrete situations.

3. *Being able to take the perspective of others.*

4. *Being able to reason morally*—to understand why some actions are morally better than others.

5. *Being able to make thoughtful moral decisions,* considering alternatives, consequences, and the moral values at stake.

6. *Having self-knowledge,* including the capacity for self-criticism.

Bringing this knowing side of character to maturity is one of the most difficult challenges in moral education. It requires clear ethical thinking by the teacher as well as a sophisticated set of teaching skills. Let's examine first a kind of unclear ethical thinking by some teachers that interferes with their ability to develop rational moral judgment in students.

THE MISTAKE OF MORAL RELATIVISM

Without ethical training, many teachers tend to treat moral judgment as if it were simply a matter of personal opinion. That is the mistake of moral relativism, an error that has deep roots in contemporary culture.

Moral relativism is an outgrowth of philosophical positivism (which denies that there can be objective moral truths) and personalism (which emphasizes individual autonomy and subjective feelings). Many teachers who might not think of themselves as "moral relativists" nevertheless talk as if they were. They routinely introduce a classroom moral discussion by saying to students, "There are no right or wrong answers . . ." In a values discussion, these teachers scrupulously avoid making any statement that could cause students to think that they might be wrong in a particular value judgment—regardless of what the students say.

Most students, unfortunately, are all too ready to believe that there are no right or wrong answers when it comes to morality. They have grown up in a world where large numbers of people think that moral values are never absolute but always relative to the individual or the society holding them. The implication of that belief is far-reaching: Nothing is objectively right or wrong; "moral" means "what's right *for me.*"

Such thinking fails to grasp a fundamental moral truth. There *are* rationally grounded, nonrelative, objectively worthwhile moral values: respect for human life, liberty, the inherent value of every individual person, and the consequent responsibility to care for each other and carry out our basic obligations. These objectively worthwhile values demand that we treat as *morally wrong* any action by any individual, group, or state that violates these basic moral values.

How is it possible to demonstrate rationally that moral values such as respect and responsibility have objective worth? First of all, such values serve the good of both the individual and society. They also survive two classic ethical tests: *reversibility* (would you want to receive this kind of treatment?) and *universalizability* (would you want all persons to act this way in a similar situation?). Behaviors that are contrary to respect, for example, clearly fail the tests of both reversibility and universalizability. If we ourselves wouldn't want to be the victim of theft, rape, or murder (the reversibility test), and if we wouldn't want people in general to go around stealing, raping, and murdering (the universalizability test), then such behaviors are self-evidently wrong.

RELATIVISM IN THE CLASSROOM: A CASE STUDY

When teachers don't grasp this basic moral logic—and when they bring instead a muddy relativism to classroom discussions—they can't help students learn how to think clearly about moral questions. Consider the following incident reported not long ago in *The New York Times*.[3]

At a Teaneck, New Jersey, high school, a female student found $1,000 in a purse and turned it in. The next day, a guidance counselor led a discussion of the incident with 15 juniors and seniors. The counselor asked them what they thought of the girl's action. They concluded that she had been foolish to turn in the money.

The students then asked the counselor what *he* thought of the girl's behavior. He told the students that he believed the girl had done the right thing, but added that he "would not try to force his values on them." The counselor later commented to the *Times* reporter: "If I come from the position of what is right and what is wrong, then I am not their counselor."

I gave this article to a class of my undergraduate education students and asked them to evaluate the counselor's moral reasoning. They were hard pressed to find anything wrong with it. One fairly bright young woman volunteered that she would have handled the situation in the same way.

Why didn't my students immediately see the holes in the counselor's reasoning? Because they themselves are used to thinking relativistically about moral questions. The counselor's statements about not wanting to "force his values" and not wanting to "come from the position of what is right and what is wrong" sound sensible enough—if you start with the premise that all values are purely personal and relative, a matter of choice rather than obligation.

My students could, however, spot the problem with the counselor's thinking when I posed the following situation: Suppose it had been the counselor who had lost the $1,000. Suppose that his money had not been turned in and that he was discussing the matter with his student group. Under that circumstance, can you imagine his saying, "Personally, I think it would be right for any of you to return my money if you find it—but, of course, I don't want to force my values on you"?

When we appeal to values that are a matter of rights and obligations, we aren't "forcing" those values on others. Rather, *the values expressing rights and obligations impose themselves on all of us.* We are all morally bound to honor such values, like it or not. Usually there's a societal law that backs up the moral requirement. Respect for somebody else's property, for example, is a both a moral and a legal obligation, not a choice.

GETTING CLEAR ABOUT BASIC MORALITY

To the extent that a teacher thinks that all values are purely personal and relative and that there are no rights and obligations that bind everyone, the teacher is incapacitated as a moral educator. There are rational, objectively valid moral requirements to which all people are accountable. Society can't exist without them. One of the primary tasks of the school as moral educator is to help students understand that moral fact and act accordingly.

The ironic thing is that virtually all teachers take a nonrelativistic approach in immediate, concrete moral situations, even if many talk like relativists in the abstract. When a child's milk money has been stolen, teachers don't lapse into rhetoric about "not imposing values." They insist that the money be returned. When children call each other degrading names, throw food in the cafeteria, bully someone on the playground, or speak disrespectfully to an adult, the adults in charge don't say, "Personally, I don't agree with your behavior, but there's no right or wrong, so you should make your own decision." Instead, they insist that the student make the morally correct decision—stop the demeaning put-downs, not throw food, not bully, speak respectfully. If they do their job well, teachers also carefully explain the *reasons* for these moral requirements, so that children's minds are changed, not just their behavior.

Once teachers abandon relativistic thinking and become convinced that the school has a right and a duty to teach nonrelative moral values, one very big obstacle to morally educative discussion is overcome.

But another remains. Here as elsewhere, teachers need tools. They don't want to stand up in front of a class and say, "This is right" and "This is wrong." They don't want to "preach." Although direct moral teaching or mentoring (see Chapter 5) has its place, teachers want and need other ways of engaging students in moral discussion.

Let's look at the various methods of encouraging moral reflection as they have evolved historically—and at how a teacher can incorporate the best features of each.

LEARNING THE SIMPLE VIRTUES

Turn back the clock to the beginning of this century. You're in second grade, and it's time for reading. The teacher says to get out your *McGuffey Reader* and turn to the story "The Honest Boy and the Thief." It goes like this:

The Honest Boy and the Thief

Charles was an honest boy, but his neighbor, Jack Pilfer, was a thief. Charles would never take anything for his own which did not belong to him; but Jack would take whatever he could get.

Early one summer's morning, as Charles was going to school, he met a man opposite the public house, who had oranges to sell. The man wished to stop and get his breakfast, and asked Charles if he would hold his horse while he went into the house.

But first he inquired of the landlord, if he knew Charles to be an honest boy, as he would not like to trust his oranges with him, if he was not. Yes, said the landlord, I have known Charles all his life, and have never known him to lie or steal.

The orange man then put the bridle into Charles' hand and went into the house to eat his breakfast. Very soon Jack Pilfer came along the road, and seeing Charles holding the horse, he asked him whose horse he had there, and what was in the baskets on the horse. Charles told him that the owner of the horse was in the house, and that there were oranges in the baskets.

As soon as Jack found there were oranges in the baskets, he determined to have one, and going up to the basket, he slipped in his hand and took out one of the largest, and was making off with it.

But Charles said, Jack, you shall not steal these oranges while I have the care of them, and so you may just put that one back in the basket.

Not I, said Jack, as I am the largest, I shall do as I please; but Charles was not afraid of him, and taking the orange out of his hand, he threw it back into the basket.

Jack then attempted to go round to the other side and take one from the other basket; but as he stepped too near the horse's heels, he received a violent kick, which sent him sprawling to the ground.

His cries soon brought out the people from the house, and when they learned what had happened, they said that Jack was rightly served; and the orange man, taking Charles' hat, filled it with oranges, as he said he had been so faithful in guarding them, he should have all these for his honesty.[4]

After the story, the teacher discusses with the children the following questions to aid their understanding of the intended moral lessons:

1. What is this story about?

2. Which was the honest boy?

3. What kind of a boy was Jack Pilfer?

4. What kind of a character did the landlord say that Charles had?

5. How can boys earn a good reputation?

6. What advantage is there in possessing a good character?

Obviously, you don't need a scorecard to tell the good guys from the bad guys in the *McGuffey Reader*. Stories like "The Honest Boy and the Thief" were designed to teach simple moral virtues—honesty, kindness, faithfulness, courage—in a simple and memorable way. To act according to these ideals was right; to go against them was wrong.

Virtue, moreover, was rewarded. Later in life, perhaps, children might learn that crime sometimes pays (at least in the short run) and that doing what's right can carry a cost (the Jack Pilfers of life can be tough to take on).

But in starting children on the road to virtue, McGuffey reasoned, we first need to get them hooked on goodness. We should try to do that by depicting what is, after all, fundamentally true: Honesty is the best policy, possessing a good character an advantage in life, and being good the surest way to be happy. When you lead a good life, you're living in a way you can be proud of, and the people who know you will be proud of you, too.

Besides tales of virtue, the *McGuffey Reader* offered children direct moral advice. Here is a lesson from the *First Reader*:

Always do to other children as you wish them to do to you. This is the Golden Rule. So remember it when you play. Act upon it now, and when you are grown up, do not forget it.

Children needed simple moral lessons like this in McGuffey's time, and they still need them. That's one reason why the original *McGuffey Reader* is making a comeback. Schools are also turning to other children's books written in the same spirit—like the contemporary *Value Tales* series based on the lives of real people (Louis Pasteur, Helen Keller, Abraham Lincoln, Harriet Tubman, Benjamin Franklin, Marie Curie, Jackie Robinson, Eleanor Roosevelt, and others).[5]

VALUES CLARIFICATION

Jump ahead to the late 1960s. By now, as we saw in Chapter 1, the schools had lost sight of a shared, public morality. Authority in general was suspect; personal freedom was the reigning societal value.

Values clarification swept onto the scene, capturing the spirit of the times and offering schools in an increasingly pluralistic society a way to talk about values while preserving their value neutrality. In values clarification's bold manifesto, *Values and Teaching* (1966, 1978), its creators proposed to replace "traditional ways of teaching values" (such as setting a good example, inspiring, using the arts and literature, religion, and appeals to conscience) with a focus on *process*.

The first step in the authors' recommended seven-step valuing process was "choosing freely." (Other steps were "choosing from alternatives," "choosing thoughtfully," "prizing and cherishing," "affirming," "acting upon choices," and "repeating" the value-based choice.) So strong was the authors' commitment to free choice that they even urged teachers to "aid children in finding values *if* they choose to do so. . . . It is entirely possible that children will choose not to develop values. It is the teacher's responsibility to support this choice also."[6]

To many parents, it came as a shock to find out that this kind of values education was being taught to their children. In the academic journal *The Public Interest*, Martin Eger presents a detailed case study of two small towns in upstate New York where parents mounted a formal protest against values clarification when they discovered it was going on in their school system. Eger writes:

These people, old and young alike, had thought until now that whether to become an engineer or a farmer was certainly their own choice—truly a "free" and personal decision. But they never believed that whether or not to cheat, for example, was quite in the same category. And this, it seemed, is what the school was saying. One mother wrote: "If I teach my child that cheating is wrong, and V.C. [values clarification] teaches a child that there are no right answers, no wrong answers but rather to choose freely, it most certainly upsets the house."[7]

Indeed, it upsets not only the individual household but also the whole human community. As we've seen, the shared belief in obligatory values like honesty is the glue that holds society together.

Values clarification thinking is still with us in the kind of relativistic language ("There are no right or wrong answers . . .") that we looked at earlier in this chapter. And basic values clarification methodology ("You have to decide what's right for you") is still very much around, though it doesn't often get called by that name anymore because of the controversy surrounding it. Even teachers who don't buy into the relativistic theory behind values clarification are often attracted to its great variety of classroom activities. These activities may get students involved and talking; but for a moral educator the bottom-line question has to be: What moral lessons do students take away? Let me give two examples of values clarification activities that illustrate some of the hazards.

One is "The Fallout Shelter." This exercise asks students to assume there has been a nuclear war and that the future of the human race depends on who gets to enter a fallout shelter. In one version, the shelter can keep alive only six people, and students are asked to decide which six of 10 candidates (which include a retarded girl, a violent policeman, a prostitute, a drug pusher, a confirmed racist, and a person just released from a mental institution) shall be saved.

The fallout shelter exercise, with its forced-choice format, is structured to lead students to ignore a basic ethical principle: All persons, as human beings, have equal worth and an equal right to live. The shelter activity invites students to rank human lives on a crass, utilitarian basis: Who will be most useful in rebuilding the postnuclear war society? In my graduate course in moral education, one teacher reacted sharply: "I have several handicapped students in my class. They would be devastated by an activity that suggested they might be the first to go because they were less useful than the rest."

Even seemingly innocuous values clarification activities can backfire. Consider "Things I Love to Do." Students are asked to list 20 things they enjoy doing, then to indicate which cost more than $3 each time they do it, which involve some type of risk, and which might not be on their list five years from now. With adults and many student groups, this exercise proves to be good for both clarifying personal values and building a sense of community.

Consider what happened, however, when an eighth-grade math teacher used this activity with a low-achieving class:

> When we shared our lists, the four most popular activities listed by students were: sex, drugs, drinking, and skipping school. I asked why these were the most popular, and these are the things my students said: "I don't need this class to graduate, so why come?"; "School isn't important"; "Everyone drinks and smokes dope"; "Pot doesn't harm you"; "All my friends do it, so why can't I?"; "Sex is the best part of life"; and "Sex, drugs, and rock and roll rule."

Not sure what to do next, the teacher asked her students to define "values." One boy responded, "What I like doing." Others agreed. The teacher comments: "The students said they enjoyed doing this activity. They said they found they had values in common with others around them."

What was the upshot of this discussion? The students had new peer support for their rule-breaking and self-indulgent life-styles, values that are neither in their own best interests nor in the best interests of society. And the school, in the person of the unchallenging, neutral teacher, had given tacit approval to their hedonistic value system.

Some of the founders of values clarification, to their credit, are now speaking publicly about the shortcomings of their original approach. In the May 1988 issue of *Educational Leadership,* on moral education, Merrill Harmin, one of the coauthors of *Values and Teaching,* has a thoughtful article titled, "Value Clarity, High Morality: Let's Go for Both." In it he says:

> Our emphasis on value neutrality probably did undermine traditional morality. . . . As I look back, it would have been better had we presented a more balanced picture, had we emphasized the importance of helping students both to clarify their own personal values *and* to adopt society's moral values. . . . It makes a good deal of sense to say that truthfulness is better than deception, caring is better than hurting, loyalty is better than betrayal, and sharing better than exploitation.[8]

ARE THERE WORTHWHILE FEATURES OF VALUES CLARIFICATION?

Is there any value in values clarification?

I believe there is. Values clarification encouraged people to close the gap between espoused values and personal action. As long as the values are good ones—such as acting responsibly toward oneself and others—value-action consistency is certainly a worthwhile goal.

Values clarification tried to promote this value-action consistency in a number of ways. Teachers were encouraged to ask students how they were acting on the values they claimed to hold. Teachers were also encouraged to personalize value issues by asking "What would you do?" questions.

- What would you do if you saw someone getting mugged and other people were just standing around watching?

- What would you do if your friends started making fun of a strange-looking schoolmate?

- What would you do if you heard that Native Americans on a nearby reservation were living in severe poverty and nobody was doing much about it?

Sometimes questions like these were part of "value sheets" that teachers could integrate into an academic lesson in social studies, science, or English. A values sheet might provide food for thought drawn from history or current events; to encourage serious reflection, students would be asked to respond in writing. Using this format, for example, I recently constructed the following value sheet on prejudice and used it in a teacher workshop to stimulate personal reflection and lively small-group discussion.

Two Arrested in Probe of Hate Graffiti in Wellesley

By James L. Franklin
Globe Staff

Wellesley police early today arrested two men in connection with a wave of Nazi-style hate graffiti painted on dozens of cars and buildings early Sunday.

. . . Beginning some time after 3 A.M. Sunday, Wellesley police received 40 to 50 complaints that a group had spray-painted swastikas and racial slurs targeting the town's Jewish, black, Hispanic, and Chinese residents.

The vandalism, which occurred just hours before the start of the Jewish holiday of Yom Kippur, defaced a shopping arcade under construction in the Wellesley Hills business district, as well as mailboxes, garages, houses, and cars parked along residential streets.

1. The above article appeared in the October 9, 1989, *Boston Globe*. But similar incidents have been occurring all over the country. What is your reaction to these incidents?

2. Suppose you were in a group conversation and someone made an anti-Semitic, racist, or other ethnic slur. What would you do? Why?

3. Have you ever done anything in the past to speak out against or otherwise combat prejudice? (Give an example if possible.)

4. What would you be willing to do in the future?

What values clarification fails to address is the crucial question, are the values espoused by the student worthwhile? If students valued combating prejudice and showing respect for the human dignity of all persons (the intent of the above value sheet), we'd certainly want them to put that value into practice. But if they valued "sex, drugs, drinking, and skipping school," as the aforementioned eighth-graders did, would we want them to do those things more consistently?

Students need help in coming to know what is good and right for themselves and others. To help students *evaluate* values—examine them critically—teachers need a theoretical framework that offers ethical criteria. Because values clarification lacks such a framework, its critics have called it "a set of methods in search of a theory."

For a better moral theory, many educators turned in the 1970s to the moral development psychology of Harvard University's Lawrence Kohlberg. Kohlberg's approach was to gain strong support among academics and researchers and eventually have worldwide impact on educators.[9]

THE CHILD AS MORAL PHILOSOPHER

Kohlberg's first contribution was to call attention to the child as a moral thinker.

During lunchtime at an elementary school in California, I gathered a small group of third-graders around a picnic table and did something that Kohlberg made famous. I read them a moral dilemma:

During recess on the playground, you see a big fourth-grader bullying a smaller kid, a second-grader. He's pushing him around, punching him in the arm, just being mean. You don't really know the kid who's getting picked on. What would you do if you saw this happening? What should you do? Why?

Here are the responses of two of these third-graders:

ANDY: You should try to stop it yourself. If that doesn't work, tell the yard duty [the adult on the playground].

ME: Why do you think you should do that?

ANDY: So that little kid won't get stomped on!

ME: I know some kids who would say, "It's none of your business, you don't even know the kid." What would you say to that?

ANDY: Even if he's not your friend, even if you *hate* the kid, you should still help him!

MIKE: I disagree.

ME: Why?

MIKE: I think it's none of your business.

ME: Why do you think it's none of your business?

MIKE: I just wouldn't want to get involved.

Although they are the same age (both 8), Andy and Mike are not at the same stage of moral development. Andy has reached what Kohlberg calls "Stage 3," where the child wants to be a "good person" in his own eyes and the eyes of those who know him. He cares about the needs and feelings of others, regardless of what's in it for him.

Mike, by contrast, is still at Stage 2, where the child's thinking is a combination of "Look out for number 1" and a narrow, tit-for-tat sense of fairness. At Stage 2, if the kid getting picked on had helped you once when you were getting picked on, well, then you'd have to pay him back by helping him. But otherwise it's not your responsibility.

Listen to how Mike's Stage 2 perspective surfaces again in a second dilemma discussion. Here's the question: "What would you do if you saw a kid, someone from another class, accidentally drop a dollar as he's walking down the hallway? He doesn't realize he dropped it, and you're the only person who sees the dollar on the floor."

MIKE: Take the dollar.

ME: Why would you do that?

MIKE: It's money!

KAREN: I'd give it back to the person who dropped it. It's not right to take someone's money and they don't know it. It's like stealing.

MIKE: No, it isn't. He *dropped* it! Finders, keepers—losers, weepers.

In this dilemma, as in the one before, Mike shows the same developmental immaturity: a very narrow, self-centered understanding of his responsibilities to others.

All children, Kohlberg argues, go through the same stages of development in their moral reasoning. Some go faster; some go farther. What determines how fast and how far they go is their moral environment. An important part of that environment is moral dialogue—interaction around moral questions, especially with people who are at adjacent, higher stages of moral development.

Wrestling with moral dilemmas, Kohlberg reasoned, would get kids really thinking, not just mouthing "right answers." And debating or listening to other kids at higher stages would, over time, stimulate the lower-stage students to revise their thinking toward the next higher level. And that is what more than a score of classroom studies actually showed for roughly half the students participating in such discussions.[10]

Kohlberg thus offered educators a nonrelativistic goal for moral education: *to stimulate moral development*. "Moral development" could be objectively, scientifically defined in terms of progress through the stages of moral reasoning. At each higher stage, a person is better able to stand in the shoes of others, integrate conflicting perspectives on a moral problem, appreciate the consequences of this or that course of action, and make a decision that respects the rights of all parties. To educators and parents who were unhappy with value clarification's empty neutrality and disturbing relativism, Kohlberg's message had a powerful appeal.

What are the moral stages Kohlberg asserted, and on what basis did he assert them? In *Raising Good Children* I describe each of these stages at length and ways that parents can stimulate stage development through everyday family life.[11] Here I'll give a thumbnail sketch of the stages, using the following dilemma:

Sharon's Dilemma: To Tell or Not to Tell?

Sharon and Jill were best friends. One day they went shopping together. Jill tried on a sweater and then, to Sharon's surprise, walked out of the store wearing the sweater under her coat. A moment later, the store's security officer stopped Sharon and demanded that she tell him the name of the girl who had walked out. He told the storeowner he'd seen the two girls together and was sure the one who left had been shoplifting.

The storeowner said to Sharon, "Come on now, come clean. You could get into serious trouble if you don't give us your friend's name."

Should Sharon give Jill's name to the storeowner? Why or why not? [12]

The accompanying box gives responses to Sharon's dilemma illustrating each of Kohlberg's five stages. Note that the same stage of moral reasoning can be used to generate different solutions; the stages represent the underlying *structure or quality of reasoning* rather than the specific content of what the person says should be done.

Kohlberg identified these stages on the basis of his 20-year study of 58 male subjects. (Subsequent research with females as well as males has confirmed Kohlberg's stages; [13] debate continues about whether there are sex differences in moral reasoning, but thus far clear empirical evidence is lacking. [14]) Kohlberg began his longitudinal interviews when his subjects were 10, 13, and 16. Every three years he went back and reinterviewed them, presenting the same set of moral dilemmas to see how and if their thinking had changed. At the conclusion of this two-decade research project, he reported:

- 56 of the 58 subjects showed upward stage change.

- Only four subjects showed a downward shift (to a lower stage) between any two testings.

- No subject skipped any stage.

- Only eight subjects in the sample (14%) showed any reasoning at the highest stage, Stage 5. [15]

DILEMMA DISCUSSION IN THE CLASSROOM

One of Kohlberg's doctoral students, Moshe Blatt, had a hunch that the moral dilemmas Kohlberg used in his research could be used to stimulate moral discussion in the classroom. Blatt was right; dilemma discussion over a period of several weeks, if directed by a teacher who posed or drew out higher-stage arguments, helped students advance in their moral reasoning. [16]

What does a moral dilemma discussion look like? Here's a glimpse of a class of eighth-graders debating Sharon's dilemma. The teacher has

---

KOHLBERG'S STAGES OF MORAL REASONING
(in response to Sharon's dilemma)

Stage 1: Avoidance of Punishment; "Will I Get in Trouble?"
　　"Sharon should tell. If she doesn't, she'll get in big trouble herself."
　　"She shouldn't tell. If she tells, she's going to be in hot water with Jill. Jill and her friends could make life miserable for her."

Stage 2: Tit-for-Tat Fairness; "What's In It for Me?"
　　"Why should Sharon have to take the rap for Jill? Jill looked out for herself, didn't she? Sharon should do the same."
　　"It depends on whether she owes Jill a favor—or whether she wants Jill to cover for her sometime."

Stage 3: Interpersonal Loyalty; "What Will People Think of Me?"
　　"What kind of a friend would turn in her best friend? She'll feel really terrible if she tells. And everybody will think she's a fink."
　　"If she doesn't tell, she's an accomplice to a crime. What's that going to do to her reputation?"

Stage 4: Concern for Societal Consequences; "What if Everybody Did It?"
　　"Sharon should tell, even though that would be very hard to do. Friendship is important, but it's just not fair for people to go around stealing. If you don't obey laws, society will fall apart."

Stage 5: "Respect the Rights of Every Person"
　　"Shoplifting would be wrong even if there were only one thief and one victim. Shoplifting violates the storeowner's rights as a person, and that's the reason for society's laws in the first place—to protect the rights of all of us."

---

asked small groups to make lists of "the best reasons why Sharon should tell Jill's name" and "the best reasons why Sharon should not tell." Note the nonrelativistic nature of the discussion that follows: attention to what Sharon *should* do (the moral question, focusing on obligation), and the premise that some reasons for telling or not telling will be better than others.

When the teacher called on the small groups to give their reports, this exchange occurred:

GEORGE: Jill could say, "I don't even know her. I just walked in the store off the street, and I don't even know where she lives."

TEACHER: So basically you're saying she should lie for a friend.

GEORGE: Yeah.

IRENE: I agree. Friendship matters more than a rule. The rules are there when you need them. But I at least would value a friend, somebody I could talk to, a lot more than a sweater. There is absolutely no comparison between emotions and material things.

TEACHER: Let's get the other group to explain "Thou shalt not steal." Perry?

PERRY: Well, you shouldn't steal. It's just not fair if everybody steals; you can't *live* if everybody goes around stealing.

ROLAND: It's like stealing from the rich and giving to the poor. It just doesn't work. The only thing that holds it together is the government, and you don't have government if everybody doesn't follow the rules.

TEACHER: What about the matter of these two reasons: "Thou shalt not steal" has been given as a reason for telling, friendship as a reason for not telling. Which is more important?

PERRY: I say if you don't tell on your friend, you will probably keep your crummy friend who left you standing there in the store. But even if you tell and lose your friend, somewhere along the line you will get some other friends, because I am sure that one or two people in this world are straight.[17]

George and Irene show the limitations of a Stage 3 interpersonal loyalty perspective. By contrast, Perry and Roland, reasoning at Stage 4, see the societywide consequences of stealing.

Note that friendship is still important at Stage 4, but it's not the *only* thing that's important. Perry, for example, indicates that he also values friends, but ones who are straight, who share his sense of responsibility and respect for the rights of others. A higher moral stage, such as Stage 4, doesn't toss out the values of lower stages; rather, it integrates them into a broader moral vision, a larger circle of concern for the welfare of others.

Does Stage 4 reasoning about this dilemma necessarily lead to the decision to tell on your friend? No. You might be very concerned about preserving your friendship and doing what's in the best long-range interest of your friend. You might try to get her to turn herself in. You might work on getting her to go straight in the future. But at Stage 4, no matter how much you cared about your friend, you'd also be concerned about the rights of the storeowner and the bigger moral issue—the societywide consequences of stealing.

The fact that several well-reasoned, higher-stage solutions are possible for Sharon's (or any other) dilemma suggests what a teacher should say to a class:

> *For this problem, there may be more than one good answer, and some answers may be better than others. Whatever solution you come up with, be prepared to support it with your best reasoning.*

With this approach, a teacher encourages students to use their own moral reasoning and allows for different responses. But at the same time the teacher challenges students to examine their reasoning and that of their peers critically.

THE TEACHER AS SOCRATES

In a moral discussion, Socratic "probe questions" by the teacher require students to go beyond just giving their opinions. Probe questions ask for the "whys."

Why should or why shouldn't Sharon tell? Would it make any difference if she and Jill were not good friends? Why or why not? Why is there a law against shoplifting? What moral issues are involved in this dilemma? Which is most important? Why? Eventually, studies show, these kinds of questions stimulate progress toward the next higher stage of moral development.

In one of the largest studies to date of moral dilemma discussions, Kohlberg and colleagues were able to bring about stage advances in moral reasoning in 20 different schools.[18] But within each school, there were some experimental classrooms where dilemma discussions produced stage gains and some classrooms where they did not. What made the difference?

Three things, the analysis showed, had to be present in a classroom for moral stage progress to occur:

1. Controversial dilemmas that provoked disagreement among students

2. "Stage mix" in the group (students at different stages of moral reasoning)

3. Extensive teacher use of Socratic "Why?" questions (which was the *only* teacher behavior on a hundred-item teacher observation inventory that differentiated "change" from "no change" classrooms).

FIRST-GRADERS TACKLE A MORAL DILEMMA

Can young children profit from moral dilemma discussion? Here's a dilemma that teacher Kathy Kittle presented to her class of first-graders:

Mark and the Movies

Mark was on the way to the movies when he met his friend Steven. Steven said he really wanted to see this movie, too, but he spent all his allowance and wouldn't be getting any more until after the movie left town. Both Mark and Steven were 12 but could easily pass for younger. If they lied about their age, they could both get in on the money Mark had.

Mark didn't know, though, if he should lie about his age. Steven said, "It's your money, so it's your decision."

What should Mark do? [19]

Here's how the discussion went with these 6-year-olds:

TEACHER: Okay, what do you think Mark should do?

JOHN: Him and Steven should tell them how old they are.

EMILY: They shouldn't lie about their age.

TEACHER: Why do you think they shouldn't lie?

TINA: Because if they *did* lie, they'd get a spanking.

JOHN: Mark shouldn't lie about his age because it leads to a mess.

TEACHER: What kind of a mess?

JOHN: His mother might find out.

SARA: The father, too.

ERIN: They'd get punished.

TEACHER: So you all think Mark and Steven *shouldn't* lie because they might get caught and punished. What if no one catches them—would it be right to lie then?

MOST: Yes!

BILLY: No, it's not. The manager of the show *might* catch them.

TEACHER: But what if no one catches them?

BILLY: Then it's all right.

The teacher comments on the amount of Stage 1 thinking brought out by the discussion so far: "I was surprised at how punishment-oriented my kids were. Fear of getting caught was their *only* reason for not lying. If they thought they wouldn't get caught, then it was okay to lie."

"Who thinks it would *still* be wrong to lie," she asked the class, "even if Mark and Steven wouldn't get caught?"

Five children raised their hands. The discussion continued:

TROY: They'd still get in a mixed-up mess.

TEACHER: How?

TROY: Steven might tell somebody that they lied.

TEACHER: He might, that's true. But would it still be wrong even if Steven *didn't* tell anybody?

TROY: Yes.

TEACHER: Why, Troy?

TROY: [reaching] I don't know . . . but it is.

EMILY: It's not nice to lie.

TROY: [in a rush] Yeah, and it's not *fair* to other people, either!

TEACHER: Who wouldn't it be fair to?

TROY: The others in the show. *They* had to pay full price.

TEACHER: You mean if other 12-year-old kids had to pay the full price for their tickets, then it's not fair for Mark and Steven to get in cheaper?

TROY: Right.

The teacher comments:

I considered Troy's comment a real breakthrough. I went back to the kids who originally said it would be okay to lie if they could get away with it. Some of them still said it would be all right to lie as long as they didn't get caught. However, two of them now said they thought it wouldn't be fair, though they had trouble explaining why.

At this point several children were getting tired, so I didn't push it. I decided to bring in some everyday dilemmas—like cutting into lunch line, and taking kids' things without their permission—that would make the issue of fairness more concrete to them.

For this teacher, the most valuable part of the discussion was her discovery of how punishment-oriented her children were in their moral reasoning. That's where most first-graders are developmentally, though they can be helped to progress beyond it. But it's also where a lot of students will remain unless they are helped, somewhere in their personal experience or education, to develop higher-stage reasons for respecting moral rules.

A case in point: Richard Gulbin, a student teacher at Cortland College, caught a seventh-grade boy cheating on a test. He took the boy's paper and asked him to see him after class. Their dialogue went like this:

STUDENT TEACHER: Why do you think I took your paper?

SEVENTH-GRADER: Because I was cheating.

Student Teacher: Don't you think it's wrong to cheat?

SEVENTH-GRADER: No, it's just wrong to get caught.

It is important for teachers to realize that students are moral thinkers, with their own moral perspective. Just because they have been bombarded for years with moral rules and expectations ("Don't lie," "Don't cheat," "Don't steal") doesn't mean they've made them their own. Many teachers, unfortunately, don't know how their students think morally because they haven't engaged them in the kind of dialogue that would reveal their moral reasoning.

Helping teachers get *inside* the minds of their students is one of the major contributions of moral dilemmas. Once teachers are in touch with how students are thinking, they can begin to take the next step: helping them develop their moral reasoning toward greater maturity.

CHAPTER 13

Raising the Level of Moral Discussion

R ichard Gulbin, the student teacher who caught one of his seventh-graders cheating, decided that the whole class would benefit from an open discussion of cheating. He opted to approach the issue by presenting a parallel hypothetical dilemma:

Mary's Dilemma

John and Mary are students in seventh-grade social studies. On a test, Mary notices that John is looking at her paper and writing down answers. Mary knows that John was at the game room in the mall the night before while she was studying hard for the test.

What should Mary do? What would you do if you were Mary?

Students suggested a variety of things Mary might do: cover her paper, tell the teacher, try to get John to tell the teacher he was cheating, or tell John after the test why it wasn't fair for him to cheat.

The main value of this discussion, the student teacher felt, was to begin to develop a student consensus that cheating wasn't fair to all the people who were working honestly for their grades.

WHAT SHOULD A TEACHER DO WHEN STUDENTS ARGUE FOR BAD VALUES?

Student teacher Gulbin was able to elicit a majority view that cheating wasn't fair. But what if most of his students had argued that cheating was okay, at least some of the time?

That's what happened in the classroom of Diane Daniels,[1] a thoughtful, articulate teacher of grades 7 to 9 English at an independent school in Colorado. She suspected two of her ninth-graders of cheating but "didn't have the goods on them." So she came at the issue obliquely, through a short story called "So Much Unfairness of Things" (by C. D. B. Bryan and originally published in the June 2, 1962 the *New Yorker*). The story is about a high school boy who cheats on a Latin exam; is reported by a classmate; and, as required by the school's honor code, is expelled.

At one point in her class's discussion of the story, teacher Daniels asked, "Do you think it's wrong to cheat?"

Most of the class argued that "it depends." If the subject being taught is important and the teacher is fair, they said, then it's wrong to cheat. But if the subject is "dumb" or the teacher isn't fair, then it's okay to cheat.

Would they ever turn somebody in for cheating? Absolutely not; friendship was more important than some "adult rule." Well, if somebody got an A on a paper at the expense of others, *that* would be unfair and they might turn that person in.

"All in all," Diane Daniels commented, "theirs was a highly situational morality." She said she was not at ease with how this discussion turned out. It certainly didn't help her cause of influencing the two suspected cheaters toward greater honesty.

Any time a teacher brings up a value issue—whether it's cheating, shoplifting, drugs, sex, or anything else—some or even a majority of the students may take a stand that is less than morally upright. Some may even argue strongly for positions that the teacher feels—and objective ethics would hold—are clearly irresponsible and unethical. Students may openly hold racist or sexist attitudes. Others may argue that cheating is okay; or that shoplifting is justified because of the high prices stores charge; or that sex, drugs, and drinking are fun, everybody does it, and nobody gets hurt.

In one sense, morally immature thinking by students is not an educational "problem"; after all, if students showed only high-level thinking about ethical issues, they would have no need of moral education (at least not in the intellectual realm). The problem comes when the teacher doesn't know what to say in response to low-level student thinking. To remain silent, not to get students to examine critically an ethically deficient position, or even to dissent unpersuasively feels like an educational failure to the teacher—and, unfortunately, it is.

The problem grows as students enter their teens and become more cynical; more likely to take and defend a position that runs counter to authority; more glib in arguing their case; and, in many cases, more experienced at and casual about irresponsible behavior.

The upshot: For many teachers, especially at the secondary level, fear of a low-level group response is the chief block to discussing moral questions. They're afraid that many, most, or even all of the students who speak will argue for undesirable values. Maybe it's better, these teachers think, to skip discussing value issues altogether.

THE TEACHER AS DISCUSSION LEADER

The solution to this problem lies in the quality of the teacher's strategies and skills as a discussion leader.

In the previous chapter we saw that Socratic questioning is one of those discussion skills. This chapter explores several other important skills and strategies that enable a teacher to respond to low-level student thinking and to structure moral discussion to draw forth the highest-level thinking of which the students are capable.

Here are five guidelines:

1. **Set a nonrelativistic context for discussion.** Teachers need to keep in mind that many students will have assimilated the moral relativism of the culture. They will come to any moral discussion with the attitude, "Who's to say what's right? It's just a matter of your personal opinion." A teacher can set the stage for discussion with a statement that affirms students' right to their viewpoint but at the same time challenges them to see that people can be mistaken in their moral judgments:

> Whenever we discuss a value issue in this class, freedom of thought gives you the right to form and express your own opinion. But remember, your right to your opinion doesn't mean your opinion is right.
> Down through history, many people have been wrong who at the time felt strongly that they were right. Many Americans once argued fiercely that they had the right to own another human being as a slave. That terrible moral mistake was even written into our original Constitution and

reaffirmed by the U.S. Supreme Court in its infamous *Dred Scott* decision. Men once argued passionately that women should not have the right to vote. Societies once practiced infanticide, especially against female babies, and in some parts of the world still do.

In view of the serious moral mistakes that even intelligent people have made in the past, all of us have a responsibility to ask: How do I *know* I'm right in what I think? And how should any of us go about deciding what's right and what's wrong?

Challenging students' relativism also requires teaching them the general ethical criteria that apply to any moral issue: Does a given action, rule, or policy respect the rights of the persons affected by it? Does it meet the tests of reversibility (would I want such a thing done to me?) and universalizability (would I want everyone to act this way?)? Does the action produce good or bad consequences—in the long run as well as the short run—for the individual and the whole society?

2. **Plan problem-specific questions that will challenge students' thinking.** Even young children can be helped to grasp objective ethical criteria if a teacher's questions are formulated correctly. For example, the *Personal and Societal Values* guide published by Ontario's Ministry of Education suggests the following simple dilemma for use in the younger grades:

> After school, Marie sees a soccer ball under a bush in the schoolyard. She has always wanted a soccer ball and thinks of how the school has lots of them and wouldn't miss this one. Should she take it?

To help children make this moral decision, the guide suggests these questions: "If someone found your soccer ball, what would you want him or her to do? . . . What would happen if all the boys and girls did what you suggest Marie do? Would it make school a better or worse place?"[2]

Teachers should also ask themselves, "What questions will I pose if students take such-and-such a position?"

What questions, for example, might have enabled Diane Daniels to get her ninth graders to examine critically their "It depends" morality concerning cheating? Here are some:

• Imagine you were the teacher of this class. Would it bother you if your students cheated? If so, why?

• How does cheating affect the trust between us?

- Is cheating fair to students who aren't cheating?

- If you think a teacher is unfair, or that his or her course is "dumb," is cheating on that teacher's tests an ethical response? What might be a better response?

- If cheating is okay because the teacher isn't fair or the course isn't important to you, does that mean people can pick and choose when they want to be honest?

- Is cheating currently a problem in our society? If so, how?

- Are your own values and character—the kind of person you are— affected in any way when you cheat? If so, how?

Some questions could be raised in an initial discussion; others could be made part of a writing assignment; others could be posed in a subsequent discussion of the issue.

A Westport, Connecticut, teacher said that one of her high school history classes recently insisted that "cheating is a victimless crime." Questions like those listed above can help students begin to see that cheating has many victims, including the person who cheats.

3. **Choose a reflection/discussion format that requires careful thinking.** A teacher does well to choose a format for moral reflection and discussion that helps students think carefully and critically about a value issue. There's a big difference, for example, between a loose, open-ended approach that simply invites students to voice their opinions and an approach requiring that they engage in research and/or systematic ethical analysis before taking or arguing a position.

4. **Challenge students to keep thinking about the issue.** Teachers may find themselves in values discussions where they don't have prepared questions and can't come up with them on the spot. In that case, they can at least challenge students to keep thinking about the issue and can indicate an intent to return to it. To encourage continuing thought, the teacher can also give students a thought-provoking reading on the topic and ask them to write a paragraph in response.

5. **Anchor discussions in a curriculum-based approach.** Finally, it's best *not* to treat difficult issues such as cheating, shoplifting, sex, drinking, etc., through off-the-cuff discussions or one-shot values activities. A superficial teaching approach almost always assures a superficial student response. Serious moral reflection is much more likely if classroom discussion is anchored in a planned, intellectually rigorous, curriculum-based approach. Such an approach (discussed at length in Chapter 9) can take several forms:

- **Ethical discussion integrated into an academic subject** such as social studies (e.g., What have been the effects of prejudice and discrimination in history?), science (e.g., How does scientific fraud—scientists faking their data—undermine the enterprise of science?), or literature (e.g., What moral choices do the characters in this story have, and do they make ethical decisions?).

- **A published program** of thoughtfully sequenced activities, with suggestions for guiding discussion.

- **A teacher-created curriculum unit,** spanning several days or weeks and centered on a particular value such as respect, honesty, compassion, or courage.

A curriculum-based approach gives a teacher much more quality control over discussion. Students are required to investigate, read, reflect, write, and form and discuss their value positions as an outgrowth of extended, serious inquiry.

Let's look at some examples of these approaches and how they help to advance students' moral thinking.

USE A STRUCTURED FORMAT THAT FOSTERS CRITICAL THINKING

Carol Lynch teaches at Roberts Street Elementary School in Canastota, New York. She illustrates the use of rational decision-making, a format that teaches students to approach a problem in a deliberate, step-by-step way. Students identify the important values at stake; think of alternative solutions; consider the likely consequences of each alternative; and then choose the best solution (the one that maximizes the positive consequences and respects the important values involved). This is a nonrelativistic approach to moral problem-solving because it assumes that there are objectively important values and objectively beneficial or harmful consequences of different courses of action.

Carol Lynch decided to apply the rational decision-making format to an issue that came up when she had her sixth-graders complete the following sheet:

What's Your Dilemma?

I would like the discussions we're having to be helpful to you. You can let me know what dilemmas you are actually facing in your lives by completing any or all of the sentences on this sheet. Don't sign your name unless you want to.

1. I never know how to decide what to do when . . .

2. The toughest decision I ever had to make was . . .

3. I don't want to lose my friends, but I disagree with them about . . .

Some students wrote flippant responses, the teacher says, but most took it seriously. In response to item 2, "The toughest decision I ever had to make was . . . ," one student wrote, ". . . whether or not to take a slug of beer."

To pursue the beer-drinking issue and the larger problem of dealing with peer pressure, teacher Lynch gave the class the following dilemma:

"Don't Be a Nerd"

Tory, Kris, and Sue, all seventh-graders, are friends. One night they're at Tory's house watching TV while her parents are out for the evening. After a few shows, they decide they're hungry. Opening the refrigerator, Tory sees some leftover chicken and a six-pack of beer. "Hey," she says, "let's have some chicken and beer!" Kris says, "Great!"

"Have you guys had beer before?" Sue asks.

Tory and Kris both say sure, they've had beer. Not to get drunk, just to have a little fun. That's news to Sue.

"I think I'll just have chicken," Sue says.

"Come on, don't be a nerd!" Tory says. "A little beer won't hurt you. Nobody will ever know! *We'll* never tell!"

Sue doesn't want to look like a nerd, but she knows her parents don't want her to drink and have trusted her to respect that. She wonders if it would be okay just this one time . . . but she feels a tightening in her stomach when she thinks of doing that.

Tory and Kris each open up a can of beer and take a swig. Tory opens a third can and holds it out to Sue: "Hey, what's the big deal? *Try* it— you'll like it!"

What should Sue do?[3]

Teacher Lynch first helped the class decide what values were involved in this situation. Having identified the key values of honesty, trust, friendship, and self-respect, students were ready to work on the problem individually. They did so by responding in writing to the following questions:[4]

1. Suppose Sue told herself she didn't have any choice but to go along with Tory and Kris. Would she be telling herself the truth or not? _____ Explain.

2. If you were Sue's conscience, what would you say to her?

3. In the following boxes, write the alternatives you think Sue has in making her decision, and the possible consequences each alternative might have.

Alternative 1: _____
Consequence: _____
Consequence: _____
Consequence: _____

Alternative 2: _____
Consequence: _____
Consequence: _____
Consequence: _____

Alternative 3: _____
Consequence: _____
Consequence: _____
Consequence: _____

4. What do you think is the *most* important value involved in this situation? _____ Why?

_____

_____

_____

5. Keeping in mind the good and the bad consequences of the different alternatives, and the most important value, what do you think is the best decision? _____

_____

_____

Explain why:

After the students completed the individual work sheets, the teacher asked them to share their thoughts in groups of three and try to come to a consensus about the best alternative and the rationale for it.

When they reconvened, the overwhelming sentiment was that Sue should turn down her friends' offer of a beer. Some students, however, offered various "compromises," such as just taking a sip, or pouring the beer down the bathroom sink when her friends weren't looking. That led to a lively discussion of whether such courses of action were consistent with the values of trust and self-respect and whether Sue would just be letting herself in for more trouble because her friends would expect her to drink in the future.

With these sixth-graders, the rational decision-making format succeeded in eliciting a consensus against violating parents' trust and against drinking. Would a teacher be able to get that same consensus with, say, high school juniors or seniors? Not likely, given how well entrenched drinking is in the current peer culture. At that age level, making even a dent in the drinking culture would require a long-term commitment to a well-designed values and health education curriculum (see Chapter 19). There is also the hope that values-based health education that begins in the elementary grades will help to steer at least some youngsters away from present patterns of alcohol use.

The rational decision-making format can be applied to a wide range of problems and issues (current events issues as well as interpersonal ones). Its basic message to young people is this: When you have an important decision to make, take the time to *think*. Think of the values that will help you know what's right and what is wrong. Think of your options. Think of the consequences. Then decide.

Appealing computer software is now available that teaches students to apply rational decision-making to a variety of problems. S.M.A.R.T. Choices (where S.M.A.R.T. stands for "Students Master the Art of Responsible Thinking"), designed for grades 5 through 12, helps students make responsible decisions about drugs, sex, and behavior in and out of school. The Choices, Choices series, aimed at kindergarten through grade 5, deals with playground conflicts, friendship issues, and truth-telling dilemmas. (For information about these and other values education software, contact Tom Snyder Productions, 90 Sherman St., Cambridge, MA 02140-9923; tel. 1-800-342-0236.)[5]

USING A PUBLISHED CURRICULUM TO DEVELOP MORAL REFLECTION

As I pointed out in Chapter 9, there are some very-well-designed published curricula in values education that talented people have spent years putting together and field-testing. The best of these published programs sequence activities so that one builds logically on another and there's a cumulative development in students' thinking about values. You can see this progression in the Grade 8 Ethics Course developed by ethics specialist Joan Engel and colleagues for the Ministry of Education of Alberta, Canada.[6] Here are sample activities from this curriculum:

1. **The ethical person.** The teacher divides the class into small groups and asks each to brainstorm "the characteristics of an ethical person" and write them on a life-sized paper cutout of a human figure.

The several cutout ethical persons are then posted around the room. The whole class goes from figure to figure, with the teacher asking students to note similarities and differences and inviting each group to explain its reasons for including particular ethical qualities.

2. **Ethics-in-action project.** Each small group selects *one* characteristic (e.g., "honest," "respectful," "courageous," "altruistic") of its ideal ethical person and brainstorms ways in which that characteristic could be demonstrated and fostered in the classroom, peer group, school, family, and community. Each group then:

• Decides on *one* way of demonstrating the selected characteristic in the peer group, school, family, and community that they would be willing to commit themselves to trying.

• Makes a list of how they could do this.

• Reports its action plan to the class.

• Carries out its plan over the next 4 to 5 weeks and reports the results to the class.

3. **Ethics in the world.** Students gather newspaper, magazine, and other articles that mention the word "ethics"; at the same time they examine codes of ethics from a variety of professions such as teaching, law, and medicine. After studying these examples, students draft a code of ethics for their own classroom and/or school.

4. **Guest lectures on ethics in the professions.** The class invites members of various professions to come in and speak about the relevance of ethics to their jobs. This can help refute the popular notion that "in the real world you can't be too ethical if you want to survive." A lot of people, young and old, think that it's okay to talk about the right thing to do, but that in a tough and competitive world you've got to play "hardball." Lawyers, doctors, political leaders, journalists, and businessmen who are both successful *and* striving to be ethical give students important role models.

Guest speakers from these fields can tell students the ethical questions they have to deal with and how it is indeed often possible to have integrity, do good in the world, and still work within the organization. They can also give examples of ethically upstanding companies and other institutions that have managed to demonstrate both success and a concern for honesty and human welfare. Finally, they can talk about the times when the prompting of their consciences put them in conflict with those around them—and how they dealt with that.

A TEACHER-DESIGNED CURRICULUM UNIT

Fifth-grade teacher Bill Van Slyke of Ithaca, New York, designed his own curriculum unit to foster thoughtful, sustained reflection about the value of honesty. He comments: "My goal in this unit was to promote my students' valuing of honesty—with parents, with friends, and with people in general—and especially as a positive attribute of their classroom community. I wanted them gradually to find it easier to be honest with each other and to recognize the benefits of honesty over time."

His unit combined media, moral dilemma discussions, and student journal entries. At one point in the unit he showed a film called *To Tell the Truth*.[7] Films have a special value: They can dramatize a moral problem in a way that arouses strong student interest and has emotional as well as intellectual impact.[8]

To Tell the Truth demonstrates both the benefits of honesty and the perils of deceit. As the film opens, 8-year-old Callie, feeling bad about a poor report card, lies to a classmate about her grades. Later she accidentally ruins classmate Tara's homework but remains silent when the teacher tries to find out what happened to Tara's paper. During recess, children shout "Liar! Liar!" when Callie denies stepping on the line in a game of foursquare.

Finally, Callie unburdens her troubled conscience to her teacher. The teacher comforts her and gently counsels, "It's hard to tell the truth sometimes, but everyone feels better in the end." Callie gets up the courage to tell Tara the truth about her crumpled paper, Tara forgives her, and the two become friends.[9]

The teacher's guide suggests stopping the film at two points and posing questions to focus children's thinking and stimulate brief discussion. For example, at the point where the teacher asks who knows what happened to Tara's paper, suggested questions include: What will happen if Callie tells the truth? What will happen if Callie remains silent? What do you think she should do?

End-of-the-film questions include: What did the teacher mean when she said, "It's hard to tell the truth sometimes, but everyone feels better in the end"? Can a lie hurt the person who tells it? Can a lie hurt someone else? How?

In the discussion that teacher Van Slyke had with his class, one boy said, "A lie is like a weight you carry around afterward." Another boy thought the movie "was a good example of what lies can do" but didn't think "just telling Tara about the homework would make them instant friends." A girl said the film reminded her of a saying she'd heard: "One lie leads to another."

At the end of the unit on honesty, the teacher asked these 10-year-olds to write a journal entry on what they thought they had gained from writing and talking about issues of honesty. One girl wrote: "I learned that all the times I've been lying, I've been making a big mistake. And I should stop because it could hurt someone." Another wrote:

I have learned that like the teacher said, you feel better when you tell the truth. Then you don't have it weighing on your shoulders. It makes the person you lied to feel better and it makes you feel better. People might find out you lied and not trust you anymore.

About this unit, teacher Van Slyke reflects:

Observing changes in behavior, as opposed to reasoning, I found more problematic. While I sometimes felt I saw students being more honest with each other when disputes arose, these changes are more difficult to pinpoint, since they occur slowly.

I could have improved this unit by integrating it more into other curricular areas—literature and social studies, for example. In the future I would also make greater use of role-playing, building on my fifth-graders' love of acting.

I do feel that honesty, lying, and trust in relationships are very real issues to my children. Giving them an opportunity to deal with them validates their thoughts, questions, and even their confusion about sometimes difficult choices. At its best moments, this did not feel at all like an "imposed" curriculum, but one that grew out of my students' interests and needs.

ROLE-PLAYING

The role-playing that teacher Van Slyke says he'd do more of is another moral reflection strategy that challenges students to go beyond superficial thinking.

Role-playing is highly involving, enjoyable for students of all ages, and does an especially good job of fostering perspective-taking. When you have to play a certain role in a moral situation, you really enter into that person's view, think how he thinks, feel how he feels. Teachers who have role-played moral dilemmas themselves in a workshop often comment on how they "really saw a situation differently" when they had to take a particular character's part. One research study found that role-playing was far and away the most effective method of stimulating student interest and involvement.[10]

Elizabeth Saenger of Fieldston Lower School in Riverdale, New York, makes use of role-playing through what she calls "ethics plays." In these miniplays, children will often act out incidents that have just happened to them. Students who were just involved in a conflict, for example, will choose the parts they wish to play in reenacting it (the parts they choose are often different from their actual roles in the incident). "The vehicle of the play," teacher Saenger says, "helps us get the issue out into the open, talk about it, and see it from different perspectives."

Role-playing is also a good way to conclude a rational decision-making activity, such as the one Carol Lynch conducted around the beer-drinking dilemma. Especially with a peer pressure dilemma, students need to be able to act out various ways in which the situation could be handled—the words to say, the moves to make. From grade 6 on, the concern with being "cool" is very strong. Role-playing helps students work out the specific behaviors needed to carry out the solutions developed through reflective decision-making.

Educating for Citizenship,[11] a curriculum that teaches students the rights and responsibilities of citizenship and gives them opportunities to practice citizenship skills, uses role-playing extensively.

"GOOD ETHICS"/"BAD ETHICS" DRAWINGS

When you walk into Elizabeth Saenger's classroom, the first thing you notice is all the children's drawings that cover the walls and partitions. Closer inspection reveals that each drawing is labeled either "Good Ethics" or "Bad Ethics" and has a caption on the bottom explaining what is depicted.

The creators of these artistic ethical statements are second-, third-, and fourth-graders who have been invited by teacher Saenger to "draw pictures based on your own experiences that show good ethics or bad ethics." From the following captions you can get an idea of the moral events children choose to represent:

"Good Ethics"
1. "This is good ethics because I am making up with my best friend after we had a fight."

2. "Two boys were teasing me about my Cabbage Patch doll. I wanted to tease back, but I didn't because that wouldn't be the right thing to do. So I just ignored them, and kept ignoring them, and soon they stopped."

3. "This is good ethics because a girl made friends with a new girl and still kept her old friend."

"Bad Ethics"
1. "I shot a basket and someone hit it away. They all laughed. That was *bad* ethics."

2. "The person sitting on my father's car just said 'Shut up!' to me even though I asked him to get off in a nice way. I don't think that was ethical because he didn't respect me."

3. "This is bad ethics because the boy broke his mother's vase and blamed it on his little sister."

The teacher comments:

The kids really like expressing their thinking about ethics in a picture. We talk about their pictures in class. . . . We come to define ethics as "the study of how people should treat each other."

This approach has several things to recommend it: It makes direct use of children's own moral experiences. It has children draw—something children like to do that puts their moral experiences and thinking into a concrete, visible form for other students to react to. Moreover, the mounted drawings provide a public, cumulative record of the children's thinking about ethical issues—an opportunity to observe progressions and themes in their thinking.

Finally, the "good ethics," "bad ethics" pictures provide an abundance of clear moral situations of the sort that children need as they build up their ideas about right and wrong. Good character, after all, is more often a matter of doing what's kind, fair, and honest in everyday situations than it is a matter of solving complex moral dilemmas.

LEARNING TO JUDGE WISELY

One of the qualities of wise judgment, philosopher Jon Moline says, is seeking the advice of more experienced persons when we have to make a difficult decision.[12]

Traditionally, people who faced hard decisions have sought advice from persons they respect: parents, grandparents, teachers, an older brother or sister, a best friend, a religious counselor. Many young persons today talk only to their peers about problems—even suicidal feelings—if they talk to anyone at all.

We should help them develop a different mind-set—one that values advice from several sources, including wiser heads. We can do that by structuring educational exercises in decision-making that encourage intelligent advice-seeking.

At the two independent schools where Bill Valentine has taught, he has specialized in values education programs for middle schoolers. Often, when he gives them a moral dilemma, he asks not only "What should you do?" and "What would you do?" but also "Who would you ask for advice? Why? What do you think they would say?"

One dilemma teacher Valentine uses in this manner is adapted from the chapter "The Price of Belonging" in the book *I'm Not Alone* by Walter Limbacher:

The Silver Sisters

Holly had finally made it. All the Silver Sisters had agreed to let her join their club. The sisters held parties and picnics at each other's houses. Still, only the neatest, best-dressed, and most popular girls belonged. The twelve Sisters were the best that the fifth and sixth grades of two schools had to offer.

At her first meeting, Holly discovered why the Sisters were called "Silver." Each wore a silver pin. Before Holly could be a club member, she would have to steal her silver pin from the jewelry counter of the department store in the shopping center.

While she was getting her pin, the other sisters would be watching from various spots around the store. That way they could be sure Holly did not buy her pin.

Holly was shocked. All the girls were from well-off families. Holly thought they had all been brought up as she had. To her, stealing was very wrong. She had never stolen so much as a pencil.

She wanted more than anything to be one of the Silver Sisters. It was the top group. Belonging would make her one of the best.

Holly wrestled with the problem for the rest of the meeting.

What should Holly do?

After some class discussion of what Holly should do, teacher Valentine asks, "If this were your problem, to whom would you go for advice? What would they say?"

He follows up with more specific questions: "What advice would your mother or father give you? Your favorite teacher? Your most trusted friend? Someone who owned a store? A relative who was a policeman? Someone who had been arrested once for shoplifting? Someone you considered your enemy?"

Another good source of material for moral questions are letters to Ann Landers or Dear Abby. One girl wrote in, "Dear Abby, I'm 16, I'm pregnant, and I'm scared to death to tell my folks. What should I do?" As a homework assignment, students could ask persons they respect, "What advice do you think Abby should give?" Sharing the various responses the next day in class should make clear the value of listening to the thoughtful judgments of others before arriving at your own.

HELPING STUDENTS DEVELOP MORAL SELF-KNOWLEDGE

Any serious program of moral reflection should also foster the kind of moral knowledge that is hardest of all to attain but is vital for character development: knowing oneself.

We should help young people realize, for example, that while it is often easy to know what is right, it is usually harder to do it. Students need practice both as moral psychologists (who understand why people act as they do) and as moral philosophers (who can judge what is right). They should reflect on why they and other people sometimes cheat, lie, put people down, or treat others unfairly, even when they know such things are wrong. In the process of reflecting on these questions, students can deepen their knowledge of their own individual characters—where they are strong, where they need to grow.

An eighth-grade English teacher at Chicago's Reilly Elementary School explains how she helps her students develop this kind of moral self-knowledge:

> We go from talking about the traits of characters in a novel to talking about their own character traits. I start them off asking them to list their physical characteristics, then a good character trait they feel they have. They list things like, "I help at home when I'm asked," and "I take care of my little brothers and sisters."
>
> Then I ask them to put down a character trait they're not so proud of, one they'd like to correct. The negative trait is often the flip side of the positive one: "I don't always do what I'm asked," "I fight with my brothers and sisters." I ask them to plan how they'll try to change that and set a time line. They tend to set the goal too soon, but that's okay; I help them focus on whatever improvements they do make.

Some teachers encourage students to keep "ethics journals." This activity can be especially helpful to students who seem to have little awareness of their own behavior and trouble translating their moral reasoning into how they respond to the world around them.

Teacher Elizabeth Saenger has her children keep "Ethics in Action" journals based on their school experiences. She gives them examples of what to write about (conflicts on the playground, problems with friends, ethical things they do that they're proud of, and so on). One third-grade girl wrote in her journal:

> I know I *shouldn't* be mean back to someone, but if I don't, it burns and burns inside of me and I can't stand it. So I write a letter to that person but don't send it. I write it every day, and at the end of the week, I crumple it up.

The teacher complimented this girl on her resourceful method of self-control.

HOW TO ENCOURAGE AND ENHANCE MORAL REFLECTION
(from Chapters 12 and 13)

1. Take time to deal with real-life moral issues from the life of the classroom and school.

2. Use stories to teach the simple virtues.

3. Discuss hypothetical moral dilemmas as a way of diagnosing and developing students' moral reasoning.

4. Use parallel dilemmas to get at real classroom problems.

5. Draw out students' own dilemmas.

6. Increase the likelihood of high-level student thinking in a class discussion by:
   - Setting a nonrelativistic context for discussion.
   - Planning problem-specific questions that challenge students' thinking.
   - Choosing a reflection/discussion format (such as rational decision-making) that helps students think critically about the issue at hand.
   - Challenging students to keep thinking about the issue.
   - Anchoring moral discussion in a curriculum-based approach (an academic lesson, a published program, or a teacher-designed unit).

7. Use role-playing to foster perspective-taking.

8. Design decision-making activities that encourage intelligent advice-seeking.

9. Help students develop moral self-knowledge through personal ethics journals, character improvement projects, and discussions of conscience.

"WHAT IS A CONSCIENCE?"

Ron Woods is a veteran fifth-grade teacher at Birch Meadow Elementary School in Reading, Massachusetts. To help his students develop moral self-knowledge, he had them write about "conscience." He gave them these thought-provoking questions:

1. What is a conscience?

2. Does everybody have one?

3. When does your conscience appear?

4. Do you listen to your conscience?

5. Which do you consider your conscience: an enemy or a friend?

6. What advice would you give to other people about their conscience?

In class discussion one girl said, "A conscience is an inner voice that tells you what's right and what's wrong. I think everyone has one, but some people don't listen to it all the time." A boy said, "A conscience is the part of your mind that has the job of decision-maker. My conscience appears just before an incident occurs. Most of the time I listen to it, but there are times when my conscience sleeps through an incident."

Clearly, there's valuable material here for moral reflection: Why does your conscience sometimes "sleep through" an incident? How can you keep it awake?

Teachers find stimulating and guiding moral reflection to be the most difficult part of values education. Partly that's because moral discussion tends to bring into the open not only students' developmental immaturity but also all of the relativistic thinking and undesirable values prevalent in the culture. Dealing constructively with that requires a repertoire of sophisticated skills: framing the moral issue; helping students move beyond relativism; preparing questions that will draw out and challenge students' moral reasoning; selecting a discussion format that is most likely to elicit students' best thinking; understanding the stages of moral reasoning; getting students to explain and justify their reasoning rather than just giving their opinions; encouraging good listening and interaction; using Socratic questioning to focus the discussion on the relevant moral issues; and helping students apply their best moral reasoning to their own behaviors.

With time, patience, and practice, however, dedicated teachers can and do develop these skills. However challenging it may be for the teacher, the effort to engage young people in thoughtful moral reflection is clearly essential. Thinking isn't all there is to morality, but there can be no morality without it.

CHAPTER 14

Teaching Controversial Issues

Most of the significant issues of the day—Central America, AIDS, South Africa, abortion—are also the most controversial. As a result, they are too often excluded from the classroom. To censor controversy is to tell our students that they will not learn in school what people care most about in life.

> —JEROLD M. STARR, Director of the
> Center for Social Studies
> Education [1]

The good of a nation demands the consideration of serious ethical questions. If education ignores the value and moral aspect of the human psyche, where will society find citizens able to make mature moral decisions?

> —A. K. BENJAMIN, Centre for
> Human Development and Social
> Change [2]

When everyone thinks alike, no one thinks very much.

> —Poster at an educational
> conference

Nothing gets attention—or stimulates thinking—like controversy. And yet most schools avoid controversy like the plague. Teachers worry about discussions getting out of hand. Administrators worry about parental objections. Everybody worries about bias in the handling of issues where feelings run deep and balanced treatment is difficult.

As a consequence, controversy tends to be kept out of the curriculum. An opportunity for high-quality moral discussion and education for democratic citizenship is thereby lost.

Now, I *don't* recommend that schools plunge into controversial issues when they're trying to get a values education program off the ground. Given our highly pluralistic, contentious society, people are already prone to expect conflict and division when you suggest teaching values in the schools. Fortunately, as we've seen, there are many noncontroversial values (e.g., respect, responsibility, honesty) that schools can and do teach in noncontroversial ways (modeling, community-building, cooperative learning, and so on).

These commonly accepted ways of teaching commonly accepted values must be kept in the forefront of any values education effort. They represent the common ethical ground that is foundational for both moral education and the building of a moral society.

But it's also true that commonly accepted values—such as life and liberty, loyalty and justice, individual freedom and the common good, economic development and protection of the environment—come into conflict. That's what creates controversy. Since controversy is a fact of life, it is artificial, and a poor preparation for citizenship, for schools to try to avoid all controversial issues. How can we hope to develop citizens capable of making reasoned judgments about the difficult moral questions of our day if students never learn to think critically about complex issues?

DEALING FAIRLY WITH A CONTROVERSIAL ISSUE: THE VIETNAM WAR

The Vietnam War was the longest, the second most costly, and, with the exception of the Civil War, the most divisive military conflict in U.S. history. For millions of Americans, the war is still an open wound. Basic questions remain: Why did we go to war in Vietnam? Was it a just war? Could we have won it? Should we have wanted to? What lessons does it have to teach us?

Despite its significance, the Vietnam War is "covered" in only one or two pages by standard U.S. high school textbooks. Many students' knowledge of the war is on a par with that of the young woman cabdriver, just out of high school, who insisted to her rider that the Vietnamese were the ones we fought in World War II.[3]

Recently, however, enterprising educators have found ways to give the Vietnam War the attention it deserves. And the approaches to that complex and emotional subject shed light on a larger question in values education: How should teachers handle controversial issues?

The most comprehensive Vietnam War curriculum is a new program called The Lessons of the Vietnam War.[4] It was meticulously developed by Jerold M. Starr, director of the Center for Social Studies Education in Pittsburgh, with the help of 150 scholars, teachers, and Vietnam War veterans representing a wide range of views on the war.

"My mission," says Starr, "is to complicate students' thinking. They do tend to come in with a Rambo mentality."[5]

Divided into 12 modules, The Lessons of the Vietnam War uses a critical thinking approach that encourages students to arrive at their own judgments by examining conflicting points of view fairly. With that goal in mind, the teacher helps students:

- Learn the facts about the controversial issues involved in the war.

- Consider all points of view and identify the assumptions behind the different viewpoints and the values behind the assumptions.

- Research the backgrounds of the persons who held the different views of the war.

Through role-playing, students are put in positions that affect the war's outcome. For example, they become government officials or members of Congress, arguing for or against military escalation.[6] "When role-playing works," Starr comments, "students begin to reframe the debate in order to question assumptions and identify needed information."[7]

At the end of the curriculum, rather than propose a solution, the teacher asks questions—ones that get students to compare and contrast the different positions and think their way through to their own conclusions.

Carol Transou is an award-winning teacher at Science Hill School in Johnson City, Tennessee. She developed her own Vietnam War course, focusing on the origins of the war, the war experience, and the war's legacies.

Classwork requires students to examine primary sources such as the *Pentagon Papers*. Another assignment requires students to interview their parents or other members of the community about their experiences during the war and what they learned from it.[8] Transou's approach, like Starr's curriculum, is designed to expose students to a diversity of views. (A resource which presents a highly critical analysis of American high school text books' treatment of the Vietnam War is *Teaching the Vietnam War* by William L. Griffin and John Marciano.)

WHAT ABOUT THE TEACHER'S VIEWS?

In guiding discussion of a controversial issue, should teachers let their own views be known? One perspective is that teachers should remain strictly impartial so they don't sway the discussion and abuse their position of influence. A counterargument holds that it would be miseducational for teachers to seem to be neutral or indifferent on matters of great moral importance; what message does that send to students?

Another guide to moral discussion in the classroom suggests that teachers should not *introduce* their viewpoint but should disclose it when and if students ask.[9]

In general I think it's appropriate for the teacher to say:

I do have views on this issue, and I'd be happy to share them with you later. But I want to stay impartial for now, because the purpose of this unit is not for you to learn what I think. It's for *you* to evaluate carefully all the arguments and evidence and come to what you think is the most supportable position.

Whether discussion of controversy is planned or spontaneous, good teachers will want to ensure balance and give students the benefit of more than one point of view. In some cases that may mean the teacher's sharing her own point of view. Sixth-grade Rhode Island teacher Lois Morris gives this example:

I am personally quite opposed to nuclear power plants. The electric company comes into the school and talks about the wonders of electricity and nuclear power. . . .

Afterward we have a general discussion. I don't bring it up, but if we flow into it, I will say I understand exactly where the company is coming from, but I personally worry about nuclear power plants. I say that's my opinion. I tell students, "You have heard both sides of the issue; you have to make up your own mind. Go home and talk to your parents, too."[10]

Teacher Morris's evenhanded, "that's my opinion" approach makes good sense when the issue is controversial. And her final exhortation—

"Talk to your parents"—is wise practice. If parents think the teacher is encouraging children to talk to *them* about the ethical issues discussed in class, that will help to alleviate parental anxieties about whether the teacher is abusing the classroom to promote her personal beliefs.

MORAL DEBATES

Structured debates are another effective way to stimulate reflection about controversial issues, especially for students at the middle school and high school levels.

Says sixth-grade teacher Tim Kent of Clovis, California:

> I want to light a fire under my kids, get them really thinking. Debates about controversial issues do that. Today they read aloud their essays about whether girls should be allowed to play boys' football. I walked by some kids outside during recess, and they were still talking about it. Often, after we debate an issue in class, kids will bring in newspaper articles on that topic.

Elizabeth Saenger uses debates with her fifth- and sixth-graders as part of her "ethics class" curriculum (see Chapter 9). Like Tim Kent, she finds students eager to discuss the controversial issues they hear about in the news. Should capital punishment be outlawed? Should seals and minks be raised for their furs? Should certain rock lyrics be censored because people find them morally offensive?

Students choose the topic. In a typical ethics class there are 12 students. Four take one side of the debate, four take the other, and four are cast as judges. (As much as possible, students decide which group they're going to be in for each debate.)

The teacher coaches the judges on the scoring criteria (logic of arguments, number of different arguments, supporting evidence) and the method of awarding points and subtracting them (teams are docked points for interrupting).

Even more important, judges have the role of calling on each side to *respond* to the other team's points as they make them. There is no set time for each side to speak; the argument bounces back and forth, creating a genuine moral dialogue.[11]

Without preparation, teacher Saenger says, a debate can flop.

> It takes two classes, one to get ready, one to have the debate. In the preparation class, we clarify exactly what we are debating. What's the

ethical issue here? Students will then do homework overnight to prepare for the debate. I'll supply background material—articles from magazines and newspapers, for example—that they'll need. I want them to learn something before they start arguing about it.

At the end of a debate, teacher Saenger gives some kind of writing assignment. For example, after the debate about the death penalty, students were asked to write on "The best ethical reason for capital punishment" and "The best ethical reason against capital punishment."

Some issues, such as abortion and euthanasia, are clearly better suited to the upper grades. Others, such as capital punishment, are a judgment call; the teacher will want to consider the maturity level of the particular group, the feelings of parents, and so on. Animal rights issues and some of the less complex science and environmental controversies are a good developmental match for upper elementary and middle school students.

DEBATING ETHICAL ISSUES IN SCIENCE

Catherine Gefell, in her monograph "Socially Responsible Science Education," argues persuasively that consideration of controversial issues has an especially important role to play in science education.[12] "Debating controversial issues," she says, "will dispel the notion that science is value-free and can always deliver 'right answers.' "[13]

Gefell identifies numerous issues in Earth science alone: *Alternative energy sources*: Should the U.S. government give as much research money for the development of solar power as it does for research and development of nuclear power? *Fossil fuels*: How much should coal-burning power companies be penalized for failing to comply with EPA regulations on smokestack emissions? Should American citizens be fined for driving vehicles that are not fuel-efficient? *Who owns the oceans?*: How should countries decide who has the right to harvest mineral-rich sea nodules or offshore petroleum deposits?

The accompanying box lists other timely issues that combine scientific learning and ethical debate.

Handled well, ethical debates about topics like these can teach students to study an issue in depth, develop reasoned arguments for a position, articulate those arguments in a public forum, and listen and respond to opposing views.

ETHICAL ISSUES FOR DEBATE IN SCIENCE EDUCATION
(abridged from Catherine Gefell's "Socially Responsible
Science Education"[14])

Earth science

1. *Environmental issues:* What should be done about overcrowded land-fills? Should the United States repay Canada for damage caused by acid rain formed by emissions from U.S. power plants?
2. *Space exploration:* Should billions of dollars be spent on a manned expedition to Mars when millions of people in the world are without food, homes, health care, etc.?
3. *Water rights:* In the arid western states, should those living along a river use all the water they want if it means severe water shortages for those downstream?

Biological sciences

1. *Genetic engineering:* If gene splicing becomes economically practical, should there be mass production of living organisms?
2. *Food supply:* If studies show that all people in the world could have enough to eat if food were better distributed and if land devoted to cattle were used to raise food for people, should we expect millions of meat-eaters to change their diets?
3. *Hunting:* Is hunting ethical? Under what conditions? Do animals have moral rights?
4. *Health issues and health care:* Is it right for some people to spend what amounts to millions of dollars a year on "luxury" operations (e.g., "nose jobs" or liposuction) when thousands of infants die each year because their mothers could not afford prenatal care? Who is responsible for caring for the increasing numbers of elderly people in the United States?

Physical science

1. *Nuclear power/nuclear arms/nuclear waste:* Should nuclear energy be used in any capacity until a safe method is found for disposal of radioactive waste? Is there any justification for further production of nuclear weapons?
2. *Ozone depletion/acid rain/greenhouse effect, etc.:* Are chemical companies doing enough to avoid widespread environmental devastation?
3. *Toxic waste and toxic emissions:* Would students be willing to live without certain consumer products if they knew that toxic waste was produced in their manufacture?
4. *Artificial intelligence/robotics:* Is it ethical for automobile manufacturers to put thousands of workers out of jobs by using robots on the assembly line? What kinds of decisions should not be left up to computers?

Science and social studies (interdepartmental)
1. *World poverty and world hunger:* How should resources be allocated on a global scale?
2. *Appropriate technology for Third World countries:* Should underdeveloped nations continue to grow cash crops for export, or should they be helped to change over to growing food for their own countries? What responsibility do wealthy nations have to poorer nations to share scientific and technological information?

SHOULD SCHOOLS DISCUSS A VOLATILE ISSUE SUCH AS ABORTION?

Of all the controversial issues that confront our society, abortion is the most divisive. Those who favor abortion rights believe that a woman's choice to end her pregnancy is among the most personal and intimate of human decisions and a reproductive freedom that is vital to the full participation of women in the economic and political walks of American life.[15] Those who oppose abortion see it as a violation of the fundamental human right to live, unjust discrimination based on age, and selective violence against the most vulnerable members of the human community, the preborn.[16]

Does the abortion debate belong in the schools? A case can be made against it: Students can cut their teeth on other controversial issues; leave the explosive subject of abortion to outside-of-school arenas; don't jeopardize community support for the school's values program by taking on such an emotional issue. But an issue as prominent as abortion is going to come up anyway. Ask high school students if they've ever discussed abortion in any of their classes; chances are good that they have. Ask them if, in classes where it came up, they know their teacher's position. Chances are they do.

If the school has a values education program in operation, that's another reason why abortion is likely to surface as an issue. Schools in Howard County, Maryland, for example, plan to promote "respect for life" as one of 18 approved values. But teachers aren't sure how they'll handle questions about abortion, which they expect to come up.[17]

The question, then, becomes not whether schools will deal with abortion but rather will they deal with it well—with thoughtful, balanced presentation of both sides.

The second reason for a planned educational approach to abortion is simply the centrality of this issue in American moral and political life. The country is in a virtual cultural civil war over the abortion issue. As ethicist John Noonan has observed, not since the Civil War over slavery has the nation been so divided over questions as fundamental as "Who is a human being?" and "Who shall be accorded human rights?"[18] If education has a role to play here, it may be to try to add, however modestly, to our capacity for reasoned public dialogue about this important public policy issue.

ESTABLISHING SCHOOL GUIDELINES
FOR THE STUDY OF CONTROVERSIAL ISSUES

Schools should establish written guidelines, approved by the Board of Education, for teaching controversial issues. Whether the issue is abortion or any other social-ethical controversy, these matters are too serious for teachers to be "making it up as they go along." Everyone benefits—teachers, students, administrators, and the community—when there's a thoughtfully developed, publicly stated, and consistently followed educational policy.

Even if a schoolwide policy is not yet officially in place, individual teachers are wise to follow general guidelines such as those in the accompanying box when they treat controversial issues in their classrooms.

MAKING THE CLASSROOM SAFE FOR DIVERSITY

An important first step in dealing with abortion or any other controversial issue is to try to make the classroom safe for diversity. The normal inhibiting effects of peer pressure and what-will-people-think-of-me? are heightened when the issue is emotionally charged. A teacher can attempt to create an atmosphere of intellectual freedom by making a statement such as:

> I want everyone here to be able to think and speak without fear of intimidation. Remember, it takes courage to take a minority position, and history often applauds those who did. Remember, too, that there is no shame in changing your mind or in withholding judgment if you're not sure what you think.

Next, the teacher can supply public opinion polls on the issue—letting students see for themselves the diversity of opinion that exists. With respect to abortion, one of the most thoroughgoing polls was

---

CONTROVERSIAL ISSUES: A SAMPLE SCHOOL POLICY
(abridged from Harry G. Miller, *The American Biology Teacher,*
November 1973)

Curriculum

1. Approval of course content should be made by departmental decision, in writing and submitted to the school administration for consideration by the School Curriculum Committee.
2. For those courses in which controversial issues are deemed especially volatile, parental persmission in a written form will be requested prior to course registration.

Faculty

1. Teachers have the instructional responsibility to assist students in examining all of the positions taken concerning a particular controversial issue.
2. When examining controversial issues, teachers have the right to express their own opinions, while recognizing that the classroom should not be used as a means for the inculcation of their own personal opinions and beliefs.
3. Teachers have the instructional responsibility to demonstrate that planning and preparation have taken place for the study of controversial issues.

Grievances

1. When course attendance is not required by state law, and if the parent feels the course is inappropriate, the parent shall have the right to request a course change in the child's program of studies.

---

commissioned by *The New York Times* and CBS News in April 1989 and based on a national sample of 1,412 adults.[19]

Like previous surveys, the *Times*/CBS poll found both men and women nearly evenly split on the abortion issue.[20] Among women, 47 percent favored "keeping abortion legal as it is now," while 51 percent wanted greater restrictions (40 percent felt that legal abortion should be limited to cases of rape, incest, or when the mother's life is in danger, and 11 percent favored a total ban). The rest were undecided.

Among men, 51 percent favored keeping abortion legal as it is now, while 46 percent wanted greater restrictions (38 percent felt it should be limited to cases of rape, incest, or threat to the mother's life, and 8 percent favored a total ban).

Conservatives and liberals were also split within their own ranks. While most people who called themselves "politically conservative" favored stricter abortion laws, nearly four of 10 conservatives wanted to keep abortion "legal as it is now." While most who called themselves "politically liberal" favored the abortion status quo, a third of liberals wanted to limit legal abortion to rape, incest, and threat to the mother's life (28 percent) or ban it completely (5 percent).[21]

Students can be given still other examples of such divisions: Liberal groups such as the American Civil Liberties Union[22] champion abortion rights in the name of privacy and personal freedom; but other liberal groups such as "JustLife"[23] advocate a "consistent life ethic" and campaign against abortion, poverty, and nuclear arms as all being violations of social justice and respect for life.

Showing that positions on abortion can't be neatly pigeonholed by gender or political ideology will help to free students from stereotypical thinking about this issue.

TWO DIFFERENT FEMINIST VISIONS
OF THE ABORTION ISSUE

Reading, reflection, and at least some writing should always *precede* classroom discussion of controversial matters if a teacher wants to move students beyond mere recitation of their original opinions. And balance requires that students read articulate, committed statements of the opposing views. For the abortion issue, there is no more effective way to do that than to assign the writings of women whose differing visions of feminism have led them to diametrically opposite stands on abortion.

Two such writings follow in the accompanying boxes, along with the kinds of sharply focused questions that help students key into what the authors are saying, identify the ethical issues, and evaluate the authors' arguments critically. The first (abridged) essay, "The Woman Behind the Fetus," is by Barbara Ehrenreich, author of the book *The Hearts of Men,* and first appeared April 28, 1989, as an op-ed column in *The New York Times.* Ehrenreich favors unrestricted abortion rights. The second essay, "A Moral Obligation," is by Sidney Callahan, editor of the book *Abortion: Understanding Differences,* and is an abridged version of her article in the November 1989 issue of the magazine *Sojourners.* Callahan asserts the primacy of the woman's obligation to her dependent fetus.

The Woman Behind the Fetus
by Barbara Ehrenreich

In the case of *Webster* v. *Reproductive Health Services,* the Supreme Court this week heard arguments about protection of the fetus and its relation to the right of privacy in using contraceptives. Almost lost in the legal tangle is that the high court is making a decision about women: their health, dignity, sexuality—even their economic well-being.

Sixteen years ago, at the time of the *Roe* v. *Wade* decision, that much was obvious. The pro-choice side was united in seeing abortion as a life-and-death issue, with both the lives and deaths at stake being women's.

The rise of the fetus as an independent figure in our national consciousness has transformed the debate—upstaging, and sometimes eclipsing, women and their stake in the legality of abortion. Today, even liberals and ostensible supporters of choice often talk as if abortion were on a moral par with shooting an intruder who enters one's home: a desperate action, to be undertaken only in extreme circumstances, and then duly regretted.

At the root of this new pro-choice, but anti-abortion position is an issue which never arose in the abortion debates of the past: the question of the legal status and possible personhood of the fetus. Contrary to the common anti-choice claim that abortion violates America's "traditional values," abortion was legal from the birth of the republic until the 1880s.

The arguments that led to its being outlawed focused almost entirely on women: the dangers of abortion to women. Nor did the omission of the fetus reflect biological ignorance. The medical profession, which led the 19th century fight against abortion, was reasonably well-informed about fetal development.

Today the fetus is viewed almost as a freestanding individual, while women have all but disappeared. Consider the misleading way we have come to visualize a fetus: a sort of larval angel, suspended against a neutral background. But no fetus—no living fetus—is suspended anywhere, but anchored to the placenta, housed in the womb, and wrapped in the flesh of a living woman.

The anguished and ambivalent ask how do we know that the fetus is not a person? A fetus is certainly a potential person. But it is also, scientifically speaking, a collection of cells—a part of a woman's body. A woman may think of her fetus as a person or as just cells depending on whether the pregnancy is wanted or not. This does not reflect moral confusion, but choice in action.

The recent belief that the fetus can be considered as separate from a woman's body, health, and life may become the basis for a compromise in which abortion will be ringed with restrictions designed to make a woman "think twice." Waiting periods might be imposed. Lectures—on anything from fetal development to the chances of winning support from a boyfriend—might be required. The intent will be to acknowledge our national ambivalence, but the effect will be to punish women.

When we talk about abortion, we are talking about women, and when we talk about women, we are talking about thinking, morally conscious human beings. The question America needs to return to is: When will women achieve their full personhood? We already know the answer to this one: Not until abortion—and contraception—are freely available to all women, without insulting restrictions and caveats. Anything less is a violation of something that goes far deeper, and cuts closer to the very meaning of "personhood," than mere privacy.

A MORAL OBLIGATION
by Sidney Callahan

I hold a feminist pro-life position on abortion, which can be characterized as a "consistent ethic of life," held by many peace and justice activists. I ground my position in the rational conviction that all human beings are of equal intrinsic worth.

This egalitarian ethic has engendered the democratic tradition of Western societies. The radical claim is made that no human being can be held to be morally inferior to another or used as a means of another's ends without consent. In this ethic, all members of the human family possess inalienable human rights—just because they are human.

When applying this moral ethic to the case of abortion, I cannot justify excluding the human embryo as a member of the human community. I see no moral reason why immaturity, size, or an early stage of development or vulnerability excludes an embryo (which I once was) from having the equal intrinsic moral worth of other human lives. It is a totally dependent human life, which, like a newborn, is on its way to being like us.

In reality all human lives are interdependent; all are in need of nurture and environmental sustenance at some point in the life cycle. The woman who alone has the power to sustain the human life in her womb has a corresponding obligation to protect and nurture it.

While humans have many intrinsic, inalienable human rights, it has long been recognized that the most fundamental and necessary for all the others is the right to life—or the right not to be killed. This intrinsic right is more basic than the right to self-determination or liberty.

Once we justify inequality and violations of intrinsic rights for pragmatic goals, then a woman's own human rights, vis-à-vis more powerful males, will be endangered. Protection of vulnerable, dependent fetal life becomes a moral imperative for the whole society, a test case of our ethical commitment to human equality, human solidarity, and human rights. People who fight for civil rights, equal rights for women, equal rights for the handicapped, and spouse and child abuse laws, will struggle for just treatment of the unborn.

First, the feminist pro-life movement will want to seek measures to ensure better choices than abortion, with provisions for waiting periods, mandatory counseling by neutral non-providers of abortion, and mandatory consultation and offering of information about alternatives such as adoption. Next, there would be support for banning late abortions—so obviously close to infanticide—in all but the gravest threat to the mother's health and life. Eventually, arbitrary social abortion on demand would be severely regulated.

As the community legally intervenes to protect the preborn, it must be politically forced to offer care and support for born women, children, and families. Parental leave, child care allowances, day care provisions, health care, housing and educational employment opportunities are long overdue pro-family measures of our political agendas.

But before these social changes come about, can we in justice struggle to restrict abortions? Yes. If we do not recognize our communal moral obligation to the dependent and helpless fetus, why should women, children, and families be helped? Unless the law changes, the ethic of domination and expediency—the law of the jungle and marketplace—will have won the day.

Questions for Student Writing and Discussion:

1. Does either author make any factual claims (as opposed to ethical arguments) that are open to question? What other sources of information could be checked to try to evaluate the accuracy of those factual claims?

2. Ehrenreich asserts that a woman may think of her fetus as a person or as just cells—and should have unrestricted freedom to decide whether to abort it. What arguments does she use to support her position? Do you agree or disagree? Why?

3. Callahan asserts that the woman does not have a moral right to abort the fetus within her. What arguments does she use to support her position? Do you agree or disagree? Why?

4. How do the two authors differ in their views of what the role of the law should be regarding abortion? What arguments do they use to support their claims? Do you agree or disagree? Why or why not?

Remaining an impartial moderator is not easy when the teacher has strong feelings about a controversial issue. It takes a deliberate commitment by the teacher not to be drawn into one side of the argument. Teachers can help themselves stick to a neutral, moderating role if they announce their intent to do so at the beginning of the discussion.

A teacher can also serve the cause of balance by bringing in two speakers on opposite sides of the issue. Alternatively, teachers can keep themselves in the background by organizing a student debate or a student-led discussion of the issue. In these approaches, the goal is to maximize the students' participation and circumscribe the teacher's. At the end of the class's investigation of the issue, after the final writing assignments have been turned in, graded, and returned, teachers may choose to disclose their views and how they came to them if students would like to know—although even that disclosure is not educationally necessary and may unduly sway students to the teacher's view.

A COOPERATIVE APPROACH TO CONTROVERSIAL ISSUES

A fresh and promising approach to controversial issues—one that prevents teacher bias from skewing the discussion, maximizes student participation, and reaps the benefits of cooperative learning—is "structured academic controversy."[24]

Developed by cooperative learning experts David and Roger Johnson, the model is simply this: Define controversies "as interesting problems to be solved rather than as win-lose situations." The Johnsons reject the classic debate format in favor of a cooperative format in which students work together rather than antagonistically.

In their article "Critical Thinking Through Structured Controversy" in the May 1988 issue of *Educational Leadership,* the Johnsons explain their cooperative format in detail. Using hazardous waste disposal as their controversial issue, they illustrate their procedure as follows:

1. **Assignment:** A teacher assigns students to groups of four, composed of two-person "advocacy teams." Each foursome is asked to prepare a report titled "The Role of Regulations in the Management of Hazardous Waste."

   Within each foursome, one team of two is assigned the position that more regulations are needed, and the other team of two the position that fewer regulations are needed.

2. **Planning:** During the first class period, the two-person teams receive materials from the teacher that support their assigned positions. Their task: "Plan how to present your position so that you *and* the opposing team in your group will learn your position so well as to find it convincing."

TEACHING CONTROVERSIAL ISSUES

1. In developing a values program, emphasize noncontroversial ways (e.g., role-modeling, moral community-building, cooperative learning, curriculum projects) of teaching noncontroversial values (e.g., respect, responsibility, honesty, compassion).

2. Justify the inclusion of controversial issues as important for developing students' critical thinking about the public policy decisions facing citizens in a democratic society.

3. Develop schoolwide guidelines for teaching controversial issues.

4. If available, use high-quality published curriculum materials on teaching a controversial issue.

5. Use the debate format to structure students' investigation and discussion of controversial issues.

6. In studying abortion or any highly controversial issue:
   - Make the classroom safe for diverse views by acquainting students with the diversity of opinion in society.
   - Provide readings on both sides of the issue and questions that guide students' critical evaluation.
   - Bring in speakers on both sides of the issue.
   - Refrain, as the teacher, from disclosing one's personal views until the students' inquiry is completed.

7. Use a cooperative learning format—"structured academic controversy"—to maximize the benefits of studying controversial issues while minimizing the divisive effects.

---

3. **Advocacy:** During the second period, the two teams present their positions to each other. Then they engage in general discussion in which they advocate their positions, rebut the other side, and try to reach the best decision possible about the need to regulate hazardous waste management.

4. **Position switch:** In the third period, each team switches positions, arguing *for* the position it originally opposed.

5. **Reaching consensus:** During the fourth period, the four group members synthesize what they see as the best information and reasoning from both sides into a *consensus solution*. They then write and submit a group report.

6. **Individual accountability:** When the consensus report is completed, each student takes a test on the factual information contained in the reading materials.

To help students develop a set of cooperative attitudes and skills, the Johnsons recommend that the teacher ask students to commit to these rules:

1. *I am critical of ideas, not people.*

2. *I focus on making the best decision possible, not on "winning."*

3. *I encourage everyone to participate and master all the relevant information.*

4. *I listen to everyone's ideas, even if I do not agree.*

5. *I restate (paraphrase) what someone said if it is not clear.*

6. *I first bring out all the ideas and facts supporting both sides and then try to put them together in a way that makes sense.*

7. *I try to understand both sides of the issue.*

8. *I change my mind when the evidence clearly indicates that I should do so.*[25]

The Johnsons have done ten years of classroom research on their process; they say their findings show that students:

- Gain in their perspective-taking abilities.

- Demonstrate greater mastery and retention of the subject matter than is true with either debate or individualistic learning formats.

- Produce higher-quality solutions to problems.

- Manifest greater liking of other student participants and higher academic self-esteem.

- Develop more positive attitudes toward the subject and the process of controversy itself.[26]

These impressive results suggest that structured academic controversy deserves a place in any program that wants students to develop the critical thinking fostered by controversy but that wishes to minimize the divisive effects of value conflict.

The many-faceted challenges of dealing with controversial issues were most recently demonstrated by the war in the Persian Gulf. Two days after hostilities broke out, I was at Gracemor Elementary School in North Kansas City, Missouri, doing a values education workshop for staff there. The workshop was interrupted by the news that a former student of the school district was one of the first casualties of the war. Counselors were called out of the session; how were the schools, the news media wanted to know, planning to handle students' questions, feelings, and concerns about the war?

In Albuquerque, New Mexico, a mother called La Cueva High School to say she was keeping her daughter home because instructors were spending too much time discussing the war. At Hempfield Area High School outside Pittsburgh, 150 students were suspended after walking out of classes to protest what they said was a lack of attention to the war.[27]

A January 23, 1991 article in *The New York Times* reported another aspect of the debate: What should be taught about the war? If teachers raised the issue of international oil supply as a factor in U.S. involvement, some parents objected; if they taught that the war was being waged solely to liberate Kuwait from Iraqi occupation, other parents objected. Discussing issues like these was compounded by the emotions arising from the fact that teachers or students often had spouses, parents, or other relatives serving in the Gulf.[28]

Joyce Briscoe, a world history teacher at La Cueva High School, said she thought it was not enough for teachers to "take a safe middle course" by just "letting kids air their feelings." In response to the Gulf conflict, she gave her students crash lessons on the long-standing hostilities in the Middle East and why they exist. Students and parents, many of whom said they had known very little about the region, generally welcomed Mrs. Briscoe's informative lectures.[29] Her approach reminds us of an important pedagogical point: The teacher's first task in approaching any controversial subject is to help students develop a solid knowledge base from which to form their opinions.

Democratic disagreement doesn't come naturally; it's learned. Giving students practice at discussing controversial issues—and simultaneously learning about the great social and ethical conflicts of our time—is a way to develop the rational components of character and at the same time educate citizens for democracy.

CHAPTER 15

Teaching Children to Solve Conflicts

I once had the unhappy experience of observing a fourth-grade teacher who became extremely exasperated with a boy in the back of the room. Despite repeated reminders to stay in his seat, Marcus kept getting up and wandering around. Finally the teacher lost her temper, grabbed Marcus by the back of the neck, and marched him down to the principal's office.

Feeling embarrassed for the teacher and sorry for the boy, I slipped out of the room and went down to the principal's office. There Marcus sat, slumped over.

I sat down next to him, not saying anything at first. Then I asked quietly, "How are you feeling?"

"Fine," he said in a quivering voice that belied his words.

I then drew four faces on a piece of paper: a happy face, a sad face, an angry face, and a face that expressed no feeling. Marcus watched as I did so. When I finished, I offered him my pencil and said, "Put an X under the face that shows how you feel."

Marcus made an X under the angry face.

"Pretty mad, huh?" I said. He nodded.

"You're angry at your teacher for what she did?" He nodded again.

"Can you tell me why you're angry at her?" I asked.

"She hurt my neck," he said, showing me where she had grabbed him. I said, "You're mad at her for hurting you like that." He nodded.

Then I said, "Marcus, can you make an X by the picture that shows how your teacher felt?" He quickly made another X below the angry face. "Why do you think she felt angry?" I asked. "Because I was out of my seat," he said.

"Tell me, Marcus," I continued, "what else do you think your teacher could have done when she was angry at you besides grabbing your neck?" I wanted to see if he could think of another, less hurtful way the teacher could have expressed her anger and dealt with his behavior.

He thought for a moment. Then he said, "She could have kicked me."

I paused and said, "Yes, I suppose she could have done that. Can you think of anything different she might have done?"

He shook his head no.

Marcus appeared to believe that when you get angry at somebody, there's only one thing you can do: hurt the person in some way. This belief was reflected in his own behavior. He was, the principal said, constantly getting into fights on the playground and in the school.

Marcus most likely had little or no experience in school or at home in working out alternative approaches to solving social problems. So when he was confronted with a conflict, he knew only one way to respond: with force. Unfortunately, his teacher's handling of his out-of-seat behavior only served to reinforce his immature thinking about dealing with conflict and anger.

Marcus's immaturity is common among students, and schools often do not do much to remedy it. From the standpoint of values education, that is a serious failure.

People who respond violently to conflict situations are a danger to themselves and to others. They are handicapped in their intimate relationships—marriage and parenting, for example—where conflict resolution skills are crucial and their absence often leads to verbal or physical abuse. As citizens, such persons do not contribute to a society or a world that seeks alternatives to violence. Indeed, they are often perpetrators of violence in society.

CONFLICT IN THE CLASSROOM

The moral life of the classroom is full of opportunities to teach children to handle conflict constructively. I asked one group of third-graders to describe situations that were causing conflict in their class. In about five minutes they came up with this list:

1. When you don't agree with what another person says and it leads to a big argument.

2. Two people want to use the same thing at the same time.

3. Two people are arguing about what to do, and somebody comes along and takes one side.

4. People tease you or call you a name, and if you tell, they just do it more.

5. You try to get in a game and they say you can't play.

6. When you're in line and somebody cuts in ahead of you.

7. Somebody gets mad in a game and tries to break it up.

8. People throw things.

9. Somebody takes something of yours without asking.

10. Somebody pushes or punches you.

11. When you get hurt, people laugh even though you're crying.

12. Somebody says bad things about you behind your back.

The class meeting, which develops a problem-solving disposition in students, is one way to help students learn to deal effectively with conflicts like these. But the class meeting can't do the whole job, for several reasons: Conflicts have to be dealt with when they happen, and a teacher can't call a class meeting every time a problem occurs; in the heat of an actual conflict, students often have trouble remembering and carrying out what they agreed in class meeting they should do; some students, low in social maturity, will require extra individual coaching in the interpersonal skills they need to solve conflicts; and with some exceptions, it's better to deal with actual conflicts by talking only with those students directly involved.

I believe an adequate approach to teaching conflict resolution includes these five elements:

1. *A planned curriculum* that has students think, write, and talk about various kinds of conflicts

2. *Structured skill training* that coaches students in conflict-avoidance and conflict-resolution skills

3. Using the *class meeting* to address common conflicts that occur among class members and to establish the *norm* of solving conflicts fairly and nonviolently

4. *Intervening* when necessary to help children apply their interpersonal skills at the moment of an actual conflict

5. Making students increasingly responsible for *working out their own conflicts* without the aid of an adult.

Let me illustrate each of these strategies.

A CURRICULUM ON CONFLICT

PREPARE, the Ontario values education program discussed in Chapter 2, is an example of a planned curriculum approach to teaching conflict resolution.

As part of the PREPARE unit titled *Fighting,* each child receives a student notebook containing seven lessons. Each lesson consists of written exercises that are the springboard for class discussion. In one lesson, for example, students are given different scenarios involving fighting and asked to give the reasons why they think fighting took place. In another lesson they are asked to write a paragraph about a time when they successfully avoided a fight.

Lesson Five, titled Physical Violence Is Usually a Poor Way of Fighting, begins with a story about two boys, Steven and Phillip. At recess, Phillip and Steven have the following conversation:

STEVEN: No one calls me a four-eyed jerk, buddy!

PHILLIP: You are a jerk! You tripped me.

STEVEN: I didn't trip you. Call me that again and I'll plow you one!

PHILLIP: I'll call you what I like, you four-eyed jerk!

Steven throws a punch and a fight is on. A crowd of kids gathers and chants, "Fight, fight, fight!"

Students are asked to complete a table indicating the possible consequences of this fight for the two boys and to show, by putting "+" or "−" in the "Value" column, whether they think a particular consequence is good or bad:

Question	Consequences	Value
What may happen to Steven?		
What may happen to Phillip?		
What might the teacher do?		
What might the principal do?		
What might other kids think about Steven and Phillip?		

After filling in this table, students are asked to "give alternatives to punching that Steven might consider just before he punches Phillip." Then they are asked to "rewrite Steven and Phillip's conversation so that a fight is avoided."

The last lesson of the unit is titled Compromise Is Usually a Better Way of Settling a Disagreement than Fighting. Students are given an example of a successful compromise and then asked to make up their own compromise solutions to hypothetical disagreements between adults, between parents and children, and between friends.

I interviewed a teacher in a Hamilton, Ontario, elementary school in a low-income area where fighting was a way of life for many students. All the teachers of grades 4 through 6 made a commitment to teaching the unit on fighting. They began with activities to build students' self-esteem and a sense of community, and introduced the unit on fighting in November. "We took it slow," the interviewed teacher said, "and made it span several months. We developed it into a language arts unit as well—students did creative writing on themes having to do with conflict. The faculty shared their experiences and supported each other. By the end of that year we had pretty much solved the problem of fighting in the school."

Says a principal in another Hamilton school that now teaches the unit on fighting:

> We used to deal with fighting where it occurred, out on the playground, but that didn't have much effect on future behavior. Now I bring kids

into the office. I have a small blackboard there, and I write down their alternatives in the conflict. Talk it over? Walk away? Clean his clock? Which of these will work best? They see.

When our teachers did the unit on fighting, there was a definite decline in the number of kids coming to my office. When they do come to the office for fighting, they are much better able to discuss their behavior and to see the other guy's viewpoint if they've had the unit on fighting.

STRUCTURED SKILL TRAINING

An academic curriculum like the unit on fighting is most effective if the teacher includes simulated situations that give students supervised practice in using the new conflict-avoidance and conflict-resolution skills. I think of this structured skill training as a kind of "moral coaching."

An example comes from the second-grade classroom of Peggy Manring in Skaneateles, New York. She brought in a bag of wood scraps from the local toy factory and dumped them on the rug in the middle of their circle meeting. She asked the children, taking turns, to use the wood pieces to make a model of the classroom as they saw it. As they did so, teacher Manring observed their interactions and intervened at opportune moments to teach more effective communication. Here is an excerpt from the dialogue that took place:

DAVID: That is the dumbest chalkboard, Martha. You put it in a stupid place.

TEACHER: (to David) You think Martha should put the block in a different place. Would you like to suggest to her where she might put it?

DAVID: Yeah, right there. The chalkboard is *behind* the table.

TEACHER: (to Martha) If you accept David's suggestion, you may move your block. If you like it where you put it, you may leave it right there.

TEACHER: (to David) When you don't use the words "stupid" and "dumbest," people like to listen to you. You had an interesting point to make about the chalkboard.

The teacher comments: "The next time David wanted to say something, he said, 'Paul, I *suggest* you look where the art table is. It's next to the teacher's desk.' Paul picked up on the 'I suggest'; so did Eddy and Alan. All the children seemed to be stretching to cooperate."

Some students will need individual or small-group coaching in a whole range of social skills (such as listening, saying thank you, asking a question, and beginning a conversation). Children who are highly impulsive and aggressive or otherwise socially immature benefit from a very structured approach to skill training. This approach has the teacher model a social skill through role-playing; "think aloud" the substeps in each skill (e.g., when facing a conflict, "Count to 10 . . . decide what the problem is . . . then think about my choices . . ."); guide the child through a similar role-play; give feedback on how well the child followed each step; and help the child plan how he or she will use the new skill in real life.

The book *Skillstreaming the Elementary School Child* by psychologists Ellen McGinnis and Arnold Goldstein[1] describes a program that grew out of their work in special education and is designed to teach 60 different prosocial skills. They cite research showing that prosocial skill deficits in children are directly related to school maladjustment and peer rejection. This is especially true for handicapped students, who tend to interact with peers less frequently and in more negative ways than nonhandicapped students do.

USING THE CLASS MEETING TO DEAL WITH CONFLICT

The class meeting can be used both to teach conflict-resolution skills and to solve conflicts occurring in the classroom.

Marty Kaminsky is an experienced teacher of a combined first- and second-grade class at Central School in Ithaca, New York. He frequently uses role-playing during his class meeting to try to prevent and solve classroom problems. He follows these self-developed guidelines:

1. During the day, the teacher listens carefully to the complaints children have about each other.

2. He brings up these problems at the morning class meeting without mentioning the particular people involved. He comments: "During role-plays and discussions, I don't allow the children to use the real names of people they're having problems with, because that shuts down people and causes them to get so defensive that they get very little out of the discussion."

3. He describes a particular conflict in enough detail to give everyone a clear picture of the problem.

4. Next he leads the class in a discussion of the reasons for the problem ("What brought this about?").

5. Then he asks, "How does each person in this conflict feel?"

6. He and the class discuss possible constructive ways to solve the problem. When they agree on the best solution, he asks for volunteers to act it out in the middle of the circle.

7. After students have acted out what they think is the best solution to the problem, teacher Kaminsky asks: "Will this work in real life? What's necessary to make it work?"

There is no shortage of hands when you ask for volunteers to act out situations. Role-playing stimulates high interest and involvement because it brings discussion close to real-life problems. And *seeing* the solutions acted out makes it more likely that students will actually use the conflict-resolution strategies when a real conflict comes along.

If role-playing is difficult for young children, the teacher can use puppets in the circle meeting to dramatize common conflicts, such as fighting over the same toy, two children refusing to let a third join their play, name-calling, and so on. After acting out a scenario, the teacher asks questions such as:

- What happened in this situation?

- How did the different characters feel?

- What are some other ways to solve this problem?

- Have we had any problems like this?

- What should you do if you have this problem?

Young children who observe and discuss these puppet dramas, studies show, offer fewer aggressive solutions as time goes on and become less aggressive and more cooperative in their own social play.[2]

DISCUSSING STUDENTS BY NAME

In general I think it's best to avoid using names when discussing conflicts in class meeting so as not to put individuals on the spot. But there are times when the growth of the individual and the growth of the group may be best served by discussing the particular parties involved.

For example: Since he started school, Tim, a 10-year-old boy in the community of Hamilton, Ontario, had been teased about having big ears. As a result, he got into lots of fights on the playground and also had poor peer relations inside the classroom.

Tim's fifth-grade teacher asked him for his permission (an ethically essential step) to raise this problem in class meeting. Since other approaches had failed, Tim was willing to try the class meeting as a way to solve his problem.

In the meeting, the teacher said that Tim was very unhappy about how people were treating him, especially on the playground. "What is Tim's particular problem?" she asked.

"Kids tease him a lot," a boy said.

"About what?"

"His ears."

"How do you think he feels about that?"

"Probably not very good."

Tim spoke up to say that kids had picked on him because of his ears ever since *first* grade. He hated it.

"Did you realize how Tim felt about this?" the teacher asked. Not really, students said. How could the class help in this problem? They agreed to stop saying things about Tim's ears, to keep a record of what was happening with him on the playground, both good and bad, and to come back to this issue at a future class meeting. The teacher comments:

> There were two good outcomes from this. The group improved; they teased Tim much less. And he learned to ignore the teasing he still got from some kids. He was less likely to get in a fight on the playground. He used to have a real chip on his shoulder. Now he's at the point where he can even say, "Okay, I do have big ears."

Teachers can lay the groundwork for discussing sensitive problems if they use the class meeting to help individuals with other, less volatile problems. We've already seen (in Chapter 6) how teachers have done this by asking the group, "Who's having a problem that the rest of us can help with?" When class meetings include this practice of helping individual members, they establish an ethic of mutual helpfulness that makes it easier to take on an emotionally charged issue.

GUIDING STUDENTS THROUGH ACTUAL CONFLICTS

Even if students have the benefit of a conflict curriculum, social skill training, and class meeting discussion, many will still have trouble applying these learnings when emotions are running high in a real conflict. In these situations the teacher usually has three tasks:

1. Helping students understand each other's point of view ("How does so-and-so feel when you do that?").

2. Helping students work out a fair solution, one that takes into account both points of view and satisfies the legitimate claims of each party ("What's a way of solving this problem that's fair to both of you?").

3. Helping children practice the behavioral skills that will help them solve such problems without the intervention of an adult ("Can you guys show me how you could have solved this problem without fighting?").

Observant teachers know the situations that tend to cause conflicts, and the kids who tend to get into them, and keep an eye out for potential problems. If a teacher can intervene early—before a negative confrontation is in full swing—there's a better chance of calling a positive conflict strategy into play.

On-the-spot intervention is also much more productive if the teacher and students have already established a framework for talking about conflict. Says one of the Hamilton teachers who uses the unit on fighting:

> For me, the greatest benefit from the unit was in how *I* dealt with their fighting. I was able to talk it through with them more effectively. We had done role-playing in class—practicing alternatives, walking away, seeing the other person's point of view. We could refer to the unit when a real fight occurred.

KIDS AS "CONFLICT MANAGERS"

A group that specializes in training children to be "conflict managers" is STASIS Conflict Management Consultants of Ithaca, New York. STASIS trains 20 children per elementary school to work in pairs as conflict managers on the playground (they wear an official badge)—looking for disputes and intervening when necessary.

Each school is asked to choose a mix of students representative of the entire student body. In eight hours of training, children learn communication and listening skills, dealing with emotion, brainstorming creative solutions, and practicing teamwork.

Teachers and administrators have been highly supportive of the program because of the real help the conflict managers provide in mediating student disputes and because of the special benefits in skill

development and self-esteem for those children who take on this responsibility.[3] (Training students as playground mediators was origi-
nated by the Community Board Program, 149 9th Street, San Francisco,
CA 94105; tel. 415–552–1250.)

INCREASING STUDENTS' RESPONSIBILITY
FOR SOLVING THEIR OWN PROBLEMS

The ultimate goal of conflict training is to enable students to solve
their conflicts without outside intervention. A teacher can help children
develop that problem-solving competence by structuring situations where
they have to take more of the responsibility for solving the conflict.

Jan Page, who teaches second grade in Modesto, California, says
that if two children have an argument or a fight, she sends them away
for a conference (some teachers have a taped "conflict circle" on the
carpet). Their assignment: "to come up with *one* story of what happened." She comments:

> This isn't easy; it usually takes several tries. Sometimes other kids will
> try to join in and help them. I'll say, "Sorry, they have to work this out
> themselves." If they can't come up with one version after five minutes or
> so, I'll say, "Okay, time's up, you can talk more later."
>
> Often that's the end of it. Sometimes during the conference they'll get
> talking about something else and forget about the fight. Often they'll come
> up to me and one will say, "It was an accident—he didn't mean it." I'll
> say, "Okay, the next time, if you didn't mean it, say you're sorry."
>
> Gradually they develop the ability to solve their own problems.

Says a fifth-grade teacher: "When my students fight, I have them
each write three paragraphs—and I don't present this as a punishment:
(1) What was the problem? (2) What were the causes? and (3) How
can you solve it in the future? I have very few second occurrences."

JoAnne Shaheen, when she was an elementary school principal in
New York, used a three-step process for students who were sent to the
office for fighting.

• First, they had to interview each other—about their lives, their interests, and their feelings—using a worksheet she provided. Her rationale: "When two children fight, it's often somewhat a function
  of their not knowing one another."

• Then she gave the two students a set time to come up with a solution to their problem. If they couldn't come up with anything, she

---

STRATEGIES FOR TEACHING CONFLICT RESOLUTION

1. Use a conflict resolution curriculum to teach students the causes of conflicts and nonviolent ways to solve them.

2. Coach students in the specific social skills needed to avoid and solve conflicts.

3. Use class meetings to discuss the causes of conflicts and to establish the value that conflicts should be solved fairly and without violence.

4. Intervene when necessary to assist students in using their newly learned conflict-resolution skills.

5. Provide special training for students who are willing to serve as "conflict managers" on the playground.

6. Reinforce classroom instruction by using a conflict mediation process with students who are sent to the office for fighting.

7. Help students gradually progress toward the goal of solving their conflicts without outside mediation.

---

offered several alternatives and had them select what they thought would work best.

- After several days, students had to report back to let her know how their solution was working.

What does the research show about the effects of conflict resolution training? In one study of first-graders, University of Wisconsin psychologist Robert Enright collaborated with the teacher on a program to teach children to be social problem-solvers. When conflicts arose in the classroom, the teacher asked the children who were directly involved to describe what they did, how it affected the other person's feelings, what else they might have done, and what they would do the next time in a similar situation.

The teacher held students accountable for following through on their new problem-solving plans. At the end of 11 weeks, first-graders who experienced this program were significantly superior to a matched class of students on measures of interpersonal understanding and ability to reason about fairness.[4] Other studies have found similar results.[5]

CONFLICT TRAINING WITH OLDER STUDENTS

The need for moral competence training is even greater in high schools, where tensions can explode into deadly violence.

"How many of you get really angry—angry enough to fight?" The questioner was Dr. Deborah Prothrow-Stith, a physician who specializes in adolescent violence. The audience was a class of teenagers at Jeremiah E. Burke High School in Boston.[6] At least one teenager a month was killed in the area where these students lived.

Slowly, the hands rose until everyone in the room, male and female, big and small, had answered in the affirmative. The rest of the class period was spent discussing crime statistics.

The 45-minute session was the beginning of a 10-week minicourse in the prevention of violence. Taught at Burke High School as part of a required health education course, the minicourse was developed by Dr. Prothrow-Stith and is designed to teach teenagers what causes violent conflict and how to avoid it. The program has caught the interest of educators in several states and is now available as a curriculum packet from the Education Development Center in Newton, Massachusetts.[7]

As yet there has been no formal research on the program's effectiveness, but early indicators are promising. "I used to carry a knife for protection, but I stopped and I don't fight as much as I did," says one 18-year-old senior at Burke High School who took the course. Says a graduate: "I had my share of fights, and I learned how to avoid them by talking things out. Otherwise I could lose my life over something really stupid like stepping on someone's shoe and not wanting to say 'Excuse me.'"

At Burke High School, the introduction of the violence prevention course coincided with other changes made by a new principal. In the past two years, assaults on teachers and students have declined and fewer students are carrying weapons.

Conflict goes with the territory of human interactions. A large part of being civilized is to be able to use reason, not force or intimidation, to settle our differences. We have not finished educating our children until we teach them this basic human skill.

One of the best resources for materials on teaching conflict resolution, grades kindergarten through eight, is the Children's Creative Response to Conflict Program, *Fellowship of Reconciliation, Box 271, 523 North Broadway, Nyack, NY 10960-0271 (tel. 914-358-4601).*

Other recommended resources: William Kreidler's Creative Conflict Resolution: More Than 200 Activities for Keeping Peace in the Classroom *(Goodyear Books, 1900 East Lake Ave., Glenview, IL 60025),* Creating Peace in Our Classrooms: Cooperative Learning, Controversy, and Conflict Resolution, *a comprehensive resource bibliography ($5) including information on training opportunities, available from Nancy and Ted Graves, IASCE, Box 1582, Santa Cruz, CA 95061–1582; and Annie Cheatham's 124-item* "Annotated Bibliography for Teaching Conflict Resolution in Schools" *(37 pp., $4) and* Directory of School Mediation and Conflict Resolution Programs *(169 pp., $15), both available from the National Association for Mediation in Education (NAME), 425 Amity Street, Amherst, MA 01002; tel. 413–545–2462.*

PART THREE

SCHOOLWIDE STRATEGIES FOR TEACHING RESPECT AND RESPONSIBILITY

CHAPTER 16

Caring Beyond the Classroom

Close to a billion people suffer from hunger and preventable diseases in a world that has the resources to assure a decent standard of living for all.

—OXFAM AMERICA

We overwhelm children with all the suffering and evil in the world, but do we enable them to act?

—SISTER JOAN MAGNETTI, RFCJ,
Headmistress, Convent of the
Sacred Heart,
Greenwich, Connecticut

Item: Harvard government professor Richard M. Hunt, in teaching a course on the Holocaust, was dismayed to learn that a majority of his students had a "no fault" view of history. They believed that the rise of Hitler and the Nazis was inevitable, that no one could have resisted it, and that in the end no one was responsible for what happened.[1]

Item: According to the U.S. Census Bureau, voter participation has dropped most sharply among 18- to 24-year-olds: Only 36 percent voted in the 1988 election, down from 50 percent in 1972. A common reason given for not voting: "It won't make any difference."

Item: According to reports such as UCLA's *The American Freshman,* college students during the past 20 years have shown a declining interest in public affairs and service and a growing preoccupation with personal wealth. Coupled with this trend is a pessimism about society's future: Many students see the idea of making a positive difference in the world as useless and naive.[2]

Of the many things that make a person a good citizen, two stand out. One is an attitude of caring about one's fellow human beings. The other is the belief that one person can make a difference.

Individuals, of course, *do* make a difference. Every day, people who care about more than their own comfort are doing all sorts of things to improve the lives of others. And as they help those in need, they experience a deeper fulfillment than can ever be found in a bank account. Helping young people realize that, grow beyond selfishness, and discover their own capacity for doing good is a crucial part of values education.

The need for caring citizens who feel empowered to act is greater than ever before. Says Joseph Califano, Jr., former federal Secretary of Health, Education, and Welfare: "Government alone cannot meet and master the great social problems of our day."[3] "The big ideas in this world," writes author Norman Cousins, "cannot survive unless they come to life in the individual citizen."[4]

How can schools foster an "I can make a difference" sense of citizen responsibility? It starts in the classroom, where children can see the results of their actions as they work to create a caring moral community. But what can be done to extend students' caring attitudes into larger and larger spheres so that they come to identify compassionately with the mainstream of humanity and do what they can to build a better world?

DEVELOPING AWARENESS OF THE HUMAN CONDITION

A social conscience begins with social awareness:

• Nearly a billion people in the world live in poverty.[5] Each year, an estimated 15 to 20 million people will die from hunger and diseases resulting from malnutrition.[6] That's the equivalent of a Hiroshima every 48 hours.

In some Third World countries, families are so poor that they send their children into the streets to pick in the dung of animals to try to find undigested grains.

- Much of the world is ravaged by sicknesses that are almost unheard of in technologically developed countries. As we approach the end of the twentieth century, more than 20 million people still suffer from leprosy. Each year, nearly a half billion people in 107 countries get malaria, the single greatest killer in the world.

- For 90 percent of people living in Third World poverty, water carries disease. In 53 countries, schoolchildren have blood in their urine. That's because they have parasitic bilharzia worms, a waterborne infection that afflicts 200 million people and can cause cirrhosis of the liver; bladder cancer; and damage to the brain, heart, and spleen.

  In some poor countries, as many as 15 children of every 100 born will die before their first birthday (compared to one of 100 in the United States).[7] Children under age 5 account for one in three of all the world's deaths; simple diarrhea is their leading killer.[8]

- Every day, thousands of people are killed, maimed, or driven from their homes in the dozen or more wars that continually rage around the globe.

  In both developed and developing countries, a large share of national resources—more than $1 billion a day worldwide—is spent on weapons. According to the Brandt Commission, *0.5 percent of one year's military spending in the world would buy all the farm equipment needed to enable food-poor countries to approach food self-sufficiency within a decade.*[9]

Poverty and its resultant suffering are not limited to distant, Third World nations. In the midst of our own affluent society, many go without. The National Coalition for the Homeless estimates that nearly three million people in the United States are without homes each winter; in the cities, one of every four homeless persons is a child.

Moreover, poverty in America is on the rise: In 1969, one in seven U.S. children was poor; in 1990 it was one in five; by the year 2000 it will be one in four. The poverty rate for white children is 15 percent; for Hispanic children, 39 percent; for black children, 45 percent.[10]

PEOPLE WORKING TO CHANGE THE WORLD

I look at the individual. I can love only one person at a time. I can feed only one person at a time. As Jesus said, "Whatever you

> *do to one of these least ones, you do to me." So you begin. If I
> didn't pick up one person, I wouldn't have picked up 42,000.*
>
> —MOTHER TERESA

Facts about human want and suffering can be demoralizing, and even destructive of the will to act. Students need to know that all over the world, people are taking effective action to alleviate suffering and restore hope and dignity to the poor and oppressed.

Students should know, for example, about the highly successful work of independent citizen groups like Oxfam America, a Boston-based international organization specializing in disaster relief and long-range strategies to reduce world poverty and hunger.

Oxfam America has improved the lot of poor people in Asia, Africa, Latin America, and the Caribbean. It provides food for the hungry; modest income grants to help the landless buy land; health care education about how to treat diseases and eliminate their sources; education in community organization; and tools, seeds, and training to help grass-roots groups become agriculturally self-reliant. Simultaneously, Oxfam America also works to educate government policymakers and the public about the root causes of world hunger and poverty—including exploitative practices of rich nations toward poor ones.

One of Oxfam America's main student activities has been participation in its annual Fast for a World Harvest Day each November. Individuals fast for a meal or a day and contribute the money saved to a fund sent to Oxfam.

Students are made aware of how much even small amounts of money can do: A sum of $13 will provide a fishnet for a Kampuchean farmer who must rely on fish for food during the rainy season; $24 will supply cooking pots for five destitute Mozambican refugee families; $120 will buy five acres of rich farmland and pastureland for a cooperative of indigenous people in Ecuador.

Here is a small sampling of the special activities sponsored by scores of schools around the country as part of Oxfam's Fast for a World Harvest Day:

- Using the slogan "Don't be greedy, feed the needy," Camelback High School students in Phoenix, Arizona, held a Fast and Hunger Banquet. In addition, students went into the community and got businesses each to pledge 10 percent of the total amount raised by the school.

- At Notre Dame High School for Girls in Chicago, math classes studied demographic facts related to hunger, and religion classes discussed the question "What is our ethical and religious responsibility for the starving people of the world?"

- At Noonewaug High School in Woodbury, Connecticut, faculty and students participated in an International Harvest Dinner, where most of the diners ate plain rice to dramatize the inequitable distribution of world food resources. Student leaders held a press conference to get publicity for the campaign to fast. They also researched the hunger problems of four countries and presented their findings to classmates.

- Elementary school children at Holy Family Primary School in Elmira, New York, gave up their ice cream and half a sandwich for the Oxfam America fast. To help pupils visualize the problem of world hunger, the school showed filmstrips of poor and hungry children in different countries. Later that day the children joined hands to form a chain around the school building and sang "We Are the World." [11]

Joseph Short, former executive director of Oxfam America, asserts that widespread hunger, poverty, and disease are "morally and politically intolerable in a world that has the resources to assure a decent standard of living for all." For Oxfam's newsletter and for information about how to get involved, write Oxfam America, 115 Broadway, Boston, MA 02116, or call 617-482-1211.

COMING TO THE AID OF PRISONERS OF CONSCIENCE

A seventh-grader from Ann Arbor, Michigan, writes to the president of Ethiopia:

Your Excellency,
 I am writing to you because I am very concerned about the imprisonment of Namat and Amonsissa Issa. They have been in jail for seven or eight years without trial. . . . *Amonsissa needs to grow up somewhere besides a prison.*

This 12-year-old student is one of hundreds across the country writing letters and postcards to presidents, prison officials, legislators, and other government leaders around the world. (Within the year, Namat and Amonsissa Issa were released.) The students' efforts are part of an around-the-clock rescue effort by Amnesty International on behalf of the unjustly imprisoned.

Recipient of the Nobel Peace Prize in 1977, Amnesty International works to free the world's "prisoners of conscience"—people who have been arrested because of their beliefs, color, sex, ethnic origins, or religion and who have not used or advocated violence. They include teachers, students, fishermen, factory workers, medical personnel, priests, monks, housewives, and even children. Half of the world's governments hold prisoners of conscience; most of these governments practice torture.[12] When Amnesty International learns of a prisoner of conscience, one of its 3,000 "adoption groups" in 51 countries immediately swings into action.

In 1988, membership in the U.S. branch of Amnesty International jumped 33 percent, largely because of hundreds of new chapters at high schools and colleges across the country. Now even elementary school children are writing letters, often movingly eloquent, on behalf of particular prisoners of conscience. In the process, they gain an education in the meaning of freedom and the extent to which others are deprived of it around the world.

Amnesty offers a special-edition *Children's Urgent Action* newsletter each month; many of the cases sent to children are about other children in danger or detention. For information about how to set up an Amnesty International chapter for children or older students, write Amnesty International/U.S.A., 322 Eighth Avenue, New York, NY 10001, or call 212-807-8400.

THE NEED FOR INSPIRING ROLE MODELS

Young people need inspiring examples of individuals making a difference in their own communities, too. Providing a wide range of positive moral role models is urgent in an age when television has for many children become the primary source of values. Says Phyllis Smith-Hansen, a fifth- and sixth-grade teacher in Lansing, New York:

> In November I do a unit on heroes and heroines. It's gotten harder and harder to do. Kids don't even understand the concept anymore. They pick TV characters. Even Garfield the Cat. The closest they come to real persons is professional wrestlers like Hulk Hogan. They value money, being on TV, being strong, and being attractive. The deeper experiences and values of humanity are lost to these kids. Nobody is exposing them to those.

Happily, help is on the way. It's coming from a simple but ingenious enterprise called the Giraffe Project.

Established in 1983 by the wife-husband team of Ann Medlock and John Graham, and the subject of national media attention, this project is an effort to identify "Giraffes"—"people who stick their necks out for the common good." Giraffes, says the project, are "ordinary people acting with extraordinary compassion and courage," tackling problems such as pollution, poverty, drugs, corruption, social injustice, and international conflict.

A volunteer committee selects the persons to receive a Giraffe award, choosing from nominations submitted by anyone who has witnessed a person's taking a risk for others. The project then sends out an individual Giraffe's story, in the form of a public service announcement, to radio stations and newspapers across the country. A sample radio announcement:

> Julie Leirich runs a checkout stand in a Los Angeles supermarket. She saw that the market threw away a lot of good food—*and* that there were a lot of hungry people on the streets. Julie stuck her neck out and started taking that good food to the homeless. When she admitted what she was doing, her boss didn't fire her—he gave her more food. Customers in Julie's checkout line volunteered to help. Today Julie and her fellow volunteers distribute six tons of food a month.
> *There's something you could do, right here in (name of city). (Name of station) and the Giraffe Project say, "Stick your neck out."*

How can schools make use of the Giraffe Project and build on its basic idea? Here are some ways:

1. *Contact the Giraffe Project* (120 Second Street, P.O. Box 759, Langley, Whidbey Island, WA 98260, or call 1-800-344-TALL) to learn about available educational materials such as a teacher's kit and classroom activities to develop Giraffe Project concepts. There is also an excellent half-hour video of a PBS TV program ("It's Up to Us") on the Giraffe Project and the activities of eight people— ranging from a high school student who launched an antidrug program to a 90-old environmental activist—who have received Giraffe Project commendations. (This inspiring video may be rented or purchased directly from the Giraffe Project.)

2. *Join the Giraffe Project (for $25).* Memberships—which pay much of the project's budget—include a subscription to the quarterly *Giraffe Gazette* (single copies are available for $3). Jam-packed with

colorful stories about Giraffes of all types and ages, the *Giraffe Gazette* is a wonderful source of role models for students. It describes people like:

- Frank Melton, a black businessman in Jackson, Mississippi, who responded to gang killings in his city by setting up a summer camp where he teaches gang rivals to respect each other and work together.
- Marion Stoddart of Groton, Massachusetts, who devoted 20 years to leading an effort that turned the once severely polluted Nashua River into a clean waterway that is now popular with picnickers and listed as a "scenic river."
- Three devout Christians who bought a secluded farm in Annapolis, California, to live in peace and prayer, felt called to set up a home for babies with AIDS, and have continued this work despite community opposition.

3. A class can undertake its own search for Giraffes, combing newspapers and magazines for examples of people sticking their necks out for others in big or small ways. Articles brought in can be discussed and then displayed on an ongoing Giraffe Bulletin Board. Giraffes in the local community can be invited into classrooms to answer questions about their work.

4. A teacher can do a curriculum unit on heroes and the concept of heroism. Biographies[13] are perhaps the best resource here, but there are other good materials as well: *Rescuers of Jews During the Holocaust: Programs and Resources*, a superb catalog of books and videos, such as *The Courage to Care* available from the Jewish Foundation for Christian Rescuers, Anti-Defamation League, 823 United Nations Plaza, New York, NY 10017: 212-490-2525; classroom exercises on heroes and heroism ("Teachable Moments," available from the Stanley Foundation, 420 East Third Street, Muscatine, IA 52761; 319-264-1500); Nat Hentoff's book *American Heroes in and out of School,* featuring heroes known and unknown, some of them high school students; the annual accounts of persons who have received the Carnegie Medal of Heroism for risking their lives to save others (write the Carnegie Hero Fund Commission, 606 Oliver Building, Pittsburgh, PA 15222); Charles Kuralt's heartwarming portraits of people who take joy in helping others (in *On the Road with Charles Kuralt*[14]); *Newsweek*'s July 4, 1988, article "A Holiday for Heroes," featuring profiles of 50 unsung heroes, one from every state in the country; and stirring videos such as *Mother Teresa,*[15] which tells the story

of her life and her Sisters of Charity's care for the world's poor. Newly available is Sara Ensor's *Purpose for Living* (for ages 9 to 13), a series of three textbooks and teachers' guides that presents stories of inspiring models, past and present, from the United States and around the world.[16]

All of these are means of bringing to the fore what is often hidden: how many good people there are, how many ways there are to do good, and how much happiness comes to those who extend help as well as to those who receive it.

KIDS WHO ARE GOOD SAMARITANS

Classes should also be encouraged to find examples of young people doing good.

The Giraffe Project has spotlighted kids who are Giraffes. One example: Justin Lebo, of Saddle Brook, New Jersey, who since age 10 has spent all his allowance, much of his summer vacation, and weekends during the school year fixing up more than 50 old bikes for children in local orphanages.

You can also find some of these stories in the regular media. A few years ago there was a newspaper story about a sixth-grader named Trevor Ferrell in Gladwyne, Pennsylvania, a suburb of Philadelphia. During a cold wave in December, Trevor watched a Philadelphia news report showing street people huddled over steam vents. "Do people really live like that?" Trevor asked his father. "Sure, right here in Philadelphia," his father said. "If you want to see for yourself, I'll take you down there." And he did.

Almost every night after that, accompanied by his parents and sometimes his brother and sisters, Trevor brought the street people blankets, sandwiches, soup, and coffee. He came to know them by name. Trevor's friends on the streets looked forward to his visits, calling him "Little Buddy" and "Little Jesus."[17]

Three months after Trevor began his nightly missions, the mayor of Philadelphia presented him with a commendation for his care of the street people. Trevor and his family went around to churches, where Trevor told of the street people's needs. Contributions of blankets, pillows, and food began to pile up on the family's front yard. Checks began to come in.

To date, more than 850 volunteers have joined Trevor's campaign for the homeless. They have distributed food, clothes, and bedding, helped to run a thrift store, and remodeled an old building into a 50-bed shelter for the homeless called "Trevor's Place."[18] Trevor, now 15, recently addressed the United Nations and met with Mother Teresa and President Bush to discuss the plight of the homeless.[19]

Trevor Ferrell's story illustrates a recurring phenomenon: One person's compassionate example is soon multiplied by the compassion it inspires in others.

Schools can establish their own programs of Good Samaritan or good citizenship awards, presented at an assembly or special banquet to students who stand out in their efforts to help others in their school or community. Nominations can come from community members, teachers, or fellow students.

Another way to use positive peer examples is to have all students in a class write an essay "A Time When I Stuck My Neck Out for Somebody Else." Essays can be posted, or the teacher can read selected essays to the whole class (the name could be withheld, with the class invited to guess who it is).

LEARNING TO CARE THROUGH SERVICE

To develop responsibility, young people need to *have* responsibility. To learn to care, they need to perform caring actions.

Simply learning *about* the value of caring may increase students' moral knowledge. But it won't necessarily develop their own commitment to that value, their confidence that they themselves can help, or the skills needed to help effectively. To cultivate caring, as with any other moral quality, requires a learning-by-doing approach that develops all three aspects of character: knowing, feeling, and action.

Consider the experience of a ninth-grade teacher in the Canadian province of Quebec. He hoped to arouse his honor students' concern for the poor by showing them a graphic film on world hunger. At the end of the film, one student raised his hand and said, "The world has an overpopulation problem, right? People have to die anyway. Starvation reduces the world's overpopulation." Nods around the room suggested that other students thought this was a good point.

Other teachers have also reported indifferent and even hostile student reactions to efforts to raise their social consciousness. Part of the problem may be defensiveness; they can't see any solution to the problem, and they don't want to have to feel guilty about it. That's why a teacher should make clear—*before* showing a film about world poverty—that groups like Oxfam America are doing something about the problem and that students can help.

But there's an even more basic need. To develop empathy and caring, students need *ongoing, firsthand experience in face-to-face helping relationships*. That's how they come to bond with other people, value them, and discover the powerful rewards of touching another's life. There is simply no substitute for person-to-person helping experience.

How can schools provide direct opportunities for helping? It begins with a school philosophy that makes service a priority. Says one private school headmaster:

> Children here are expected to care for others. The older students are all involved in teaching something to the younger ones. They're achievers, to be sure, but they get the message "It's not just your own education you're here for. You're here to contribute to other people's education as well."

There are simple ways to promote helpfulness that any school could readily implement. At Emily Carr Elementary School in Scarborough, Ontario, older students referee noon-hour games for the younger pupils and coach them in sports such as soccer and basketball. In Beecher Elementary School in Elmira, New York, good classroom behavior is rewarded by free time to teach a younger child to read, or to help out in the cerebral palsy resource room.

CLASS BUDDIES

Another way to extend caring beyond the classroom is a "class buddies" program, wherein an older class "adopts" a younger one.

Kim McConnell, sixth-grade teacher at Walt Disney Elementary School in San Ramon, California, has been "doing buddies" for four years. Her sixth-graders get together with their second-grade buddies two or three times a month and have done everything from working on math skills, to camping overnight, to a field trip to Chinatown.

Louise Lotz, who teaches in the same school, says her third-graders greatly value their friendships with their fifth-grade buddies. In turn, her third-graders have buddied up with a kindergarten class and read to their younger schoolmates once a week.

At Ontario's Emily Carr School, kindergarten teacher Dee Bent has her 5-year-olds buddy with 9- to 12-year-old students who have learning disabilities. For the learning-disabled students, she says, being able to assume the responsibilities of older buddies has had dramatic effects:

> It makes them feel so valuable. Their reading scores have shot up; they've spent a lot of time looking for books to read to the little ones. In the fall they organized a science treasure hunt for their little buddies. There is real affection; the older kids will poke their heads in to say "Hi" when they go by, and my children will say to me, "I saw my buddy on Saturday!" The experience has been especially important for one older boy who has virtually no support at home. Here he has three little ones who love him.

In one-to-one relationships like these, the older children are learning to care by caring; the younger ones are learning to care by being cared for.

CROSS-AGE TUTORING

A growing number of schools are discovering the benefits of cross-age tutoring as an opportunity for children to render meaningful service.

In the cross-age tutoring relationship, an older student takes on regular responsibility for instructing a younger child in a particular subject or skill. Cross-age tutoring can be set up between two classes (e.g., as an extension of a buddies program) and may involve selected students rather than the whole class.

To increase chances of success, schools typically provide a training program for the student tutors, giving tutors their own "teacher's manual" and taking them step-by-step through specific lesson plans. Tutors are also shown what to do if the tutee makes a mistake or seems restless or bored.

The Child Development Project (see Chapter 2) has put together an excellent four-session training program for cross-age tutors in its three participating elementary schools. In these schools, any fourth-, fifth-, or sixth-grader can volunteer to give up one or two recesses a week to tutor a first-, second-, or third-grader who needs extra help. Two years after the program went into effect, some 70 children were giving up free time to tutor younger schoolmates.

I interviewed a fifth-grade girl who was in her second year of tutoring. "It makes me feel important to help other people," she said. "If they need help, you know *how* to help them."

Not all tutors continue after their first year; some find it's harder than they expected. But among the young children who have had the experience of being tutored, the project finds, there's a high probability that they go on to be tutors themselves when they are old enough. (For information on this program, write to the Child Development Project, 111 Deerwood Place, Suite 165, San Ramon, CA 94583.)

All of these cross-age programs, besides enabling children to grow through serving others, do a lot to develop a positive, schoolwide moral community.

OLDER FRIENDS FOR YOUNGER CHILDREN

At the high school level, Big Brother/Big Sister programs give older students a chance to get involved in a caring relationship with a younger child.

Older Friends for Younger Children is one of the oldest Big Brother/Big Sister programs in Massachusetts. It began in 1976 in the Salem-Marblehead area when six divorced mothers approached a local counseling center for help in finding male companionship for their sons. Susan Maynard, a counselor at the center who is also a school psychologist, responded by pairing single-parent children under 14 with mature 14- to 19-year-olds she worked with at Marblehead High School.[20]

The big brothers and big sisters typically see their younger friend once a week, play ball, take a walk, go for an ice cream, or just talk. Says one 16-year-old big brother: "You're aware of trying to be a good example, maybe one of the only examples these little kids have of someone older. It makes you think more about your own values."[21]

REACHING OUT TO THE COMMUNITY

A few years ago Ernest Boyer, former U.S. commissioner of education, made headlines with a bold proposal: Require all high school students to complete a community service term, taken for school credit.[22]

Before they graduated, students would be asked to volunteer in the libraries, parks, hospitals, nursing homes, day-care centers, social agencies, or programs for the handicapped and retarded of their communities. They would learn to care about the common good by contributing to it.

Others before Boyer have argued that the way to solve the problem of youthful alienation is to give young people meaningful ways to participate in society.[23] But this time the idea of student community service is riding a wave of concern about national values and character.

According to a 1987 Carnegie Foundation study,[24] most public high schools offer some type of community service program (either voluntary or required). By the mid-1980s, one of five public high schools—including the school systems of Detroit, Atlanta, and St. Louis—had mandated some form of community service as a graduation requirement.

Students in these schools sometimes work individually, sometimes together on special service projects. For example, in Bergenfield, New Jersey, 15 to 18 high school juniors and seniors staff an aid-to-senior-citizens project. Each morning, between 7:30 and 8:30, the students phone elderly people who live alone and say, "Good morning, this is Bergenfield High School. Are you okay today?" In just one year, Bergenfield's program resulted in 37 emergency aid visits to senior citizens who had fallen out of bed and couldn't respond to their phone.

Sometimes service projects are for academic credit, part of a course. Juniors in a history class in Connecticut, for example, learned that a schoolhouse built in 1799 was to be demolished. They responded by raising money and doing the work to renovate it and move it to its original location.[25] (For helpful thumbnail sketches of how five high schools have implemented community service courses for academic credit, see "A Profile of High School Community Service Programs" by Fred Newmann and Robert Rutter in the December 1985/January 1986 issue of *Educational Leadership*.)

Sometimes a community-school umbrella organization supports this kind of effort. For example: The cities of Evansville, Fort Wayne, and Indianapolis, Indiana, have been the testing grounds for a concept designed by the National Crime Prevention Council and funded by the Lilly Endowment. In each city, a board consisting of local citizens offers modest grants for community service projects that teens play a substantial role in designing and implementing.

One group of teens learned that a day-care facility in a low-income area was about to be closed because it didn't have adequate outdoor play space. The teenagers sought a community grant to buy materials and did all the design, permit-seeking, and construction for the needed play facility. As a result, a much-needed service remained available to hard-pressed working parents.[26]

CHILDREN HELPING THEIR COMMUNITIES

Even before service became a national trend among high schools, many elementary and middle schools were demonstrating that children could also be involved in reaching out to the human community, both near and far.

• At Mountville Elementary School in Pennsylvania, teachers and students planned a major community environmental project around three activities: recycling, fieldwork, and conservation. Recycling activities included viewing a film on recycling, turning bottle caps into coasters, and making egg-carton wastebaskets. Field experiences included painting the fence in the community park, raking the leaves on the nursing home grounds, cleaning up the three-corner downtown area, and planting bulbs at the reservoir. Conservation activities included viewing a slide show on land use conservation, creating a wildlife refuge on school grounds, and making energy-saving reminders for home use.[27] (See Chapter 9 for other examples of environmental projects carried out by children.)

• At Westwood Elementary School in St. Cloud, Minnesota, students develop one-to-one relationships with elderly and often depressed patients at the nearby Veterans Administration Medical Center. During twice-weekly visits, the children and the vets play cards, plant seedlings, chop wood, discuss travel or current events, or talk about the differences between growing up today and 60 years ago. Since the program's inception in 1972, more than 2,000 veterans have developed a renewed interest in life through their relationships with Westwood students.

• At Heritage Heights Elementary School in Sweet Home, New York, during a recent school year students organized a fund-raising drive to aid earthquake and hurricane victims. At South School in Andover, Massachusetts, students gathered a truckload of clothing for children in Romania with AIDS.

• One of the most successful community service programs—one that has received national recognition—can be found at the Shoreham-Wading River Middle School in Shoreham, New York. Since 1973 hundreds of sixth-, seventh-, and eighth-graders each year have done community service, usually for one hour a week, as an integral part of their middle school curriculum. When community service is woven into the school curriculum in this ongoing way, it has the greatest chance of deep and lasting impact on a child's character.

Students are involved in serving four groups: (1) young children in neighboring day-care centers, Head Start centers, and district kindergartens; (2) elementary school classes, where middle schoolers team up with lower grades to lead a variety of learning activities; (3) handicapped children at a local hospital and special education centers; and (4) elderly who reside in adult homes and nursing homes.

A school publication, *Children and Their Community,* gives touching examples of what these experiences have meant to the participating students. Gains in self-esteem are common; said one girl who worked at a local nursing home, "This is the very first time I have been able to prove what I can do." Another girl outgrew her initial pity for old people through community service. She said: "The elderly aren't ashamed of what they are and they aren't worried about their futures; they just want to share their pasts. The past was when they lived; now I see how crazy I was to want to grow up so fast, wishing my life away."

Work with handicapped children, the school reports, has provided some of the most difficult and challenging community service opportunities. Work with these children goes slowly. In the beginning, many of the middle school students are reluctant to touch the handicapped children, or even to look at them. But continued exposure breaks down the students' fear and prejudices. One child who made regular visits to a school for the retarded said, "When I used to see retarded kids, I was afraid of them. Now the retarded have become people to me, with needs and wants."

(For how-to manuals on Shoreham-Wading River community service projects, write Winnie Pardo, Shoreham-Wading River Middle School, Randall Road, Shoreham, NY 11786. Other resources: *Wingspread: Principles of Good Practice for Combining Service and Learning,* The Johnson Foundation, Inc., Racine, WI 53401; *The Generator: National Journal of Service Leadership,* NYLC, 1910 West County Road B, Roseville, MN 55113; and the award-winning film *Close Harmony*—information available from Kay Edstene, Friends Council of Schools, 1507 Cherry Street, Philadelphia, PA 19102; tel. 215-241-7245.)

SCHOOLING FOR SOCIAL JUSTICE

Another dimension to community service is called to mind by the following parable:

A man saw a person drowning in a river and dove in to save him. The next day, another person was swept down the river, and once more the

---

CARING BEYOND THE CLASSROOM

Schools can foster students' caring attitudes and active citizenship beyond the classroom if they:

1. Make students aware of the needs and suffering of others in their own country and around the world.

2. Offer examples of groups such as Oxfam America and Amnesty International working effectively to help the poor and oppressed; organize student action projects to help.

3. Provide inspiring role models, such as Giraffe Project heroes, of people helping others in their own communities.

4. Provide positive peer role models.

5. Give students the opportunity to render school service, especially in face-to-face helping relationships such as class buddies and in cross-age tutoring.

6. Enable students to participate in community service; where possible, integrate such service into the academic program.

7. Provide education in social justice, the politics of change, and citizen action.

---

courageous bystander plunged into the waters to save the struggling victim.

The following day, there were three people drowning, and this time the bystander had to get help to make the rescues. The day after that, ten people needed saving, and many citizens had to join the rescue effort. Soon the river was full of drowning people, and the whole town worked ceaselessly to save them.

Finally someone said, "We should go upriver to find out where all these drowning people are coming from." But others answered, "We can't—we're too busy saving their lives down here."

Educating students to care about others ultimately means educating them in social justice. That means going upriver to find the source of the problem.

Robert Starratt is a Fordham University professor who has worked with high schoolers on social justice concerns. It's necessary, Starratt says, to teach students to distinguish between "works of mercy" and "works of justice." Visiting someone who is unjustly imprisoned and commiserating with him in his plight is an act of mercy. Making an effort to restore his political rights is an act of justice. Bringing food to the poor at Christmas is a work of mercy; trying to change the social conditions that trap people in poverty is an act of justice.[28]

Self-giving on the part of students, Starratt says, will often begin with personal works of mercy. But we must help them understand the need to go beyond mercy to works of justice. Students must understand "that while we can and should offer succor to those suffering because of unjust laws, we serve them far better by getting the unjust laws changed."[29] The best educational experience, Starratt says, would be for students to work with the poor, and then, back in the classroom, analyze the social structures that adversely affect the lives of the poor people they deal with.

Some schools have a tradition of developing social-political awareness as a source of social action. An example is Princeton, New Jersey's Stuart Country Day School, part of the Order of the Sacred Heart Schools. The school's then headmistress, Sister Joan Magnetti, says of their high school students:

> Our students read to the blind, work with kids in inner-city neighborhood houses, help in soup kitchens, rebuild houses, and spend two weeks in Appalachia. Many have also interviewed their congressional representatives regarding social issues. Since we believe this kind of education should ideally have an international dimension, we've also sent many students to Bogotá. Our goal is to prepare our students for leadership by exposing them to the moral imperatives in the world today.

Resources for educating students in social justice are available to teachers. *Educating for Citizen Action,* by Professor Fred Newman of the University of Wisconsin at Madison,[30] lays out for students the steps and skills for analyzing and attacking a social problem. Using a systematic approach like Newman's, high school students have in fact carried out sophisticated citizen action, including proposing and lobbying for bills in the state legislature.

The well-known project Facing History and Ourselves (see Chapter 2) has recently developed a minicourse called Facing Today and the Future: Choosing to Participate. The original project began with a Holocaust curriculum for eighth-graders. But many students, after learning about Nazi genocide and examining prejudice in their own lives, wanted to know what they could do to help prevent prejudice and improve society.

The new course on participation is an answer to that; it looks at all the ways down through history that people have participated—through human service, politics, social activism, and other voluntary activity—in creating a society that seeks justice and dignity for all its members. (For materials on the Choosing to Participate course, contact Facing History and Ourselves, 25 Kennard Road, Brookline, MA 02146; tel. 617-232-1595.)

"Moral education must include political education," argues West German educator Michael Miller; "how else will moral values become real in society?" Miller maintains that even grade-school children can begin to develop a critical political awareness that will eventually guide their citizen action.

In a West German moral education project, third-graders read and discussed a novelette about a gang of street children in Bolivia. In the story, the street children survive by selling rubber "flip-flop sandals," which they make from tires they steal. One boy refuses to join in the stealing. The story becomes a vehicle for discussing moral choices and the social conditions that send thousands of children into the street to live.[31]

Comments Miller:

> Children this age really enter into the plight of the poor; they have a very strong feeling for justice. Global education with them doesn't mean talking about something abstract like the parliament of Bolivia but about concrete experiences they can identify with.

Educating for caring citizenship beyond the classroom is not without its stumbling blocks. For example, in high schools where community service has been made a graduation requirement, many program coordinators say that transporting students to community sites is a "major problem."[32] Strong administrative and community support is needed to work out the logistical difficulties. Another problem: Many high school students have shown little or no desire to get involved in community service. That points to the need to start sooner, in the elementary years, to develop their participatory spirit and help them discover the pleasures of helping other human beings.

In his prophetic book *Democracy in America,* nineteenth-century Frenchman Alexis de Tocqueville said that American democracy, for all of its strengths, tended to foster individualism because of its emphasis on personal freedom. That individualism, Tocqueville said, first saps the virtues of public life and ends in pure selfishness.

Teaching students to be caring, public-spirited citizens—in their school, community, nation, and world—is one of the most promising antidotes to the selfish individualism that afflicts our culture. This participatory citizenship education has students learn to care by giving care.

In so doing, it teaches young people to see themselves as capable of goodness. It teaches them to feel membership in a single human family. It teaches them to pay attention to the social conditions that bring about suffering and to use the political system to create a more just society and world. And it teaches them the truth of Edmund Burke's famous statement some two centuries ago: "The only thing necessary for the triumph of evil is for good people to do nothing."

CHAPTER 17

===

Creating a Positive Moral Culture in the School

If we want our students to take moral education seriously, the school itself must be a moral institution.

—JANET BRODESSER, teacher,
Brockport, New York

S ays a mother whose son goes to private high school in the Midwest:

> There are many problems at the high school. Besides drinking—and there's a lot of that—there's a tremendous amount of stealing. Kids wear ratty sneakers to school because they might be stolen; you can't leave anything around. It seems as if any time you go to get a book out of the library, it's been stolen. The teachers at the high school seem to care about the kids, but the kids don't seem to pick up on their example. They feel you're just responsible for yourself.
>
> And these are kids who come out of wonderful, warm, caring elementary schools where the students appear to be learning kindness and respect for others. But then they go to high school and seem to lose it all. What causes the regression? Do they have moral reasoning that they're just not using?

High school students who behave in self-centered, irresponsible ways (including students at academically "top" schools) very often do have higher moral reasoning available. Why don't they use it? One answer: The surrounding environment—the ethos or "moral culture" of the school—doesn't evoke students' best morality and may even discourage them from operating at their highest moral levels.

Just how the school's moral culture affects students' moral functioning has been studied by psychologists Clark Power, Ann Higgins, and Lawrence Kohlberg. In their book *Lawrence Kohlberg's Approach to Moral Education* (1989), they report this finding: When a high school strives to be a "just community," students see their school as being governed by high-stage moral norms (e.g., "Care about others"). Under that condition students bring into play their highest level of moral reasoning when asked how they would solve an everyday school-related moral dilemma.

Not so in high schools that are not experienced by students as just and democratic communities. There, the research shows, students given a school-related moral dilemma are likely to show a reasoning gap—using moral reasoning (e.g., "Look out for yourself") that is lower than the level of which they are capable.[1] In short, students' operative moral reasoning level tends to rise—or fall—to match what they perceive to be the moral environment of the school.

A MEASURE OF THE MORAL CULTURE

Elementary schools, like high schools, differ markedly in their moral cultures.

One morning a fourth-grade teacher in Ontario left a $5 bill on her classroom desk in plain sight. Over recess, unobserved, she removed the bill from the desk. When the students had all come back, she pointed out that the bill was gone and said to the class, "Write down what you think happened to the $5."

Not a single student suggested that somebody might have stolen the money. Instead the children said things such as, "It's got to be here somewhere," "The wind must have blown it away," and "Maybe our rabbit [the classroom pet] got it." The fact that it seemed not to occur to these children that somebody in the school might have taken the money showed that a high level of trust characterized their school's moral culture.

The same $5 bill experiment was carried out by this teacher's husband. He also taught a fourth-grade class but at a different school in the community—one lacking a good school climate and where there was no consistent effort to foster positive values. When he reported to his class that the $5 was missing from his desktop, *all* of his students said, "Somebody must have stolen it." In this school, students obviously perceived dishonesty to be the norm: Given the chance, people would steal.

We want students to become the kind of people who will do what's right even when they're surrounded by a rotten moral culture. But *forming* that sort of character is much easier in a moral environment where being honest, decent, and caring is perceived to be the norm—what everybody simply expects of everybody else.

THE SIX ELEMENTS OF A POSITIVE MORAL CULTURE IN THE SCHOOL

How can a school create a positive moral culture? Six elements, I believe, are important:

1. Moral and academic leadership from the principal

2. Schoolwide discipline that models, promotes, and upholds the school's values in *all* school environments

3. A schoolwide sense of community

4. Student government that involves students in democratic self-government and fosters the feeling "This is *our* school, and we're responsible for making it the best school it can be"

5. A moral atmosphere of mutual respect, fairness, and cooperation that pervades all relationships—those among the adults in the school as well as those between adults and students

6. Elevating the importance of morality by spending school time on moral concerns.

Progress in one element usually brings progress in another. However, a school doesn't have to be equally strong in all six dimensions to have a good moral culture. I think it's useful to think of these elements as ideals to work toward.

Let's look now at schools in this country and Canada that exemplify one or another of these six elements.

ELEMENT 1: THE PRINCIPAL'S LEADERSHIP

Find a school with a healthy moral environment and a program for teaching good values and you'll find a principal who is leading the way or supporting someone else who is.

An effective principal is typically involved in all of the activities common to values education success stories: creating a council or steering committee that identifies the school's target values and provides ongoing leadership for implementing the program; setting up workshops, sharing sessions, curriculum development time, resource centers, and other opportunities for school staff to develop skills as moral educators; involving *all staff*—including aides, secretaries, cafeteria workers, custodians, and bus drivers—in sessions that introduce them to the goals and strategies of the values program and show them how everyone has a role to play; eliciting the support and participation of parents; and modeling the school's espoused values through the principal's interactions with staff, students, and parents.

Effective principals also have vision. In a study of school leadership styles, University of Texas at Austin researchers asked principals, "What is your vision for this school—your long-range goals and expectations?" Without hesitation, effective principals began to list their goals for their schools. When less effective principals were asked the same question, they usually responded with a long pause and a vague statement such as, "I think we have a good school, and I'd like to keep it that way."[2]

In this study, when a principal had a vision of a school's future, teachers were likely to describe the school as a good place for both students and teachers. By contrast, teachers working under less effective principals seldom spoke of their school or of their own work with enthusiasm or excitement.[3]

Profile of an Effective Principal

Carl Campbell, principal of Dry Creek Elementary School in Clovis, California, fits the profile of an effective school leader. Projecting warmth and optimism, he explains that his school's mission is to help students develop their potential in five areas: academics, athletics, performing arts, citizenship in the school, and citizenship in the community. And that commitment, he says, goes for *every* student:

> Our philosophy is that we do everything we can do while we've got a kid. When he walks through that door, we're responsible for the quality of his experience. We may not be able to control his environment elsewhere, but we can control the environment here.

Dry Creek was one of the places I visited during my research on schools reputed to be making a deliberate effort to teach moral values.

On the morning I arrived, Carl Campbell was on the public address system thanking a third-grade boy for turning in $20 he had found. When he finished, I said, referring to the boy's act, "That's pretty impressive."

"That happens all the time," he said. Honesty of that sort, he explained, is encouraged by making it one of the values of the month in the school's character development program and by giving public recognition to acts of honesty that children perform.

In Dry Creek's Value of the Month program, the whole school—every teacher at every grade level—focuses on a particular value (e.g., friendship, cooperation, loyalty) each month. Principal Campbell elaborates:

> I have many teachers who do a terrific job with the Value of the Month. They talk to their kids about it. They work it into the writing assignments. They do special projects around it. They make special displays in the classroom. They bring in books or articles that tell about a person or incident that exemplifies the value.

Many people wonder, "Can the school teach values effectively if kids are getting different values at home?" I asked Carl Campbell: "Do you think your Value of the Month program would be effective in, say, teaching honesty in a community where a significant number of students were not taught that value outside the school?" He responded:

> Before coming to Clovis, I was principal in a poverty pocket. Stealing was an everyday occurrence at the school when I arrived. The attitude among students was that it was okay to steal as long as you didn't get caught. There was also a problem of kids being intimidated for their lunch money.
>
> I said to the faculty, "How can we change this?" We selected basic values to teach, ones that wouldn't get us in trouble. Honesty was one. As time went on, kids started turning in money they found on the playground. Intimidation became less and less of a problem. By the end of our second year with the program, stealing was a rare event at this school.

Even when there is not a supportive moral culture outside the school, it's still possible to create one within the school. If teachers at every grade level are simultaneously teaching the same moral value, doing so in different and creative ways, and doing so all school year long, year after year, the school has a cumulative effect with the power to change students' moral behavior.

There will certainly be individual differences in how much students generalize positive moral behavior beyond the school. In part, that generalization will depend on the extent to which improved moral behavior reflects genuine growth in character—in children's reasoned understanding of a moral value, for example, and in their emotional commitment to it. That's why it's important to teach a value in a way that fosters not only desirable behavior but also the cognitive and affective underpinnings of moral conduct.

CHILDREN AS *AMIGOS*

To the northwest of Clovis, in the city of Modesto, California, is Sonoma Elementary School. It was lunchtime when I arrived there. In the cafeteria, children in wheelchairs intermingled with physically normal children.

Then I noticed that the children were in pairs. I learned that this was part of the *Amigo* Program, wherein students in grades 2 through 6 sign up to be *amigos* to physically handicapped children. They are buddies to the handicapped kids, assisting them in the cafeteria, on the playground, and on and off the bus. Mostly they are just friends. It was clearly not a chore for these *amigos;* their lively chatter and happy faces were evidence of that.

None of this was an accident, of course. Mayris Baddell, the principal, explained that Sonoma is a school of 600 students that thoroughly integrates its 70 handicapped children. "Our goal here," she said, "is to treat children as children. We want to foster appreciation of all people, whatever their handicaps and whatever their gifts."

Once a month, Sonoma has a school pride assembly at which awards are given for citizenship as well as academic achievement. Fourth-, fifth-, and sixth-graders can earn points toward a school letter through various kinds of service—tutoring a younger child, serving on the traffic patrol, being an *amigo,* and so on. As part of each assembly, students sing the "Sonoma Spirit Song." All of this contributes to a school environment that emphasizes caring for others as much as good grades.

THE POWER OF THE PRINCIPAL'S EXAMPLE

At Reilly Elementary School in Chicago, Rosemary Culverwell's leadership demonstrates the force of the principal's personal example and direct involvement in getting things done.

Reilly's enrollment of 700 students includes children from 38 different countries of origin. Approximately 200 children, 75 percent of them black, are bused in from other parts of the city. Yet racial or ethnic hostilities are rare.

Mrs. Culverwell has high praise for what she feels is a first-rate faculty: "We have a marvelous staff—diverse, very talented, very-well-educated, very open. You have to be in order to deal effectively with so many cultures and nationalities."

When I spoke with individual teachers at Reilly, all emphasized that they tried constantly to model, by how they treated students, the acceptance and affirmation of individual differences.

The climate at Reilly was not always so positive. The school is in a neighborhood that is home to one of Chicago's most violent white gangs. When Rosemary Culverwell became principal in the mid-1970s, there was hardly a window in the school that wasn't broken "and the building looked as if it was falling down." By enlisting the help of the teachers' union, principal Culverwell got the building in good shape. (The gang still frequents school grounds after hours but no longer vandalizes the school.)

Principal Culverwell was still distressed, however, by the prevalence of graffiti. So one day she brought some rags and a can of "vandal spray" to school, took them out on the playground during recess, and asked some children to help her clean some graffiti off a wall.

"I didn't do it!" they all said.

"I know," she said. "Neither did I. But I need your help." They did help, and pretty soon some other kids who were watching volunteered. She explains:

> After that, every so often I'd go around with the vandal spray and rags and ask kids to help me clean a wall. Sometimes I'd stick my head in a classroom and ask, "Who will help me clean some markings off a wall?" After a while, kids started coming up to me and telling me about marks that needed cleaning. When we started this, there was a lot of writing on both inside and outside walls. Now there is virtually none.

Principal Culverwell also began picking up litter—again, during recess, because she wanted the children to see her.

The Student Council was given the responsibility of inspecting each classroom once every three months. When I visited a fifth-grade class at Reilly, the teacher explained that the children each had their own plastic pail and that at the end of every day they each washed their own desktops.

"What do you like about this school?" I asked these fifth-graders.

"The teachers," was their first answer; "they help you learn, and they don't scream at you." "It's a clean school," was the second answer.

"Why is it clean?" I asked.

"Because we take care of it," they said.

During a recent year, in a competition with more than 200 other Chicago schools, Reilly Elementary won first place as the cleanest school in the city. A year later, in recognition of the many things it does to foster student responsibility, Reilly won a citywide award from the organization For Character for excellence in both character development and academic achievement.

Rosemary Culverwell's style illustrates another characteristic of good principals: They are highly visible. That maximizes their personal contact with both teachers and children and their ability to create a high level of accountability. Says Fred Gula, principal for more than 20 years at Glendale Elementary School in Scotia, New York:

> I go into *every* classroom two times a day. I can tell the temper of a class—whether learning is taking place. If I think there's a problem, the teacher and I will meet.
>
> I'm also in the halls a lot. I'm in the cafeteria every day—what we call the combat zone. Kids know me in different ways. If I discipline someone, I'll make it a point to get back to that kid before the end of the day to say something positive—something totally unrelated to the offense.

Sylvia Peters is another high-profile principal; she won a Whitman award for excellence in education by dramatically turning around the Dumas Elementary School (kindergarten through eighth grade) in inner-city Chicago. Under her leadership, Dumas has been recognized by the U.S. Department of Education and featured on NBC television for its drug-free environment and values education program. Like other outstanding principals, Sylvia Peters makes her presence felt throughout the school. She comments:

> I used to collect guns and knives when I first came here. We had sixth-graders getting pregnant. One of the first things I did was to put my hands on everyone. I'd take their faces and talk to them. That calmed things down and stopped a lot of bad behavior. Kids let you know what they need: They want to have a friend, to be loved, to be safe, and to learn.

What these principals have done at the elementary level, other principals have done in the larger, more formidable setting of the secondary school. Witness, for example, the stories (see Chapter 19) of high school principals who have come into drug-infested, crime-ridden, low-achieving schools and created an environment for learning and good values.

ELEMENT 2: SCHOOLWIDE DISCIPLINE

Effective schoolwide discipline is a second vital ingredient in the total moral environment of the school.

In the book *Fifteen Thousand Hours,* British researcher Michael Rutter and colleagues report their study of 2,700 students they followed from elementary school through 12 different high schools in London. Rutter's team identified children who at age 10 were at high risk of becoming juvenile delinquents.

Controlling for social class, the researchers found that if an at-risk child subsequently went to a high school with poor order and discipline, there was a 48 percent probability that the child would become a juvenile delinquent. But if the child went to a high school with good order and discipline, the probability of delinquency dropped dramatically, to only 9 percent.[4]

How rules are enforced makes all the difference in how seriously students take them—and whether a rule violation becomes an occasion for a student's moral growth.

Using school discipline to promote moral development is an important goal at Emily Carr Elementary School (kindergarten through grade 8) in Scarborough, Ontario. Principal Bill Fleming explains: "We involve both staff and kids in helping to set the rules. When a student is sent to me for a serious rule violation, I use a contract approach that requires the student to take responsibility for improving his or her behavior."[5] Principal Fleming asks these four questions:

1. What happened to bring you here? ("Ninety-five percent can tell you.")

2. Is that behavior helping you? ("Students can usually see that it isn't.")

3. Do you want to do something about it? ("Here we usually talk some more.")

4. What do you do well to gain recognition? ("I want to build that into the plan for improvement.")

Following this discussion, Mr. Fleming and the student:

1. Work out and sign a mutually agreed-upon plan by which the student can improve his or her behavior.

2. Meet within a week's time to review the plan to see how it's working, and continue to do this weekly for the next two to three weeks.

3. Touch base once a month over the course of the next few months.

Says Bill Fleming: "If you involve kids in thinking, in taking an active part in solving their problem, you get more commitment and responsibility. This approach works for 90 percent of kids who are sent to my office. For the other 10 percent we involve other resources [such as parents or the school psychologist]."

Teachers are also important in making a schoolwide discipline policy work. The role they play in communicating expected behavior was clear from my conversation with students at Emily Carr. For example, two eighth-graders, both members of the Student Council, talked about the difference between Emily Carr and schools they'd gone to before. Marlena said:

> I came from a school where you fought if somebody said something to you. One girl called me a name, and I punched her out.
>
> The first time I got in a fight here, the teacher told me, "Fighting won't help you solve your problems, and it encourages the younger ones to start it. It's a bad habit for them to get into." The teachers here really stress that the younger ones will follow your example.

I asked Marlena, "How have you changed as a person since you came to this school?" She answered: "I don't pick fights anymore. I used to pick fights so people would notice me. Here you don't have to prove anything. You're just accepted for who you are."

ACTING TO STOP ABUSIVE BEHAVIOR

Creating a good moral environment in the school requires treating as serious any behavior that violates respect for persons. That means responding swiftly when children abuse others. Teacher Josine Nocula gives an example of that kind of vigilance at Chicago's Reilly Elementary School:

> We don't close our eyes to what goes on before and after school. Last week a grandmother called and said some kids were ganging up on her 8-year-old granddaughter on the playground before school. The assistant

principal immediately got on the case of the guilty students, and I called the grandmother back to tell her what we had done. She felt better. We take action.

Last year some third-grade boys were picking on some of the first-grade children in my Polish language class. I confronted them about it. But I also wanted to build positive relations between them and my students, so I asked them, "Would you like to learn Polish?" They joined the class. Now some of them are walking their little friends home.

Unfortunately, such vigilance is far from universal. In many schools, for example, there is little or no effective supervision of children's playground behavior, and cruelty reigns. There are several solutions to playground problems, but all of them call upon adults to resume responsibility for providing the supervision that children definitely need:

- Organize clubs, sports, and other games during recess so that all students are involved in some kind of constructive activity.

- Have classes at all grade levels brainstorm ideas for preventing and solving playground problems. They can then implement their best ideas or submit their proposals, if it's a cross-class issue, to the Student Council and school administration.

- Teach playground aides techniques for effective supervision and for handling discipline problems in a way that's consistent with the values the school is trying to teach.

- Recruit and train older students in assisting with supervision of playground activities (e.g., at Emily Carr students in the upper elementary grades coach teams of younger pupils and officiate at their lunchtime volleyball, hockey, and baseball games).

With some thought and effort, any school can transform the playground from a *Lord of the Flies* situation, where the lowest common denominator prevails, to a positive part of a school's total moral environment.

MORALITY ON THE SCHOOL BUS

The school bus is another trouble spot. One mother said her second-grade daughter was terrified to ride the bus because of a 14-year-old boy who repeatedly cursed her, ripped her book bag, warned that he "was going to get her if she told," and one day stomped on her hand hard enough to break several blood vessels. A father told of how his fourth-grade son had been intimidated on the bus by one or another older student every year of elementary school. In both cases, complaints to the principal had produced little effective action—an all-too-common story.

Mark Flint, who teaches kindergarten in a small rural school in central New York, was disturbed when several of his students complained that they were being picked on by older students on the bus. He is now trying to start a "bus buddies" program whereby each of his children will have an older student to watch over them—and even read to them—during their bus ride.

Seeing to it that children feel safe and secure on the school bus is an absolutely fundamental responsibility of a school administration. Not to do so is a serious failure on several counts—not the least of which is that it sends a terrible moral message to both bullies and victims: that children are allowed to be cruel and menacing to other children, and adults will look the other way.

Some schools are beginning to wake up to the problem of school bullying, which is a growing concern in many countries. In Norway, many schools have begun a new program that combines clear rules against bullying behavior, greater adult supervision, classroom discussion of the problem, and parental awareness. Early reports are that this program has reduced school bullying by an average of 50 percent. The program notes another reason to pay attention to bullying: Children who bully are five times as likely as other children to end up with criminal records.[6]

If a school truly wants to teach values such as respect and responsibility, behavioral expectations need to be spelled out and enforced for *all* school environments—the corridors, the bathrooms, the library, the cafeteria, the auditorium, the playground, and the school bus.

ELEMENT 3: DEVELOPING A SCHOOLWIDE SENSE OF COMMUNITY

A strong, schoolwide sense of community is often the best way to prevent abusive behaviors such as bullying, which breed easily when the bonds of community are weak and positive group norms are absent.

At Winkelman Elementary School north of Chicago, the high level of student diversity could easily lead to friction. Economic levels of families range from millionaires to families on welfare. There's also a good deal of racial and ethnic mix; represented groups include Orientals, Jews, Indians, Brazilians, blacks, Mexicans, Pakistanis, and Greeks.

From all this diversity, however, Winkelman has fashioned a cohesive and caring school community. This is evident in how the school integrates a new student—a telling indicator of how much attention a school pays to community-building. A mother of a third-grade girl describes her daughter's experience:

> It was February when we moved here. I was impressed by the way they greeted Dana at the door when she came to visit the school, and how they took her around and introduced her to all the different classes. By the end of the day, she said, "I want to go to school here, Mommy." When she arrived for her first day, there were great big WELCOME DANA banners hanging outside the classrooms.

Winkelman students, this mother points out, feel valued when they're in school and valued when they're absent. She comments:

> If a child is sick here for more than a few days, cards start to come to the house. And when the child returns, they make him feel that he's the most important person on Earth—that he was really missed.

Another of Winkelman's community-building traditions is the Winkelgram, a note of appreciation written on a yellow, preprinted, five-by-eight message form. Stacks of blank Winkelgrams are readily available—on all teachers' desks, for example—and anyone may send one to anyone else.

On the day I visited the school, the principal had just sent a Winkelgram to a staff member thanking her for her work on a special school bulletin board display. The principal had also just sent the following Winkelgram to a girl who had helped a younger schoolmate who fell on the playground:

> Dear Lori,
> Thanks for being a super person and helping somebody in trouble.
>
>   Mrs. Sechrist

A teacher explained how she uses Winkelgrams: "If another class gives a play for us, we'll write a Winkelgram as a class. If the custodian makes an extra effort to help us clean up after a project, we'll send one to him." Children now frequently help themselves to Winkelgrams and send them to each other on their own.

Messages like these go a long way toward generating a strong sense of school community and norms of respect and caring.

Community-building also means creating opportunities for students to get to know people beyond their own classroom, including the various adults who are part of the school. In an elementary school in San Ramon, California, as part of a unit on helping, various school helpers—principal, nurse, janitor, and secretary—visit second-grade classrooms to talk about what they do.

EXTRACURRICULAR ACTIVITIES

Extracurricular activities are another effective way to help students develop the feeling of being valued members of their school community.

Virtually all schools offer a variety of extracurricular activities, but elementary schools in Clovis, California, give that effort a unique twist. They elevate the importance of extracurricular activities by calling them their "cocurricular program," and they try to get all students in grades four through six to participate. Principal Carl Campbell explains:

> It might be sports—volleyball, football, cross-country, basketball—or chorus, student government, or the school play; it doesn't matter what it is as long as the youngster is involved in something. Our experience tells us that every child benefits—in skill development, self-confidence, and peer relations—by being part of the cocurricular program.
>
> When we find some kids who aren't getting involved, we'll talk to the child, contact the child's parents, explain our philosophy regarding the cocurricular program. Eventually we'll get that child involved.

He gave an example of a student who at first didn't participate in any cocurricular activity:

> This year we have a boy in fourth grade who is legally deaf. Before this year he was in special education schools. At the start of this year he's had a little trouble with his peers—making friends. I've seen him out on the playground standing alone, bouncing a ball.
>
> Well, we talked with his parents, and we've got this boy started in cross-country track. He's got a group now, he's part of a team, he's involved.

A month later I wrote to Carl Campbell to ask how this boy was doing. He wrote back:

Evan Adair, our deaf student, continues to run cross-country at Dry Creek. His participation in a cocurricular activity has improved his behavior and his rapport with his peer group.

On November 1, Pat McCormick, a former U.S. Olympic diving champion, will be presenting a motivational assembly at our school on goal-setting and becoming a champion. Evan has been selected to hold the Olympic torch that Pat brings to assemblies.

The cocurricular program also contributes to good discipline. If students don't have their homework done for a particular day (and have no valid excuse), or are involved in certain kinds of behavior problems, a note goes home and they must go to "supervised study" the next day after school. That means missing their after-school cocurricular activity. They usually buckle down after that.

TEACHING GOOD SPORTSMANSHIP

If schools are going to sponsor competitive sports—which, as the Clovis story illustrates, can be the source of much good—it's essential that they stress the value of good sportsmanship. No school that is serious about developing a good moral atmosphere can turn a blind eye to the kinds of deplorable player, coach, and fan behaviors that increasingly mar athletic events.

Rippowam-Cisqua, an independent school (kindergarten through grade 9) in Bedford, New York, cares very much about the values its students learn from sports. Richard Wade, the headmaster, explains:

For us, the coach is an educator, first and foremost. Our *primary* concern is sportsmanship. We do not yell at kids, and we do not allow them to yell at each other, opposing players, or referees.

Sadly, this is not the case with some schools we play. We've had opposing coaches berate the umps or refs. There have been coaches who have totally lost it. Last year the refs had to call a game because the cursing by the other team got so bad.

Interscholastic leagues should, with input from all member schools, draft sportsmanship codes for player, coach, and fan behavior, including consequences for violations. Participating schools can then give such a code a high profile in their own school communities.

If there isn't leaguewide action, a school can ask its student council, with input from all homerooms, to come up with a strong sportsmanship code. The code can then be given prominence through a school assembly where coaches and student leaders explain the expected behaviors, the values underlying those behaviors, and how the code will be enforced.

Clovis schools, which start competitive athletics in the elementary grades, motivate sportsmanship in the following way. At the end of every competitive game between schools, officials are asked to rate, for each side, the sportsmanship of adults present at the game, students, players, and the coach.

SPORTSMANSHIP RATING

	Satisfactory	Unsatisfactory
Adults		
Students		
Players		
Coach		

At the end of the school year, each school's overall percentage of satisfactory ratings for all team sports is tallied. The school with the highest percentage wins the district Sportsmanship Championship.

Elementary schools in Hamilton, Ontario, teach sportsmanship through an intermediate-level curriculum unit called Winning (part of the PREPARE program; see Chapter 2). This unit consists of activities designed to teach key ideas about sportsmanship such as "feel good about yourself when you win, but consider the feelings of others" and "you may be a winner even when it seems you're not." Teachers report positive schoolwide effects of using this curriculum-based approach.

THE SCHOOL ASSEMBLY AS A COMMUNITY- AND CHARACTER-BUILDER

School assemblies are a versatile vehicle for transmitting values. And they are one of the very few times in which the whole school is visibly constituted as one community.

Here are glimpses of how various schools have used assemblies to foster school solidarity and good values:

• At the Scarborough Village Public School in Scarborough, Ontario, all grades—kindergarten through eighth—helped to plan and carry out an assembly on the theme of world peace.

Students and staff took turns singing songs and reading prayers like this one written by seventh- and eighth-graders: "We pray for the freedom of every land and for civil rights. We pray that families may not be divided either by political borders or thoughts. We pray that we may all be free to exist in love and peace in the country of our choice."

Comments the principal, Bruce Carmody: "Our assemblies are a way we hold up a value to our children and say, 'This is important. This matters.'"

• A community on Long Island, New York, had a serious problem with shoplifting. Its high school responded by organizing an assembly that featured storeowners, police, and a judge talking about the effects of such theft on merchants, customers, and offenders who were caught. Individual classrooms had follow-up discussions. Subsequently, shoplifting declined in the community.

• Many junior high and high schools present special assemblies aimed at motivating students to avoid drugs, drinking, and premature sexual involvement. A private school in downstate New York demonstrated that an assembly can also be used to address a school crisis stemming from irresponsible behavior such as alcohol abuse. At a drinking party in the woods held by eighth-graders, several students got sick, and one girl passed out. Panicking, other students hosed her down in an effort to revive her—and induced a near-fatal case of hypothermia.

Says the headmaster: "After calling the parents of all the students involved, we had an assembly of the whole upper school [grades 6 through 9] to talk about what had happened. We got it right out into the open and treated it as an educational opportunity."

Many schools let the tradition of school assemblies slide because it became too much of a hassle to manage students' rude audience behavior. A better response is to have students take responsibility, on a rotating basis, for planning and putting on the assemblies.

Jade Reitman, principal of South School in Andover, Massachusetts, has used this approach. Over the course of the year, each class performs a play, skits, songs, or a curriculum-related presentation for the rest of the school. Comments principal Reitman: "We have had no problems with audience behavior. You can hear a pin drop."

SCHOOL JOBS

South School also has every class perform an ongoing job that contributes to the common good of the school.

At the beginning of the school year, classes at each grade level discuss the kinds of jobs they would like to do for the school. All the teachers then get together with the principal to decide which jobs are developmentally appropriate for which grades. Then each classroom meets again: to develop a specific plan for carrying out its job and to select a "foreman," who meets with the principal to go over the plan.

Sample school jobs for a year: two second-grade classes worked on "beautifying the bathrooms"; two third-grade classes, on keeping the cafeteria clean; a fourth-grade class, on creating and maintaining a wildlife atrium; a fifth-grade class, on helping the office secretaries; another fifth-grade class, on putting out the school paper; another on running the school store.

During the year, individual classes use the class meeting to evaluate how well they are doing their jobs and what, if any, improvements need to be made.

ELEMENT 4: DEMOCRATIC SCHOOL GOVERNMENT

Another schoolwide character development strategy, greatly under-used, challenges students to help govern the life of their school.

Dr. JoAnn Shaheen has pioneered in bringing democracy to the world of the elementary school child. She has found that children, operating within decision-making structures designed by adults, can assume increasing responsibility for the welfare of their school community.

As principal at Cottage Lane Elementary School in Blauvelt, New York, Dr. Shaheen had this goal: to "have the total school environment reflect the principles of a democratic, pluralistic society based on the rule of law."[7] That meant involving children in rule-making, rule-evaluating, rule-enforcing, and rule-changing.

She began by setting up two student councils. The Little Student Advisory Council (Little SAC) was made up of first- through third-graders; two delegates were elected by each classroom, and a third delegate was jointly selected by the principal and the classroom teacher. The Big Student Advisory Council (Big SAC) was made up of delegates from grades 4 through 6, plus officers elected by the entire student body. As principal, JoAnn Shaheen was convener and secretary to both SACs and met with them weekly over lunch, usually for 30 to 35 minutes.

The classroom-council link. From a values education perspective, the link between the student advisory councils and the classrooms is critical. Principal Shaheen's Little SAC and Big SAC get everyone involved because classroom delegates vote as their individual classrooms instruct them. SAC delegates can't take formal action on any issue without first having input from class meetings.

Moreover, classrooms at the various grade levels have class meetings at least once a week, where they propose agenda items for SAC meetings and provide input into discussions currently under way. Because *all* students are in this way involved in the governance of the school, they all have the opportunity to grow in perspective-taking, problem-solving, and their sense of being active, caring citizens of their school.

At one Little SAC meeting, third-grade delegates complained about the messy tables they found when they came in for their lunch hour. Other grievances quickly followed: "If you don't look out, you'll sit in peanut butter!" "People are always pinging peas!" "Sometimes you have to stand in line so long to get your food, you don't have any time left over to go out and play!" Others argued that they shouldn't have to buy food they didn't like and therefore wouldn't eat.

Principal Shaheen helped the SACs take action. They set up subcommittees, conducted a survey of all students, and then brainstormed what an ideal cafeteria would be like. The results: "Menus were changed as much as possible; a new lunch schedule cut down on crowds; a new system of lunch lines speeded service; and kids at each grade level assumed responsibility for a clean, neat cafeteria."[8]

Children in schools like Cottage Lane, as Dr. Shaheen points out, know they have the power to affect the quality of their school community but that they must operate within guidelines and requirements provided by the principal and staff. The adults are ultimately in charge, but within that framework, children are given real responsibility for making decisions about certain school matters and for experiencing the growth in character that such decision-making can produce.

CAN DEMOCRACY WORK IN THE HIGH SCHOOL?

Big, traditional high schools are now also experimenting with involving students in greater decision-making and responsibility for their schools. These high school experiments help students form community bonds through small-scale support groups and enable students to participate—town meeting–style—in making just decisions about problems and policies affecting the school as a whole. (See Power, Higgins, and Kohlberg for narrative descriptions and research evaluations of several "just community schools."[9])

Success with this democratic community approach has been demonstrated in places as challenging as the South Bronx. Just a few years ago, Theodore Roosevelt High School there was plagued with the usual problems, including violence, that beset inner-city schools. Then it became home for a just community school-within-a-school where 200 students, alongside faculty advisers, work at governing themselves.

When the experiment began, about half of these students were at high risk of dropping out of school or being expelled. Luis, 15, is one. He was interviewed in a 1989 television special that included a segment on the just community at Theodore Roosevelt. He explained how his mother did drugs and didn't care where he was, how he used to skip school a lot, and how he had had a 20 to 30 average in all his subjects. Now Luis and others like him talk about how the just community has taught them responsibility and given them a reason for coming to school.[10]

As Clark Power notes, more than a decade of research on high school climate has pointed to the need for more responsive school organizational structures and increased opportunities for adolescent decision-making. These were the same conclusions reached by no fewer than seven national task forces and commissions on school reform in the 1980s.[11]

The school, as moral educator David Purpel points out, "is the only social institution charged with preserving and enriching our democratic heritage. The destiny of our schools and the destiny of our democracy are intertwined."[12]

ELEMENT 5: CREATING A GOOD COMMUNITY AMONG ADULTS

In good schools, the research tells us, there is also a strong moral and intellectual community among the adults.[13] Staff collegiality flourishes. Teachers share ideas. Experienced faculty coach new teachers. The school administration provides time and support for all of this.

In effective schools, teachers and administrators also work together to set school policy, improve instructional practice, select textbooks, strengthen discipline, and create a good program for character development.

In less effective schools, there is not this spirit of collaboration. Let me give a small example.

A few years ago I was working with several student teachers in an urban elementary school. The school had had a lot of vandalism in the bathrooms. Students swung on doors, ripped them off, plugged the toilets, and the like. The teachers I spoke with said the principal dealt with this by unilaterally announcing a new policy: "This year you must take your students to the bathroom as a class."

That idea did not have the consent or support of the faculty. To me they said, "You can't toilet 30 7-year-olds at the same time. There's also the problem of noise control in the hall. It's been very frustrating."

Now, principals obviously can't consult teachers on every decision they make, and teachers wouldn't want them to. But when a decision affects teachers directly and how they work with their students, they want and deserve to have their voices heard. If you respect and value people, you consult them.

Happily, shared decision-making is now on the rise in schools—one of the most promising new directions to emerge from the recent critiques of American schooling. When teachers feel empowered, they're in a better position to empower their students. When their critical thinking is valued, they're more likely to foster critical thinking by young people. And when teachers are treated with respect and given a greater measure of responsibility, those moral values are more likely to flourish in classrooms.

ELEMENT 6: MAKING TIME FOR MORAL CONCERNS

Says the headmistress of a private school (kindergarten through grade nine) in Ohio: "I found a moral vacuum when I came to this school. There was no attention paid to the moral significance of small things— the minor acts of teachers and students."

Time spent on moral concerns, this headmistress went on to say, "is terribly important. There is no quick way to develop a positive moral climate in a school."

She gave an example of how spending time on moral matters, however small, builds a moral culture:

> In our school we have a lost-and-found table. I didn't pay much attention to it. Then a parent came to me and said she overheard one girl saying, "I always wanted a sweater like that" and another saying, "Take it." Other students were not claiming things that were actually theirs ("I never liked that blouse my mother got me"). There was a complete disregard for actual ownership.

Disquieted by this report, the headmistress brought the matter up for discussion at a meeting with faculty. She says: "We decided that the children needed guidance in this area. They needed to discuss property and the question 'What do you have a right to?' before we put things out for claiming on the lost-and-found table. Some wonderful discussions with the children did in fact take place."

Barbara Kobrin is a fourth-grade teacher at Curtis School, outside of Los Angeles. She says that one year, the fourth-grade boys "were killing each other, verbally and physically. A lot of them, as a consequence of this kind of behavior, were getting bad comments on their report cards, and it bothered them. They felt the situation was out of control."

So Barbara Kobrin initiated a voluntary meeting, every Monday lunch hour, open to all fourth-grade boys. Students could bring up any problem. They talked about what bugged them—what started arguments and fights. They got better, teacher Kobrin says, at problem-solving. At the end of a meeting, some would say, "Can I bring a friend the next time?" They felt especially good when other kids in the group would tell them that their behavior had improved.

This lasted for four consecutive Mondays, teacher Kobrin says, and then as the need arose. "It worked so well for the boys that I did the same thing for all the fourth-grade girls. They had their own problems—cliques, backbiting, exclusiveness—and we made good progress in that group, too. With kids this age, you certainly don't have to manufacture problems to talk about; they're there."

Barriers to taking time for morality. What prevents schools from taking the time to pay attention to moral matters small and large? Currently, two related impediments exist: inappropriate academic pressures, and a preoccupation with test scores as a measure of school success.

Academic reform was certainly needed, especially at the high school level, where the U.S. curriculum has not been nearly as rigorous as that of many other industrialized countries. But our push for greater academic rigor has in many school systems resulted in a hurry-up, pressure-cooker atmosphere, especially in the elementary grades. This atmosphere is counterproductive from an intellectual as well as a social-moral standpoint. Says a veteran teacher who teaches science in grades four through six at a small school in upstate New York:

> The amount of material to be covered is just impossible. There's no time for kids really to *think* about what they're doing. We keep pushing more information at them; teachers' attitude is, "I've only got two weeks to cover this!" The slower kids suffer the most, but it takes a toll on the brighter ones as well.

In this school, the way teachers and children interact—what does and what doesn't get talked about—has been markedly altered by the new time pressures. "There's certainly no time," this teacher says, "for group moral discussions, and not even for the one-to-one talks that kids need."

"Fragmentation is killing us," says another elementary school teacher. The tyranny of the clock and the chopping up of the school day into smaller and smaller chunks guarantee a more stressful school climate. We know what stress does to human relationships. A school that wants to develop a positive moral culture must schedule the day so as to minimize fragmentation and allow time for the group and one-to-one conversations so important to moral community.

The school building principal is the single most important person in creating the conditions that nurture a positive school culture. But principals, like teachers, need relief from unreasonable academic pressures imposed from without. Most often those pressures take the form of demands for better student performance on standardized tests of achievement.

Nobody publishes students' human decency scores in the town newspaper. But these days, a school's scores on statewide achievement tests often do get published. Community members look to see how they compare with other communities, and the principal, superintendent, and school board feel the heat if the comparison is not flattering. Concerns such as values education become low priorities; test scores become the tail that wags the educational dog.

To resist this tunnel-vision focus on test scores, a school needs a strong philosophical commitment to educational goals that are truly in students' best interests. In the intellectual realm, most would agree that those goals should include creative and critical thinking, even if that doesn't show up on standardized tests. In the moral realm, most would acknowledge the importance of good citizenship, positive values, and good character.

Besides a clear philosophy, schools need community support for making teaching values an educational priority. Parents and other citizens need to let school boards and school administrations know that they want the schools to do everything they can to help young people become caring, honest, responsible members of society.

Finally, state education departments can help. They can help schools balance their educational agenda by asking them to be accountable for doing values education, just as they are now accountable for meeting state requirements for science, math, and so on. State education departments can ask schools: "What is your district's plan for helping

ELEMENTS OF A POSITIVE MORAL CULTURE IN THE SCHOOL

1. **The principal provides moral and academic leadership by:**
   - Articulating a vision of the school's goals.
   - Introducing all school staff to the goals and strategies of the values program.
   - Recruiting parent support and participation.
   - Modeling the school's values through interactions with staff, students, and parents.

2. **The school creates effective schoolwide discipline by:**
   - Clearly defining its rules and consistently and fairly enforcing them.
   - Handling discipline problems in a way that fosters students' moral growth.
   - Ensuring that the school's rules and values are upheld in all school environments and moving swiftly to stop abusive behavior wherever it occurs.

3. **The school creates a schoolwide sense of community by:**
   - Encouraging members of the school to express their appreciation of the caring actions of others.
   - Creating opportunities for students to get to know students and staff outside their own classroom.
   - Getting as many students as possible involved in an extracurricular activity.
   - Upholding good sportsmanship.
   - Using school assemblies to foster community and good values.
   - Having every classroom be responsible for a job that contributes to the life of the school.

4. **The school can use democratic student government to promote citizenship development and shared responsibility for the school by:**
   - Structuring student government to maximize student participation and the interaction between classrooms and student councils.
   - Making student councils responsible for dealing with problems and issues that have a tangible effect on the quality of school life.

5. **The school can create a moral community among adults by:**
   - Providing time and support for school staff to work together on instructional matters.
   - Involving staff in collaborative decision-making when they are directly affected by the issue at hand.

---

6. **The school can elevate the importance of moral concerns by:**
   - Moderating academic pressures so they do not cause teachers to neglect children's social-moral development.
   - Encouraging teachers to spend time on moral concerns.

---

students develop the values necessary for responsible citizenship in a democratic society?"

"THAT'S WHAT WE ARE"

Says a ninth-grader at Rippowam-Cisqua School in Bedford, New York: "Here you really try to be nice to new people. Kids are nervous enough if they're new. So we try to help them. That's what we do; that's what we are."

At a public school in Ontario, a black boy, a third-grader, was a new arrival. On his first day at school, another boy, also new, called him a derogatory name.

On hearing this, a third student, who happened to be white, came over to the boy who had called the offending name. "Don't do that," he said; "we don't call people names here."

It *is* possible to develop a school where people define normative behavior—"who we are"—in terms of values such as mutual respect and caring. It doesn't happen overnight, but as the schools described here attest, that kind of moral culture can be fostered.

Attention must be paid to the shared moral life of the school; that is the stuff of which a school's moral culture is made. If a school succeeds in creating a moral environment where many phases of collective life converge to support good values, it does much to help young people make those values part of their enduring characters.

A helpful collection of essays that describe schoolwide approaches (including democratic student government) as well as classroom strategies is Jacques Benninga's Moral, Character, and Civic Education in the Elementary School *(New York: Teachers College Press, 1991).*

A useful guide to creating a positive school ethos at the high school level is Gerald Grant's fine book, The World We Created at Hamilton High *(Cambridge, MA: Harvard University Press, 1988).*

CHAPTER 18

Sex Education

Recently, I went to a center for teenage girls where the teacher asked what they would like to discuss most. Human biology? Care for their infant? Physiology of childbirth? Family planning? The girls showed no interest. Then the teacher asked, "Would you like to discuss how to say no to your boyfriend without losing his love?" All hands shot up.

—EUNICE KENNEDY SHRIVER [1]

Seventh- and eighth-graders who have chosen not to engage in intercourse say that the greatest influence on their decision is the fact that "It is against my values for me to have sex while I am a teenager."

—WILLIAM J. BENNETT, "Why
Johnny Can't Abstain" [2]

In all of values education, no topic stirs as much debate as sex education. Under that heading come the sensitive subjects of the morality of premarital sex, contraceptives, school-based clinics, abortion, homosexuality, and AIDS.

But in the midst of the pitched battles over these issues, there is a consensus about this: Sexual behavior is determined by values, not mere knowledge. Consequently, sex education must educate young people about the moral dimensions of sexual conduct.

There is also now a consensus among experts in adolescent development and those who have witnessed the destructive effects of premature sex: Sex is not for kids, and abstaining from sexual relationships is in the best interests of teenagers themselves and society at large.

The challenge now before schools is to help young people in every way possible to make the moral decision not to get sexually involved. Happily, large numbers of teenagers are relieved to be given good reasons for staying away from sexual involvement and strategies for doing so, even if they have already been sexually active.

CURRENT PATTERNS OF YOUTHFUL SEXUAL ACTIVITY

There is a clear and present need to help young people understand the moral issues involved in sex and to develop sexual self-control:

- By age 15 more than one in four girls and one in three boys has had sexual intercourse. By age 17 more than half of girls and two- thirds of boys are sexually active.[3]

- The proportion of all girls aged 15 to 19 who had sexual intercourse rose from 30 percent in 1971[4] to 47 percent in 1982 to 53 percent in 1988.[5] Between 1982 and 1988 the increase in sexual activity was greatest among whites and in higher-income families. Among sexually active 15- to 19-year-old girls, nearly six of ten report having intercourse with two or more partners.[6]

- According to the Centers for Disease Control, sexually transmitted diseases are now at an all-time high among teenagers.[7] Each year, 2.5 million adolescents will contract a sexually transmitted disease.[8] Nationwide, about 1 million women become sterile each year because of STDs. Says Dr. Vicki Alexander, an authority on teenage sexually transmitted disease: "We could be bringing up a generation of infertile women."[9]

- Although, according to the Alan Guttmacher Institute, more teenagers (47 percent) "regularly used" contraceptives in 1988 than in 1982 (22 percent), the overall teen pregnancy rate remained the same[10]—one reason being that more teens were having sex. Each year one of every ten U.S. teenage girls becomes pregnant.[11]

- Nearly a third of all abortions in this country are performed on teenagers—more than 400,000 a year.[12]

- Each year, approximately 500,000 teenage girls give birth; about 60 percent of them are unmarried.[13] Between 1986 and 1988 the number of babies born to 15- to 17-year-olds showed a sharp increase—

jumping 10 percent in just that three-year period.[14] One of every four babies in the United States is now born out of wedlock (compared to one of 20 in 1960).[15]

• Most teen mothers will spend at least part of their lives as single parents, often on public assistance. Teenage childbearing is now recognized as one of the root causes of poverty.[16]

• The babies of teenage mothers, compared to infants born to women in their twenties, are more likely to be abused; held back in school; exhibit behavior disorders; have emotional problems; become drug-addicted; and, later in life, become teenage parents themselves.[17]

THE ROOTS OF THE PROBLEM

Facts and numbers, however, don't tell the whole story. Talk to teachers and others who are close to children and adolescents and you will hear story after sad story testifying to the changes that have taken place in the sexual attitudes and behavior of the young.

• A nurse who does substitute teaching in central New York health education classes told of high school students who, before the start of one class, "talked and joked openly about their sexual activities, who was doing what with whom, what went on the night before, and so on. I was speechless. When I finally asked them if they didn't ever worry about AIDS, they just laughed."

• At an Indiana high school a teacher says, "The air is thick with sex talk. Kids in the halls will say—boy to girl, girl to boy—'I want to f—— you.' And the girls will call to each other, 'Hey, slut!' One girl wrote a poem to a boy that was unbelievably filthy. When I talked to her about it, she just looked at me and said, 'Didn't you write things like that to your husband?' "

• A ninth-grade teacher in Alberta, Canada, told of a 14-year-old boy in her class who watched pornographic movies at home with his father. "He's going to see it later anyway," was the father's comment. After months of watching such movies, this boy sexually abused his cousin, a 3-year-old girl.

• In Rochester, New York, after watching pornographic movies, a 10-year-old boy raped and sodomized two girls, aged 8 and 4.

• In a central New York village, a mother said that in third grade, a boy sent her daughter Kelly notes saying, "I love you, let's have sex." Kelly came home very upset by this, her mother told the teacher, and the boy was not allowed to go near Kelly for the rest of the school year. But this year, in fourth grade, many boys are writing such notes to girls, and the girls, Kelly says, like getting them.

• A kindergarten teacher says she has a boy who dives for her legs and grabs at her in other sexually inappropriate ways. When she asked the boy's mother to come in to see this for herself, the mother did—and "thought it was funny that he was 'getting it on' with the teacher."

Not all children and teenagers, of course, fit the disturbing patterns described in these stories. But virtually all young people have been af-fected, in some way, by the eroticized environment that is the legacy of the "sexual revolution." A generation of children has grown up in a society in which large numbers of adults, preoccupied by sex them-selves, no longer try to protect children from premature exposure to sex or even from exposure to pornographic and perverted forms of sexuality. Moreover, television, movies, and supermarket magazines all send the message that sex is the central and indispensable source of human happiness and that sex between uncommitted persons is stan-dard human behavior. Rock lyrics—in songs such as "I Want Your Sex"—beckon young listeners toward early sexual gratification.

One could describe all this, without exaggeration, as a kind of psy-chological sexual abuse of children. From very early ages, children are immersed in a culture that inundates them with sexual information and images they are not developmentally ready to evaluate, overstim-ulates them sexually, divorces sex from moral values, and conse-quently reduces their chances of growing up sexually in a healthy, moral way.

To this pervasive distortion of childhood, add child sexual abuse as traditionally defined—the physical violation of a child by an adult (or, with increasing frequency, by an older child). Physical sexual abuse in this country is rampant. A major study by the University of New Hampshire's Dr. David Finkelhor, author of *Child Sex Abuse* and *Sex-ually Victimized Children,* estimates conservatively that one in four girls, and at least one in seven boys, is sexually abused at least once before they reach age 18.[18] Here, too, examples better than numbers tell this painful story:

• In Indianapolis, an assistant high school principal and a high school teacher were both arrested for sexually abusing the teacher's son. Ac-cording to charges made by the son at age 19, the teacher, who was his adoptive father, forced the boy to have sex as often as three times a day from the time of his adoption at age 11.[19]

• A librarian and her husband were convicted of sexually assaulting a teenage girl; the coupled forced the girl to view pornography before sexually assaulting her.

• A boys' summer camp operated by a community's police department came under heavy attack from parents who objected to an "initiation rite" in which rookie camp members (from age 12) were required to run down a field without any clothes on and with their underwear atop their heads. Boys at the camp also testified that one supervisor read *Hustler* magazine to them.[20]

What have been the effects on children of all these betrayals of trust and assaults on their bodies and spirits? "Childhood Sexual Abuse Cited as Root of Adult Ills" ran the headline of a 1988 Toronto newspaper story about the long-term effects of such abuse. It reported findings of a study of 930 adult women linking childhood incest and other sexual abuse with a higher-than-average incidence of a host of adult problems: beatings or rapes by their husbands, anorexia, alcoholism, drug addiction, prostitution, imprisonment, mental illness, and suicide.[21]

We also know that children who are sexually abused suffer fear and mistrust, develop feelings of worthlessness, often become precocious in their sexual behavior, sometimes (especially in the case of boys) sexually abuse younger children, and are vulnerable (especially in the case of girls) to later sexual exploitation.

TAKING THE MEASURE OF THE CHALLENGE CONFRONTING SCHOOLS

All these changes in the total sexual environment and in children's formative experiences within it must be understood if we wish to take the measure of the challenge confronting schools. It is increasingly common to hear that teen sexual activity and teen pregnancy are due to factors largely beyond the school's control—such as the sexual abuse already cited, lack of family structure, negative influence of the mass media, poor role-modeling by adults, and social class-related values that do not support sexual restraint or actually encourage teen pregnancy.

These factors suggest that if schools are to succeed in teaching sexual responsibility, they will need a broad-scale approach—plus all the help they can get from families, religious institutions, and other community groups that work with young people.

WHAT *HASN'T* WORKED

Most surveys of schools through the mid-1980s showed that about three of four teens received some kind of formal sex education.[22] Did it do any good?

In his article "Sex and School Reform," Stanford University education professor Larry Cuban states: "Schools started to offer sex education courses in the 1930s. Decade after decade since then, statistics have demonstrated the ineffectiveness of such courses in reducing sexual activity, unwanted pregnancy, and venereal disease among teenagers."[23]

A national study designed by the Centers for Disease Control evaluated 14 separate sex education programs (ranging from 6-day courses to year-long programs).[24] The study found that "none of the sexuality courses had a measurable impact on whether or not the participants had experienced sexual intercourse . . . or the number of times participants had sexual intercourse."[25]

Why didn't sex education reduce teenage sexual activity? Until recently—and this comes as a surprise to many parents—the purpose of sex education has *not* been to get teenagers to refrain from sexual intercourse. It has not been to help students arrive at the moral judgment that sex outside a committed love relationship is wrong because it violates caring—caring about oneself, one's partner, the child that might result, and society as a whole. Here, for example, is one prominent sex educator, author of the *Curriculum Guide for Sex Education in California Schools,* explaining why, in her view, schools could not present a moral perspective on sex:

> "Right" or "wrong" in so intimate a matter as sexual behavior is as personal as one's own name and address. No textbook or classroom teacher can teach it.[26]

The morally relativistic assumption in this position—which went unchallenged for a long time—was that because sexual behavior is an intimate or personal decision, there can be no objective, rational ethics to guide it. But upon closer examination, that logic breaks down. No one would argue, " 'Right' or 'wrong' in so intimate a matter as sex between 13-year-olds is too personal for any textbook or classroom teacher to teach it." All actions, however personal, are subject to moral judgment.

But most sex education, operating with a relativistic and privatistic notion of morality, skirted the hard moral questions and encouraged students to "make your own decision." Sex education did supply information about the physiology of sex, pregnancy, birth control, venereal disease, and the like—and hoped that with all of this and with practice in decision-making exercises, teens would make a "responsible" decision. But "responsible" all too often translated only as, "If you do it, don't get pregnant or catch a disease." It wasn't likely to translate, especially in the minds of teenagers, as "You shouldn't have sex." As one high school senior put it: "No one says not to do it, so by default they're condoning it."[27]

THE CASE FOR A PRO-ABSTINENCE APPROACH

AIDS changed the status of abstinence, in society and in schools. Here was a sexually transmitted disease that would kill you. As the title of one new sex education curriculum announced, *Suddenly Sex Has Become Very Dangerous.*[28] Teachers now felt they could stand up in front of a class of adolescents and say without embarrassment, "Don't have sex if you don't want to get AIDS."

A 1989 survey found that 86 percent of sex education teachers say they now teach their students that abstinence is the best way to prevent pregnancy and avoid sexually transmitted disease.[29] Most of these teachers also say that they try to help their students avoid intercourse by providing instruction in how to resist peer pressure and how to say no to a boyfriend or girlfriend.[30]

Why does a pro-abstinence approach to sex education make good ethical sense from the standpoint of both moral education and public policy?

1. Abstinence is the only 100 percent effective way to avoid pregnancy and sexually transmitted disease.

2. Abstinence is also the best protection against the emotional hurts—feelings of loss, guilt, betrayal, and being used—that very often follow sex outside a committed relationship.

3. Abstinence is consistent with a long-term goal of character development: self-control. Teen sexual activity is often part of a larger pattern of self-indulgence that can carry over into adulthood. Marital infidelity now occurs in one of every two marriages. If adolescents do not learn to say no to premarital sexual opportunities, what habits of

self-control will they have to draw on when faced with extramarital temptations?

4. A pro-abstinence approach recognizes that sex is powerful and attempts to teach that truth to young people. Sex can create the illusion of intimacy with a person you don't really know. Sexual attraction can inspire and uplift and be part of a beautiful love; but uncontrolled it can lead to broken hearts, exploitation, promiscuity, rape, prostitution, pornography, and the sexual abuse of children.

5. Helping teens avoid premature sex also supports families in their values and hopes for their children. True, many parents fail to teach their children sexual morality, and many others do harm by exposing their children to unwholesome sexual influences. But two-thirds of all Americans 18 and older now say that schools should "urge teenagers not to have sexual intercourse."[31]

6. Finally, an unambiguous commitment to the value of abstinence for teenagers gives sex education the clear ethical viewpoint needed to engage, and positively influence, students' sexual moral values. Adolescents tell researchers that it's their *internally held values* that keep them away from sexual involvement.[32] Even peer pressure is not as powerful as these internalized beliefs and values.

THE NEW SEX EDUCATION: PROGRAMS THAT TEACH ABSTINENCE AND PROMOTE DEVELOPMENT

The best of the new sex education programs teach abstinence in the context of an approach that supports the student's total growth as a valuing, confident, capable person. Here are some examples of the new sex education and the results it has been able to achieve:

• In 1980, the teen services program at Atlanta's Grady Memorial Hospital surveyed the thousand or so girls it saw each year. It found that the overwhelming majority (87 percent) wanted to learn how to "say no to sex without hurting anyone's feelings."

Grady responded by developing a program for eighth-graders called Postponing Sexual Involvement, offered in more than a score of Atlanta-area schools. Of those students taking the course, 70 percent say it taught them that they can "postpone sexual activity without losing their friends' respect."[33]

• Community of Caring programs, sponsored by the Joseph P. Kennedy, Jr., Foundation, are recommended by the U.S. Department of Education for their emphasis on teaching sex education "within the context of family and ethical values."[34] This approach also seeks to create, within classrooms and schools, a strong sense of community as a way of meeting the intimacy needs that for many teens go unfulfilled in their natural families. Of the unwed teenage mothers who partici- pate in Community of Caring programs, only 3 percent experience re- peat pregnancies, compared to a national average of 15 percent.[35]

• Project Respect, with federal grant support, has developed a pro- abstinence curriculum that as of 1989 was being used in six midwest- ern states. Project director Kathleen Sullivan rejects the theory that "hormones are destiny" when it comes to sex. "Nobody's ever died from not having sex," she says; "it's the one appetite that's not neces- sary to fulfill."[36]

Before participating in the Project Respect program, 38 percent of the students agreed with the statement, "It's important for me not to have sex before I get married"; after the program, 56 percent agreed with it. Says a nurse-teacher from Kansas: "During the 1987–88 year, we've had no pregnancies in eighth or ninth grades, nor with sopho- mores who had the [Project Respect] program as freshmen."[37]

• Some of the most impressive results come from an imaginative pro- gram carried out in the San Marcos, California, school system. San Marcos faced a serious teen pregnancy problem: 147 high school girls known to be pregnant in the 1984–85 school year. The school opted for a positive, multifaceted approach that it called Decision-Making: Keys to Total Success. It included these components:

1. A 6-week course for seventh-graders on developing study skills.

2. Another 6-week course for seventh-graders aimed at developing self-esteem and positive moral values.

3. A 6-week course for eighth-graders, including a curriculum titled Sexuality, Commitment, and Family.

4. Daily ten-minute lessons for both seventh- and eighth-graders on "how to be successful" (from the Thomas Jefferson Research Cen- ter; see Chapter 9).

The entire program emphasized goal-oriented behavior and helping young people develop the necessary self-confidence to abstain from sex. Says then principal Joe DeDiminicantanio: "A quick knee-jerk reaction to our teen pregnancy problem would have been to haul all the girls into the gym and all the boys into another gym and show them some movies and tell them where to buy prophylactics. But what we really wanted to do is influence attitudes and change behaviors, and that takes time."[38]

The component of the San Marcos program that focused explicitly on sexuality used a popular pro-abstinence curriculum known as Teen-Aid. Teen-Aid's six-week course Sexuality, Commitment, and Family offers these messages to young people:

1. The only real, safe sex is having sex *only* with your marriage partner who is having sex *only* with you.

2. Abstinence offers freedom *from* guilt, doubt, and worry; sexually transmitted disease; pregnancy; the trauma of abortion; loss of reputation; and pressure to marry early.

3. Abstinence offers freedom *to* become more creative in sharing feelings; develop skills and abilities; develop healthy self-appreciation; achieve financial stability before having a family; and develop greater trust in marriage.

4. After having been sexually active, it is possible to regain the advantages of abstinence. Decide to change; forgive yourself and others; change old habits; and develop ways of sharing that do not include sexual activity.

These ideas are developed through discussions and videos such as *Why Wait?* (a classroom simulation leading students to discover for themselves the advantages of avoiding premarital sexual activity); *Window to the Womb* (ultrasound footage of fetal development, graphically demonstrating to students that their sexuality has the power to create new human life); and *AIDS—Learn and Live* (on how AIDS is transmitted and the reasons why monogamy and premarital abstinence are the best methods of prevention). Teen-Aid's program also sends summaries of lessons to parents and offers them a workshop on teaching responsible sexual behavior. (For information on Teen-Aid materials, contact Teen-Aid, Inc., N. 1330 Calispel, Spokane, WA 99201-3220; tel. 509-328-2080.)

After implementing the Teen-Aid curriculum and the other parts of its Keys to Total Success program, San Marcos experienced a dramatic drop in student pregnancies: from 147 known pregnancies in 1984–85 to 20 known pregnancies in 1986–87.

• SEX RESPECT is a sex education curriculum developed by Colleen Kelly Mast, a Bradley, Illinois, high school teacher, under a grant from the federal Office of Adolescent Pregnancy Programs. The program is now used by scores of schools across the country. Its goal is to encourage students to choose chastity as a positive life-style, one that gives them "the freedom to grow up without the pressures of sex."

SEX RESPECT uses humorous slogans to get its point across: "Pet your dog, not your date"; "Control your urgin', be a virgin"; and "Sex is good, sex is great, save it for your permanent mate." One version of the program is aimed at middle school students, another at high schoolers. Activities in the SEX RESPECT curriculum include:

1. **What's My Line?** Thinking up and role-playing quick comebacks to standard one-liners (e.g., "We'll only do it this one time," "I'll stop whenever you say.")

2. **"Lanny Anders" letters:** Writing replies to letters from teenagers seeking advice about sexual dilemmas.

3. **Brainstorming:** Making a list of "fun, interesting things to do on a date that do not lead to sexual activity."

4. **Discussing "sex-cess stories"** such as: "My high school and college dating years were the best years of my life. I learned that *no* to sex meant *yes* to fun. My reputation as a virgin got out fast. I had more dates, better grades, and good, quality friendships. Guys knew they didn't have to perform for me, so we could concentrate on getting to know each other and having a great time. I believe that virginity is the key to successful dating."

5. **Viewing and discussing films** such as *Second Thoughts,*[39] a well-made movie about high school students that, without being moralistic, portrays the dangers of sex without commitment and the advantages of saving sex for marriage; it also offers hope and comfort for teens who have been sexually active and wish to change.

6. **Parent involvement,** including a parent guidebook with home assignments for enhancing parent-teen communication about sexuality and the value of chastity.

Of course, some teenagers, especially boys, will resist the idea of saving sex for marriage or even forgoing sexual activity in their present relationships. Overall results, however, are hopeful; a formal evaluation of SEX RESPECT by the U.S. Department of Health and Human Services reports "positive and encouraging changes in attitudes toward sexual behavior, including the ability to control sexual desire."[40] For example: At Wilson High School in Appleton, Wisconsin, before taking the SEX RESPECT course, only 32 percent of students agreed with the statement "Sexual feelings are *always* controllable." After the course, 68 percent agreed. Before the course, only 37 percent agreed that "There are a lot of benefits to waiting until marriage to have sexual intercourse." After SEX RESPECT, 63 percent agreed.

Students' personal statements reveal other ways in which SEX RESPECT affected their thinking and values. A 16-year-old boy wrote: "Teens today really need a lot of help with sex respect. Most important was the part about dating." A girl who was openly skeptical at the start wrote: "Outwardly I said, 'Forget it!' But inside I was listening. I never had a class explaining how sex can cause problems and how this can affect your whole life."

Information about the SEX RESPECT curriculum and staff development workshops is available from Respect, Inc., P.O. Box 349, Bradley, IL 60915-0349 (tel. 815-932-8389).

There are also pamphlets that present the chastity message in a concise and appealing way: *How to Say No Without Losing His/Her Love* and *Secondary Virginity: A New Beginning* (available from Womanity, 1700 Oak Park Blvd. Annex, Pleasant Hill, CA 94523); *Love Waits* (Christian Action Council, 101 West Broad Street, Suite 500, Falls Church, VA 22046); and *No Is a Love Word* (Human Life Center, University of Steubenville, Steubenville, OH 43952). All of these materials are non-sectarian in their content and written for a general audience. Another practical resource is Mary Rosera Joyce's book *Friends: for Teens* (available from SEX RESPECT), which shows young people how to develop close relationships that do not involve sexual intimacy.

COUNSELING TEEN BOYS ABOUT SEX

A 1988 Children's Defense Fund report on teen sex confirms what many teachers have found: Boys present special challenges to educators attempting to promote sexual restraint and responsibility.[41]

Although by the late teens the proportion of sexually active girls is now nearly as high as for boys, half of males have had sex by age 16, compared to 34 percent of females that age. Moreover, says National Research Council member Robert Mnookin, there's a tendency for many young boys to stay detached. Their attitude is, "You take the pill, you take the risk. If you don't want to have a baby, you have an abortion."[42]

Charles Ballard, who runs the Teen Fathers Program in Cleveland, says that one day he asked a group of 15 boys how many were fathers.

Only two raised their hands. When he asked how many had babies, 14 hands went up. Says Ballard: "They don't connect pregnancy with marriage or husbanding or fatherhood."[43]

Attitudes like these led the Children's Defense Fund to conclude that sex education falls short when it fails to recognize the special problems posed by boys. For many adolescent boys, their first sexual experience may be the primary symbol of manhood—a rite of passage—and changing this male value is critical to reducing teenage pregnancy.[44] Sex education programs should target male-only classes, the report recommended, and use more men to deliver the message.

SEX AND MARRIAGE

As part of Virginia's new sex education mandate, state regulations require that schools present marriage as the proper context for sexual intercourse and include the fact that intercourse outside of marriage violates Virginia law.

Education writer Sarah Glazer reports on the controversy surrounding this requirement.[45] Among those supporting it is Jacquelyn Henneberg of Falls Church, Virginia: "We feel sex is really for marriage, and for marriage alone. Thus sex should be taught in this context." Another Falls Church citizen, Barbara Jansy, objects to this requirement because, she says, it doesn't match reality: "By the time students reach the eighth grade, many will be brought face-to-face with a conflict: Despite what the curriculum says [about sex belonging in marriage], not all single parents or unmarried adults are celibate."

One response to this concern is to point out that historically it's been the job of schools to hold up ideals to young people—to point the way to a better life and world.[46] Another relevant point is that in other areas of values education, especially health education, schools try to persuade students not to do things—smoke cigarettes, use drugs, abuse alcohol—that many of their parents may be doing. In all of these areas, teachers can say, "You may see many adults doing things that are different from what we're saying is best for your health and happiness. Our business here is to challenge you to think hard about what is best for *your* life, now and in the future."

To try to avoid the sex-and-marriage question, some sex education programs talk simply about "postponing sexual involvement." That's a step in the right direction, but it begs an important question: Postpone until when? Says one teenage mother: "I thought I did great because I waited two years to have sex with my boyfriend—until we were

17. Then we had sex, and a little while later we broke up. The next guy I went out with, I had sex on the third date and got pregnant."

The lack of clear guidance in talking only about "postponing" sex points to the wisdom of programs that promote not only teenage abstinence but also the benefits of saving sex for marriage. If schools really want to help students develop well-defined values that will guide their sexual decisions, they should offer them a clear goal that answers the question "What am I waiting *for?*" A sex education curriculum can offer students this vision:

> Sex is most fulfilling when it's part of something bigger—a continuing, loving relationship between two human beings. Down through history, societies all over the world have said the same thing: Marriage is the relationship in which sex should occur.
>
> Marriage is the most serious, total, and public commitment between two people that any human society has been able to devise. It's within that committed relationship that sex is most likely to be loving, the dangers of disease and hurt are minimized, and a family is available for raising a child if pregnancy should result from the sexual union.

Here is what one guest speaker said to a class of high school juniors when asked by a student, "What are your views on premarital sex?"

> When you're married, sexual union is part of the total commitment you've made to each other. Your sexual intimacy expresses your complete commitment, your complete giving of self.
>
> When you aren't married, sexual intercourse is different. Not being committed to each other changes the meaning of the sex act. Then it's not part of the complete giving of yourself; you're holding back. Even if you're engaged, you can always get disengaged. You're keeping your options open.
>
> Totally giving love means this: You join your bodies when you join your lives. Really join them. From this viewpoint, sex before marriage is wrong because it separates sexual love from the committed love relationship that it's meant to express.

After the class, a young woman came up to thank the speaker for what he had said. "I never heard anyone talk like that about sex before," she said. "Now I know what I think."

Adolescents are also interested to learn what recent studies in both this country and Europe have shown: Couples who do not live together before getting married are at least 50 percent *more* likely to remain married than those who do live together.[47]

THE CONTRACEPTION ISSUE

Can schools credibly teach students that they ought to abstain from sex if they simultaneously instruct students in condom use as a way to reduce the risks of sexual activity? The case for trying to do both goes like this: "Many kids are going to have sex no matter what we do to promote abstinence. Given that reality, we have a responsibility to teach them to use contraceptives as protection against pregnancy and disease."

At first hearing, this argument may sound sensible and realistic. But I believe there are very serious ethical and educational problems with this approach:

1. **How far should the school go in teaching about condoms?** Should teachers, as some do, pass around various kinds of contraceptives so students "become comfortable" with them? Should classes do role-plays where, for example, girls are asked to develop responses to boys who say, "But using a condom is like taking a shower with a raincoat on!" Should the curriculum include, as is sometimes the case, explicit instructions in when and how to put on a condom, demonstration of proper condom use with a model, and discussion of the pros and cons of different lubricants? Should the curriculum provide, as is also sometimes the case, instruction in effective lubrication for anal as well as vaginal intercourse?

Clearly, large numbers of parents—not to mention teachers—would have problems with a no-limits approach to teaching about condom use. But once you accept the premise that how-to condom instruction is a good thing, how do you logically argue that it ought to go only so far?

2. **The mixed-message problem.** Schools may claim to encourage abstinence at the same time that they teach students how to use condoms, but trying to do both inevitably sends a mixed message: "Don't have sex" and "Here's how to do it fairly safely." If parents were to tell their teenage son or daughter that, morally speaking, they shouldn't have sex, but in the next breath give a matter-of-fact, here's-how lesson on using contraceptives, how seriously would the teenager take the parents' moral counsel about abstinence? Why should it be any different in the classroom?

The school further undermines the credibility of its advocacy of abstinence if it not only offers condom instructions but also distributes condoms to students through school-based clinics, school counselors, and the like. As long as the school is either teaching how to use condoms or passing them out, its recommendation of abstinence loses all moral force and is reduced to merely stating a medical fact ("Abstinence is the only 100 percent safe method . . ."). The school is then back in the position of seeming to be neutral about the morality of teenage sex itself—a value-neutrality that has demonstrably failed in the past to curb teen sexual activity, pregnancy, or sexually transmitted disease.

3. **Teaching students how to use condoms and distributing them creates a false sense of security about the protection they provide against pregnancy and AIDS.** What are teenagers already prone to think "It won't happen to me" likely to conclude if the school—in spite of the announced risks—explains how to use condoms and offers them on request? Many students will conclude that the risks are tolerable.

The risks, of course, are not tolerable. That's why the New York State Board of Regents, when it mandated AIDS education in 1987, characterized "the use of condoms as *extremely high-risk behavior. The view that condoms should or can be used as a way to reduce the transmission of AIDS should not be supported*" (emphasis added).[48] That was responsible public policy then and remains so now. Schools must not convey the idea that "protected sex" is a responsible "second option."

It follows that only one kind of condom instruction is educationally justifiable: that which teaches students all the reasons why condoms do *not* make sex safe. Condoms have a 10 percent failure rate in preventing pregnancy, and the protection they provide against AIDS transmission may well be considerably lower.[49] That's because the AIDS virus is much smaller than the sperm; it can infect either partner; and it can infect a victim any day each month (whereas a woman can become pregnant only a small number of days each month). In a study conducted by the University of Miami Medical School, 17 percent of wives of AIDS-infected husbands contracted AIDS themselves within 18 months, despite their husbands' use of condoms.[50] And a government report warns that condoms have higher-than-average failure rates among homosexuals (one reason being that condoms are more likely to tear and fail in anal intercourse than in vaginal intercourse).[51]

Promoting reliance on condoms is bad AIDS education because, in the words of Presidential AIDS Commission member Dr. Theresa Crenshaw, "Putting a mere balloon between a healthy body and a deadly disease is not safe."[52] Or as a *Newsweek* headline put it, "Counting on Condoms is Flirting with Death."[53]

4. Contraceptives do nothing to make sex emotionally safe. If we care about children, we will help them understand all the emotional hurts (discussed in the next section) that can come from premature, uncommitted sex. Condoms provide no protection whatsoever against these emotional consequences. When the school offers condoms as a way to make sex physically safer, it makes the emotional dangers of uncommitted sex seem irrelevant or relatively unimportant.

5. By appearing to sanction "protected" sex, the school fails in its responsibility to support parents in teaching their children to abstain from sex. The public opinion polls, as we have seen, show that parents want the schools to teach their children not to have sexual intercourse during this period of their lives. When the school in any way undermines that value, it violates a basic public trust.

Moreover, if the school distributes condoms to students without their parents' knowledge and consent—as called for by the recent New York City School Board decision (February 27, 1991)[54]—the betrayal of trust is even more profound. It also violates at least the spirit of public health law, which recognizes the right of parents to be involved in decisions affecting the health, safety, and welfare of their minor children.

Even if a school's plan to distribute condoms without parental consent were to survive a court test, what happens to the trust and partnership between school and home, so important to the long-range success of values education? Said Michael Petrides, a father and one of three New York City School Board members who voted against the City's condoms without parental consent proposal: "If a neighbor gave a condom to one of my children without telling me or my wife, I'd probably pick up the phone and call the cops."[55]

6. The school cannot, in the pursuit of other aims, set aside its educational obligation to teach good values and character. I think many of those schools that are trying to promote both abstinence and the use of condoms sense the internal contradictions of that approach but feel that it's a compromise necessary to combat teen pregnancy and AIDS. Teenage pregnancy and AIDS are serious social problems, to be sure, but schools must never engage in bad education in an effort to ameliorate social problems. The school is first and foremost an *educational* institution; as such its first duty must always be to teach children the truth and good values. The truth is that sexual activity by unmarried teenagers is harmful to them and harmful to society. The morally right value is for young people to avoid such activity.

Schools must not even appear to approve of something which is clearly wrong for students to do. No school would consider passing out clean needles as a means of reducing AIDS transmission among intravenous drug users. Schools must have the same clarity about their mission in sex education. Efforts to reduce teen pregnancy and AIDS must not be carried out at the expense of children's values and character.

The most important goal of sex education is to help young people learn to act as they should—with control over their desires, respect for self, respect for others, and a view to the future—in their sexual lives as in all other areas of their lives. If they learn to resist the temptations of premature sex just as they say no to drugs and other self-damaging activities, we will make progress against teen pregnancy and sexually transmitted disease. And our children will have developed the kind of values and character that will someday serve them well as marriage partners, parents of their own children, and citizens of society.

As an encouragement to embracing unqualified abstinence education and avoiding "safe-sex" messages, schools should keep in mind that pro-abstinence sex education is not a hypothetical proposition; it is going on—and succeeding—in many parts of the country.

THE EMOTIONAL RISKS OF UNCOMMITTED SEX

A big part of making the ethical case for abstinence is helping young people understand the serious psychological consequences of sex outside a committed love relationship. How do you make the emotional dangers real to kids?

Regret. As a counselor, psychologist and lecturer Dick Purnell hears over and over about the guilt and emptiness and regret people experience after uncommitted sex: "People come to me, and in the privacy of my office they pour out their hearts and talk about the emotional scars that fill their lives. What they say usually goes something like this: 'At first it was very, very exciting. Then I started to feel bad about myself. Then I started to feel bad about the person I was with. We started to argue and fight a lot. Then we broke up, and now we're enemies.' "[56]

Adolescent girls need to know the sharp regret that so many young girls feel after getting sexually involved. Says a high school junior: "I get upset when I see my friends losing their virginity to some guy they've just met. Later, after the guy's dumped them, they come to me and say, 'I wish I hadn't done it.' "[57] Says a ninth-grade girl who slept with eight boys in junior high, "I'm young, but I feel old."[58]

George Eager, author of *Love, Dating, and Sex* (one of the best-written books for teens on this subject), offers this advice to boys:

"When the breakup comes, it's usually a lot tougher on the girls than on the guys. It's not something you want on your conscience—that you caused someone else to have deep emotional problems."[59] At a high school assembly, Eager says, a well-known speaker was asked, "What do you most regret about your high school days?" Instantly he replied, "The thing I most regret about that time in my life is that I single-handedly destroyed a girl."[60]

Regret over uncommitted sexual relationships can last for years. I recently received a letter from a 33-year-old woman, now a psychiatrist, who is very much concerned about the sexual pressures and temptations facing young people today. She told about the lessons she learned the hard way. After high school, she says, she spent a year abroad as an exchange student.

> I was a virgin when I left, but I felt I was protected. I had gotten an IUD so I could make my own decisions if and when I wanted. I had steeled myself against commitment. I was never going to marry or have children; I was going to have a career. During that year abroad, from 17 ½ to 18 ½, I was very promiscuous.
>
> But the fact is, it cost me to be separated from myself. The longest-standing and deepest wound I gave myself was heartfelt. That sick, used feeling of having given a precious part of myself—my soul—to so many and for nothing, still aches. I never imagined I'd pay so dearly and for so long.

When you share your body with someone, Dick Purnell points out, you're giving part of yourself. When they leave your life, something of you goes with them. You'll never get it back.

Disruption of marital intimacy. Dr. Kevin Leman, a clinical psychologist, describes the "sexual flashbacks" that trouble a number of the married women he has counseled.[61] When they make love with their husbands, they suffer—sometimes 10 to 15 years into the marriage—involuntary mental images of premarital sex with other partners. Men are also vulnerable to these disruptive flashbacks. Says one young husband:

> I am married to one of the most wonderful women I've ever met. I would do anything for her. And I would do anything, ANYTHING, to forget the sexual experiences I had before I met my wife. When we start having intercourse, the pictures of the past and the other women go through my head, and it's killing any intimacy. I'm to the point where I don't want to have sex because I can't stand those memories. The truth is, I've been

HELPING YOUNG PEOPLE DEVELOP SEXUAL MORAL VALUES

Schools can help students develop respect and responsibility in their sexual attitudes and behavior if they:

1. Implement a sex education program that promotes the value of teenage abstinence, the ideal of sex within marriage, and the student's total development as a valuing, confident, and capable person.

2. Teach why contraceptives do not make uncommitted sex responsible or "safe."

3. Teach that love means wanting what is best for the other person.

4. Help students understand the emotional as well as the physical risks of sex outside marriage.

5. Encourage students to bring the values and teachings of their religious faith to bear on sexual questions.

6. Offer programs for boys that deal with the special challenges boys pose (e.g., the attitude that sex is a necessary part of dating relationships).

7. Handle questions about homosexual sex in a way that acknowledges differing views; emphasize the obligation to treat homosexual persons with respect regardless of one's personal views; and teach that regardless of sexual orientation, the best way to avoid AIDS and other sexually transmitted diseases is to refrain from sex outside of an adult, monogamous, mutually faithful relationship.

8. Seek parents' help in teaching healthy sexual attitudes by sending home copies of the school's sex education lessons, conducting workshops for parents on talking to kids about sex, and making parents aware of the harmful effects of exposing children to inappropriate sexual material.

9. Make sure that teachers of sex education classes are appropriate role models, with strong personal convictions about the importance of teenage abstinence.

10. Provide special programs for high-risk youth that develop their self-esteem and improve their life options.

married to this wonderful woman for eight years and I have never been "alone" in the bedroom with her.[62]

Stunting effects on a teenager's development as a person. Girls, especially, risk hurting their development through absorption in a sexual relationship. Says New York psychiatrist Samuel Kaufman: "A girl who enters into a serious relationship with a boy very early in life may find out later that her individuality was thwarted. She became part of him and failed to develop her own interests, her sense of independent identity."[63]

Dr. Reo Christenson of Miami University, Ohio, identifies still other emotional hazards of teenage sex: the frequently unsatisfying nature of initial sexual experience, especially for girls; the guilt feelings many teens will experience; the anguish of parents if pregnancy occurs or if sexual activity becomes known; the termination of normal adolescent activities and the premature arrival of adult cares and burdens if pregnancy occurs; and the probable abandonment of the mother by the teenage father.[64]

One of the most important tasks of sex education is to help young people gain a central ethical insight: *Love is wanting what's best for the other person, now and in the future.* You can hardly claim to love someone if you're gambling with that person's health, welfare, and present and future happiness.

Teens need to know that if someone pushes for sex by saying, "If you loved me, you would," they can truthfully reply: "If *you* loved *me,* you wouldn't ask."

WHERE DOES RELIGION COME IN?

Reo Christenson, writing in *Christianity Today,* raises still another sensitive issue: the role of religion in sex education. He points out that many parents dissent from public school sex education because they believe that crucial ethical and religious principles will be excluded from consideration. How could a religious perspective be included, he asks, in a way that is consistent with the Constitution?

Christenson's proposal: Structure students' inquiry into the issue of sex so that religious questions are raised right along with other relevant questions. For example, when exploring moral considerations, students would investigate questions such as: What does the Christian or Jewish or Muslim faith say about premarital sex? What do these traditions say about the morality of abortion?

Inquiry into such matters, Christenson observes, would be well within the Constitution. Teachers would not presume to tell students whether their religious beliefs are valid or not, but would encourage students to bring whatever religious beliefs they may have into the discussion. "That in turn," Christenson points out, "would oblige parents, pastors, priests, and rabbis to make sure that students' religious heritage in this area was clarified, so that students could accurately take it into account while formulating their views."[65]

Two recent findings support the wisdom of helping teens bring their religious traditions to bear on questions of sexuality. One is that teens who say they "attend religious services frequently" report a rate of sexual activity that is significantly lower (18 percent among 12- to 17-year-olds) than the rate for those who say they "seldom or never" attend religious services (38 percent sexually active).[66] Another poll, however, found that a surprisingly high percentage (43 percent) of 17-year-olds in evangelical Protestant families had had sexual intercourse. Three quarters of these sexually active teens said they got "little or no information about sex from their church."[67] Schools could help by encouraging students to investigate their faith's teachings about sex.

Sensitivity to religious beliefs is also important when the school deals with an issue such as masturbation. I have spoken with sex educators who think schools should teach children that masturbation is healthy and normal and a safe alternative to intercourse. But that ignores the view that sex was meant by God to be relational, an expression of love between two persons. While it is generally recognized that masturbation is common childhood behavior, many parents nevertheless want gently to encourage their children to try to resist that temptation. Teachers are obliged to respect that parental value and should encourage children who ask about masturbation to talk to their parents.

WHAT SHOULD SCHOOLS SAY ABOUT HOMOSEXUALITY?

On April 22, 1988, *The New York Times* ran a story titled "Sex Education Manual Prompts Moral Outrage."[68] The manual, produced with a federal grant by a New Hampshire family planning clinic, contained the following statement: "Gay and lesbian adolescents are perfectly normal, and their sexual attraction to members of the same sex is healthy."

Critics of the manual, including the governor of New Hampshire, objected to homosexuality's being presented to students as "healthy" and "normal." The author of the manual defended it by stating that his purpose was to "help teachers give support to homosexual teenagers in the classroom . . . and to respond to disparaging remarks against homosexual teenagers. We say that homophobia is the problem."[69]

To decide what to say about homophobia, it's necessary first to clarify language. "Homophobia" has been used to mean at least three different things. One meaning is "irrational fear of homosexuals," such as the belief that one can get AIDS through casual, nonsexual contact with gay persons. That is in fact an unfounded, irrational fear which schools should correct with accurate information.

"Homophobia" is also used to mean hatred of or unjust and uncharitable treatment of homosexual persons. Such acts, ranging from verbal harassment to murder, are on the rise and must be condemned for the same reason that hatred and mistreatment of any group must be condemned: They violate justice, human dignity, and respect for life.

But "homophobia" is also used in a third way: to mean that a person who disapproves of homosexual behavior is "prejudiced" in the same way that a person with racist or sexist attitudes is prejudiced. However, whether homosexuality is right and normal, "just another life-style," is a matter of moral and/or religious judgment (as opposed to "prejudice") about which honorable persons can and do disagree.

Some persons, for example, believe that a homosexual life-style is ultimately self-damaging behavior. Others object on religious grounds: Homosexual sex violates what they view as God's imperative that sex be reserved for a man and a woman united in marriage.[70]

One can require all citizens, regardless of their private views of homosexuality, to respect the civil and human rights of homosexual persons. However—and this point is lost in much of the current debate—one cannot in fairness accuse someone of being a bigot because that person, in good conscience, makes the judgment that homosexual activity is not healthy or right behavior. The ethical obligation to treat every person justly does not mean that one must approve all of a person's behaviors, sexual or otherwise.

Schools are, I believe, within the bounds of truth, sensitivity to pluralism, and sound moral education if they:

1. Make it clear that homosexual behavior is highly controversial in our society, with some people regarding it as normal and others viewing it as contrary to what is right or normal. (Sex educators must respect the fact that there is not public support for the posi-

tion that schools should "tell students that homosexuality is just an alternate sexual activity"; that position was endorsed by only 24 percent of American adults in a national poll for *Time* magazine.[71])

2. Distinguish between moral *judgments* of homosexual behavior, about which people may in good conscience disagree, and *treatment* of homosexual persons, which must be governed by the same principle of respect for human dignity that governs treatment of all people; and give concrete examples of the kinds of mistreatment (name-calling, degrading graffiti, harassment, violence) that are wrongful violations of respect for homosexual persons as human beings.

3. Stress that, regardless of sexual orientation, the best way for young people to avoid AIDS and other sexually transmitted diseases is the recommendation made by the U.S. Department of Education's guidebook *AIDS and the Education of Our Children:* "to refrain from sexual activity until as adults they are ready to establish a mutually faithful monogamous relationship."[72]

WHAT IS THE ROLE OF PARENTS?

Research shows that when parents talk openly with their children about sex, children's sexual attitudes and values are more likely to reflect their parents'.[73]

If schools wish to maximize their chance of affecting young people's sexual values, they must recruit the help of parents. To do this, schools can:

• Mail to all parents a written statement of the goals of the sex education program and at least an outline of the curriculum; invite interested parents to come in and examine the curriculum materials to be used; and provide the option for a family to have their child not participate in any parts of the curriculum, not mandated by the state, that they find objectionable.

• Send home copies of the school's lessons on sex, as Teen-Aid, Sex Respect, and Atlanta's Postponing Sexual Involvement course all do.

• Welcome parents as observers in sex education classrooms as a further way of building trust.

• Conduct a workshop for parents on talking to kids about sexual values and behavior.

- Let parents know that many schoolchildren are showing evidence—in their sexually precocious conversations, attitudes, and behavior—of premature and unhealthy exposure to sexual stimuli. Cite examples of cases where pornography has been harmful to children. Give parents support for saying no to TV shows and movies that include explicit sexual material or that take a favorable attitude toward sex outside of committed relationships. Stress that if kids pick up the wrong attitudes toward sex early, it makes it that much harder for the school to teach positive attitudes and sexual restraint later.

- Tell parents, "You are your children's most important sex educator, the chief influence on their sexual attitudes and conscience." Encourage parents to communicate with their children about sex—openly, often, and early.

  Age 3, for example, is not too soon to teach children how to recognize, resist, and report "bad touching."[74] At age 4 or 5, children can be introduced to the facts about reproduction through a book such as Andrew Andry and Steven Schepp's tasteful and gentle *How Babies Are Made* (a Time-Life publication). Some parents have used advice-column letters (e.g., "Dear Abby, I'm pregnant but scared to death to tell my parents") to get dinner table discussion going ("What advice do you think Abby should give?") and have found that a good vehicle for communicating family values regarding sex.

- Let parents know what studies show: Young people who have positive attitudes toward themselves are less likely to get sexually involved.[75] That means helping children, at home as well as at school, to build a positive self-image.

THE IMPORTANCE OF THE TEACHER

Both parents and schools must pay attention to who is teaching children about sex.[76] The pro-abstinence programs recommended earlier in this chapter all stress the importance of the ideals and convictions of the teacher as role model. Unfortunately, many sex educators still teaching were formed in a more permissive era and do not possess strong personal convictions about the desirability of teenage abstinence, much less saving sex for marriage.

I recently had an encounter with such an educator when I took part in a television talk show on the problems of teenagers. After I spoke about the dangers of teenage sexual activity and the wisdom of chastity, a woman in the audience stood up and said with cheerful enthusiasm:

> I am a sexuality educator. I have a teenage daughter; she's sitting right here. In our kitchen at home, I have colored condoms on the walls—all different colors. I want our children to grow up being comfortable with condoms. In school, we pass around condoms in class. At first the kids pull back and say "Oooh!" but gradually they become comfortable with them.

After the show, I went over to this person and initiated a conversation that went like this:

> ME: By focusing so much on condoms, aren't you sending kids the message that the only thing they need to be concerned about is avoiding pregnancy and disease? You don't seem to be dealing with the morality of the teenager's initial decision about whether to get sexually involved.
>
> WOMAN: We do deal with that decision.
>
> ME: How?
>
> WOMAN: We ask students what their values are—and whether having a sexual relationship is consistent with their values.
>
> ME: What if a student says, "Having sex with my boyfriend or girlfriend is consistent with my values"?
>
> WOMAN: Then that's their decision.
>
> ME: But you wouldn't use that approach with drugs, drinking, or shoplifting, would you? You wouldn't say, "If these things are consistent with your values, it's okay for you to do them."
>
> WOMAN: Sex isn't like any of those things. I believe sex is healthy.
>
> ME: For teenagers?
>
> WOMAN: Yes.

Obviously this woman's values do not reflect those of the majority of adults who say they want schools to teach teenagers that they should not have sexual intercourse. Schools clearly have a responsibility to their communities—as well as to the moral growth and well-being of young people—to select sex educators who do not approve of sexual involvement by their students.

Fortunately, the new sex education is gaining ground. And new creative strategies are being developed all the time: combining sex education with career planning and community service (as in St. Louis's Teen

Outreach Program); a citywide Teenage Pregnancy Prevention Week (as in Pittsburgh), featuring teen-produced "raps," skits, dances, and posters that say "Parenthood Is Permanent; Decide Today, Choose Delay"[77]; involving responsible older students in helping to conduct sex education classes; guest speakers—teenage mothers and fathers, for example—who talk candidly with young people about the mistakes they made and how to avoid them[78]; assemblies featuring speakers, like Pennsylvania's Molly Kelly (a mother of four teens who has given hundreds of high school talks in the U.S. and Canada), who can make the case for chastity with a light touch and in a way that gets through to teens[79]; programs that target especially vulnerable youth, such as potential dropouts, by getting them involved in productive activities that build their basic skills, self-esteem, and hope for the future; and laying the foundations for sex education in the early grades, where discussion can deal with topics such as the positive physical affection that families show and how to say no to inappropriate touching.

In the stormy waters of sex education, schools can steer a true course— one that serves children's best interests now and in their futures—if they keep this clear in mind: The school's goal in values-based sex education is not just to reduce teen pregnancy and sexually transmitted disease, important as that is. The school's goal is also to help teens avoid all the emotional hurts to self and others that come from premature, uncommitted sexual activity; to help students develop the self-control that will serve them well throughout their lives; to foster the ideal of sex as part of the marriage commitment; and to help students develop an ethical understanding of the relationship between sex and love.

The best way to pursue all of these character development goals is to adopt the well-designed pro-abstinence curricula now available. These programs help students come to the conclusion that abstaining from sex is the *only* truly responsible choice for them to make.

Happily, a growing segment of society appears to be recovering what used to be shared cultural wisdom: Children are incompletely developed human beings needing special guidance and protection. That is nowhere more true than in the area of sex. Acting on that wisdom, there is much we can do to help our children learn about the moral dimensions of sex and to make a safe passage to sexual moral maturity.

CHAPTER 19

Drugs and Alcohol

S tation KYW/TV in Philadelphia recently aired a program called "How Honest Are Kids Today?" I served as one of several panel members who were asked to comment on issues such as why kids lie and whether that's a bigger problem than it used to be. When the discussion turned to drugs, the host took phone calls from the viewing audience. The first caller was a girl, and the dialogue went like this:

GIRL: I'm a teenager, and I do drugs.

HOST: You do drugs.

GIRL: Yes.

HOST: How old are you?

GIRL: Fifteen.

HOST: Why do you do drugs?

GIRL: I like them. I like the way I feel when I take them.

HOST: What drugs do you take?

GIRL: Cocaine. Pot. Speed.

HOST: Uh . . . do your parents know you take these drugs?

GIRL: No. If they ever knew, they'd say, "You're outa here!" I wouldn't want that.

HOST: Where do you get the drugs? How do you pay for them?

GIRL: I don't. My friends give them to me. Sometimes I get them from my boyfriend.

HOST: How are your grades in school?

GIRL: They're okay.

HOST: Wouldn't you like to stop doing drugs?

GIRL: No.

HOST: Don't you consider yourself an addict?

GIRL: I'm not addicted. I haven't done cocaine in two weeks. Right now I'm just smoking pot and drinking.

I reported this dialogue to a class of my undergraduate education students, only two years out of high school themselves.

"I'm not shocked by that," one of my students said. "I knew a lot of kids in high school who did drugs all the time, and their parents didn't have a clue."

Others explained that it's easy to hide marijuana and alcohol use with perfume and breath fresheners, and that a lot of kids just go to their rooms and don't see their parents very much anyway. I asked about what percentage of their friends in high school would they say did drugs on a regular basis—at least once a week. About half, they said. How many were into drinking on a weekly basis? More than 75 percent. When did the drinking start? Eighth grade. How about the drugs? Ninth grade.

Studies find that drug use by young people is *ten* times more prevalent than parents suspect.[1] A recent U.S. Department of Education handbook on drug education states flatly: "In America today, the most serious threat to the health and well-being of our children is drug use."[2] Consider the following:

- The United States has the highest rate of teenage drug use of any industrialized nation (ten times greater than that of Japan).[3]

- Nearly six out of 10 high school seniors say they have used illegal drugs (not including alcohol). According to a 1990 national report, more than 3.5 million children aged 12 to 17 have used marijuana (now the leading cash crop in this country).[4]

- During the past decade, according to the Centers for Disease Control, total U.S. consumption of cocaine nearly doubled.[5] Although overall cocaine use is down among high school students, the use of crack, the most potent form of cocaine, has increased dramatically.[6]

- AIDS researchers fear that drug-using teens, who feel invulnerable when they're high, will emerge as a new AIDS risk group. Says Robert Fullilove, a researcher at the University of California at San Francisco: "Crack use is helping to fuel an epidemic of sexually transmitted diseases among adolescents."[7]

• LSD is returning to the drug scene. One in 12 high school students admits to experimenting with this hallucinogenic drug.[8]

• According to the December 1988 issue of the *Journal of the American Medical Association,* one in 15 high school senior boys has used steroids.

• Students are getting into drugs at younger and younger ages. The percentage of children using drugs by the sixth grade has tripled since 1975.[9] In a survey by *Weekly Reader,* 25 percent of fourth graders said they experienced "some" to "a lot" of peer pressure to try drugs or alcohol.

• There has been a surge in the number of students using inhalants—children as young as second graders sniffing the fumes of everything from spray paint to typewriter correction fluid. A Texas A&M study found that one third of inhalant users were injecting harder drugs four years later; nearly half were using alcohol in amounts equivalent to five cans of beer a day.[10]

• In a 1989 Gallup poll, six in 10 teenagers ranked drugs as the greatest problem facing their generation.[11]

KIDS IN THE GRIP OF DRUGS

As always, the statistics, grim as they are, pale by comparison with the stories.

• In Fayetteville, a suburb of Syracuse, New York, a group of teenagers reeling from beer, cocaine, and LSD sliced apart a cat and collected the blood for a Satanic rite.[12]

• Bob is 17 and a junior at a suburban high school in central New York. His drug habit started when he was in ninth grade. By his junior year he became so desperate for cocaine that he began having sex with his male dealer.[13]

• Maria is 16. Two years ago she had her first experience with inhalants—sniffing a gasoline-soaked rag on a school bus. From there, friends persuaded her to try spray paint and Liquid Paper. It made her "forget a lot of things," she says, including problems at home. Soon she was into stealing to support her habit. Then she began having withdrawal symptoms—red eyes, pains in her stomach and legs, and a near inability to walk. Afraid she would die, she quit using inhalants, but soon after discovered she was pregnant.[14]

• Theresa got into drugs and prostitution at age 15. Her baby daughter Candace was born addicted to cocaine. Theresa had injected coke right up to labor.[15]

• Mike was the stereotype of suburban boys. He earned merit badges as a Boy Scout, won the Pinewood Derby car competition, got good grades in school, and played trumpet in his high school's marching band. His father sold advertising; his mother took care of the family of five.

At 16, Mike passed out in school after snorting Freon from air conditioning refill canisters. He began stealing pills and painkillers from his family's bathroom cabinet. Then money. Soon he was into pot, speed, and LSD as well as Freon. His parents got him into counseling, which helped for a while. Then one night he went to his room, turned on the stereo, and hanged himself.[16]

HOW DRUGS WREAK THEIR HAVOC

At first, kids take drugs to feel good. Then they take them to keep from feeling bad. Eventually the drug itself leaves a wake of bad feeling. More than half of all teenage suicides are drug-related.[17]

Drugs block, retard, and distort the most crucial human capacities: perception, planning, physical coordination, and moral judgment.[18] Drugs scramble sensory information, lessen self-control, and give users the false sense that they're at their best when they're on the drug—an illusion that can lead them to harm themselves and others.

Most insidious, the user's self-imposed disruption of key mental and motoric capacities is reinforced by highly pleasurable sensations.[19] With continuing drug use, messing up one's mind and body becomes physically or psychologically addictive.

Drugs can remain in the body and produce negative side effects long after they are taken. Fat-soluble drugs such as pot, PCP, and LSD go straight for the body organs that are high in fatty tissue—such as the brain and the testes and ovaries. Once there, they build up. Their slow release over time can cause delayed effects such as flashbacks weeks and even months after drug use has stopped.[20]

The accumulation of THC, the main mind-altering ingredient in marijuana, can inhibit formation of DNA, the genetic material that tells the body's cells how to grow. DNA damage can mean abnormal offspring.[21]

In 1981 the American Medical Association stated that "even moderate use of [then available] marijuana is associated with psychoses, panic states, and adolescent personality disorders." Since the time that statement was issued, most marijuana has contained double to triple the amount of THC capable of causing serious psychic damage.[22]

Crack, a smokable form of pure cocaine available for as little as $10, produces an immediate rush of euphoric feeling. It can cause addiction within a few days. Crack has led many young people into stealing, prostitution, and drug-dealing to pay for their habit. Like any form of cocaine, it can also kill by causing cardiac arrest or interrupting the brain's control over the heart and lungs.

Some of the new "designer" drugs—slight chemical variations of existing illegal drugs—have caused permanent brain damage with a single dose.[23]

Drugs also undermine learning and the school environment necessary for learning. Liz, 19, says pot-smoking was widespread in her suburban high school. "This one kid used to do cocaine in the back of study hall. People would drop acid in class."[24]

Students who use pot, one study found, are twice as likely to average D's and F's as other students.[25] Heavy drug-using students are three times as likely to skip school as nonusers. Four of five school dropouts in a Philadelphia study used drugs regularly.[26]

With many students, drug use is a symptom of deeper difficulties—trouble at home, low self-esteem, no goals, no hope. But drugs compound the original problem and accelerate a downward spiral. One of three teen callers to a national cocaine hot line said they sold drugs. Nearly two of three said they stole from family, friends, or employers to buy their drugs.[27]

Adolescents face a whole array of new challenges and stresses—physical changes, mood swings, tensions with parents, academic demands, peer pressure, relating to the opposite sex, developing a sense of adequacy, and finding values and goals worth living for. If teenagers face these developmental challenges and work through them, they mature intellectually, emotionally, socially, and morally. But to the extent that they use drugs as an escape or crutch, their maturation is slowed and their future imperiled.

GROWING UP IN A DRUG CULTURE

A 1987 *Weekly Reader* survey shed light on what leads elementary school-age children to get involved with drugs. For children in grades

4 through 6, the most important reason for using marijuana was "to fit in with others."

"To have a good time" was the second main reason, followed closely by a desire "to feel older." Students also indicated that TV and movies played a big role in making drugs and drinking seem attractive.[28] And children grow up in a world where drug busts are almost daily news events. Revelations of drug use by star athletes and other celebrities are equally routine. So are reports of drugs in the workplace.

By their midtwenties, says University of Michigan's Social Research Institute, 75 percent to 80 percent of young adults have tried an illicit drug. More than half have experimented with an illegal drug other than marijuana.[29]

One student in our teacher education program—a man in his early thirties who wants to be a junior high school English teacher—stopped by my office one day and brought up the problem of drugs. "I did drugs for five years," he said, "starting when I was 20 and working as a carpenter. The construction industry is loaded with drugs. I'd wake up in the morning and smoke a joint. I knew I had to go out and pound nails, and I didn't want to do it. I'd have another joint at lunch, and another one later on.

"It slowed my brain, and not just for the years that I did it. I'm okay now when I write, but when I speak, I still have trouble organizing my thoughts, expressing my opinions. When I was smoking, I didn't care about anything—not my job, not my marriage, not anything. I nearly ruined my life."

He says he sees kids now who are into drugs by the sixth, seventh, or eighth grade. "They're sitting there in a daze, waiting for the bell to ring so they can go and smoke another joint. And nobody is really *talking* to them about this, how they're ruining their lives, how much better life could be without drugs.

"One reason is that a lot of their teachers are doing it, too. There's an enormous drug subculture out there. Some people my age will even speak to kids in ways that encourage them to do drugs. . . . I know a married couple who have fourth- and fifth-grade children, and they do drugs in front of them. I know parents who smoke pot with their teenage kids. These are people who got into the drug culture in the sixties, and they're still in it. Nobody talks about this, but it's a big problem."

It's not true that *nobody* is talking straight to kids about drugs; many teachers do teach about drugs in an honest, heartfelt, and credible way. But this student's larger point is sadly valid.

Many of the parents who do drugs also abuse their children while they're under the influence. A father in Syracuse, New York, repeatedly raped his two daughters, 11 and 10, when he was high on crack. The National Committee for the Prevention of Child Abuse reported a 10 percent jump in 1989 in known cases of child abuse (up to 2.4 million)—the largest increase in five years. According to committee spokesperson Anne Cohn, the increase was "caused primarily by an explosion in parents' substance abuse, especially crack cocaine."[30]

WHAT CAN SCHOOLS DO?

The good news is that there are schools and communities across the country that have met the drug problem head-on and are making discernible progress.

The stories of schools that have set their sights on a totally drug-free environment are told in the U.S. Department of Education guidebook *Schools Without Drugs*.[31] Each school's story is used to illustrate a basic principle in comprehensive drug education. Some examples:

Principle 1: Establish clear and specific school rules regarding drug use that include strong corrective actions.

Case study: The Anne Arundel County School District in Annapolis, Maryland, found it had a serious drug problem. It moved to implement a new policy that directs school officials to take strong steps when students are found using or possessing drugs:

- The school immediately notifies the police, calls the parents, and suspends the student for one to five school days.

- A special assistant to the superintendent meets with the student and parents together. To return to school, students must state where and how they obtained the drugs. They must also agree to take the district's Alternative Drug Education program at night and at least five hours of counseling accompanied by their parents.

- Students are expelled if caught using or possessing drugs a second time or if caught distributing or selling drugs.

After this policy was implemented, the number of drug offenses declined 60 percent over the next six years.

Principle 2: Reach out to the community for help in making the school's antidrug program work.

Case study: Gompers Vocational-Technical High School is in the South

Bronx in New York City. Ninety-five percent of its 1,500 students are from low-income families.

A *New York Times* article in 1979 called Gompers a "war zone." Students smoked pot and sold drugs both inside the school and on school grounds. Police had to be called in daily.

The school board hired a new principal, Victor Herbert, who took these actions:

- He established a drug education program for teachers, students, and parents that emphasized recognizing the signs of drug use.

- To provide students with positive alternatives to drugs, he persuaded companies such as IBM to hire students for after-school and summer work. Students had to be drug-free to participate.

- A computerized attendance system was installed to notify parents of their child's absence. "Family assistants" were hired to locate absentees and bring them back to school.

- In cooperation with the police captain, Herbert arranged for the same two police officers to respond to all calls from the high school. These officers came to know the students, and eventually students confided in the police about drug sales occurring near the school.

- Herbert stationed security guards and faculty outside each bathroom. He organized "hall sweeps" to make sure all students were in classes and no longer allowed students to leave the premises at lunchtime.

The current principal at Gompers High School reports that in 1986 there were no known incidents of students using alcohol or drugs in school or on school grounds, and only one incident of violence. Moreover, the percentage of students reading at or above grade level rose from 45 percent in 1979–80 to 67 percent in 1984–85.

Principle 3: Involve students in encouraging other students to resist drugs.

Case study: R. H. Watkins High School in Jones County, Mississippi, generates positive peer pressure against drugs by training students as drug education peer counselors. Students selected as peer counselors receive drug education credit for meeting these responsibilities:

- Remaining drug-free
- Maintaining a C average or better in all classes

- Successfully completing training for the counseling program, including units on identifying drug abuse, reasons for drug abuse, and the legal and economic aspects of abuse

- Presenting monthly programs on drug abuse in each of the elementary and junior high schools and to community groups and churches

- Participating in group rap sessions or individual counseling for students.

Here is a high school senior in Liverpool, New York, who is a student counselor in her community's elementary schools:

> We go into the fifth and sixth grades. The teacher stays in the room, but the kids still really open up to us. Teachers say their students talk to us more easily than they talk to them. They listen to us when we tell them about the problems we faced and how to handle peer pressure.

Older students helping to teach younger ones in this way is now part of a national movement to make greater use of students as an educational resource. There is even the National Peer Helpers Association (2730 Market Street, Suite 120, San Francisco, CA 94114; tel. 415-626-1942), which will advise schools on how to develop their own program. When it comes to student counselors, careful selection, training, and supervision of the counselors have proven to be the ingredients for success. With proper preparation and adult guidance, students have been able to help both agemates and younger schoolmates with issues as varied as drug and alcohol problems, loneliness and friendship needs, violence and vandalism, academic difficulties, language and cultural barriers, and conflict resolution.

Principle 4: Implement a comprehensive drug prevention program, beginning in kindergarten, that teaches why drug use is wrong and harmful and how to resist drugs successfully.

In Los Angeles, the school district and the police department have teamed up to create DARE (Drug Abuse Resistance Education), now operating in more than 400 schools from kindergarten through eighth grade. More than 50 carefully selected and trained frontline police officers come into the classroom to teach students how to say no to drugs, increase their self-esteem, manage stress, resist prodrug media messages, and develop other skills to keep them drug-free.

Officer Bill Guerrero holds up a bright red balloon in front of his sixth-grade DARE class. "This is our self-esteem balloon," he says, smiling. "When good things happen to us, our self-esteem balloon grows." He blows up the balloon.

"But when bad things happen to us, what happens to our self-esteem balloon?" "It goes down," the class says. "That's right," says Officer Guerrero, letting out all the air, making a loud rasp. The class laughs.[32]

Officer Guerrero then makes his point seriously. "Everyone does something well," he says. "Identifying our own strengths is important in building a positive self-image. We don't have to rely on others to blow up our self-esteem balloon. By pumping up our own self-esteem, we can take more control over our own behavior."[33]

DARE instructors like Officer Guerrero also spend time on the playground at recess so students can get to know them. And they participate in meetings with teachers, principals, and parents to discuss the drug-education curriculum.

DARE has improved students' self-esteem, sense of responsibility to themselves and to police, and resistance to drugs. In one evaluation study, 51 percent of fifth-grade students before DARE equated drug use with having more friends. After the program, only 8 percent reported this attitude.[34]

DARE also has an evening program that teaches parents about drugs and ways to increase family communication. Before taking this program, 61 percent of parents thought there was nothing parents could do about their children's use of drugs. Only 5 percent said that after the program. Before DARE, 32 percent of parents thought it was all right for children to drink alcohol at a party as long as adults were present; after DARE, no parents reported such a view.[35]

DARE's partnership between schools and police also points to the importance of incorporating law education into drug education. "There are a lot of kids walking around who think smoking marijuana is legal," says Eric Mondchein, director of the New York State Bar Association's Law, Youth, and Citizenship program. "Much of the present drug-education curriculum deals with health-related aspects of abuse. But kids also need to be made aware of the consequences of a drug conviction. If you're busted, it can affect whether you can go to certain colleges, what jobs you can get—the rest of your life."[36]

"DRUG-FREE YOUTH"

Bennington High School in Bennington, Oklahoma (population, three hundred), is a totally drug-free school.

It wasn't always that way. "A lot of people around here always said

Bennington had a drug problem," says Christie Wilson, a sophomore at the school.

In 1989, in an effort to rid their school of drugs completely, all 75 students in Bennington High School volunteered for a countywide drug testing program. Students who pass the test receive a drug-free identification card, good for discounts at restaurants, bowling alleys, and other local establishments. Students who fail subsequent, random tests (given to 10 percent of the students each month) lose their cards and receive counseling but no other disciplinary action.

"The program has generated peer pressure for kids to stay clean," says school superintendent Olan Ispell. Katy Morris, Bryan County's youth services education coordinator, says that 1,400 hundred students in the county's 10 high schools have volunteered for the test, and only about a dozen students have failed in the whole county. But Bennington High School is the only school so far at which 100 percent of the students agreed to give a urine sample. Morris adds that she has not received a single complaint about the project from the community.

"It feels good to say you're from Bennington now," says Christie Wilson. "I hope schools start doing this all over."[37]

"COMMUNITY SCHOOLS"

In 1990 a New York City mayoral commission set out to find new ways to try to strengthen communities and stem the tide of drugs.

One of the commission's best-received proposals: Turn existing schools, at relatively modest cost, into "community schools" by having them remain open 16 hours a day every day. Such schools would serve as home base for a host of local services: drug enforcement efforts, treatment outreach, welfare and employment offices, tenant organizations, public health classes, and youth groups. Organized and supervised recreation programs would bring many youngsters off the streets.

As an approving *New York Times* editorial observed, drugs flourish where families, churches, and schools don't supervise youth.[38]

VALUING PERSONAL HEALTH

Valuing personal health means respecting and caring for one's body as part of overall self-respect—and understanding the role of drugs in either aiding or damaging health. Some drugs, such as medicines, can help the body get well and stay well. Other drugs, such as illegal narcotics, are banned by law because they harm the body. This is a big idea, one that children should be exposed to in the earliest grades.[39]

At the junior and senior high levels, the study of drugs and health can examine how drugs affect the circulatory, digestive, nervous, reproductive, and respiratory systems. Students can learn about the properties of drugs from experts (community physicians, scientists, pharmacists, or police); do research on the drug problem as it exists in the school, the community, and the sports and entertainment fields; and visit an open meeting of Alcoholics Anonymous or Narcotics Anonymous[40] (this last activity, testifies one health educator, produces a level of awareness that students can't get out of a book).

MAKING A MORAL JUDGMENT ABOUT DRUGS

Many health curricula and antidrug media campaigns stress that doing drugs is "not smart" ("Why do you think they call it 'dope'?").

A good curriculum will also help students make a *moral* judgment: Doing drugs is wrong for at least four reasons:

1. It's self-destructive—a violation of our obligation to respect and care for ourself, develop our potential, and not throw away our future.

2. Drug abuse almost always leads to some other wrongful behavior, such as lying, stealing, pushing drugs to pay for the habit, or reckless and violent behavior.

3. Drug abuse causes much suffering to those people, especially families, who care about the drug abuser.

4. Drug abuse by minors or adults contributes to an enormously destructive societal problem. If you're dealing in drugs—buying or selling—you're part of that national problem.

Helping students make this clear moral judgment about drug abuse is a more powerful deterrent for them than simply to think it's "not smart." With drugs, as with sexual behavior, students' moral values govern their decision-making.

ALCOHOL

America's most serious drug problem, because it is so widespread, is alcohol abuse.

COMBATING DRUGS AND ALCOHOL

Schools can fight drug abuse by:

1. Establishing and enforcing clear school rules regarding drug use.

2. Seeking the community's help (e.g., jobs for drug-free students and the involvement of police in drug instruction) in making the school's program work.

3. Involving students in encouraging other students to resist drugs.

4. Implementing a kindergarten-through-twelfth-grade drug prevention curriculum that teaches children to value their personal health, know the laws about drugs, and understand all the reasons why drug abuse is irresponsible.

5. Getting students to set the goal of making their school totally drug-free.

6. Becoming a neighborhood-building "community school" that is open after school hours for a wide range of community uses.

Schools can try to reduce student alcohol use by:

1. Implementing an alcohol-education curriculum that teaches students to:
   - Value their health and understand the destructive effects of alcohol abuse and dependency.
   - Understand how advertising manipulates young people into drinking.
   - Confront problems rather than escape them through alcohol.
   - Respect the law regarding alcohol use.
   - Never drink and drive.
   - Understand the moral obligation to maintain self-control and how getting drunk destroys that.

2. Seeking the help of parents in discouraging underage drinking.

3. Encouraging the formation of student groups that promote the value of teenagers' staying away from alcohol.

- More than half of American high school seniors say they get drunk at least once a month.[41] Two of five get drunk at least once a weekend.

- One of three teenagers drinks enough to hurt school performance seriously or to get in trouble with the law.[42]

- Nearly half of tenth-graders and one third of eighth-graders say that during the past month they have ridden with a driver who used alcohol or drugs.[43]

- The average age of first alcohol use has dropped to 12.3 years (seventh grade).[44]

- An estimated 100,000 ten- and eleven-year-olds get drunk at least once a week.[45] As early as fourth grade, one of three children say they experience peer pressure to drink beer, liquor, wine, or wine coolers.

The personal and societal costs of alcohol abuse are staggering:

- Drinking and driving is the number-one killer of adolescents.[46]

- Mixing alcohol and other drugs is the cause of an additional 2,500 deaths in the United States every year.

- Alcohol commonly serves as a gateway drug, leading to other forms of substance abuse.

- Young people who drink regularly risk developing a mind-set that their problems are soluble in alcohol. "When I drank," says one teenage problem drinker, "I lost my fears. I could talk to people."

- An estimated 10 million to 20 million Americans suffer from alcoholism or alcohol-related problems. An alcoholic's life span is shortened by an average of 10 to 12 years. For every one person who suffers from alcoholism, another four persons (usually family) are directly affected in adverse ways.[47] Fetal alcohol syndrome has become the leading cause of mental retardation in the Western world.

- According to the *Harvard Medical School Health Letter Book,* alcohol is involved in half of all automobile deaths, half of all murders, half of all rapes, and 25 percent of all suicides.[48] Drinking by young people contributes to violence, vandalism, impulsive sexual behavior, suicide, and a variety of serious crimes and accidents.

In short, alcohol abuse leads to more problems for individuals, families, and society as a whole than any other drug use.[49]

WHY DO SO MANY TEENS DRINK?

Young people use alcohol because they like the feeling of being high or drunk; they experience peer pressure to drink; they're asserting their independence; they suffer from high stress or low self-esteem; their parents fail to set and enforce rules regarding alcohol use or are openly permissive; they're from alcohol-troubled families where the parents themselves set a bad example; they underestimate the dangers of alcohol; they lack good decision-making skills.

Another big factor makes alcohol use by the young a particularly tough problem: Alcohol, because it's legal for adults, is constantly promoted through advertising. *Myths, Men, and Beer,* a recent study published by the AAA Foundation for Traffic Safety, estimates that by the time they reach driving age, American children have seen close to 100,000 beer commercials. This study concludes by recommending that beer commercials be banned from television—or at least kept from using images that link beer with driving and speed.[50] That is a proposal that the educational establishment should vigorously back.

SCHOOLS FIGHTING STUDENT DRINKING: "WE CANNOT DO THE JOB ALONE"

A good classroom curriculum is a start in alcohol education, but the available evidence says it won't do the job alone. For example, a January 1988 article in the *Journal of Studies on Alcohol* reports a thoroughgoing research evaluation of an alcohol-education curriculum called Here's Looking at You.[51] Considered state of the art, this kindergarten- to twelfth-grade curriculum uses a variety of participatory activities designed to enhance self-esteem, improve decision-making, develop students' coping skills, and provide information on alcohol and other drugs. In spite of all this, the evaluation study found that the program had only "minimal" impact on the psychosocial variables assumed to be involved in drinking behavior and had *"essentially no measurable carry-over effect on problem [drinking] behavior"* (emphasis added).[52]

The difficulty schools face in controlling students' alcohol use is expressed well by Bill Baldwin, a recently retired principal at Cortland Junior-Senior High School in Cortland, New York. In an interview for that school district's newsletter he was asked, "How is the high school helping students with the problem of alcohol?" His answer:

> We have 56 extracurricular clubs and activities in the junior-senior high for students to participate in and stay out of trouble. We have resource people such as the school-community relations counselor, the guidance counselors, and the school social worker. We have our SADD (Students Against Drunk Driving) program; our recently instituted peer counseling program; educational programs; special events and materials we bring in from outside the schools; and finally, the school curriculum itself. Yet it is not enough. We cannot do the job alone.

What is needed, Mr. Baldwin went on to say, is the cooperation of parents. But in a recent survey of his school's students, 59 percent said they most often do their drinking at parties, and 47 percent said their parents allowed them to drink at home.

The biggest job in alcohol education is parent education. Parents need to be made aware that alcohol is a drug, can hurt school performance, is very often a factor in irresponsible and high-risk activity (e.g., drinking and driving, sex) by teens, can become a dependency, and frequently leads to the use of illegal drugs, sometimes in combination with alcohol. And parents need to know the law:

- Parents who host parties at which alcohol is served to minors can be sued if any underage person leaving their home is injured in an accident, and can also be sued for any damages caused by an alcohol-impaired minor. Case law exists establishing the liability of parents for underage drinking in their home even if the parents are not home at the time.[53]

- Even if no accident occurs, host parents can be charged with the crime of providing alcohol to minors or endangering the welfare of minors by allowing it to be served to them.

Schools can help parents prohibit drinking by suggesting the words to say, which should be essentially the same message the school is transmitting:

> These are critical years when you're laying the foundation for your whole future. You don't need drinking when you're learning how to drive. You don't need drinking when you're learning how to relate to the opposite

sex and handle the feelings that go with that. You don't need drinking when you're learning how to stand up to peer pressure.

If you drink now, you also won't be learning other ways to enjoy yourself in life. You'll get so you think that if there's no drinking, there's no fun.

We care about you too much to permit you to use alcohol during these years. Save drinking for later, when you'll be more mature, you'll be better able to handle peer pressure, and it will be legal for you to drink.

Some schools have implemented programs that teach parenting skills that help prevent alcohol and other drug abuse.[54] In these programs, parents learn how to communicate more effectively with their teenagers, set clear rules prohibiting drinking, supervise where teens go and what they do, and spot the warning signs of drinking. These programs also inform parents of an important fact: Teens who are "taught to drink responsibly" grow up to be adults who have just as many alcohol-related problems as teens who are not allowed to drink.

A very hopeful movement—one that is spreading to school districts across the country—is Safe Homes. In this community-based program, participating parents pledge:

- I will not serve nor will I allow anyone under the legal drinking age to consume alcohol in my home or on my property.

- I will not allow the use of illegal drugs in my home or on my property.

- I will not allow parties or gatherings in my home without proper adult supervision.

For more information write Safe Homes, Guilderland Central Schools, District Office, State Farm Road, Guilderland, NY 12084.

THE IMPORTANT MORAL MESSAGES IN ALCOHOL EDUCATION

Schools need to know that when they are doing alcohol education, as with drug education in general, they are doing values education. These are the most important moral messages to try to get across to students:

1. Value your personal health, and don't abuse it through alcohol.

2. Don't drink and drive; to do so is to risk other people's lives as well as your own. (The booklet *Fighting Drinking and Driving: Tips from America's High School Students* describes dozens of award-winning educational strategies and projects and is available from The National Association of Secondary School Principals, 1904 Association Drive, Reston, VA 22070.)

3. Don't use alcohol to try to solve problems; solve problems by confronting them and getting help if you need it.

4. Respect the law by waiting until you're of legal age to drink.

5. When it's legal for you to drink, do so in moderation so as to maintain responsible control over your judgment and actions. Make it a goal for yourself never to get drunk.

Everyone knows that many adolescents are going to drink alcohol no matter what the law or the school says. But some authors take that fact and use it as a justification for talking to young people about "responsible" underage drinking. Here, for example, is advice to teens from Susan and David Cohen's 1986 book *A Six-Pack and a Fake I.D.*:

> If you're planning a drinking party, and your parents accept the idea, then at least try to make your party a safe, pleasant, and interesting one, instead of a drunken bash. . . . Don't overdo the amount of alcohol in the punch, and don't let anyone else add to it.[55]

Such advice, however well-intended, is faulty on two counts. First of all, telling high schoolers to "go easy on the drinking" is unrealistic because, as teenagers themselves will testify, most of their peers at a party drink to get drunk. Second, advice such as the Cohens' amounts to telling teens and their parents, "Go ahead and break the law."

The school has an obligation, as an institution entrusted with citizenship education, to promote respect for and compliance with the law. Rather than send the message "Hey, kids, we know you're drinking—here are some tips for doing it moderately," schools would do better to pose the question "Why is society asking you, through its laws, to postpone drinking?"

The personal obligation to maintain self-control is a moral concept that should be at the center of any alcohol education program. To begin with, young people need to know that alcohol acts first on those parts of the brain that affect self-control and other learned behaviors.

That's why heavy drinking often leads people to be violent, take risks, and do other things they would be unlikely to do when sober.

Author Colleen Reece tells the story of 16-year-old Jennifer. She was thrilled when Kevin, a star athlete at her school, asked her to a victory party at his house. His folks were gone and, she discovered upon arrival, "there was a regular river of liquor." Jennifer didn't ordinarily drink, but everybody else was drinking and "it didn't seem like a drink or two would hurt."

> The basement lights were really low and everyone was making out, then making off into other rooms. Kevin kept giving me drinks and edging me toward his parents' room. I always thought girls who started having sex on dates were stupid. I think I tried to leave, sort of, and I did say no. But Kevin just smiled and pulled at me and said, "Don't you want to be my girl, Jennifer?"
>
> I couldn't think clearly. All my ideas about waiting until marriage were fuzzy and hard to remember. What if Kevin never asked me out again? I don't remember much else except waking up the next morning feeling sick over what I could remember.[56]

A chaplain at a well-known Catholic university says that in confession these days, college students rarely confess, as students once did, the sin of getting drunk (always considered a grave sin in Catholic moral theology). It's not that today's students at this university never get drunk; many do. But apparently they do not think, as their predecessors did, that getting drunk is a serious moral wrong.

Students won't view drunkenness as a serious wrong unless they are taught a moral principle that has fallen into neglect: A person has a moral responsibility to remain in control of his or her will. The will is the critical faculty that links moral judgment to behavior; our will is what enables us to act in accordance with what we know to be right. Weaken the will, as excessive drinking does, and you weaken control over moral decision-making and moral behavior. That's why getting drunk is morally irresponsible, often criminally and tragically so.

In the long run, the battle against underage drinking will be won, if it is won, through changes in the peer culture. Those will come slowly. But as progress in shifting attitudes toward sexual abstinence shows, peer-group norms can and do change. In the Sweet Home school district outside of Buffalo, New York, sixth-graders campaign against both drugs and drinking. In some secondary schools there are "youth to youth" groups where the message is that it's "uncool" to drink.

The long-term battle against drug and alcohol abuse will also require a shift in cultural values—away from the frantic pursuit of pleasure and self-gratification toward a deeper, more spiritual sense of what life is about.

In this connection I think of a conversation I had with a student who is working on his master's degree in physical education and who was taking my course in moral education as an elective. He stayed after class one night to talk about something he found very distressing. "I lift weights competitively," he said, "but it's getting harder and harder to compete because everybody takes steroids. I don't and never will. But everyone I know does, and nobody gets caught."

I said, "What about all the health hazards? You can't pick up a paper or a magazine without reading about how steroids cause sterility and cancer and all kinds of other problems."

"People know all that," he said, "but it doesn't faze them." Then he told about an article he had just read in one of his physical education classes.[57] It reported the results of a survey of more than 100 amateur athletes who were asked this question: "If you could take a drug that would guarantee you'd win an Olympic gold medal but would kill you within the year, would you take that drug?" Over half the athletes surveyed said yes.

Large numbers of young persons, growing up in a society that makes gods of money, power, pleasure, and success, are spiritually adrift. As one mother commented upon hearing the results of this survey, "They don't know why they're here."

Public school values education clearly won't, by itself, fill the spiritual void that causes so many people to look for life enhancement in drugs or alcohol and to risk their health and futures in the process. But in this difficult area, as elsewhere, schools must contribute what they can. They can help young people develop a sense of responsibility to themselves and others and begin to think about what it truly means to live life well.

CHAPTER 20

Schools, Parents, and
Communities Working
Together

*The school system can't make up for family failure. The total
education of our children is a cooperative effort requiring community solidarity. Apathetic parents who foster a permissive home
atmosphere create a problem for everyone.*

—JOHN HANSGATE, father, Buffalo,
New York [1]

*In a national survey of 22,000 public schoolteachers, 90 per-
cent say lack of parental support is a problem, 89 percent report
abused or neglected children in their classes, and nearly 70 percent cite sick and undernourished students.*

—Report of the Carnegie
Foundation for the Advancement
of Teaching [2]

The long-term success of the new values education depends on forces
outside the school—on the extent to which families and communities join schools in a common effort to meet the needs of children
and foster their healthy development.

In a time of many moral troubles, the crisis in the family is arguably

395

the most serious problem we face. One who shares that view is Dr. Steven Sample, president of the University of Southern California. He observes, "It's very unusual in any advanced society to have large numbers of children born for which the father asserts no ownership at all."[3] And that particular social pathology, as Sample points out, is only part of a wider societal trend: "a dissolving sense of responsibility on the part of parents to children and the almost total absence of a sense of responsibility to the larger community."[4]

"We've somehow forgotten where quality comes from," says Dr. Thomas Delaney, a psychologist in Olean, New York, who counsels upwardly mobile families and their troubled children. "We somehow have to get back to a position where parents see their major priority in their children."[5]

SUPPORTING FAMILIES

How can we support and strengthen the family in its time-honored role as the primary caregiver and moral teacher of children?

NEEDED: A NATIONAL CAMPAIGN

We should begin with a national campaign to convince parents how important they are to their children.

Parents need information and images concerning all the ways in which they affect their children's health, happiness, self-esteem, and character. Parents are powerful people, but great numbers sadly underestimate their importance to their children. Says a third-grade teacher: "Parents need to know that they can make a big difference in their child's life just by making sure they know their math facts."

Japan now uses appealing 30-second television spots that promote kindness in children by showing a child doing a good deed and feeling happy about having helped another person. In a similar way, American television and other media can be used to promote both the responsibilities and the pleasures of parenting. Parents would speak in their own voices about how they try to raise their children to be good and decent people. Here, for example, is a mother talking about how she teaches her children to be helpful:

> When we found we were expecting another baby, I explained to them that I would be very busy with the baby and I would need their help. My 3-year-old brings the wash downstairs every day and gets diapers, etc., for me when I need them. He feels good about helping and being part of the

family. And he also understands that by helping me do things around the house, he gives me more time to do things with him.

A father tells how he was able to establish a channel of communication with his first son:

> Don and I go out for breakfast on Saturday mornings. We started back when he was 10, and I worried that we didn't have enough in common. We found out we like each other in spite of our being different in many ways. . . . It's amazing what I learned, and it's been good in making Don feel open about talking to his mother and me about all sorts of things: school problems, girls, sex, fears. . . .

And here is a mother speaking about how she and her husband, through family traditions, try to pass on a religious heritage to their children:

> We want our children to understand that God has created them for goodness. We have a tradition of a fasting dinner on Monday night— usually an apple or orange for the kids and a cup of broth for us. Everybody has a snack before bed to quiet growling stomachs, but the idea is to deprive ourselves a little so we have a better appreciation of world hunger. The money we save by not having a regular meal is put in a jar and sent to Oxfam America at the end of the month.
>
> Sometimes we'll read a letter from Oxfam about progress in relieving hunger in one country or the outbreak of a crisis somewhere else. We want our children to know how much suffering there is in the world, and that God calls us to love our neighbor, wherever our neighbor is.

In all of these vignettes, the underlying message to parents would be: "You—and the life you create as a family—are indispensable to your child. Nothing can take your place. And as a parent, you are engaged in the most important work there is: raising up new human life."[6]

HELP FROM THE TOP

Government must be part of the solution instead of part of the problem. Current policies often contribute to the subversion of parenting and family life.

For example: Women who work are not encouraged by job leave policies to stay home with their newborns for a long enough period to allow bonding to occur. The well-known Harvard pediatrician T. Berry

Brazelton has reported a new and disturbing phenomenon he has seen in his practice: Expectant mothers who knew they would be returning to work up to three months after the baby was born did not show the usual excitement about or commitment to the anticipated birth. "It was as if they were guarding themselves against the turmoil of attachment," Brazelton said of 60 expectant mothers who showed this flat emotion.

He does not, however, observe this problem among expectant mothers who are planning to stay home with their infants for at least four months. "An obvious solution," Brazelton says, "is to push for paid maternity leave for four months. It's a goal we must pursue nationally."[7] It's a modest goal; many European countries already provide more.

Government, fortunately, is gradually coming to recognize how wide and deep the crisis in the family is, but social policies are needed to provide families with support that will make a difference.

THE YEAR OF THE FAMILY AND PARENTS AS TEACHERS PROGRAMS

Some states have taken the lead in showing what can be done to focus public attention on parenting and provide parents with practical help and support.

In Wisconsin, the Department of Public Instruction launched a state-wide campaign in 1987 called The Year of the Family in Education. It had three goals: (1) to educate teachers about their role in promoting greater parent involvement; (2) to share information with schools on how they could improve home-school communication; and (3) to get information directly to parents on their role in the education of their children. (For information on this program and available information packets, contact the Department of Public Instruction, Family in Education Program, Box 7841, Madison, WI 53707; tel. 608-266-9757.)

In Missouri, with initial support from the Danforth Foundation, the State Department of Elementary and Secondary Education organized a highly successful program called Parents as Teachers (PAT). PAT is based on a compelling idea: to help children get the best possible start in life by supporting parents as their child's most important teachers during the crucial early years—birth to age 3.[8]

Parents as Teachers, which is voluntary and available without cost or restriction to parents of all children, includes:

- Monthly home visits by trained parent educators who present simple tasks for the child to do (such as matching games or reassembling a puzzle). By observing, parents learn new ways to play with their children and help them learn. The home visitor also offers observations on how the child has developed since the last visit, what new things he or she is doing, and so on.

- Group sharing meetings with parents of like-age children.

- Periodic monitoring to assure that children do not reach age 3 with an undetected handicap or developmental problem.

In Missouri, Parents as Teachers has grown rapidly, from a program for 380 families in 1981 to a state-funded service provided by all 543 Missouri school districts and reaching more than 50,000 thousand families a year. PAT has also been replicated in more than 80 sites across the nation. (For more information, contact Parents as Teachers National Center, 800 Natural Bridge Road, St. Louis, MO 63121; tel. 314-553-5738.)

SCHOOLS OF THE TWENTY-FIRST CENTURY

According to U.S. Bureau of Labor Statistics, as of 1990 a total of 70 percent of all mothers of children 6 to 17 are in the labor force at least part time.

In response to the great need for reliable, high-quality child care, Dr. Edward Zigler, director of Yale's Center in Child Development and Social Policy, came up with this idea: Take the public school building that is already in existence and use it for five much-needed services:

1. On-site day care for 3- to 4-year-olds.

2. Before- and after-school care provided by trained personnel for 5- to 12-year-olds.

3. Support and training for neighborhood persons who offer day care in their own homes.

4. Home visits and group meetings for new and expectant parents (similar to Missouri's Parents as Teachers program).

5. Information and referral services for parents starting as early as pregnancy.[9]

Zigler called this model the "school of the twenty-first century." Missouri schools, since they already had the Parents as Teachers component in place, were among the first to latch on to Zigler's idea. It soon spread to schools in Colorado, North Carolina, Wyoming, and Connecticut.

Says Elliot Ginsberg, Connecticut's human resources commissioner: "Rapid changes in the world of children and parents have threatened the ability of families to raise healthy, successful children. Family resource centers address these changes." [10]

Says one mother who has taken advantage of a twenty-first-century school: "I feel lucky to live in a place where the neighborhood school started caring about my child before she was even born!" [11]

SCHOOLS AND PARENTS AS PARTNERS
IN VALUES EDUCATION

In addition to these broad-based efforts to help parents and children, there are many things schools can do to recruit parents as partners in the special task of developing moral values and good character. That challenge is twofold: (1) encouraging and helping parents to carry out their role as their child's primary moral educator and (2) getting parents to support the school in its effort to teach positive moral values.

How are schools in the values education movement going about that task?

ASKING PARENTS, "WHAT KIND OF A PERSON WOULD YOU
LIKE YOUR CHILD TO BE?"

If you are a parent, it gives you pause to be asked, "What kind of a person would you like your child to be?"

Asking that question was a wise first step by the Child Development Project (see Chapter 2). The Child Development Project began its values education efforts in San Ramon, California, in a district that draws its students from several affluent, high-powered San Francisco suburbs. Academically the district ranks in the top 10 percent of California systems.

"We had expected that parents and the school board would be primarily interested in students' academic achievement," says project director Eric Schaps.[12] But Schaps and his colleagues let San Ramon parents speak for themselves. They surveyed 2,300 parents in six schools, giving them a list of 20 characteristics representing "ways you would like your child to be." Parents were asked to rate each of these characteristics on a scale of 1 ("not important") to 4 ("essential"). Here, in their order of finish, are the 10 characteristics that got the highest ratings:

1. Being self-confident

2. Being responsible, dependable

3. Being curious, eager to learn

4. Being independent, self-directing

5. Being able to work well with other children

6. Being sensitive to others

7. Being kind and considerate

8. Being a hard worker

9. Getting good grades

10. Being amiable, good-tempered.

Finishing lower, in the bottom 10, were qualities such as "having a quick mind, being intelligent," "being liked by others," "being assertive, not getting pushed around," "being a leader," and "being athletic."

Such a survey is likely to reveal the extent to which most parents, even those who are living in the fast lane, still want their children to be kind and sensitive people as well as competent. That gives the school something solid to build on in seeking support for its efforts in values education. The school can say to parents, "The values we'd like to teach in classrooms—responsibility, kindness, cooperation, hard work—are the same ones you say you want for your children."

PARENTS IN LEADERSHIP ROLES

Schools with strong parental support for their values programs usually have parents serving in leadership roles.

In Baltimore County, Maryland, for example, parents sit on each school's values education committee and help to shape their school's plan. In the southeastern part of the county, which was experiencing high unemployment among steelworkers, parents stressed the need to emphasize self-esteem. However, at Pikesville High School, where students compete fiercely for good grades, parents argued for an emphasis on academic honesty issues, such as cheating, plagiarism, and lying or exaggerating on college applications.[13]

In San Ramon's Child Development Project, for each participating school there is a parent group that plans how families can implement the same goals that teachers are working on in classrooms. At Rancho Romero Elementary School, the parents' group spoke enthusiastically about a recent special event they had helped to plan: "Grandparents' Day," conceived in the recognition that grandparents are an important source of values.

During the three weeks leading up to this event, children investigated the question "What influences do our grandparents and other relatives have on us?" They interviewed their grandparents, and read books and saw films about their grandparents' generation. On Grandparents' Day, those grandparents who lived in the community came to school and took part in classes. (Children without grandparents could invite another older person.)

One of the best-attended events organized by Rancho Romero parents was the Family Science Fair. On the night of the school's spring open house, nearly 150 families displayed science projects they had worked on together at home. One father commented: "Working together with the kids on our project and making sure they all had active roles gave me a better understanding of cooperation than I've ever had." In a survey of Child Development Project schools, approximately 50 percent of parents say they have made positive changes in family life as a result of their participation in activities like the Family Science Fair.

SCHOOL-SPONSORED PARENTING EDUCATION

It's a commonplace observation that being a parent is the toughest job in the world—and one for which we get no training.

Memphis, Tennessee, schools addressed that problem head-on. They put together a parent training program, selected for commendation in the U.S. Department of Education's *Schools That Work*[14] and notable because it has had success in high-poverty areas where the majority of the students come from single-parent homes.

Ten elementary schools participate. Weekly parent workshops are held at the schools and other convenient locations in the community. Each workshop deals with a specific issue, including topics such as:

- Discipline

- Planning and monitoring home study

- Building self-esteem

- Communication skills

- Drug and alcohol abuse

- Nutrition

The parent training program has attracted an average of 20 to 40 parents in each school. Parents report a renewed sense of control over their children—and personal satisfaction at being directly involved in their children's education.[15]

In Los Angeles, the Center for the Improvement of Child Caring (CICC) offers an array of parent training services. Widely recognized for its success in working with abusive parents, CICC now runs a national parent training program for child care workers. CICC also offers something of special interest to schools: Learning About Parenting, a program that teaches school personnel how to set up a course for high school students to prepare them for the realities of being a parent. If we are serious about preparing the next generation for the responsibilities of parenting, we should require *all* high school students to take a course in child development and parenting. (For information on CICC's programs, write Dr. Kerby Alvy, director, Center for the Improvement of Child Caring, 11331 Ventura Boulevard, Suite 103, Studio City, CA 91604; tel. 818-980-0903.)

EPIC—Effective Parenting Information for Children—is designed to prevent child abuse, teen pregnancy, school dropout, and drug and alcohol abuse. The program combines workshops for parents of young children and parents of adolescents with a pre-kindergarten through grade 9 classroom curriculum *Growing Up Together*. (For more information, write EPIC, State University College at Buffalo, 1300 Elmwood Avenue, Buffalo, NY 14222; tel. 716-884-4064.)

VALUES EDUCATION HOMEWORK

At least some school systems are beginning to act on the principle that if you have trouble getting the parents to the program, take the program to the parents. Send the materials into the home.

Here's how San Ramon's Child Development Project does that: Every two to three weeks, teachers send home "family homework" with the children. Family homework consists of short stories or poems for families to read together and talk about. These literature selections poignantly or humorously illustrate common family situations involving issues such as helpfulness, fairness, and sibling conflict. Discussion suggestions accompany each assignment.

One family homework assignment: "List four rules you must follow at home, then discuss with your parents the reason behind each rule and whether it's fair." Another assignment: Discuss family chores, using the following poem as a lighthearted opener:

Sarah Cynthia Sylvia Stout
Would Not Take the Garbage Out!

Sarah Cynthia Sylvia Stout
Would not take the garbage out!
She'd scour the pots and scrape the pans,
Candy the yams and spice the hams,
And though her daddy would scream and shout,
She simply would not take the garbage out.
And so it piled to the ceilings:
Coffee grounds, potato peelings,
Brown bananas, rotten peas,
Chunks of sour cottage cheese.
It filled the can, it covered the floor,
It cracked the window and blocked the door. . . .[16]

Parents have expressed appreciation of these activities. Says Sheila Garcia, whose son Joey is a third-grader:

I keep saying "I don't have the time," but somehow I find 10 minutes to sit down—and once you begin, it turns into fun. Joey gets to talking about emotions and feelings, and I learn things I never would have known about him. Instead of the usual, "What did you do in school today?" kind of discussion, conversations started by family homework let me discover the inside part of him.[17]

Schools wishing to receive a sample packet of family homework assignments can write the Child Development Project, 111 Deerwood Place, Suite 165, San Ramon, CA 94583.

Through a publication called *Family Guide,* the Scotia-Glenville school system, north of Schenectady, New York, shows parents the value lesson that was taught that day in their child's classroom—and suggests how to follow through at home.[18] For grades four to six, the *Family Guides* have been written by a team of mothers.

For each grade, there are 12 classroom units dealing with values such as getting along with others, good work habits, self-confidence, empathy, and making good decisions. A unit lasts for a week and consists of five lessons, which take about 15 to 20 minutes to teach at the start of the day. (During the rest of the day, teachers reinforce these learnings as opportunities arise.)

For example: The first-grade values curriculum focuses on membership in groups. Teasing is one of the topics discussed. *Family Guide* suggestions for parents include:

- We are all teased sometimes. Record two incidents when your child was teased. Ask your child to tell you how he or she felt at the time.

- Role-play a teasing situation with your child.

- Talk about how another child would feel if your child teased him.[19]

At Back-to-School Night in September, each teacher personally gives parents their copy of the *Family Guide* and explains the objectives of the character curriculum at that grade level. Fully 90 percent of the parents, says Assistant Superintendent Dr. Ruth Kellog, turn out for this meeting. And in November, at parent-teacher conferences, teachers talk individually with parents about the values program and the role the family plays. About 90 percent of parents come out for these conferences.

Out of respect for a child's privacy, Dr. Kellog says, a teacher will never ask, "How many of you did the family activity last night?" But the district gets a rough measure of family follow-through from a questionnaire it sends to parents at the end of each year's program. In a recent year, slightly more than half the parents returned the questionnaire; of those who did, most said they used the *Family Guide* "on a regular basis."

The end-of-the-year questionnaire asks parents to evaluate the effects of the past year's curriculum on their child. It also asks: "What did your child like best about this year's program? What things did your child like least? What suggestions do you have for improving the program?" Asking for and making use of parents' input deepens their feeling of ownership of the program. (For information on the *Family Guides* and a helpful resource on intergenerational programs, *The Connection Dimension,* contact Scotia-Glenville Central Schools, Scotia, NY 12302.)

CONTROLLING TV AS A MORAL TEACHER: WHAT FAMILIES AND SCHOOLS CAN DO

Down through history, three formative institutions—family, school, and church—have been responsible for the moral education of children. This century, however, has seen the dramatic rise of the mass media as shapers of values.

No mass medium is as omnipresent as television. At its best, television is a window on the world, expanding our intellectual, aesthetic, and moral horizons. But at its worst—and the worst is increasingly pervasive—television is part of a rising tide of cultural sleaze. It inundates the young with shoddy values and diverts them from family relationships and healthy pursuits. In many ways, television is the most insidious and ubiquitous moral miseducator in the lives of children.

In the average American family, the TV set is on seven hours and five minutes a day (a figure that's going up, not down). The typical elementary schooler watches 32 hours a week. A recent *Weekly Reader* survey found that elementary school children prefer watching television to any other leisure activity. Reading was their least favorite.

Says a father of three: "I'll come home from work and want to talk to my kids, and they'll be watching TV. I'll turn it off, and a few minutes later it's back on again. I've gotten so I hate the TV." A few years ago, *Bill Moyers' Journal* asked elementary school children, "If you had to give up one of these two things for the rest of your life, which would you give up: watching TV or talking to your father?" About half answered, "Talking to my father."

The following pattern has been identified by Yale's Family Television Research Center: "The child wakes up, immediately turns on the set, goes to school, comes home, and turns on the TV again. Next, he or she is joined by the parents, who eat dinner with the set on. Then all watch television together until relatively late at night. There is little verbal interchange among family members during the evening. The child is finally put to bed, with no quiet time between television viewing and bedtime."[20]

Children, as we've seen, acquire moral values through human interaction. A vital part of that interaction is face-to-face communication with significant adults. Television robs parents and children of the crucial conversation—the table talk, the confidences, the moral corrections, the bedtime reading, even the arguments—through which relationships develop and so much moral learning takes place.

But lost communication is only half the problem of television. The other half is the negative values, role models, and life-styles it routinely presents to young viewers. Here is Sam Proctor, a noted black educator, talking about the effects of TV's glitzy world on kids in the ghetto:

> TV shows them just pretty people. There are no poor people on TV; everybody's rich and good-lookin'. Kids see this, and they want to skip over the details and leap into that kind of a world. That's one reason why all over Harlem, kids are rammin' around in BMW's that they bought with money made from selling crack—not thinking about how they'll be dead at 25 or serving a 15-year jail term.

TV violence takes another toll. By the midteens, the typical American child has witnessed literally hundreds of thousands of violent acts on television.[21] The effect is either to increase children's own violent tendencies or to desensitize them to the violent acts of others.

It is now the official position of the American Psychological Association—supported by scores of studies—that viewing TV violence has a *causal* effect on aggression in both children and teens.[22] Such generalizations take on concrete meaning when we hear reports of children who have tragically imitated televised violence. One recent news story told of a 5-year-old Boston boy who watched *Friday the 13th* and *Nightmare on Elm Street,* talked incessantly about the movie characters and their gory exploits, and then stabbed a 2½-year-old girl 17 times with a kitchen knife.

Much television also serves up a steady diet of casual sex (eight of 10 prime-time references to sex are to sex outside of marriage), law-breaking, drinking (the highest rate of alcohol consumption occurs during prime time), sensationalism, in-your-face verbal aggression, put-downs as humor, and the unremitting message of commercials that things make you happy. Finally, TV entertainment programming presents a worldview that is strikingly bereft of any sense of the ultimate. Nationwide, polls show that more than 90 percent of the adult population professes to believe in God; yet, as Benjamin Stein observes in *The Wall Street Journal,*[23] almost never is a TV character seen to pray, go to church or temple, seek spiritual counsel, or invoke a religious precept when making a moral decision.

What can parents do about television, and how can schools help?

Parents need some basic guidelines:

- **Set a good example.** Research shows that parents who watch little television tend to have children who watch little.
- **Require children to ask permission to watch television.** Children must be taught that watching TV is a privilege, not a right. That's essential for establishing parental control. (If parents aren't around to supervise, they can have recourse to the Plug-Lok, a simple device that locks on to the TV's plug and is available at two for $4.95 from the Kenny Company, 20 Ridgemoor, St. Louis, MO 63105.)
- **Regulate what children watch.** Parents need to take a stand for the values they believe in—like the mother who said, "We don't let you put trash into your stomachs; we certainly don't want you putting trash into your minds."
- **Reduce the amount of time the set is on.** Some families do this gradually, by designating one or two nights a week as "quiet times" when the set stays off all evening. Some schools have sponsored "No TV for a Week" (or two weeks), assigning this as a classroom project; students brainstorm positive alternatives to TV-watching and keep track of how family members spend their time. At the end of the experiment, many families restore television at a level significantly below what it was before the trial shutdown.

In some schools, the principal has sent a letter home asking parents to consider adopting school-recommended TV guidelines—such as *no more than one-half hour a day for children in second grade or below,* and *no more than an hour a day for kids in third grade or above.* The letter makes the point that children are better-rested, have better concentration spans, become better readers, and get along better with classmates when they watch less television. Many parents, finding it hard to clamp down on TV on their own, have expressed gratitude for the extra leverage that the letter from school gives them.

The library can also lead the way. A few years ago, the Farmington, Connecticut, Library Council, with the backing of the Board of Education, persuaded more than 1,000 Farmington residents to turn off the television for the entire month of January. Farmington was delighted with the effects on family life and classroom performance—and got so many inquiries from around the country that it now provides the TV Turn-Off Kit, outlining how any community can undertake a similar project. (The kit is available from the Farmington Library Council, 6 Monteith Drive, Farmington, CT 06032.)

All of these school-supported efforts help parents feel they're not alone if they curb TV.

Schools can also teach children to view TV more critically. A good example of this "media literacy" approach is the curriculum *Children and TV: Teaching Kids to Watch Wisely,* developed by teacher Claudine Goller at the Scarborough Alternative School in Ontario. (For information write Claudine Goller, 5 Pegasus Trail, Scarborough, Ontario, Canada M1G 3N3.)

• **Make television a special event rather than a daily routine.** When I talk to parent groups about television, I recommend a "specials only" policy: You watch TV only if there's a special program worth viewing (e.g., a *National Geographic* nature program, a good documentary, a holiday special, a particular sports event). The advantage of a specials-only policy is that turning on TV becomes a deliberate decision rather than a mindless habit. Kids learn that the television is like most other household appliances: Its normal state is "off."

The problem of television, however, is bigger than getting parents to exercise control. In our country, network television is accountable to no one but its sponsors; cable TV to no one but its paying customers. Neither is accountable to any standards of social responsibility. England offers a contrast: BBC television began with a public mission— to transmit the best of British culture and history.

Widespread moral pressure—from educators, parents, public interest groups, and our national political leaders—is needed to get television to show a greater measure of responsibility for the welfare of the society that supports it. And a prudent measure of government regulation (e.g., restricting sex and violence during prime-time hours) is another way to proceed.

MOVIES

Within the past decade, with few exceptions, movies have regrettably become unwholesome moral influences for children and teens. It's a rare contemporary film that doesn't include graphic violence, premarital or extramarital sex depicted approvingly as normal behavior, foul language, or generally unsavory characters in lead roles. The PG rating must be taken literally: Parental guidance *is* required.

The VCR, a boon to parents who want to pick out decent movies to show at home, has in other ways compounded the problem. The typical neighborhood video store stocks, along with the standard offensive pornography, items such as *Terror on Tape,* an anthology of scenes of sexual violence against women, and *Filmgore,* a compilation of clips from slasher movies (promotional blurb: "See bloodthirsty, butcher killers and sadistic slayers slash, strangle, mangle, and mutilate bare-breasted beauties in bondage").

As Tipper Gore points out in *Raising PG Kids in an X-Rated Society,*[24] these sex-and-violence tapes are bought and rented primarily by kids—especially 11- to 15-year-olds—and are available without restriction. "In some fraternity houses on college campuses," says a *Time* magazine report, "slasher movies play continually in lounges, along with pornographic films."[25] In a society where sexual and other violence toward women is already a serious problem, it is madness to be injecting this kind of poison into the cultural bloodstream.

Permissive or neglectful parents are part of the problem. Says one mother: "My 10-year-old daughter was recently invited to a friend's birthday party where the planned entertainment was a movie about three teenage girls competing to see who could lose her virginity first. I was furious, but I wasn't sure what to do."

What to do is suggested by another mother who faced a similar problem. Her fifth-grade daughter was invited to a classmate's sleepover where an R-rated movie was to be shown. This mother called the host mother and said in a friendly way, "I don't permit Lisa to see R-rated films; should I pick her up before the movie, or would you rather I not send her at all?"

The host mother quickly back-pedaled and said, "Oh, no, I'll get another movie." Parents who stand up for their values, besides setting a good example for their children, may positively influence other parents as well.

With movies as with television, the school can help to establish community norms that are in children's best interest. It can encourage parents to monitor the movies their children see, think about their impact, and enforce guidelines consistent with the positive values that both school and home presumably want children to develop. (Recommended resource: *PREVIEW: Movie Morality Guide,* a biweekly newsletter for parents that reviews and rates newly released films and also provides specific information, for each film, on language, violence, sexual content, nudity, etc. It is available for $25 a year from PREVIEW, 1309 Seminole Drive, Richardson, TX 75080. Also available from the same source: *Recommended Movies on Video,* a booklet on more than 500 hundred videocassette movies judged to be wholesome in content for young viewers.)

SCHOOLS AND PARENTS AS PARTNERS IN DISCIPLINE

Chapter 7 looked at ways in which teachers can recruit parents' help in dealing with a child's discipline problem. School administrators can do the same.

One imaginative example of this kind of home-school partnership can be found at Wilson Junior High School in Hamilton, Ohio, an industrial city with a diverse population. "I got the idea accidentally," says principal John Lazares. He explains:

> A kid came into my office whom I had seen a number of times for discipline problems—talking in class, being late, not bringing materials, driving the teachers crazy. I just got fed up and said, "The next time I see you, we're going to have your mother come in and see what we have to put up with all day." "The reaction I got from him was, "Do *anything* you want, but don't have my mother come in." Something lit up in my head.[26]

After that, principal Lazares began what he calls his parent involvement program: If a student's behavior has earned him or her a suspension, he calls the parents and says, "If you'll come in and spend one day in class with your child, I'll take the suspension away." Dozens of parents have put in their day at Wilson, and their children's behavior improves dramatically.

"It's also preventive discipline," says Lazares; "students who have seen other kids' parents in school stop causing problems because they don't want their own parents to sit with them all day." What's more, many of the parents now call once a week to check on their child's progress. And if a student who had been a discipline problem goes for a stretch of time without causing trouble, Lazares says, "I'll call the parent and say, 'You're doing something right.' "[27]

Since putting his parent involvement program into effect, Lazares says, after-school detentions have dropped from 20 a day to zero on some days, and expulsions are also way down.

Cooperating on discipline can be something as simple as a parent conference. Says a New Hampshire elementary school principal:

> A parent conference can have such a positive effect on a child. The people most important to him have *talked* about the difficulty. They care enough. We always see an upswing in a child's behavior both before and after a parent conference.

PARENTS HELPING CHILDREN TO LEARN

A child's first job in school is to learn, and the most basic backup schools need from parents is support for that learning. As we saw in Chapter 12, learning to work and developing the self-discipline to do your best are part and parcel of character education.

Parental involvement in their children's learning is one of the leading edges of current school reform. At Horace Mann Elementary School in St. Paul, Minnesota, for example, every Friday teachers write home to parents about each child's progress—and expect a signed letter in return on Monday.

Some schools send parents a letter outlining how they can help their child develop good homework habits (e.g., "Establish a homework study area and a daily homework time").[28] There's mounting evidence that when parents and teachers work closely together in this way, students do better and like school more.[29]

A growing number of schools also now hold workshops to show parents how to supplement their children's education. Dr. Malcolm Astley of Heath Elementary School (kindergarten through eighth grade) in Brookline, Massachusetts, has pioneered one such home-school partnership, the Great Expectations program. "We wanted to help those students who seemed to be working below their potential," Astley explains. A letter went out to parents:

> Your son [daughter] has been identified by staff members as having more ability than he [she] seems to be putting to effective use in school. We would like to work with you and your child on this matter by inviting you to join your child in a new program at our school.
>
> If you decide to take part, instead of having study halls, your child will meet for two periods a week in a class designed to help students better fulfill their potentials. The class will include training in basic organizational skills, academic skills, and "tricks" for survival and success in the school environment.
>
> Because success for such students is much more likely if parents and staff work together, we will meet with parents for six breakfast classes to review skills to use in helping your child meet higher expectations. These skills include motivating students, monitoring schoolwork, and supervising homework effectively. . . .

The first round of Great Expectations was a solid success. On a questionnaire evaluation, participating students gave it moderately to strongly positive ratings, and their parents gave it even higher marks.[30]

HELPING PARENTS NETWORK

Sandra Adams is the "developmental counselor" at Summit School (kindergarten through ninth grade) outside Winston-Salem, North Carolina. She leads "rap" groups for sixth- to ninth-graders (about 12 students to a group). They meet several times a week, for about 45 minutes a session, to talk about drugs, drinking, sex, peer pressure, and other issues facing young people of this age.

But as one mother explained, "The concern for children at Summit extends beyond the school." A few years ago, she said, a lot of fifth-graders started to "go with" each other. Counselor Adams invited all concerned parents to a meeting at one parent's home.

Parents agreed that they would host no boy-girl parties until the seventh grade. They also exchanged phone numbers and agreed to call each other if they needed to check on what was happening with their kids on a given night—or for any other reason.

"The basic message," says one mother, "was 'Please call.' " She herself has had several calls. One was to inform her that her son planned to sneak out and join a group of other 14-year-olds who were planning to go driving around in the night in a couple of their parents' cars (unbeknownst to their parents).

When the school helps parents network in this way, it helps to rebuild the kind of cohesive communities that used to be the norm—where parents felt they had permission to let other parents know if their children were up to no good.

THE SCHOOL AS SUPPORT GROUP

Support groups for children experiencing family upheaval are becoming increasingly common in schools. Since 1981, for example, the Ballston Spa Central School District in upstate New York has operated Banana Splits, a program for elementary school-age children whose families are in transition because of separation, divorce, death of a parent, or remarriage. Elizabeth McGonagle, the program's founder and director, explains:

> When kids join [parental permission is required], the first thing they do is to hang a banana on our banana tree. It's reassuring for them to see all the bananas already on the tree; they're not alone. They begin to see themselves as survivors, not losers.

When Banana Splits children meet, they talk about and help each other cope with many kinds of problems: visitations (or lack of them), custody battles, parental anger, child anger, adjustment to parental dating, and the acquisition of a new stepparent. "Through drawings, special projects, discussion, humor, and books," McGonagle says, "the children are helped to face their hurts and change what they can."[31] The Banana Splits program includes a support group for parents, "which the parents basically run themselves."

The hardest part in setting up the program, McGonagle says, is "getting administrators to take on 'one more thing.' "[32] But once they're on board, she says, the rest is not difficult. (The Banana Splits manual for both the children's and the parents' groups is published by Interact, Box 997, Lakeside, CA 92040; tel. 619-448-1474. Elizabeth McGonagle may be reached at Ballston Spa Central School District, Wood Road School, 100 Wood Road, Ballston Spa, NY 12020; tel. 518-885-5361. For information on another fine program for helping children deal with parental separation or loss, write to Rainbows for All God's Children, Inc., 111 Tower Road, Schaumburg, IL 60173.)

INVOLVING THE WHOLE COMMUNITY

Since the whole community has a stake in the character development of the young, it's important for a school undertaking values education to involve more than just parents.

Broad community involvement is helpful in several ways: It helps to identify and gain support for the values that should be taught; it taps valuable ethical expertise in the community; and it informs the public and generates positive publicity for the school's efforts in this area. School systems that have tried to put a values program in place without informing and involving the community have often faced a backlash of misunderstanding, mistrust, and opposition.

The accompanying box tells a success story about community involvement in values education. As you read this account, adapted from a report by then Baltimore County Associate Superintendent Mary Ellen Saterlie,[33] keep in mind that many school systems have proceeded more modestly, but look for ways in which you might incorporate pieces of Baltimore's successful model.

There are all sorts of ways to reach out to the community for input and support. The important thing is that schools make a visible, good-faith effort to do so.

In the fall of 1982, Superintendent Robert Dubel named the Task Force for Values Education to represent Baltimore County's 148 schools. The task force included principals and central office staff, community leaders, two PTA Council Executive Board members, three representatives appointed by the Teachers' Association, and the president of the Baltimore County Student Council Association. This diverse membership was politically important as well as educationally productive.

The task force then invited respected leaders from the Baltimore area to present their perspectives on values education. Guests included a law school dean, who discussed ethics in the legal profession and how schools might try to develop ethical behavior; the president of a large chain of department stores, who discussed shoplifting, internal theft, the work ethic, and the effect of all three on the economy; and a television news analyst, formerly a county executive, who discussed ethics in politics and the media and urged educators and parents to recognize and influence the role of TV in shaping the values of the young. One of the most stimulating sessions brought together the executive director of the American Civil Liberties Union and a fundamentalist minister—for a dialogue to clarify liberal and conservative thought in the community regarding values education.

An unexpected spin-off: All the community leaders who testified before the task force became so interested in its mission that they continued to work with the project and support the implementation of values education in the schools.

Task force members debated the proposals of the guest speakers, and read and discussed articles about existing approaches to values education. They analyzed current school policies and practices to identify ways in which values were already being promoted and taught in Baltimore schools. The *Student Behavior Handbook,* the policy manual of the School Board, and the prekindergarten through grade 12 curriculum were all found to be value-laden, even though the word "values" was rarely used.

A survey was conducted of teachers and parents, and it revealed strong support for values education in both of those groups.

After much discussion, the task force agreed that the U.S. Constitution should provide the major source of a "common core of values" (e.g., honesty, human worth and dignity, justice, due process, equality of opportunity) to be taught in the schools. This decision won widespread support—from the PTA, the School Board, the ACLU, the teachers' union, the churches, and other community groups—because it drew on a broad base of civic values without infringing on or promoting religious beliefs.

The task force then gave this charge to each of Baltimore County's 148 schools: Set up your own values education committee and find creative ways to teach the core values through all phases of school life. A booklet provided by the task force offered general guidelines.[35]

School-based committees were chaired by the principal (to give them the desired visibility and importance) and included staff, parents, community members, and students. Individual schools have since designed projects around themes ranging from computer ethics to coaches as role models to the search-for-truth incentive in science.

How did the schools inform all parents and try to win their support for the new values program?

First, the central PTA Council developed an informative brochure, *Values Education in the Baltimore County Public Schools: Questions Parents Ask,* which was sent to every home.[35] This stressed the importance of a partnership between home and school to teach positive values.

Second, the PTA Council has also sponsored a Values Fair each year in which schools display the values projects and materials they have developed. The fair has paid double dividends: Parents are able to see how their children are being taught values, and schools are able to learn from each other. The first Values Fair was a great success, drawing more than 1,000 people in the southeastern portion of the county.

SCHOOLS AND COMMUNITIES WORKING TOGETHER TO FIGHT DRUGS AND ALCOHOL

There is at least some research to indicate that school-home-community cooperation pays off, even when the problem is as tough as drug and alcohol abuse.

The June 9, 1989, issue of *The Journal of the American Medical Association* reported this heartening finding: A comprehensive school-community program that encouraged preteens and teens to avoid cigarettes, alcohol, and marijuana was far more successful than a program that relied only on the schools.[36]

This ambitious study involved 22,500 sixth- and seventh-graders in forty-two schools in Kansas City, Missouri, and Kansas City, Kansas. The schools were randomly divided into two groups: (1) an experimental group, which used the new, school-community approach and (2) a control group, which continued with the usual, school-based health education programs.

In the experimental, school-community approach:

- Students were taught, in school health and science classes, about the negative effects of drugs and how to resist using them.

- Students did homework assignments (which were subsequently discussed in class) that involved role-playing with family members and interviewing them about family attitudes and rules regarding drug use.

- Community newspapers ran a series of articles on resisting drug use, and TV and radio stations sponsored news clips and talk shows in which school staff discussed the new program.

One year after the study began, students (now seventh- and eighth-graders) were asked whether they had used tobacco, alcohol, or marijuana during the past month. The main finding: The usual rate of increase in use of these substances for this age group was significantly slowed for students in the experimental program. Among those students:

- 17 percent said they had smoked cigarettes, compared to 24 percent of the students in the conventional program.

- 11 percent said they had drunk alcohol, compared to 16 percent in the conventional program.

- 7 percent said they had used marijuana, compared to 10 percent in the conventional program.[37]

Dr. Charles Schuster, director of the National Institute on Drug Abuse, called the study "one of the most important primary prevention studies that we've seen."[38]

VALUE CONFLICT

Even in the most cooperative of school-home-community partnerships, some value conflicts will arise.

Carol Nylen now teaches at Helene Dyer Elementary School in South Portland, Maine. She remembers how, at another school, one of her first-grade children enthusiastically shared during show-and-tell that he had a new bike. When teacher Nylen said, "That's exciting, Bill—how'd you get it?," he matter-of-factly explained that he and his dad went for a ride, saw the bike on a sidewalk, and tossed it in their trunk.

A third-grade teacher in central New York tells of teaching a unit on racism and having a girl come in the next day with tears in her eyes. The night before, she had corrected her father at the table for saying "damn niggers" and was sent to bed without dinner.

The teacher's challenge in cases like these is to lead the child gently to adopt or maintain the correct moral judgment—stealing is wrong, racism is wrong—while avoiding public comment on the parents'

HOW SCHOOLS, PARENTS, AND COMMUNITIES CAN WORK TOGETHER

Providing community support for family life:

1. A national campaign highlighting all the ways in which parents are important to their children.

2. Government policies, such as parental job leaves, that support parent-infant bonding and family life.

3. State initiatives, such as Wisconsin's The Year of the Family in Education and Missouri's Parents as Teachers, that help parents be their child's most important teacher.

4. Following the "schools for the twenty-first century" model to provide before- and after-school child care and other support for parents.

School-parent partnerships in values education:

5. A parent values survey that asks parents to identify the qualities of character they want their children to develop.

6. Leadership roles for parents in planning the school's values program, designing parent participation programs, and encouraging parents to teach good values at home.

7. School-based workshops on parenting skills.

8. A required course for high school students in child development and parenting.

9. Home-based values discussion materials, given to parents, that build on classroom lessons.

10. Controlling the negative influence of TV and movies.

11. Parental involvement in supporting the school's discipline.

12. Workshops (like the Great Expectations program) that teach parents how to help their children do better academically in school.

13. Helping parents network to discuss common concerns.

14. School-based support groups like Banana Splits, for children and parents of families in transition.

Other cooperative strategies:

15. Involving the whole community in identifying consensual values to be taught in the schools.

16. Communicating with parents through a brochure on the school's values program.

17. Creating a cooperative school atmosphere within which schools and parents can constructively address value conflicts when they arise.

wrongful behavior. In private the teacher can help the child understand that all of us, parents and teachers included, sometimes say and do things that aren't good, but that doesn't mean we're bad people.

Sometimes it's the parents who have a complaint about the school. Says a mother who called in to a radio talk show on values education:

> The schools in our district are not teaching the values parents want taught. During homeroom period students sit around discussing questions like "When is lying okay?" and "Pick a law you would break." Kids are being taught that there are no absolutes, there is no right or wrong.

These kinds of value conflicts are minimized, however, when schools and parents have worked together to articulate the values they want children to learn; that, plus creating the kind of climate that fosters respect, trust, and open communication.

Says Peggy Tharpe, principal of Sullivan Elementary School outside St. Louis: "Little things—like how you answer the phone—do a lot to set the tone. We say, 'Thank you for calling the elementary school—how can we help you?' " When there's that kind of welcoming school atmosphere, tensions around values and other issues have a better chance of being resolved or at least being addressed in a civil, constructive manner.

As we approach the end of this century, the mood in at least some places is one of hope. Says Ron Woods, a teacher at Birch Meadow Elementary School in Reading, Massachusetts, who has taught for more than 30 years:

> When I started teaching, it seemed to me we had the support of maybe 80 percent of the parents. Then each year it kept declining until it was about half and half, and then it seemed as if it was maybe 80–20 *against* teachers. But in the last few years I've seen a change, until now I think we're getting the support of most parents again.
>
> Sometimes you feel like a very small influence as a teacher, shoveling against the tide. But then you find out there are more people like you than you realize, people who share your values. They're out there.

Enormous problems persist—a culture in which selfishness masquerades as "life-style," countless families are in crisis, and millions of children suffer from neglect of their most basic needs. But in many communities parenting is becoming a higher priority, and schools and families are coming together in ways that strengthen both.

It remains for other communities to forge the same alliance, so that all children might have what ought to be their birthright: the opportunity to grow into healthy, capable, and upright human beings.

Getting Started and Maintaining Momentum

1. **Develop a leadership group.** Form a values education council or task force that will help select target values, develop program guidelines, and take responsibility for long-range planning and program implementation. This group should be broadly representative, including the principal; teachers; a counselor or psychologist; parents; a secretary, custodian, or other member of the school's support staff; and others who can help develop, implement, and gain widespread support for the values program.

2. **Do a needs analysis survey.** Send a questionnaire to all school staff, parents, community leaders (e.g., political and business leaders, clergy, heads of youth services), and students. Suggested questions:

   - On a scale of 1 to 5 (where 1 is "not important" and 5 is "very important"), how important do you think it is for the school to try to teach moral values and develop good character? Why do you think so?

   - Choose the *five* values from the following list (e.g., respect, responsibility, honesty, compassion, justice, integrity, courage, courtesy, hard work, self-worth) that you think our school should most emphasize in a values education program.

- What do you think is the most appropriate name for a school-based effort to foster good values and character?

_____ Values education
_____ Character development
_____ Ethics education
_____ Teaching the fourth and fifth Rs
_____ Other _____

3. **Assess how your school already tries to teach values.** Ask school administrators, teachers, support staff, and parents, "What do you think our school is already doing to teach moral values and foster good character? How might we improve on our efforts in this area?" (As one way of assessing the comprehensiveness of the school's efforts, respondents could use the 12 components of values education described in this book.)

4. **Develop a plan.** Using the results of the needs analysis survey and the school assessment, develop a plan that includes short-range goals (e.g., for the first year) and long-range goals (e.g., for the next three years). For example:

FIRST YEAR PLAN

Goal 1: _____

Steps to be taken: *Who will do it:*   *When:*

Goal 2: _____ (etc.)

5. **Get feedback on the plan.** Present the plan to the staff, parents, and others for feedback; where desirable, incorporate suggestions for improvement; disseminate the revised plan.

6. **Set up a parent committee.** Ask parents serving on the values education steering committee also to establish their own parent committee and recruit members for that. This parent group then takes responsibility for keeping all parents informed about the school's values program (e.g., through a newsletter); organizing parent participation programs; and encouraging parents to foster at home the values the school is trying to teach.

7. **Create special-focus subcommittees.** Form one or more subcommittees focusing on a high-priority schoolwide issue or problem where there is the chance of making visible progress in the near future. Possibilities:

   • Developing a schoolwide discipline policy
   • Improving the cafeteria
   • Improving playground behavior
   • Fostering good sportsmanship at athletic events
   • Student-run assemblies
   • An anti-vandalism campaign
   • Community service.

8. **Create a values education resource center.** Make a place in the school where books, curricula, materials, magazines, and other resources on values education can be kept for staff and parent use.

9. **Provide staff development.** Sponsor a series of workshops, each focusing on a particular values education strategy. Encourage *all* school staff (including secretaries, cafeteria workers, custodians, playground aides, and bus drivers) to attend at least the introductory session on the school's overall approach and reasons for undertaking values education. Allow teachers the freedom to choose those strategies they feel most comfortable implementing.

10. **Set up a "buddy" system.** Have teachers pair up so everyone has a "buddy" with whom to compare notes on activities tried after the workshops (What worked? What didn't?) Encourage voluntary peer visitations. Make time for crossgrade sharing as well.

11. **Develop or expand democratic student government.** Set up a governance structure that gives students meaningful responsibilities for decision-making that affects the life of the school (see Chapter 17). Establish a system of school jobs so that each class has a special task.

12. **Work toward a values-centered curriculum.** Arrange for teachers to meet in grade-level groups to:

    • Identify developmentally appropriate values to emphasize at each grade level
    • Define educational objectives for each value
    • Develop corresponding classroom activities.

Here are two examples of what this planning method produces when applied to different grade levels:

SECOND GRADE

VALUE: Rule of law
CURRICULAR AREA: Social Studies
OBJECTIVE: To develop the understanding of the importance of rules
ACTIVITY: Play a game such as kickball without any rules. After a few minutes of play, stop and evaluate how the game was played and the need for rules. After playing the game *with* rules, discuss the need for rules and laws in different areas of life.

FIFTH GRADE

VALUE: Truth
CURRICULAR AREA: Language Arts
OBJECTIVE: To develop an understanding of choices and consequences
ACTIVITY: Predict a course of action for a character in a story who accidentally breaks a window. Suggest possible outcomes for each choice.[1]

Write up activities tried and found successful; put them in a Values Curriculum/Activities File Box in the values education resource center.

13. **Get publicity.** Early on, arrange for positive media coverage (including photographs) of the school's values education efforts. Provide press releases for media outlets at regular intervals.

14. **Evaluate the program.** How will the school evaluate progress toward the goals it has established? (See Chapter 2 for some evaluation methods.) What indicators will be used to gauge improvement in students' moral attitudes and behavior? To gauge the extent to which teachers are implementing the various aspects of the values education program?

---

[1] These examples are taken from the booklet *1984 and Beyond: A Reaffirmation of Values* (Baltimore County Public Schools, Towson, Md. 21204: 1984). Available on request.

Notes

Chapter 1

1. Edward B. Fiske, "U.S. Schools Put New Stress on Teaching of Moral Values," *The New York Times* (September 15, 1986), p. B-8.
2. *Age-Specific Arrest Rates and Race-Specific Arrest Rates for Selected Offenses, 1965–1988* (Washington, D.C.: FBI, 1990).
3. Ibid.
4. Pat Smith and Marianne Goldstein, "Teens Seized in Human Torch Horror," *New York Post* (August 28, 1987), p. 4.
5. "5 Youths Held in Sex Assault on Mentally Impaired Girl, 17," *The New York Times* (May 25, 1989), p. 1.
6. Lance Morrow, "Children," *Time* (August 8, 1988), p. 3.
7. "So Long Wonder Years," *Newsweek* (June 26, 1989), p. 8.
8. Anastasia Toufexis, "Our Violent Kids," *Time* (June 12, 1989), p. 55.
9. Estimate based on the studies of television researcher Warren Farrell, cited in Robert Hutchinson, "Cleaning Up Trash TV," *Catholic Twin Circle* (July 9, 1989) p. 1.
10. Reported by Jacqueline Jackson Kikuchi, staff member of the Rhode Island Rape Crisis Center, at the 1988 National Symposium on Child Victimization in Anaheim, California.
11. Cited in Rushworth M. Kidder, "Public Concern for Ethics Rises," *The Christian Science Monitor* (January 2, 1990), p. 13.
12. Ellen Graham, " 'Values' Lessons Return to the Classroom," *The Wall Street Journal* (September 26, 1988), p. 25.
13. Thanks for this point to my friend and colleague Professor Henry Johnson of Pennsylvania State University.
14. H. Hartshorne and M. A. May, *Studies in the Nature of Character* (New York: Macmillan, 1928).
15. See, for example, Roger Burton's chapter "Honesty and Dishonesty" in T.

Lickona (ed.), *Moral Development and Behavior* (New York: Holt, Rinehart, & Winston, 1976).

16. I am indebted for this point to philosopher David Nyberg's thoughtful speech "Teaching Values in School: The Mirror and the Lamp," presented at the Values Education Conference, State University of New York at Buffalo, October 1988.

17. I am indebted for this discussion of personalism to Father George F. McLean, secretary of the Council for Research in Values and Philosophy, Catholic University, Washington, D.C.

18. Daniel Yankelovich, *New Rules: Searching for Self-Fulfillment in a World Turned Upside Down* (New York: Random House, 1981).

19. L. Raths, M. Harmin, and S. Simon, *Values and Teaching* (Columbus, OH: Charles E. Merrill Publishing Co., 1966).

20. S. Simon, L. Howe, and H. Kirschenbaum, *Values Clarification* (New York: Hart, 1972).

21. Thanks for this point to Rick Ellrod's fine essay "Contemporary Philosophies of Moral Education" in G. McLean, R. Ellrod, D. Schindler, and J. Mann (eds.), *Act and Agent: Philosophical Foundations for Moral Education and Character Development* (University Press of America, Washington, D.C.: 1986).

22. "Ethics in the Boesky Era," *Yale Alumni Magazine* (Winter 1987), p. 37.

23. George Hassett, "But That Would Be Wrong . . ." *Psychology Today* (November 1981), pp. 34–50.

24. Ibid.

25. Based on 1987 data from the National Center for Health Statistics.

26. FBI statistics, 1990.

27. Ibid.

28. Ibid.

29. Ibid.

30. Lou Jacquet, "Juvenile Sex Offenders: Distressingly Commonplace," *Our Sunday Visitor* (June 25, 1989).

31 Toufexis, op. cit., p. 52.

32. News item, *National Catholic Register* (September 10, 1989), p. 2. Father Brenner's *Kingdom of Darkness* is published by Acadiana Publishing Co., P.O. Box 52247, Lafayette, LA 70505.

33. *The Ethics of American Youth: A Warning and a Call to Action* (Marina del Rey, CA: Josephson Institute of Ethics, 1990).

34. Ibid.

35. Ibid.

36. "Bigotry in the Ivory Tower," *Time* (January 23, 1989), p. 54.

37. *The Ethics of American Youth,* op. cit.

38. *The American Freshman: National Norms for Fall 1990* (Los Angeles: Higher Education Research Institute, UCLA, 1990).

39. *The Ethics of American Youth,* op. cit.

40. National Research Council, *Risking the Future: Adolescent Sexuality, Pregnancy, and Childbearing* (Washington, D.C.: National Academy Press, 1987).

41. Victoria Churchville, "Youth Crime a Quandary for Police," *The Washington Post* (May 28, 1988), p. B-1.

42. "Sex, Cruelty, and Children," *The New York Times* (June 13, 1989), p. A-26.

43. Quoted in Haven Bradford Gow, "Moral Education Needed to Prevent Crime," *New York City Tribune* (August 18, 1989).

44. *The Ethics of American Youth,* op. cit.

45. *The American Freshman,* op. cit.

46. Ibid.

47. Associated Press, "Rich-Poor Gap Is Widening," *Cortland Standard* (November 5, 1988), p. 1.

48. *The Ethics of American Youth,* op. cit

49. *The American Freshman,* op. cit.

50. Peter James Spielman, "U.N. Report: U.S. Teens Have Most Abortions," *Cortland Standard* (December 14, 1988), p. 24.

51. Estimate by Dr. Vicki Alexander, medical director of the Albany, New York, Community Family Planning Council, quoted in Elizabeth Edwardsen, "One in 7 Adolescents Has Sex-Related Disease," *Cortland Standard* (January 25, 1989), p. 7.

52. *The American Freshman,* op. cit.

53. *Schools Without Drugs* (Washington, D.C.: U.S. Department of Education, 1987), p. 5.

54. Richard Halloran, "Student Use of Cocaine Is Up," *The New York Times* (August 8, 1986), p. A-12.

55. Source: *Newsweek* (April 10, 1989), p. 21.

56. Hal Block, "Ben's Dirty Testing Not That Shocking," *Cortland Standard* (September 27, 1988), p. 11.

57. Reed Bell, M.D., "Alcohol: A Gateway Drug," *The Challenge* (newsletter of the U.S. Department of Education, 1987).

58. Source: National Institute on Alcohol Abuse and Alcoholism.

59. Source: National Center for Health Statistics.

60. Based on a 1988 survey carried out by the U.S. Department of Health and Human Services of 11,000 eighth- and tenth-grade students in 20 states.

61. Patrick Donohue, "The Case for Values Education," *Hamilton This Month* (December 1984), p. 22.

62. Morrow, op. cit., p. 4.

63. Gerald Grant makes this point about pluralism in his article "Schools That Make an Imprint: Creating a Strong Positive Ethos" in J. H. Bunzel (ed.), *Challenge to American Schools: The Case for Standards and Values* (New York: Oxford University Press, 1985).

64. I am grateful to Rexford Brown, a member of the Education Commission for the States, who made this observation at the 1989 Navajo Education Summit for the Year 2000.

65. Marilyn Braveman, *Teaching Democratic Values in the Public Schools* (New York: The American Jewish Committee, Institute of Human Relations, 1988), p. 3.

66. A 1976 Gallup poll (reported in *The New York Times,* April 18, 1976) found that 79 percent of all respondents and 84 percent of parents with school-age children endorsed "instruction in the schools that would deal with morals and

moral behavior." Four years later Gallup found the same percentage of parents in support of moral education in the schools. In 1984 Gallup asked the public to rate the relative importance of various goals for the public schools. Of 25 possible goals, "To develop standards of what is right and wrong" came in second, only barely behind the school's classic academic mission—"To develop the ability to speak and write correctly"—and ahead of goals such as "To prepare students for a high-paying job"; cited in Bill Honig's *Last Chance for Our Children* (Reading, MA: Addison-Wesley, 1985), p. 95.
67. Kidder, op. cit.

Chapter 2

1. Perry London, "Character Education and Clinical Intervention: A Paradigm Shift for U.S. Schools," *Phi Delta Kappan* (May 1987), pp. 668, 672.
2. For another overview of values education programs currently under way in schools, see the January 1991 *Ethics* magazine, special issue on "Teaching Ethics in Our Schools." *Ethics* is a publication of the Josephson Institute of Ethics, 310 Washington Blvd., Suite 104, Marina del Rey, CA 90292 (tel. 213-306-1868).
3. For further information, write Citizenship Education Clearinghouse, 5234 Wells Avenue, St. Louis, MO 63113, or call 314-367-6613.
4. See, for example, Edward Wynne's *For Character: Chicago Area Award-Winning Schools, 1984–85* (Chicago, IL: University of Illinois at Chicago, 1985). (For information about obtaining a copy of this booklet, write Dr. Edward Wynne, College of Education, University of Illinois at Chicago, M/C 147, Box 4348, Chicago, IL 60680.)
5. For a detailed account of the Birch Meadow story, see the article by former principal Dennis Murphy, "The Just Community at Birch Meadow Elementary School," *Phi Delta Kappan* (February 1988).
6. Law in a Free Society is part of the California Bar's Center for Civic Education in Calabasas, California.
7. Joan Libman, "Building Better Kids," *Los Angeles Times* (November 8, 1988), p. V-1.
8. Another excellent resource in law-related values education is Arlene Gallagher's *Living Together Under the Law*, available at no cost from the Bureau of Social Studies Education, New York State Education Department, Albany, NY 12234.
9. For further information on PREPARE or PREPARING ADOLESCENTS FOR TOMORROW, contact Steve Barrs, Values Education Consultant, Board of Education for the City of Hamilton, P.O. Box 558, 100 Main Street West, Hamilton, Ont. L8N 3L1, Canada (tel. 416-527-5092).
10. The Child Development Project disseminates a helpful resource book *Creating a Caring School Community* (available free from the Child Development Project, 111 Deerwood Place, Suite 165, San Ramon, CA 94583; tel. 415-838-7633).
11. Margot Stern Strom, "Facing History and Ourselves: Holocaust and Human

Behavior" in Ralph Mosher (ed.), *Moral Education: A First Generation of Research and Development* (New York: Praeger Publishers, 1980).

12. For information about Facing History and Ourselves write to Facing History and Ourselves National Foundation, 25 Kennard Road, Brookline, MA 02146.

13. Quoted in Peter Simon, "Values Education Makes the Grade in Schools: Sweet Home Enjoys Success in Teaching Students Respect, Honesty," *The Buffalo News* (January 14, 1990), p. B-6.

14. For an overview of Sweet Home's program and its handbook of values education activities, write Sharon Banas, Values Education Coordinator, Sweet Home Middle School, 4150 Maple Road, Amherst, NY 14226 (tel. 716-837-3500).

15. Ellen Graham, " 'Values' Lessons Return to the Classroom," *The Wall Street Journal* (September 26, 1989), p. 2-1.

16. For information on the many excellent resources—including a bimonthly newsletter—available from the Values Education Centre, write Judy Clarke, coordinator, Values Education Centre, St. Andrews Jr. P.S., 60 Brimorton Drive, Scarborough, Ont. M1P 3Z1, Canada.

17. For information about Winkelman's program, write Winkelman Elementary School, 1919 Landwehr Road, Glenview, IL 60025.

18. For a recent overview of values education research, see James Leming's monograph "Curricular Effectiveness in Character Education: What Works, What Doesn't, What Might, and What We Still Need to Know," a paper presented at the September 1987 working conference "Moral Education and Character" sponsored by the U.S. Department of Education. For a copy of the paper write to Dr. James Leming, Department of Curriculum and Instruction, Southern Illinois University, Carbondale, IL 62901.

   For a copy of Ivor Pritchard's *Moral Education and Character,* summarizing the discussions of this two-day conference, write U.S. Department of Education, Office of Educational Research and Improvement, Washington, D.C. 20208-5646.

   A still useful compendium of research on earlier moral education programs, especially interventions in the 1970s that were derived from Lawrence Kohlberg's theory of moral development and/or John Dewey's theory of democratic education, is Ralph Mosher's edited collection *Moral Education: A First Generation of Research and Development* (New York: Praeger Publishers, 1980).

19. Strom, op. cit., pp. 23–24.

20. Marilyn Watson et al., "The Child Development Project" in Larry Nucci (ed.), *Moral Development and Character Education* (Berkeley, CA: McCutchan Publishing Corporation, 1989).

21. For a recent review of research on family influences on moral development, see William Damon's chapter "Parental Authority and the Rules of the Family" in his book *The Moral Child* (New York: The Free Press, 1988).

22. Rainer Dobert and Gertrud Nunner-Winkler, "Moral Development and Personal Reliability" in Marvin Berkowitz and Fritz Oser (eds.), *Moral Education: Theory and Application* (Hillsdale, NJ: Lawrence Erlbaum Associates, 1985).

23. Several studies by Diana Baumrind point to the effectiveness of "authorita-

tive" parenting; see, for example, Diana Baumrind, "Early Socialization and Adolescent Competence" in S. E. Dragastin and G. H. Elder (eds.), *Adolescence in the Life Cycle* (New York: Wiley, 1975).

24. Carol Holstein, "The Relationship of Children's Moral Judgment Level to That of Their Parents and to Communication Patterns in the Family" in R. C. Smart and M. S. Smart (eds.), *Readings in Child Development and Relationships* (New York: Macmillan, 1972).

25. Mary D. Ainsworth et al., *Patterns of Attachment* (Hillsdale, NJ: Lawrence Erlbaum Associates, 1978).

26. James Q. Wilson and Richard J. Herrnstein, *Crime and Human Nature* (New York: Touchstone Books, 1986).

27. Perry London, "Character Education and Clinical Intervention: A Paradigm Shift for U.S. Schools," *Phi Delta Kappan* (May 1987), pp. 667–73.

28. These data are based on preliminary reports from the National Survey of Families and Households, funded by the National Institutes of Health and carried out by University of Wisconsin at Madison researchers Larry Bumpass, James Sweet, and Elizabeth Thomson.

29. Thanks for this point to my friend and colleague Kevin Ryan, director of the Center for the Advancement of Ethics and Character, School of Education, Boston University, Boston MA.

30. Judith S. Wallerstein, *Second Chances: Men, Women, and Children a Decade After Divorce* (New York: Ticknor and Fields, 1989), p. xv.

31. "National Survey Asks: Whither the American Family?," *On Wisconsin* (December 1988).

32. London, op. cit.

33. James Coleman, "Reflections on Developing Character," unpublished remarks at "Symposium on Developing Character," annual convention of the American Educational Research Association, Chicago, April 1985.

34. N. Harter and R. Lodish, "Parent Peer Groups at Sidwell Friends," *Independent School* (May 1985), pp. 21–22.

35. Coleman, op. cit.

Chapter 3

1. George Basler, " 'Little Monsters': Schools Urged to Teach Kids Mercy, Morality," *Press and Sun-Bulletin* (July 16, 1989), p. 1.

2. Research and Forecasts, Inc., *The Connecticut Mutual Life Report on American Values in the 80s: The Impact of Belief* (Hartford, CT: Connecticut Mutual Life Insurance Co., 1981).

3. Thanks for this point to the helpful booklet *Moral Education in the Life of the School*, a report from the ASCD Panel on Moral Education, April 1988 (for a copy, send $6 to: Association for Supervision and Curriculum Development, 1250 N. Pitt Street, Alexandria, VA 22314–1403).

4. Barbara Jones, "Transmitting Values in the Family," *The Fessenden School Parents and Alumni News* (Fall 1986), pp. 22–28.

5. John Adams to Benjamin Rush (October 25, 1789). I am indebted for this and the Washington quote to Walter Nicgorski's excellent article "The Moral Cri-

sis: Lessons from the Founding," *The World and I* (September 1987), pp. 75–85.

6. Gilbert Sewall, "Religion in Textbooks: A Sensitive Subject Slighted," *Social Studies Review* (Winter 1990). This whole issue is devoted to examining the treatment and neglect of religion in American social studies and history textbooks.

7. Paul Vitz, *Censorship: Evidence of Bias in Our Children's Textbooks* (Ann Arbor, MI: Servant Books, 1986), pp. 3–4.

8. For examples, see the above-cited issue of *Social Studies Review.*

9. *Moral Education in the Life of the School,* op. cit.

10. Larry Nucci, "Children's Conceptions of Morality, Societal Convention, and Religious Prescription" in C. Harding (ed.), *Moral Dilemmas: Philosophical and Psychological Issues in the Development of Moral Reasoning* (Chicago: Precedent Press, 1985).

11. Larry Nucci, "Teaching Children Right from Wrong," in *Teacher Education Quarterly* (Autumn 1984), pp. 50–63.

12. I am indebted for this point to New York University philosopher Gabriel Moran.

13. Jon Moline, "Classical Ideas About Moral Education" in Edward Wynne (ed.), *Character Policy: An Emerging Issue* (Lanham, MD: University Press of America, 1982).

14. Christopher Derrick, "We Hold These Duties . . . ," *National Catholic Register* (June 22, 1986), p. 4.

15. I was reminded of the central contribution of tolerance to civil society by the thoughtful commencement address of Dr. James Clark, president of Cortland College, New York, on the occasion of the college's May 1987 graduation.

16. From a meditation by John Donne, poet and preacher, in *Devotions upon Emergent Occasions,* 1624.

17. Burle Summers, "Ontario Moral Values in Education Position Paper," *Ethics in Education* (January 1990).

Chapter 4

1. Walter Nicgorski, "The Moral Crisis: Lessons from the Founding," *The World and I* (September 1987) p. 7.

2. James Q. Wilson noted this deepening concern for character in his article "The Rediscovery of Character: Private Virtue and Public Policy," *The Public Interest* (Fall 1985), pp. 3–16.

3. James Stenson, "Is Life Too Easy For Them?," *National Catholic Register* (August 27, 1989), p. 1.

4. For a thorough and illuminating exposition of Aristotle's views on character, see Jody Palmour's *On Moral Character: A Practical Guide to Aristotle's Virtues and Vices* (Washington, D.C.: The Archon Institute for Leadership Development, 1986).

5. Michael Novak, "Crime and Character," *This World* (Spring/Summer 1986) p. 1.

6. My thanks to Jim Sorenson for this story.

7. My thinking about this model of character was much influenced by the colle-

gial interaction of an interuniversity moral education project in which I was fortunate to participate. Sponsored by the Council for Research on Values and Philosophy (George F. McClean, secretary, Washington, D.C. 20064), this project brought together teams of philosophers, psychologists, and educators over a period of four years to address questions of the nature of morality, moral development, and moral education. Readers interested in the work of this project may wish to consult the three books it produced: George F. McClean et al. (eds.), *Act and Agent: Philosophical Foundations of Moral Education and Character Development* (Lanham, MD: University Press of America, 1986); Richard T. Knowles and George F. McClean (eds.), *Psychological Foundations of Moral Education and Character Development* (University Press of America, 1986); and Kevin Ryan and George McClean (eds.), *Character Development in Schools and Beyond* (New York: Praeger, 1987).

8. Readers wishing to familiarize themselves with recent research in the field of moral development can consult the following sources: Lawrence Kohlberg, *Essays on Moral Development, Vol. 2: The Psychology of Moral Development* (San Francisco: Harper & Row, 1984); Carol Gilligan, *In a Different Voice* (Cambridge, MA: Harvard University Press, 1982); William Damon, *The Moral Child* (New York: The Free Press, 1989); William Kurtines and Jacob Gewirtz, *Morality, Moral Behavior, and Moral Development* (New York: Wiley, 1984) and *Moral Behavior and Development* (Hillsdale, NJ: Erlbaum Associates, 1990); Nancy Eisenberg, *The Roots of Prosocial Behavior in Children* (New York: Cambridge University Press, 1989); James Rest, *Development in Judging Moral Issues* (Minneapolis: University of Minnesota Press, 1979); and Mary Brabeck, *Who Cares? Theory, Research, and Educational Implications of the Ethic of Care* (New York: Praeger, 1989).

9. For a description of the stages of moral reasoning from early childhood through young adulthood, see my book *Raising Good Children* (New York: Bantam Books, 1983).

10. G. Spivak and N. Shure, *Social Adjustment of Young Children: A Cognitive Approach to Solving Real-Life Problems* (San Francisco: Jossey-Bass, 1974).

11. D. Goldman, "Exclusive Interview with John Dean," *Comment,* Boston University School of Law (February 1979), p. 7.

12. My colleagues in this endeavor were C. R. Narayan, Len Cohen, and Bill Hopkins. Professor Narayan provided the impetus for the study, designed the sampling procedure, and completed the data analysis.

13. For a copy of the full questionnaire, write to me at: Education Department, Cortland College, Cortland, NY 13045.

14. See, for example, research reported by Stanley Coopersmith, *The Antecedents of Self-Esteem* (San Francisco: W. H. Freeman, 1967).

15. For psychological theory and research supporting the relationship between self-esteem and prosocial behavior, see Ervin Staub, *Positive Social Behavior and Morality* (New York: Academic Press, 1979).

16. Marion Radke-Yarrow and Carolyn Zahn-Waxler, "Roots, Motives, and Patterns in Children's Prosocial Behavior" in Ervin Staub et al. (eds.), *Development and Maintenance of Prosocial Behavior* (New York: Plenum, 1984).

17. William Kirk Kilpatrick, "Moral Education" in his book *Psychological Seduction: The Failure of Modern Psychology* (Nashville: Thomas Nelson Publishers, 1983).
18. Nicgorski, op. cit., p. 77.
19. C. S. Lewis, *Mere Christianity* (New York: Macmillan, 1952).
20. M. Scott Peck, *People of the Lie* (New York: Simon & Schuster, 1983).
21. Staub, op. cit.
22. Daniel Goleman, "Great Altruists: Science Ponders the Soul of Goodness," *The New York Times* (March 5, 1985), p. C-1.
23. William Bennett, "The Teacher, the Curriculum, and Values Education Development" in Mary Louise McBee, *New Directions for Higher Education: Rethinking College Responsibilities for Values* (San Francisco: Jossey-Bass, 1980), p. 30.
24. George Bear, "Children and Moral Responsibility," *Children's Needs: Psychological Perspectives* (Washington, D.C.: National Association of School Psychologists, 1987).
25. Thomas C. Hayes, "Ethics in Business: Answers by a Values Consultant to Top Companies," *The New York Times* (October 12, 1986), 1987 National Employment Report, sec. 12.

Chapter 5

1. Haim G. Ginott, *Teacher and Child* (New York: Avon, 1976), p. 13.
2. William Bennett and Edwin J. DeLattre, "A Moral Education," *American Educator* (Winter 1976), p. 6.
3. The title of this five-part series is *Effective Management for Positive Achievement in the Classroom,* produced by Universal Dimensions, Inc. (4621 North 16th Street, Suite 608, Phoenix, AZ 85016).
4. Session II, "Creating a Positive Classroom Atmosphere," *Effective Management for Positive Achievement in the Classroom*. Phoenix, AZ: Universal Dimensions, Inc.
5. Ibid.
6. Session V, "Discipline Approaches in the Classroom," *Effective Management for Positive Achievement in the Classroom*. Phoenix, AZ: Universal Dimensions, Inc.
7. This research is cited in the excellent chapter by Marilyn Watson et al., "The Child Development Project," in Larry P. Nucci (ed.), *Moral Development and Character Education* (Berkeley, CA: McCutchan, 1989).
8. For an example of research supporting the role of direct cognitive instruction in forming the conscience of children as young as two, see Carolyn Zahn-Waxler et al., "Childrearing and Children's Prosocial Orientations Toward Victims of Distress," *Child Development* 50 (1979), pp. 319–30. For evidence of the effectiveness of moral advocacy with teenagers, see Dobert and Nunner-Winkler (complete citation in note in Chapter 2).
9. Zahn-Waxler et al., op. cit.
10. Thanks for these points about stories to the Portland, Maine, moral education

project—in particular, to material shared with me by Carol Nylen of the South Portland schools.

11. Adapted from the original 1985 story in *Reader's Digest.*
12. Quoted in Louise Bernikow, "Alone—Yearning for Companionship in America," *The New York Times Magazine* (August 15, 1982).
13. One example of this "sleeper effect" comes from a Canadian study reported in the book *Moral Learning* by Ed Sullivan (New York: Paulist Press, 1975). A moral discussion program was implemented in an upper elementary classroom, and gains in students' moral reasoning were assessed at the end of the year. At this point, when the program ended, the experimental group showed no superiority over the control group. A follow-up evaluation a year later, however, showed the experimental group more advanced in moral reasoning than the control group.
14. Thanks for this felicitous phrase to Alan Tom, author of *Teaching as Moral Craft* (New York: Longman, 1984).

Chapter 6

1. Quoted in R. Archambault (ed.), *John Dewey on Education* (New York: Random House, 1964), p. 431.
2. Robert Fulghum, *All I Really Need to Know I Learned in Kindergarten* (New York: Villard Books, 1989), p. 20.
3. Ron Harris, "Children Who Dress for Excess," *Los Angeles Times* (November 12, 1989), p. A-1.
4. John Dewey, "The Need for a Philosophy of Education," *The New Era in Home and School,* 15 (1934), pp. 211–41.
5. Kristen Field and Virginia Holmes describe the partners activity and other classroom strategies in their chapter "Teaching Co-operation: A Beginning Step Toward a Democratic Classroom" in a book on school and classroom democracy. (T. Lickona, M. Paradise, and R. Mosher, eds.; in prep.)
6. Good feelings/bad feelings is adapted from an activity in Sidney Simon et al., *Values Clarification Through Writing* (New York: Hart Publishing Co., 1973).
7. See, for example, *Values and Teaching,* L. Raths, M. Harmin, and S. Simon (Columbus, OH: Charles E. Merrill, 1978).
8. "Positive word power" is a variation of an activity called "strength bombardment," which has been popular in group-building for some time.
9. The phrase "hugs for health" comes from the work of psychotherapist Virginia Satir.
10. Herve Varenne, "Symbolizing American Culture in Schools" in E. Wynne (ed.), *Character Policy* (Lanham, MD: University Press of America, 1982).
11. "Student of the Week" as described here is a composite of ideas from three elementary school teachers: Lori Gallerani, DeRuyter Elementary School; Linda Nickels, Belle Sherman Elementary School; and Eleanor DeVall, Port Byron Elementary School.
12. Michael Walzer, *Spheres of Justice* (New York: Basic Books, 1983).
13. Robert N. Bellah et al., *Habits of the Heart: Individualism and Commitment in American Life* (San Francisco: Harper & Row, 1985).

Chapter 7

1. Emile Durkheim, *Moral Education* (New York: The Free Press, 1973), p. 148.
2. Lee Canter and Marlene Canter, *Assertive Discipline* (Los Angeles: Lee Canter & Associates, 1976).
3. Marilyn Watson, "Classroom Control: At What Price?," *Teacher Education Quarterly* (Autumn 1984).
4. Jean Piaget, *The Moral Judgment of the Child* (New York: The Free Press, 1965), p. 362.
5. Forrest Gathercoal, *Judicious Discipline* (Davis, CA: Caddo Gap Press, 1989).
6. Barbara McEwan, *Practicing Judicious Discipline: An Educator's Guide to a Democratic Classroom.* (Davis, CA: Caddo Gap Press, 1991).
7. Larry Nucci, "Synthesis of Research on Moral Development," *Educational Leadership* (February 1987), pp. 86–92.
8. Canter and Canter, op. cit.
9. I am indebted for this idea to Donna Funk, a special education teacher who has guest-lectured in our classroom discipline course.
10. See, for example, T. N. Fairchild, "The Daily Report Card," *Teaching Exceptional Children*, 1987, vol. 19, pp. 72–73.

Chapter 8

1. Jean Piaget, *The Moral Judgment of the Child* (New York: The Free Press, 1965), p. 366. Originally published 1932.
2. The name of the school has been changed.
3. The name of the teacher has been changed.
4. John Dewey, *Problems of Men* (New York: Greenwood Press, 1968), pp. 59–60.
5. Ibid., p. 58.
6. National Assessment of Educational Progress, 1990, cited in "Missing the Basics," *Cortland Standard* (April 9, 1990).
7. Thanks for these questions to Gaynell Knowlton, a teacher at Birch Meadow Elementary School, Reading, Massachusetts.
8. Thanks to Virginia Satir for this idea.
9. Thanks to Carol Lynch for the "sticky situations" name.
10. Thanks for these questions to Carol Wertheim, a teacher at Birch Meadow Elementary School.
11. Richard Lauricella and his colleague Paula Verel are the authors of an award-winning program The Parent Connection, on home-school communication. For information, write Richard Lauricella, Lakeland Elementary School, Bury Drive, Solvay, NY 13209.
12. Adapted from a feedback form in Sidney Simon et al., *Values Clarification Through Writing* (New York: Hart Publishing Company, 1973).
13. Thanks to the Tacoma, Washington, moral education project for the class meeting evaluation form.
14. Janet Clauson, "Class Meetings," unpublished paper, State University of New York at Cortland (1981).

Chapter 9

1. The Institute for Democracy in Education now counts more than 300 teacher members in southeastern Ohio and publishes *Democracy and Education: The Magazine for Classroom Teachers.* Subscriptions are $12 a year for four issues; make check payable to Ohio University and send to Institute for Democracy in Education, College of Education, 119 McCracken Hall, Ohio University, Athens OH 45701-2979.
2. Nancy Roe, "It Works: Democracy in the Classroom—Theory into Practice," *Ohio University Today* (Fall 1988), p. 6.
3. Ibid.
4. This quote is a composite of children's statements taken from Nancy Roe's article in *Ohio University Today* and Bill Elasky's own report.
5. Edward B. Fiske, "U.S. Schools Put New Stress on Teaching of Moral Values," *The New York Times* (September 15, 1986), p. B-1.
6. Lorraine Keeney, "Teaching Values and Self-Esteem Through the Environment," *Connect: The Newsletter of Practical Science and Math for K-8 Teachers* (Spring 1990) (Teachers' Laboratory, Inc., P.O. Box 6480, Brattleboro, VT, 1990).
7. Ibid.
8. Ibid.
9. Dorothy J. Gaiter, "School Children Learn to Treat Animals Kindly," *The New York Times* (January 9, 1984), p. B-6.
10. For information, call the SPCA's headquarters at 92nd Street and York Avenue, New York (tel. 212-876-7700).
11. Ibid.
12. Ibid.
13. David Hill, "Crusaders in the Classroom," *Teacher Magazine* (November 1989), p. 58.
14. Ibid.
15. Ibid., p. 58.
16. Taken from "The Year of Self-Discipline" in *Ethical Models in the Classroom* (Portland, ME: Portland Public Schools, 1983), p. 8.
17. Carol Nylen, "Integrating Ethics in History," *Ethics in Education* (March, 1984).
18. Alan L. Lockwood and David E. Harris, *Reasoning with Democratic Values; vol. 2, 1877 to the Present.* (New York: Teachers College Press, 1985), p. vii.
19. Abridged from Lockwood and Harris, op. cit., pp. 74–76.
20. Nat Hentoff, "Daring to Teach Values in the Public Schools," *The Washington Post* (April 17, 1989). Thanks to my colleague Barbara McEwan for calling this article to my attention.
21. This account has been adapted from an article by Muriel and Thomas Ladenburg, "Moral Reasoning and Social Studies," *Theory into Practice* (special issue on moral education, April 1977), pp. 112–17.
22. The Ethical Culture Schools are: Midtown School, Fieldston, and Fieldston Lower School. Fieldston Lower School is on Fieldston Rd., Riverdale, NY 10471 (tel. 212-543-5000).

23. "The Elementary School Curriculum as Moral Educator," special issue of *Moral Education Forum* (Summer 1983). To subscribe ($25 per year) write *Moral Education Forum,* Prof. Lisa Kuhmerker, Editor, 1580 Massachussets Avenue, 8A, Cambridge, MA 02138.

24. Susan Resneck Parr, *The Moral of the Story: Literature, Values, and American Education* (New York: Teachers College Press, 1982).

25. A. C. Garrod and G. A. Bramble, "Moral Development and Literature," *Theory into Practice* (special issue on moral development) (April 1977), pp. 105–111.

26. For further information on the Child Development Project's "read aloud guides," contact Marilyn Watson, Developmental Studies Center, 111 Deerwood Place, Suite 165, San Ramon, CA 94583 (tel. 415-838-7633).

    Other valuable guides to children's literature are Sharon Dreyer's *The Bookfinder: A Guide to Children's Literature About the Needs and Problems of Youth Aged 2–15* (Circle Pines, MN: American Guidance Service, 1977) and Arlene Gallagher's *Living Together Under the Law: An Elementary Education Law Guide,* a book of classroom activities that correlates children's books with ten themes about rules, laws, and values (available free from the Bureau of Social Studies Education, New York State Education Department, Albany, NY 12234).

    Finally, Frances Kazemek of Eastern Washington University has written a beautiful essay, "Reading and Moral Development: From a Feminine Perspective," singling out children's and young adults' books that exemplify the "morality of connectedness" that Fieldston takes as its theme. Her article is published in ERIC (ED 268 510, October 1985).

27. Elizabeth Saenger, *Ethical Values: Lessons for Lower-School Students Grades Two Through Six (A Teacher's Guide)* (New York: The Council for Religion in Independent Schools, 1985). Distributed (cost: $8) by The Council for Religion in Independent Schools, P.O. Box 40613, Washington, D.C. 20016.

28. Beverly Cleary, *Ramona the Pest* (New York: William Morrow, 1968). This is one of the series of *Ramona* books that make wholesome reading for young children.

29. Ann Petry, *Legends of the Saints* (out of print).

30. Gloria Frey, "The Middle Ages: The Social Studies Core of the Fifth Grade," *Moral Education Forum* (Summer 1983).

31. Ibid., p. 33.

32. Barbara Leonie Picard, *One Is One* (New York: Holt, Rinehart, and Winston, 1965).

33. Ibid., p. 169.

34. Peter Sommer, "Children as Historians," *Moral Education Forum* (Summer 1983), pp. 34–43.

35. Philip Shabecoff, "Loss of Tropical Forests Is Found Much Worse Than Was Thought," *The New York Times* (June 8, 1990), p. 1.

36. William A. Henry III, "Beyond the Melting Pot," *Time* (April 9, 1990), pp. 28–31.

37. Patricia B. Flach, Eleanore, N. Gettleman, Barbara A. Lanke, and Patricia K.

Wood, *Heartwood* (available from the authors at 155 Cherrington Drive, Pittsburgh, PA 15237; contact Patricia Flach at 412-486-2160).

38. For information about Understanding Handicaps, where you can get training in the program, and how you can purchase the full curriculum book (only $35 as of 1986), write Understanding Handicaps, Inc., c/o Newton Public Schools, 100 Walnut Street, Newtonville, MA 02160.

39. For further information about the "Grade 8 Ethics Course," contact Joan Engel, program manager, Curriculum Branch, Alberta Education, Devonian Building, West Tower, 11160 Jasper Avenue, Edmonton, Alta. T5K 0L2, Canada (tel. 403-422-9720).

40. For information on materials available from the Thomas Jefferson Research Center, contact the center at 1143 North Lake Avenue, Pasadena, CA 91104 (tel. 818-798-0791).

    For information on the Living the Constitution unit, contact Clare Robert, East Coast coordinator, P.O. Box 1202, Old Tavern Road, Orange, CT 06477 (tel. 203-387-2700).

41. Write Sheldon Berman, president, Educators for Social Responsibility, 23 Garden Street, Cambridge, MA 02138 (tel. 617-492-1764).

42. *Philosophy for Children, 1985–1986* (program information booklet) (Institute for the Advancement of Philosophy for Children, 1985).

43. To inquire about Philosophy for Children materials or staff development services, contact the Institute for the Advancement of Philosophy for Children, Montclair State College, Upper Montclair, NJ 07043 (tel. 201-893-4277).

Chapter 10

1. Robert Marquand, "Powerful Idea: Learn from Each Other," *The Christian Science Monitor* (January 30, 1987), p. B-2.

2. William J. Warren, "Education's Fast-Rising New Wave," *Daytona Beach Sunday News Journal* (March 5, 1989), p. B-1.

3. To subscribe to, or order back issues of, *Cooperative Learning,* write the editors: Drs. Nancy and Ted Graves, IASCE, Box 1582, Santa Cruz, CA 95061-1582 (tel. 408-426-7926).

4. For comprehensive reviews of cooperative learning research, see David and Roger Johnson's *Cooperation and Competition* (Edina, MN: Interaction Book Co., 1989) and Robert Slavin's *Cooperative Learning: Theory, Research, and Practice* (Englewood Cliffs, NJ: Prentice Hall, 1990).

    For a step-by-step guide to implementing cooperative learning, see Dee Dishon and Pat O'Leary's *A Guidebook for Cooperative Learning* (Learning Publications, P.O. Box 1326, Holmes Beach, FL 33509).

    For staff development ideas, see *What Is Cooperative Learning? Tips for Teachers and Trainers* by Nancy and Ted Graves (available directly from the authors: write 136 Liberty Street, Santa Cruz, CA 95060).

5. Marilyn Watson et al., "The Child Development Project: Combining Traditional and Developmental Approaches to Values Education" in Larry P. Nucci

(ed.), *Moral Development and Character Education* (Berkeley, CA: Mc-Cutchan, 1989).

6. D. W. Johnson, R. Johnson, and G. Maruyama, "Interdependence and Inter-personal Attraction Among Heterogeneous and Homogeneous Individuals," *Review of Educational Research* 53, pp. 5–54.

7. James Leming, "Research on Social Studies Curriculum and Instruction: Inter-ventions and Outcomes in the Socio-Moral Domain," *Review of Research in Social Studies Education, 1976–1983*, NCSS Bulletin 75.

8. R. E. Slavin, *Cooperative Learning: Theory, Research, and Practice* (Engle-wood Cliffs, NJ: Prentice Hall, 1990).

9. Ibid.

10. R. T. Johnson and D. W. Johnson, loc. cit.

11. Ibid., p. 23.

12. Slavin, op. cit.

13. Jeanie Oakes, *Keeping Track: How Schools Structure Inequality* (New Haven: Yale University Press, 1985).

14. For a fuller exploration of the negative effects of competition and the positive effects of cooperation, see two recent books by popular speaker and author Alfie Kohn: *No Contest: The Case Against Competition* (Boston: Houghton Mifflin, 1986) and *The Brighter Side of Human Nature: Altruism and Empa-thy in Everyday Life* (New York: Basic Books, 1990).

15. Marilyn Burns' cluster-group system was first described in her article "Groups of Four: Solving the Management Problem," *Learning* magazine (September 1981), pp. 46–51. I am indebted to a helpful summary of this article that appeared in "Easing Painlessly into Cooperative Learning" by Nancy and Ted Graves (unpublished).

   For an extended interview with Marilyn Burns and her latest available co-operative learning materials (e.g., *The Good Time Math Event Book*), see the October 1989 issue of *Cooperative Learning*.

16. Adapted from Robert Slavin, "Learning Together," *American Educator* (Sum-mer 1968), pp. 10–11.

17. This report was adapted from Craig Pearson, "Cooperative Learning: An Al-ternative to Cheating and Failure," *Learning* (March 1979), pp. 34–37.

18. Ibid.

19. Elliott Aronson, *The Jigsaw Classroom* (Beverly Hills, CA: Sage, 1978).

20. Warren, op. cit.

21. There is a useful book by this title: Robert Slavin et al. (eds.), *Learning to Cooperate, Cooperating to Learn* (New York: Plenum Press, 1985).

22. Personal conversation, 1990.

23. Catherine C. Lewis, "Cooperation and Control in Japanese Nursery Schools," *Comparative Education Review*, vol. 28, pp. 69–84.

24. Judy Clarke, "Cooperative Learning: A Powerful Way to Teach Values," *Co-operative Learning* (March 1990), p. 26.

25. Ibid.

26. Pearson, op. cit., p. 36.

27. For further information about Phyllis Smith-Hansen's Adolescent Issues course,

write to her at Lansing Middle School, Lansing, NY 14882. For information about Quest, which offers an elaborate teachers' guide along with training programs in how to use it, write Quest International, 537 Jones Road, P.O. Box 566, Granville, OH 43023-0566 (tel. 614-522-6400).

Chapter 11

1. "Conscience of craft" is the name given by Syracuse University educator Thomas Green to one of four voices of conscience. Green elaborates on this idea in his provocative article "The Formation of Conscience in an Age of Technology," *American Journal of Education* (November 1985), pp. 1–38.
2. William Glasser, "The Quality School," *Phi Delta Kappan* (February 1990), p. 426.
3. *Investing in Our Children: Business and the Public Schools* (New York: Committee for Economic Development, 1985).
4. Taken from Albert Shanker, "Kids Who Work Are Taunted by Peers," *The New York Times* (March 6, 1983).
5. Judith Guttman, letter to the editor, *The Washington Post* (September 19, 1987), p. A-22.
6. Ronald L. Zigler, letter to the editor, *The Washington Post* (September 19, 1987), p. A-22.
7. *America's Challenge: Accelerating Academic Achievement* (Princeton, NJ: National Assessment of Educational Progress, 1990).
8. Irene Stanlis, "Back to Basics: A Necessary Refrain," *The Christian Science Monitor* (July 11, 1989), p. 18.
9. *The Nation's Report Card on Science* (Princeton, NJ: National Assessment of Educational Progress, 1987).
10. Charles Green, "East Is . . . ?" *The Times Union* (February 8, 1990), p. A-1.
11. Bruno Bettelheim, "Education and the Reality Principle," *American Educator* (Winter 1976), p. 12.
12. Green, op. cit., p. 5.
13. Adapted from *What Works: Research about Teaching and Learning* (U.S. Department of Education, Consumer Information Center X, P.O. Box 100, Pueblo, CO, 1986) and Richard Hersh, "The Politics of School Change," theme address, Annual Conference of the Association for Moral Education, Harvard University (November 1987).
14. Personal communication.
15. *What Works*, op. cit.
16. Thanks to Sara Early, a graduate student, for this story.
17. Daniel Goleman, "I.Q. Tests Ignore 'People Skills,' Experts Claim," *Syracuse Herald-American* (December 7, 1986), p. AA-11.
18. Howard Gardner, *Frames of Mind: The Theory of Multiple Intelligences* (New York: Basic Books, 1983).
19. *What Works*, p. 41.
20. Ibid.
21. Ibid.

22. Ibid.
23. I am indebted for this idea to David Darrow of Cortland Junior-Senior High School, Cortland, New York.
24. Thanks to Sue Cunliffe for this idea.
25. Thanks to Julie Rick for this story.
26. John I. Goodlad, *A Place Called School* (New York: McGraw-Hill, 1983); also see John Goodlad, "A Study of Schooling: Some Findings and Hypotheses," *Phi Delta Kappan* (March 1983), pp. 465–70.
27. Mary Ann Lindley, " 'Overwork' Ethic Is Getting Tired," *Syracuse Herald-American* (June 26, 1988), p. AA-2.

Chapter 12

1. S. Pfeiffer, "Is Eichmann in All of Us?," letter to *The New York Times* (June 30, 1974), p. 10.
2. Ibid.
3. Jonathan Friendly, "Ethics Classes Avoid Teaching Right and Wrong," *The New York Times* (December 2, 1985), p. B-2.
4. Condensed from "The Honest Boy and the Thief" in Harvey Minnich (ed.), *Old Favorites from the McGuffey Readers* (New York: American Book Co., 1936).
5. Spencer and Ann Donegan Johnson, *ValueTales* (ages four to nine). A series of twenty-seven colorfully illustrated books, each dealing with a particular value— such as patience, kindness, humor, truth and trust, caring, courage, and respect—exemplified by the life of a famous person. (La Jolla, CA: Value Communications, Inc., 1976–1979). For further information, write ValueTales, P.O. Box 1012, La Jolla CA 92038.
6. Louis Rath, Merrill Harmin, and Sidney Simon, *Values and Teaching* (Columbus, OH: Charles E. Merrill, 1966), p. 48.
7. Martin Eger, "The Conflict in Moral Education: An Informal Case Study," *The Public Interest* (Spring 1982), pp. 62–80.
8. Merrill Harmin, "Value Clarity, High Morality: Let's Go for Both," *Educational Leadership* (May 1988), pp. 24–30.
9. For an introduction to the moral development theory and research of Lawrence Kohlberg, see his chapter "Moral Stages and Moralization: The Cognitive-Developmental Approach" in Thomas Lickona (ed.), *Moral Development and Behavior* (New York: Holt, Rinehart, and Winston, 1976), pp. 31–53.
10. For scholarly research reviews that find positive results of moral dilemma discussions but no clear evidence in support of values clarification, see Alan Lockwood, "The Effect of Value Clarification and Moral Development Curricula on School-Age Subjects: A Critical Review of Recent Research," *Review of Educational Research* 48 (1978), pp. 325–64; and James Leming, "Curriculum Effectiveness in Moral Values Education: A Review of Research," *Journal of Moral Education* 10 (1981), pp. 147–64.
11. See T. Lickona, *Raising Good Children* (New York: Bantam Books, 1983). The supporting research for Kohlberg's stages is also presented in his own books: Lawrence Kohlberg, *Essays on Moral Development, vol. 1: The Phi-*

losophy of Moral Development (1978), and *Essays on Moral Development, vol. 2: The Psychology of Moral Development* (San Francisco: Harper & Row, 1984). The latter volume also presents at length the several criticisms of Kohlberg's theory and research and his responses to them.

12. Based on a story created by Dr. Frank Alessi, a member of the staff of the Carnegie-Mellon/Harvard Values Education Project and quoted in Barry K. Beyer, "Conducting Moral Discussions in the Classroom" in Peter Scharf (ed.), *Readings in Moral Education* (Minneapolis, MN: Winston Press, 1978), pp. 62–63.

13. See, for example, James Rest, "Morality," in J. Flavell and E. Markman (ed.), *Carmichael's Manual of Child Psychology*, 4th ed. (New York: John Wiley & Sons, 1983). Rest reports a review of studies using the Defining Issues Test (Rest's short-answer adaptation of Kohlberg's moral reasoning interview): "Over 90% show no sex difference. The evidence at hand hardly supports the view that the stage model [of Kohlberg] is biased against women. Where sex differences occur, they are likely due to differences in educational opportunity, suggesting a bias in the social system, not in the stage scheme."

14. Carol Gilligan first raised the issue of sex differences in moral reasoning in her book *In a Different Voice* (Cambridge, MA.: Harvard University Press, 1982). For a summary of Gilligan's criticisms of Kohlberg, and Kohlberg's response, see L. Kohlberg, *Essays on Moral Development, vol. 2: The Psychology of Moral Development* (San Francisco: Harper & Row, 1984).

15. Ann Colby, Lawrence Kohlberg, John Gibbs, and Marcus Lieberman, "A Longitudinal Study of Moral Judgment," *A Monograph for the Society of Research in Child Development* 48, no. 4. (Chicago: The University of Chicago Press, 1983).

16. Moshe Blatt, "The Effects of Classroom Discussion on the Development of Moral Judgment," Ph.D. dissertation, University of Chicago, 1969.

17. Barry Beyer, "Conducting Moral Discussions in the Classroom" in Scharf, op. cit., pp. 63–64.

18. A. Colby, L. Kohlberg, E. Speicher-Dubin, and M. Lieberman, "Secondary School Moral Discussion Programs Led by Social Studies Teachers," *Journal of Moral Education* 6 (2), pp. 90–117.

19. Adapted from "Mark's Dilemma" in Dennis Adams, "Building Moral Dilemma Activities," *Learning* (March 1977), p. 46.

Chapter 13

1. Not the teacher's real name.

2. *Personal and Societal Values: A Resource Guide for Primary and Junior Grades* (Province of Ontario: Ministry of Education, 1983), p. 15.

3. Adapted from an activity sheet on alcohol use developed by the American National Red Cross, 1980.

4. These questions are adapted from those in the *Making Decisions* unit of Hamilton, Ontario's, PREPARE curriculum.

5. Thanks for making me aware of computer software in moral education to my

colleague Joe Braun, editor of the helpful book *Reforming Teacher Education* (New York: Garland Publishing, 1989).

6. All of these activities have been taken from the "Grade 8 Ethics Course," Joan Engel, program manager, Curriculum Branch, Alberta Education, Devonian Building, West Tower, 11160 Jasper Avenue, Edmonton Alta. T5K 0L2, Canada.

7. *To Tell the Truth* is available from Churchill Films, 662 North Robertson Boulevard, Los Angeles, CA 90069-5089.

8. An extensive annotated bibliography of films, videocassettes, and filmstrips dealing with a wide range of social-moral issues is available as part of the middleschool and junior high school curriculum *Skills for Adolescence.* Write Lions-Quest Program, Quest International, 537 Jones Road, P.O. Box 566, Granville, OH 43023-0566 (tel. 1-800-446-2700).

9. A film focusing on another aspect of honesty is *That's Stealing.* Heather, a sixth-grader, has developed a bad habit of taking things that do not belong to her. Write: FilmFair Communications, 10900 Ventura Boulevard, P.O. Box 1728, Studio City, CA 91604.

   A filmstrip on promise-keeping is part of a moral dilemma series for the elementary grades, *First Things: Values* (New York: Guidance Associates, 1972).

10. Patricia Grimes, "Teaching Moral Reasoning to 11-Year-Olds and Their Mothers" (unpublished doctoral dissertation, Boston University School of Education, 1974).

11. Carolyn Pereira, "Educating for Citizenship in the Elementary Grades," *Phi Delta Kappan* (February 1988), pp. 429–31. The curriculum *Educating for Citizenship* is available from Aspen Systems Corporation, 1600 Research Boulevard, Rockville, MD 20850.

12. Jon Moline, "Classical Ideas About Moral Education" in E. Wynne (ed.), *Character Policy* (Washington, DC: University Press of America, 1982), p. 197.

Chapter 14

1. Jerold M. Starr, "Classrooms Need Controversy," *Teacher Magazine* (March 1990), p. 64.

2. A. K. Benjamin, "Values in Primary Science Education" in M. J. Frazer and A. Kornhauser (eds.), *Ethics and Social Responsibility in Science Education* (Elmsford, NY: Pergamon Press, 1986).

3. This story is told by Bill Honig in his fine book *Last Chance for Our Children: How You Can Help Save Our Schools* (Reading, MA: Addison-Wessley, 1985).

4. Copies of *The Lessons of the Vietnam War: A Modular Textbook* ($38.45 including shipping) are available from: Center for Social Studies Education, 115 Mayfair Drive, Pittsburgh, PA 15228.

5. Karen Franklin, "Making Peace with Vietnam," *Teacher Magazine* (March 1990), p. 31.

6. Ibid.

7. Starr, op. cit., p. 66.

8. Franklin, op. cit.

9. This advice is offered by Ronald Galbraith and Thomas Jones in their helpful book *Moral Reasoning: A Teaching Handbook for Adapting Kohlberg to the Classroom* (Minneapolis, MN: Greenhaven Press, 1976). Thanks to Catherine Gefell for her summary of the different positions on the teacher's disclosure of her personal views.

10. Quoted in Lorraine Keeney, "Teaching Values and Self-Esteen Through the Environment," *Connect: The Newsletter of Practical Science and Math for K– 8 Teachers* (Spring 1990).

11. These procedures are described in Elizabeth Saenger's monograph *Ethical Values: Lessons for Lower-School Students Grades Two through Six* (Washington, DC: The Council for Religion in Independent Schools, 1985).

12. Thanks to Catherine T. Gefell for her summary of these positions in her monograph "Socially Responsible Science Education" (unpublished paper, State University of New York at Cortland, 1990).

13. Ibid., p. 29.

14. Ibid., pp. 31–34.

15. This position is set forth, for example, by Justice Harry Blackmun in his dissenting opinion in the U.S. Supreme Court's *Webster* ruling, *The New York Times* (July 4, 1989), p. 13.

16. This position is set forth in the book *Pro-Life Feminism*, edited by Gail Grenier Sweet (Life Cycle Books, 2205 Danforth Ave., Toronto, Ont. M4C 1K4,: 1985).

17. Sonia L. Nazario, "Schoolteachers Say It's Wrongheaded to Try to Teach Students What's Right," *The Wall Street Journal* (April 6, 1990), p. B-1.

18. John T. Noonan, Jr., *A Private Choice: Abortion in America in the Seventies* (New York: The Free Press, 1979).

19. E. J. Dionne, Jr., "Poll on Abortion Finds the Nation Is Sharply Divided," *The New York Times* (April 26, 1989), p. 1.

20. Donald Granberg, a University of Missouri sociologist who has written extensively on opinion polls regarding abortion, cites a study of 12 different national surveys. On nine of the surveys, men and women showed no statistically significant difference on abortion. On the other three, men were slightly more in favor of legal abortion than women were.

21. Ibid.

22. American Civil Liberties Union, 132 West 43rd St., New York, NY 10036 (tel. 212-944-9800).

23. JustLife Education Fund, 10 Lancaster Avenue, Philadelphia, PA 19151 (tel. 215-645-9388).

24. David W. Johnson and Roger T. Johnson, "Critical Thinking Through Structured Controversy," *Educational Leadership* (May 1988).

25. Ibid., p. 63.

26. Ibid., pp. 63–64.

27. William Celis 3rd, "What Should Be Taught About War in the Gulf?," *The New York Times* (January 23, 1991), p. B-6.

28. Ibid.

29. Ibid.

Chapter 15

1. Ellen McGinnis and Arnold Goldstein, *Skillstreaming the Elementary School Child* (Champaign, IL: Research Press Co., 1984).
2. See T. Lickona, "Moral Development and Moral Education" in J. M. Gallagher and J. A. Easley (ed.), *Knowledge and Development: Piaget and Education.* (New York: Plenum Press, 1979).
3. Adapted from an article by Barbara Woods, "Elementary Students Solving Problems the Peaceful Way," *Cortland Standard* (October 6, 1989), p. 10.
4. Robert D. Enright, "An Integration of Social Cognitive Development and Cognitive Processing: Educational Applications," *American Educational Research Journal* (Spring 1980), *17,* pp. 21–41. For reprints of Enright's study, write to: Professor Robert Enright, Educational Psychology, University of Wisconsin, Madison, WI 53706.
5. For a review of the research on the effects of classroom problem-solving on children's social and moral development, see T. Lickona and M. Paradise, "Democracy in the Elementary School" in R. Mosher (ed.), *Moral Education* (New York: Praeger Publishers, 1980).
6. This account has been adapted from a report by Kathleen Teltsch in *The New York Times* (October 13, 1986), p. A12.
7. For information on the minicourse on what causes violent conflict and how to avoid it, write Education Development Center, 55 Chapel Street, Newton, MA 02160.

Chapter 16

1. Cited in Christina Hoff Sommers, "Ethics without Virtue," *The American Scholar* (Summer 1984), pp. 381–89.
2. "Giraffe Project Sends Apathy-Busting Message to U.S. Campuses," *The Giraffe Gazette* (Spring 1987), p. 1.
3. Quoted in *The Giraffe Gazette* (Fall 1987), p. 3.
4. Quoted in *The Giraffe Gazette* (Winter 1987–88), p. 3.
5. UNICEF Report, *The State of the World's Children, 1989.*
6. Oxfam America (115 Broadway, Boston, MA 02116) publishes a variety of materials documenting levels of poverty, hunger, and sickness in poor countries of the world.
7. Source: World Health Organization, Agency for International Development.
8. UNICEF Report, op. cit.
9. Oxfam America, op. cit.
10. Based on 1987 data; cited in Interim Report of the National Commission on Children (April 1990).
11. Accounts of these Fast for a World Harvest activities have been taken from *Campaign Connection* (Spring 1987), an Oxfam America publication.
12. For a copy of Amnesty's report, *Torture in the 80s,* write to Amnesty International/U.S.A., 322 Eighth Avenue, New York, NY 10001.
13. At the early elementary level, useful biographical material is the *ValueTales*

series (La Jolla, CA: Value Communications, Inc., 1977). For further information, write ValueTales, P.O. Box 1012, La Jolla, CA 92038.

14. Charles Kuralt, *On the Road with Charles Kuralt* (New York: Ballantine Books, 1985).

15. The *Mother Teresa* video is available in many video rental stores and for purchase from Servant Book Express, P.O. Box 7455, Ann Arbor, MI 48107; tel. 313–761–8505.

16. For more information about the *Purpose of Living* series, contact Sara Ensor, president, Purpose, Inc., 407 Russell Avenue, Suite 306, Gaithersburg, MD 20877 (tel. 301-963-4166).

17. William Robbins," 11-Year-Old Ministers to Needs of Homeless," *The New York Times* (March 12, 1984).

18. Persons wishing to help can contact Trevor's Campaign, 120 West Lancaster Avenue, Ardmore, PA 19003 (tel. 215-642-6452).

19. *The Giraffe Gazette* (Summer/Fall 1988), pp. 14–15. (This and other back issues of *The Giraffe Gazette* are available from the Giraffe Project.)

20. Carol Stocker, "From Kid to Kid, Positive Power," *The Boston Globe* (June 5, 1980), p. 57.

21. Ibid.

22. Ernest Boyer, "Education Today and Tomorrow: What We Need to Do," *PTA Today* (October 1986), pp. 10–12.

23. See, for example, Mary Conway Kohler, "Youth Participation: The Key to Responsibility," *Phi Delta Kappan* (February 1981), and National Commission on Resources for Youth, *New Roles for Youth in the School and Community* (New York: Citation Press, 1974).

24. Cited in *Working Together,* newsletter of the Child Development Project (Spring 1987), p. 4.

25. Kohler, op. cit.

26. John Calhoun and Jean O'Neil, "Communities Benefit by Tapping Teens' Talents," *PTA Today* (December 1989–January 1990), pp. 13–14.

27. "These Kids Perform Community Service," *Instructor* (January 1978).

28. Robert J. Starratt, *Sowing Seeds of Faith and Justice* (Jesuit Secondary Education Association, 1717 Massachusetts Avenue, N.W., Suite 402, Washington, DC 20036).

29. Ibid., p. 23.

30. Fred F. Newman, *Educating for Citizen Action: Challenge to the Secondary Curriculum* (Berkeley, CA: McCutchan, 1975).

31. Michael Miller, personal communication.

32. Fred F. Newman and Robert A. Rutter, "A Profile of High School Community Service Programs," *Educational Leadership* (December 1985/January 1986), pp. 65–71.

Chapter 17

1. Clark Power, Ann Higgins, and Lawrence Kohlberg, *Lawrence Kohlberg's Approach to Moral Education* (New York: Columbia University Press, 1989), p. 172.

2. William L. Rutherford, "School Principals as Effective Leaders," *Phi Delta Kappan* (September 1988), pp. 31–34.

3. Ibid., p. 32.

4. Michael Rutter et al., *Fifteen Thousand Hours: Secondary Schools and Their Effects on Children* (Cambridge, MA.: Harvard University Press, 1979).

5. The "contract approach" is based on the work of William Glasser. See, for example, Glasser's book *Schools Without Failure* (New York: Harper & Row, 1979).

6. Source: "Bullying in the Schools," *Values Education,* newsletter of the Values Education Centre (September/October 1988). (The newsletter is free; to request this or other issues, write Values Education Centre, St. Andrews Junior Public School, 60 Brimorton Drive, Scarborough, Ont. M1P 3Z1, Canada.)

7. JoAnn Shaheen, "Cottage Lane: A Student Government That Works," *Social Education* (May 1980), pp. 387–90.

8. Ibid., p. 387.

9. Power, Higgins, and Kohlberg, op. cit.

10. The Theodore Roosevelt Just Community School is among the character education programs featured in an hour-long television special produced by Arnold Shapiro Productions. To order a videocassette of this uplifting program, which profiles successful values education efforts around the country, call Pyramid Film and Video at 1-800-421-2304.

11. Power, Higgins and Kohlberg, op. cit.

12. David Purpel, paper presented at the annual conference of the Association for Moral Education, Boston University (November 1984). Purpel enlarges on this theme in his fine book *The Moral and Spiritual Crisis in Education: A Curriculum for Justice and Compassion* (Westport, CT: Bergin and Garvey Publishers, 1988).

13. *What Works: Research About Teaching and Learning,* U.S. Department of Education, 1986. (For copies of this report, write Consumer Information Center, Department ED, Pueblo, CO 81009.)

Chapter 18

1. Eunice Kennedy Shriver, "Teenage Pregnancy: Something Can Be Done," *Philadelphia Inquirer* (July 10, 1986), p. 7-E.

2. William J. Bennett, "Why Johnny Can't Abstain," *National Review* (July 3, 1987), p. 37.

3. Source: 1988 data summarized by *Newsweek* (Special Issue, Summer/Fall, 1990).

4. Based on Johns Hopkins University study of 1,717 girls aged 15 to 19 by Drs. Melvin Zelnik and John Kanter.

5. Data on increased sexual activity among girls from 1982 to 1988 are based on a 1990 study by the Alan Guttmacher Institute.

6. Ibid.

7. Cited in *The Ethics of American Youth: A Warning and a Call to Action* (Marina del Rey, CA: Josephson Institute of Ethics, 1990).

8. Source: Centers for Disease Control, 1989.

9. "1 in 7 Adolescents Has Sex-Related Disease," *Cortland Standard* (January 25, 1989), p. 7.
10. Alan Guttmacher Institute, 1990 report.
11. Ibid.
12. *Newsweek,* op. cit.
13. *The Ethics of American Youth,* op. cit.
14. Source: National Center for Health Statistics, 1988.
15. Ibid.
16. Asta M. Kenney, "Teen Pregnancy: An Issue for Schools," *Phi Delta Kappan* (June 1987), pp. 728–36.
17. Ibid.
18. Dr. David Finkelhor is director of the Family Violence Research Program at the University of New Hampshire. His study of childhood sexual abuse was reported by Jane Brody in her column "Personal Health," *The New York Times* (February 18, 1987).
19. Reported in the *Indianapolis Star* (June 15, 1989), p. 1.
20. These instances of sexual child abuse, cited by the columnist Haven Bradford Gow, were reported in the Fall 1989 issue of *Police Times,* published by the American Federation of Police.
21. Ann Rauhala, "Childhood Sexual Abuse Cited as Root of Adult Ills," *The Globe and Mail* (May 27, 1988), p. A-3.
22. Kenney, op. cit., p., 732.
23. Larry Cuban, "Sex and School Reform," *Phi Delta Kappan* (December 1986), p. 321.
24. Cited in Douglas Kirby, *Sexuality Education: An Evaluation of Programs and Their Effects* (Santa Cruz, CA: Network Publications, 1984).
25. Douglas Kirby, "Sexuality Education: A More Realistic View of Its Effects," *Journal of School Health* (December 1985), p. 421.
26. Susan Cronenwett, "Response to Symposium on Sex and Children and Adolescents" in E. A. Wynne (ed.), *Character Policy: An Emerging Issue* (Lanham, MD: University Press of America, 1982), p. 101.
27. William J. Bennett, "Sex and the Education of Our Children," *America* (February 14, 1987), p. 122.
28. Previews of "AIDS: Suddenly Sex Has Become Very Dangerous" are available from Goodday Video, Inc., P.O. Box 111, 115 North Esplanade Street, Cuero, TX 77954 (tel. 1-800-221-1426).
29. Jacqueline D. Forrest and Jane Silverman, "What Public School Teachers Teach About Preventing Pregnancy, AIDS, and Sexually Transmitted Disease," *Family Planning Perspectives* (March–April 1989), pp. 56–72.
30. Sarah Glazer, "Sex Education: How Well Does It Work?," *Editorial Research Reports* (June 23, 1989), pp. 338–50.
31. Based on poll of 1,015 Americans 18 years and older, conducted for *Time* magazine by Yankelovich, Clancy, and Shulman and published in *Time* (November 24, 1986), pp 58–59.
32. Bennett, op. cit., p. 122.
33. U.S. Department of Education, *AIDS and the Education of Our Children: A Guide for Parents and Teachers* (Washington, D.C.: Office of Public Affairs,

U.S. Department of Education, 1988), p. 12. For a free copy of this useful book, which describes various pro-abstinence sex education and AIDS education resources, write Consumer Information Center, Department ED, Pueblo, CO 81009.

34. Ibid., p. 10.
35. "Will 'Safe Sex' Education Effectively Combat AIDS?," a position paper prepared by the staff of the U.S. Department of Education (Washington, DC, 1987), p. 7. Special thanks to Jack Klenk, former senior policy analyst at the White House, for making this position paper available.
36. Glazer, op. cit., p. 346.
37. For more information, write Project Respect, P.O. Box 97, Golf, IL 60029.
38. "Will 'Safe Sex' Education Effectively Combat AIDS?," op. cit., p. 7.
39. The video *Second Thoughts* is available from Bethany Productions, 901 Eastern Avenue, N.E., Grand Rapids, MI 49503-1295 (tel. 616-459-6273).
40. Nabers Cabiniss, director, Office of Adolescent Pregnancy, U.S. Department of Health and Human Services statement (March 26, 1987), cited in "Will 'Safe Sex' Education Effectively Combat AIDS?," loc. cit. The evaluation of SEX RESPECT, based on 2,200 students at various sites, was carried out by the Institute for Research and Evaluation, Stan E. Weed and Joseph A. Olson, principal investigators. For more information about the evaluation, write SEX RESPECT, P. O. Box 349, Bradley IL 60915-0349.
41. For a copy of the Children's Defense Fund report on teenage sex and male-specific sex education programs, write Children's Defense Fund, Pregnancy Prevention Policy Division, 122 C Street, N.W., Washington, DC 20001.
42. "Kids and Contraceptives," *Newsweek* (February 16, 1987), p. 60.
43. Ibid.
44. Based on a summary of the Children's Defense Fund report in *Psychology Today* (May 1989), pp. 11–12.
45. Glazer, op. cit., p. 348.
46. Thanks for this point to William Bennett, "Sex and the Education of Our Children," op. cit.
47. National Survey of Families and Households carried out by Larry Bumpass and colleagues at the University of Wisconsin at Madison, 1989.
48. *Health: AIDS Instructional Guide, Grades K–12* (Albany, New York: The State Education Department, 1987), p. 162.
49. Bruce Voeller and Malcolm Potts, *British Medical Journal* (October 1985), p. 1196; and UPI story "Condoms May Not Prevent AIDS Transfer, Expert Says," *San Francisco Examiner* (November 7, 1985).
50. Cited in *AIDS and the Education of Our Children: A Guide for Parents and Teachers* (Washington, DC: U.S. Department of Education, 1987).
51. See Alan Poarachini, "Koop Warns on Risk of AIDS in Condom Use," *The Los Angeles Times* (September 22, 1987); and Robert Noble, "There Is No Safe Sex," *Newsweek* (April 1, 1991), p. 8.
52. Theresa Crenshaw, M.D., "Condom Advertising," testimony before House Subcommittee on Health and the Environment (February 10, 1987), p. 2.
53. "A Warning to Women on AIDS: Counting on Condoms Is Flirting with Death," *Newsweek* (August 31, 1987), p. 72.

54. Joseph Berger, "School Board Approves Plan for Condoms," *The New York Times* (February 28, 1991), p. B-1. Thanks also to William Schickel for a helpful conversation on this issue.

55. Kiley Armstrong, "New York Narrowly Approves Liberal School Condom Plan," *Cortland Standard* (February 28, 1991), p. 5.

56. I highly recommend, both for its humor and wisdom, a taped talk to teens by Dick Purnell called "Sex, Love, and Intimacy." Write to Dick Purnell Ministry, P.O. Box 850846, Richardson, TX 75085.

57. Bennett, "Sex and the Education of Our Children," op. cit., p. 124.

58. Patricia Freeman, "Risky Business," *People* (November 5, 1990), p. 54.

59. George Eager, *Love, Dating and Sex: What Teens Want to Know* (available for $9.95 from Mailbox Club Books, 404 Eager Road, Valdosta, GA 31602).

60. Ibid., p. 192.

61. Dr. Leman reported his clinical experience with sexual flashbacks in a Focus on the Family radio program hosted by Dr. James Dobson, 1988. For a copy of this tape write Focus on the Family, Ponoma, CA 91799.

62. Josh McDowell and Dick Day, *Why Wait?* (San Bernardino, CA: Here's Life Publishers, 1987), p. 288.

63. Quoted in Howard and Martha Lewis, *The Parent's Guide to Teenage Sex and Pregnancy* (New York: St. Martin's Press, 1980).

64. Reo Christenson, "Sex Ed.: Why Wait?," *Christianity Today* (September 22, 1989), p. 19.

65. Ibid., p. 20.

66. Untitled Associated Press story (September 14, 1987).

67. "Teen Sex Survey in the Evangelical Church," reported in "Conservative Church-Going Teenagers Affected by Sexual Revolution," *American Family Association Journal* (May 1988), p. 5.

68. Rod Paul, "Sex Education Manual Prompts Moral Outrage," *The New York Times* (April 24, 1988), p. 39.

69. Ibid.

70. For an elaboration of this view, see, for example, Donald J. Weeren, "Education in Inclusive Sexuality," *Ethics in Education* (May 1988), p. 2.

71. John Leo, "Sex and Schools," *Time* (November 24, 1986), p. 59.

72. *AIDS and the Education of Our Children*, p. 17.

73. Vincent Bozzi, "Home Sex Ed," *Psychology Today* (May 1987), p. 14.

74. For a preschool through high school curriculum on protecting children against sexual abuse, write for information about "What Our Kids Don't Know Can Hurt Them" (The Committee for Children, P.O. Box 51049, Seattle, WA 98115).

75. National Research Council, *Risking the Future: Adolescent Sexuality, Pregnancy, and Childbearing* (Washington, DC: National Academy Press, 1987).

76. Bennett, "Sex and the Education of Our Children," op. cit., p. 125.

77. For more information on this idea, contact Dr. Huberta Jackson-Lowman, director, Mayor's Commission on Families, Health and Welfare Planning Association, 200 Ross Street, Pittsburgh, PA 15129.

78. For information on this approach write Community of Caring, 1350 New York Avenue, N.W., Suite 500, Washington, DC 20005-4709.

79. Lisa Ferguson, "When Molly Kelly Talks About Sex . . . Teens Listen!," *New Covenant* (July/August 1990). For information about chastity or Molly Kelly's lectures, write Molly Kelly, 311 Roumfort Road, Philadelphia, PA 19119. For her video, "Let's Talk—Teens and Chastity" ($29.95), contact St. Paul Book and Media, 50 St. Paul's Avenue, Boston, MA 02130 (tel. 1-800-876-4463).

Chapter 19

1. *Schools Without Drugs* (Washington, DC: U.S. Department of Education, 1987), p. 3.
2. Ibid., p. v.
3. Ibid., p. 5.
4. Kenneth Eskey, " 'Code Blue': A Health Emergency for American Teenagers," *The Times Union* (June 9, 1990), p. 1.
5. CBS *Evening News* report (April 19, 1990).
6. *The Ethics of American Youth: A Warning and A Call to Action* (Marina del Rey, CA: Josephson Institute of Ethics, 1990).
7. Matthew Spina and Steven Billmyer, "Children See Drugs Everywhere," *Syracuse-Herald American* (October 8, 1989), p. A-14.
8. Ibid.
9. *Schools Without Drugs*, p. 5.
10. Howard LaFranchi, "Legal Substances, Illegal Use," *The Christian Science Monitor* (August 31, 1988), p. 1.
11. Harry F. Rosenthal, "Adults and Teens Worry About Drug Abuse," *Cortland Standard* (August 15, 1989), p. 1.
12. Spina and Billmyer, op. cit., p. A-1.
13. Ibid.
14. LaFranchi, loc. cit.
15. Spina and Billmyer, op. cit., p. A-1.
16. Steven Billmyer, "Drugs Led Teenager to Suicide," *Syracuse Herald-American* (October 8, 1989), p. A-1.
17. *Schools Without Drugs,* p. 6.
18. Richard A. Hawley, "Schoolchildren and Drugs: The Fancy That Has Not Passed," *Phi Delta Kappan* (May 1987).
19. Ibid., p. K-4.
20. Ibid., p. K-6.
21. Peggy Mann, "Marijuana Alert: Brain and Sex Damage," in *Raising Kids* (New York: Berkley Books, 1981).
22. *Schools Without Drugs,* p. 9.
23. Ibid.
24. Spina and Billmyer, loc. cit.
25. *Schools Without Drugs,* p. 10.
26. Ibid.
27. Ibid.
28. Ibid., p. 7.
29. Richard Halloran, "Student Use of Cocaine Is Up as Use of Most Other Drugs Drops," *The New York Times* (August 7, 1986), p. A-12.

30. Associated Press, "Increased Child Abuse," *Cortland Standard* (May 14, 1990), p. 9.

31. Available at no charge by writing to Schools Without Drugs, Consumer Information Center, Department ED, Pueblo, CO 81009.

32. Adapted from William DeJong, "Los Angeles' Project DARE: Saying No to Alcohol and Drugs" in *Schools Without Drugs: The Challenge* (Washington, DC: U.S. Department of Education, May 1987).

33. Ibid., p. 5.

34. Ibid., p. 36.

35. *Schools Without Drugs,* p. 36.

36. Alan Llavore, "Students Need to Respect Law, Conference Told," *Times Union* (May 27, 1988), p. B-4.

37. Farrell Kramer, "High School Students Test Drug Free," *Cortland Standard* (March 5, 1990), p. 1.

38. "Fight Drugs with Community Schools," *The New York Times* (May 23, 1990), p. A-2.

39. See *Schools Without Drugs* for specific suggestions for the content of elementary school drug education.

40. Ibid., pp. 44–45.

41. Eskey, op. cit.

42. Source: *What Parents Must Learn About Teens and Alcohol,* pamphlet published by the National Federation of Parents for Drug-Free Youth (1820 Franwall Avenue, Room 16, Silver Spring, MD 20902).

43. Source: 1988 National Adolescent Student Health Survey, U.S. Department of Health and Human Services.

44. Dr. Donald Ian Macdonald, Deputy Assistant to the President for Drug Abuse Policy, quoted by Reed Bell, "Alcohol: A Gateway Drug," *The Challenge* (U.S. Department of Education publication: 1988).

45. Source: National Council on Alcohol Abuse and Alcoholism.

46. Eskey, op. cit.

47. Joanne Ross Feldmeth, "Life with an Alcoholic," *Focus on the Family* (February 1986), p. 11.

48. G. T. Johnson and S. E. Goldfinger (eds.), *The Harvard Medical School Health Letter Book* (New York: Warner Books, 1982).

49. Robert G. Yasko, "Alcoholics Anonymous: The Utilization of Social Experience in the Classroom," *Health Education* (February/March 1988).

50. Reported in "Hot Cars, Cold Beers," *University of California, Berkeley Wellness Newsletter* (May 1988), p. 2.

51. Ronald H. Hopkins et al., "Comprehensive Evaluation of a Model Alcohol Education Curriculum," *Journal of Studies on Alcohol,* 49 (1988), pp. 38–50.

52. Ibid., p. 46.

53. Source: *Safe Homes* brochure, Guilderland Central Schools, Guilderland, NY. Thanks to Walter Sullivan, superintendent of Skaneateles, N.Y., schools for sharing this material.

54. Ron Fagan, "Schooling Children About Alcohol Abuse," *School Safety* (Winter 1988), p. 25.

55. Quoted in Hawley, op. cit., p. K-7.

56. Adapted from Colleen L. Rice, "What Are You Drinking?," *Youth Update* (Cincinatti, OH: St. Anthony's Messenger Press, 1983).
57. Michael Clark, "A Realistic Approach for Strength and Conditioning Coaches to Deal with Steroids," *NSCA Journal*, 10 (1988), pp. 28–30. Thanks to Larry Martin for referring me to this article and to Florence Brush for her help in locating this source.

Chapter 20

1. John Hansgate, letter to *The Buffalo News* (September 1988).
2. "Teachers' Problems in Schools Surveyed," *Los Angeles Times* (December 13, 1988), p. 1.
3. David Briggs, "Changes in Family Leave Less Room for Children," *The Buffalo News* (September 14, 1988), p. A-9.
4. Ibid.
5. Ibid., p. A-1.
6. Thanks for this formulation of this point to psychologist W. Peter Blitchington's *Sex Roles and the Christian Family* (Wheaton, IL: Tyndale House Publishers, 1981).
7. Glenn Collins, "A Dean of Pediatricians Looks at Today's Family," *The New York Times* (May 28, 1984).
8. Many thanks to JoAnn Davidson, a Westport, Connecticut, teacher and former parent educator in Parents as Teachers, for sharing information on both PAT and "schools of the 21st century."
9. Adapted from Rita Watson and Karen FitzGerald, "21st Century School," *Parents* (October 1989).
10. Elliot Ginsberg, "Family Resource Centers," press release of the state of Connecticut Department of Human Resources, Office of the Commissioner, 1049 Asylum Avenue, Hartford, CT 06105 (tel. 203-566-3318).
11. Watson and FitzGerald, op. cit., p. 113.
12. Eric Schaps, Daniel Solomon, and Marilyn Watson, "A Program That Combines Character Development and Academic Achievement," *Educational Leadership* (December 1985–January 1986), pp. 32–34.
13. Joan Libman, "Building Better Kids," *Los Angeles Times* (November 8, 1988), p. V-1.
14. *What Works: Schools That Work—Educating Disadvantaged Children* (Washington, DC: U.S. Department of Education, 1987).
15. Ibid.
16. "Homework That Helps Families Communicate," *Working Together* (newsletter of the Child Development Project) (Summer 1986), p. 5.
17. Ibid.
18. The family guides for grades one through three, and the classroom curriculum for the Scotia-Glenville project, have been adapted from materials developed by the Character Research Project of Schenectady, New York.
19. *The Scotia-Glenville Experience: Family Guide for First-Grade Students* (Schenectady, NY: Character Research Project, 1981).

20. Dorothy G. Singer, "How Much Television Is Too Much?," *Families* (January 1982), reprint, p. 1.
21. Anastasia Toufexis, "Our Violent Kids," *Time* (June 12, 1989), p. 55.
22. American Psychological Association, *Violence on TV: A Social Issue Release from the Board of Social and Ethical Responsibility for Psychology.* (Washington, DC: American Psychological Association, 1985).
23. Stein, B. J., "TV: A Religious Wasteland," originally published in *The Wall Street Journal* and reprinted in *Focus on the Family* (April 1985), p. 5.
24. Tipper Gore, *Raising PG Kids in an X-Rated Society* (Nashville, TN: Abingdon Press, 1987).
25. Toufexis, op. cit., p. 57.
26. Michael Ryan, "How One School Straightens Out Students Who Act Up," *Parade* (January 18, 1987), p. 10.
27. Ibid.
28. For excellent ideas on how teachers and parents can help students develop good homework habits, see Lee Canter, "Homework Without Tears," *Instructor* (September 1988), pp. 28–32.
29. Robert Marquand, "U.S. Education: Reform Still at Top of Agenda," *The Christian Science Monitor* (December 16, 1988), p. 21.
30. For other helpful, specific ways to get parents involved in their children's learning see *What Works: Schools That Work—Educating Disadvantaged Children.*
31. From an article by Stephen Allas, "In Ballston Spa: Banana Splits Heals," originally published in *The Times Union.*
32. From a letter to Brad Pollack, Groton Central Schools; thanks to Mr. Pollock for sharing this letter with me.
33. Mary Ellen Saterlie, "Developing a Community Consensus for Teaching Values," *Educational Leadership* (May 1988), pp. 44–47.
34. Mary Ann Pentz et al., "A Multicommunity Trial for Primary Prevention of Adolescent Drug Abuse," *JAMA* (June 9, 1989), pp. 3259–66.
35. For a copy of this booklet, *1984 and Beyond: A Reaffirmation of Values,* write to the Baltimore County Public Schools, Towson, MD 21204.
36. For a copy of *Values Education in the Baltimore County Public Schools: Questions Parents Ask,* write to the PTA Council of Baltimore County, Baltimore County Public Schools, Towson, MD 21204.
37. Ibid., p. 3259.
38. Gina Kolata, "Community Program Succeeds in Drug Fight," *The New York Times* (June 11, 1989), p. 33.

Index

A

Aberth, Sally, 163

Abortion, 18, 19, 20, 47, 349; addressing in the classroom, 275, 276-82

Abortion: Understanding Differences (Callahan), 278

Abuse/abused children, 32, 73, 75, 127, 130, 165, 350, 381

Academic achievement, 22, 24; cooperative learning and, 187; decline in American, 210; effective schools and, 214; pressures, inappropriate, 344-46; and values education, 29-30

Activities. *See* Exercises and activities, classroom.

Adair, Evan, 336-37

Adams, John, 40

Adams, Marie, 145

Adams, Sandra, 413

Advertising, influence of, 16, 82-83, 389

"Adolescent Issues" (Smith-Hansen), 204

Affirmation in the classroom, 96-102. *See also* specific exercises.

Age of Indifference, The, 18

AIDS, 18, 310, 317, 350, 354, 362-65, 367, 371; drug use and, 375-76

AIDS and the Education of Our Children, 371

AIDS: Learn and Live (video), 357

Alan Guttmacher Institute, 349

Albert Einstein College of Medicine, 83

Alberta, Canada, 350; Ministry of Education, 182-83, 258

Albuquerque, New Mexico, 285

Alcohol abuse, 4, 13, 19, 32, 43, 50, 212, 376, 386, 388-89; driving and, 13, 25; guidelines for combating, 387; moral messages in educating about, 391-94; parents and, 380-81, 390; Safe Homes program, 391; in school, 323; school assembly on, 339; school-community partnership and, 416-17. *See also* Drugs.

Alcoholics Anonymous, 386

Alexander, Vicki, 349

Altruism, 7, 78, 206

Alvy, Kerby, 403

American Biology Teacher, The, 277

American Civil Liberties Union, 278

American Freshmen, The: National Norms for Fall 1990, 17, 304

American Heroes In and Out of School (Hentoff), 310

American Jewish Committee, 21

American Medical Association, 379
American Psychological Association, 407
American Psychologist, 81
Americans United for the Separation of Church and State, 40-41
Amesville, Ohio, 161-62; "Amesville Sixth-Grade Water Chemists," 161-62
Amherst, New York, 26
Amnesty International, 308
Andover, Massachusetts, 317, 339
Andry, Andrew, 372
Angelini, Molly, 44
Anger, 109, 286-87
Animals: rights, 165-66, 272; respect/responsibility, teaching of, 163-66, 183
Ann Arbor, Michican, 307
Annapolis, Maryland, 381
Anne Arundel Country School District, 381
"Annotated Bibliography for Teaching Conflict Resolution in Schools" (Cheatham), 299
Apathy, fruits of in education, 210
Appleton, Wisconsin, 358
"Appreciation time" exercise, 99
Aristotle, xiii, 50
Arnieri, Christine, 218-19
Aronson, Elliott, 192
Assertive discipline, 110, 119
Astley, Malcolm, 412
Atlanta, Georgia, 24; community service programs, 316; Postponing Sexual Involvement Program, 355
Austin, Texas, 192
Authority, 9, 15, 24, 30, 34, 43-44, 110; anti-, 9-10, 235; moral, 111-12
Awareness moral, 53-54, 56, 124-25, 229. *See also* Moral knowing; Social awareness/activism.

B

Bad language, 16, 34, 125-26, 159-60
Baddell, Mayris, 328
Baldwin, Bill, 389-90
Ballard, Charles, 359-60

Ballston Spa Central School District, New York, 413-14
Baltimore County, Maryland: booklet by, 424; parent involvement in, 401-02; school survey, 33; success story, 414, 415-16
Banana Splits program, 413-14
Banas, Sharon, 26
Barno, Sister Paul, 181
Barry Elementary School, 74
Becker, Judith, 17
Bedford, New York, 93, 197, 337, 347
Beecher Elementary School, 114, 313
Behavior: abusive, 15, 32, 76, 332-33, 344; academic, 57-58; aggressive, 146, 194, 287, 289-91, 293; classroom, 29, 96-99, 110, 113-28, 135-38, 194-95; control of, 110, 115; home-school plan, 132, 134; moral, 7-8, 12-13, 22, 27, 57, 98; respect/responsibility and, 43-44; self-destructive, 17-19, 33, 46, 83, 386; self-discipline and, 46, 121-25; situation specific, 8, 58, 63. *See also* Alcohol; Class meetings; Conflict resolution; Cooperative learning; Discipline; Drugs; Moral discipline; Sexual behavior; Violence.
Behavior improvement plan, 122-23, 124
Bellah, Robert, xiii, 107
Belle Sherman Elementary School, 75, 145
Benjamin, A. K., 268
Bennett, Amy, 113-14
Bennett, William, 62, 348
Benninga, Jacques, 347
Bennington High School, Oklahoma, 384-85
Bent, Dee, 101, 313-14
Bergenfield, New Jersey, community service programs, 316
Betinas, Claire, 106, 140
Bettelheim, Bruno, 211-12
Big Brother/Big Sister, 315
Bigelow, Martha, 143-44
"Bigotry in the Ivory Tower," 15
Bill Moyers Journal, 406
Binenbaum, Joe, 164-65

Birch Meadow Elementary School, 24, 84, 106, 140, 266, 419

Blatt, Moshe, 242

Blauvelt, New York, 340

Boston: Oxfam America, 306; violence prevention program, 298

Boston University, 22; Center for the Advancement of Ethics and Character, 59-60

Bourne, Irene, 84

Boyer, Ernest, 315

Brabeck, Mary, 55

Bradford, Ohio, 165

Bramble, Guy, 174

Brandt Commission, 305

Brazelton, T. Berry, 397-98

Brennan, Father Joseph, 14

Briscoe, Joyce, 285

Brockport, New York, 323

Brodesser, Janet, 323

Brody, Patti, 145-46, 147-48

Brookline High School, 172-73

Brookline, Massachusetts, 25-26, 91, 92, 148, 155, 172, 197, 412

Brown, Larry, 165

Brown, Rexford, 226

Bruner, Jerome, 217

Bryan, C.D.B., 250

Buffalo, New York, 395

Bullying, 334. *See also* Behavior.

Burlington, Ontario, 102

Burke, Edmund, 322

Burns, Marilyn, 190-91

Burton Street Elementary School, 113

Butler, Barb, 96

C

Califano, Joseph, Jr., 304

Callahan, Sidney, 52, 278, 280-81

California: Law in a Free Society Project, 24-25, 182; sex education in, 353; State Bar Association, 24; textbook guidelines, 163. *See also* Child Development Program.

Cambridge, Massachusetts, 21, 183

Camelback High School, 306

Campbell, Carl, 326-28, 336-37

Canada: values education programs in, 25, 26, 27; violence and vandalism in, 13

Canastota, New York, 254

Capital punishment, 11, 20, 272

Caring: acts of, 106; atmosphere of, 214; moral norms and, 324-25, 328, 335-36; one-to-one relationships and, 313-15, 317; sex and, 353; teaching, 26, 28, 42-43, 96, 137. *See also* Relationships; Sex education; Social awareness/activism.

Carlone, Ed, 193-94

Carmody, Bruce, 339

Carnegie Corporation study, 4

Carnegie Foundation for the Advancement of Teaching, 395; study, 316

Carnegie Hero Fund Commission, 310

Cazenovia, New York, 113, 146

Censorship: Evidence of Bias in Our Textbooks (Vitz), 40

Center for the Improvement for Child Caring (CICC) parent training services, 403

Center for Research on Elementary and Middle Schools, 191

Center for Social Studies Education, 268, 270

Centers for Disease Control, on STD, 349, 353, 376

Central School, 221, 292

Centre for Human Development and Social Change, 268

Chappelle, Sherry, 93

Character, 7, 10, 20, 22, 24, 49-50; definition, 50-51, 68; developing, 22, 62-63, 72, 138, 227, 239-45; diagram, 53; educating for, 7, 22, 56-57, 70; example, 51-52; highest form, 59-60; moral environment and, 63; three components of, 51-62, 139, 229-30. *See also* Conscience of craft; Family; Kohlberg; Moral action; Moral feeling; Moral knowing; Schools; Teacher(s).

Character Policy: An Emerging Issue (Wynne), xiii

Charlotte Kenyon Elementary School, 159
Cheatham, Annie, 299
Cheating, 11, 13, 14-15, 35, 45, 47, 153, 248; causes, 78; delaing with, 76-78, 252-53; conscience and, 57-58; Hartshorne and May study, 7-8
Chenango Forks, New York, 159
Chicago, Illinois, 28, 127, 129, 265, 307, 328-30, 332, 334; assignment book requirements, 224-25; T.I.M.E., 218-19
Child Development Project (CDP), 25-26, 28-30, 112, 174, 199, 206, 314-15, 402, 403-04; sample family homework packet, 404; survey of values, 400-401
Child Sex Abuse and Sexually Victimized Children (Finkelhor), 351-52
"Children and Mother Earth," 163
Children and Their Community, 318
Children and TV: Teaching Kids to Watch Wisely (Goller), 409
Children's Creative Response to Conflict Program, 299
Children's Defense Fund, 359, 360
Children's Urgent Action newsletter, 308
"Choices, Choices" (software series), 258
Christenson, Reo, 369-70
Christian Action Council, 359
Christianity Today, 368
Christopher, Cindy, 216
Citizenship, xiii, 7, 20, 25, 43, 47, 54; awards, 28, 312; caring and, 304; curriculum based, 24, 310-12; democratic, 20, 24, 135, 161; PREPARE program, 25-26, 182, 289, 338; Preparing Adolescents for Tomorrow, 25; teaching, 21, 38, 163, 303-04. *See also* Social awareness/activism.
Clarke, Judy, 201
"Class applause" tradition, 104
Class buddies, 313-14
"Class business box," 142, 145
"Class constitution" activity, 112
"Class council" exercise, 149-50
"Class directory" activity, 92-93
Class meeting, 102, 105, 113, 136-38, 157-60, 200, 205; for character development,
138; community building and, 140, 143; conflict resolution and, 288, 289, 292-94, 340-41; consequences for rule-breaking, 153; for decision-making, 147-50; defined, 138-39; developing participation skills, 154-57; developing a successful, 150-53; "emergency," 137; evaluation, 157, 158; feedback form, 148-49; goals, 139; kinds, 141-42, 149-50, 225-26; problem-solving and, 143-47; ten steps in, 151; values education and, 159-60; ways to close, 152
"Class pen pals" activity, 93-94
Class projects, 196-97
"Class symbols" activity, 103
Classroom, 107-08; control, 143-44, 148; democratic environment, 68, 135-38; discipline plan, 128-29; building a moral community in, 68, 89-108, 134, 139, 140, 143, 162, 187, 198-99; guidelines for moral community, 100; management, 145-46; moral discipline in, 111-34; problem behavior, 86, 96-99, 114, 117, 120-25, 126-27, 185-86, 289-91, 295, 296-99; rituals and traditions, 102, 335. *See also* Class meetings; Conflict resolution; Cooperative learning; Moral authority; Moral discipline; School.
"Classical Ideas About Moral Education" (Moline), xiii
Clauson, Janet, 158-59
Cleary, Beverly, 175
Cleveland, Ohio, 359-60
Cliques, social, 94
Close Harmony (film), 318
Clovis, California, 81, 215, 272, 328, 336, 338
Cluster group seating, 190-91
"Coat of arms" activity, 95-96
Cocurricular program, 336-37
Cohen, Susan and David, 392
Cohn, Anne, 381
Columbia University, 10
Columbus, Kansas, 219
Communication: class meetings and, 139, 154-57; listening skills, 139, 154, 155,

199; structured skill training and, 291-92; television and, 407

"Communities of character," 107

Community, 9; building with older students, 94-96, 107; creation of a learning, 95-96; guidelines for parent-community-school cooperation, 418; moral, in the school, 22, 89-108, 110, 112-13, 134, 290, 334-40; as partner in drug/alcohol programs, 381-82, 385, 389-91; as partners in values education, 70, 345; parents and, 36, 70; positive experience of, 107-08; responsibility/respect and, 41, 45; service programs, 24, 28, 60, 70, 312-13, 315-18; *See also* Classroom, building a moral community in; Social awareness/activism.

Community Board Program, 296

Community of Caring programs, 355-56

Community Schools, 385

Compassion, 45, 46, 54, 62

Competence, 61-62

Competition, 188-89; team learning and, 196

Condoms, teaching about, 362-65

Conference: parent-teacher, 130-31, 411; teacher-student, 80, 86, 122-23, 133

"Conflict circle" activity, 296

Conflict managers, kids as, 295-96

Conflict resolution, 28, 70, 286-87; class meeting and, 288, 292-94; conflict managers, kids as, 295-96; curriculum on, 289-91; effects of training, 297; five elements to teaching, 288-89; guiding students through conflicts, 294-95; material available for teaching, 299; older students and, 298-99; strategies for teaching, 297; structured skill training, 291-92; students' responsibility for solving, 296-97

Connect, 163

Connecticut, schools as family resource centers, 400

Conscience, 9, 30, 57-58, 61, 266-67. *See also* Reflection, moral.

Conscience of craft, 70, 208-227; defined,

213; guidelines for developing, 220. *See also* Work ethic.

Consequences (logical): class meetings and, 153; enforcement as teachable moment, 117; fixed vs. variable, 119-20; group involvement in setting, 117-18; teacher set, 118-19

"Controversial Issues: A Sample School Policy" (Miller), 277

Controversial issues, teaching of, 268-69; abortion as, 275, 276-82; current news issues and, 285; debating as teaching strategy, 272-75; ethical issues in science education, 273-75; guidelines, 283; impartiality vs. position-taking of teacher, 271-72; intellectual freedom and, 276-78; planned educational approach, 275-76; school guidelines, 276, 277; structured academic controversy approach, 282-84; Vietnam war as, 269-71

Convent of the Sacred Heart, 303

Cook-Barriero, Katsi, 179-80

Cooperation: definition sheet, 200; skills of, 199-200, 293; teaching, 46, 187

Cooperative consequence setting, 117-19

Cooperative learning, 25, 70, 74, 136, 181, 185-86; benefits, 186-89, 206-07, 284; classroom example, 204-07; evaluation, 201-02; guidelines, 198; kinds, 189-97, 225; learning strategies, 203-04; maximizing success in, 197-204; roles in group, 202-03; structured academic controversy, 282-84; work ethic and, 213

Cooperative Learning magazine, 186, 197

Cornell University, xiii

Cortland Junior-Senior High School, 193, 194

Cortland, New York, 74, 193, 389

Cottage Lane Elementary School, 340-41

Counseling, peer, 382-83

"Counting and charting" activity, 124-25

Country Club Elementary School, 145, 196

Courage, 7, 45-46, 49, 54, 172, 310

Courage of Their Convictions, The (Irons), 172

Courage to Care, The (film), 310

Courtesy, 28, 44, 54, 117

Cousins, Norman, 304

Cox, Gloria, 153

*Creating Peace in Our Classrooms: Cooper-
ative Learning, Controversy, and Conflict
Resolution* (Graves & Graves), 299

*Creative Conflict Resolution: More than
200 Activities for Keeping Peace in the
Classroom* (Kreidler), 299

Crenshaw, Theresa, 363

Crime, 2-3, 5, 6-7, 11-14, 17, 21, 24, 25,
153; lack of empathy and, 59; religious
teaching and, 41-42; responsibility and,
44; teaching honesty and, 45-46, 76

Crisis, coping with, 106-07

Critical thinking, 269, 270, 282-84. *See also*
Controversial issues, teaching of; Decision-making; Moral reflection.

"Critical Thinking Through Structured
Controversy" (Johnson & Johnson), 282

Cruelty, 15, 43, 98-99; prevention/stopping,
47, 96-102

Cuban, Larry, 353

Culture, American, 40-41, 50; diversity in,
180; moral, 63, 70, 324-25, 326-41, 343-
47; religion in, 41

Culverwell, Rosemary, 328-30

Curriculum, 7, 8; on animals, 163-166,
183; *Children and TV: Teaching Kids to
Watch Wisely,* 409; citizenship program,
24-25; computer software, 258; conflict
resolution, 288, 289-91; "covering," 216;
Decision-Making: Keys to Total Success
program, 356-57; discussion, 253-54; *Educating for Citizenship,* 262; ethical is-
sues/values in subject areas, 167-70;
feedback form, 148-49; Facing History
and Ourselves program, 26, 28-29, 182,
320, 321; Fieldston Lower School ethical
curriculum, 163, 173-80; good materials,
170-72, 204, 270; *Growing Up Together*
(parent-child education), 403; heroes and
heroism, 310; I CAN COURSE, 218;
Law in a Free Society Project, 24-25;
"Lessons of the Vietnam War, The," 270;
as moral educator, 162-63; PREPARE,
25, 182, 289, 338; pressure of mandated,
344-45; Project Respect, 356; published
curricula, 181-83; school-wide approach,
166-67, 226; sex education, 355-59, 361,
367, 374; student input, 148; teacher-designed units, 259-62; teaching strategies,
172-73; Teen-Aid: Sexuality, Commitment, and Family, 357; values and, 27,
68, 161-84; violence prevention, 298;
"Winning," 338. *See also* History; Science; Social Studies; Writing.

*Curriculum Guide for Sex Education in
California Schools,* 353

Curtis School, 344

D

"Daily report card" approach, 132

Daley, Jo, 216

Damon, William, 55

Danforth Foundation, 398

Daniels, Diane, 250, 252

DARE (Drug Abuse Resistance Education),
383-84

Darwinism, 7

de Boer, Yvette, 133

Dean, John, 56-57

Debating as teaching strategy, 272-75

Debs, Eugene, 170-72

Decision-making, 10-12, 41; adolescent, 55-
56, 356-57; class meeting for, 147-50;
democratic, 92, 139, 342; moral knowing
and, 55-56; program for, 27; student
government and, 340-42; teaching, 254-
58, 261-62. *See also* Kohlberg; Sex education.

Decision-Making: Keys to Total Success,
356-57

DeDiminicantanio, Joseph, 27, 356-57

Delaney, Thomas, 396

Delinquency, 19; parents and, 30

Democracy/democratic values, 6, 20, 39-40,
135-38, 139-40; and CDP, 28-29; and
moral education, 6-7, 46-47, 161; re-
spect/responsibility and, 43-45; school
government and, 340-42. *See also* Child

Development Program; Class meetings; Classroom; Cooperative Learning; Moral Discipline.

Democracy in America (Tocqueville), 321-22

Derrick, Christopher, 45

Detroit, Michigan, community service programs, 316

Dewey, John, 89, 90, 139, 140

Dignity, 43, 152; in the classroom, 74

Directory of School Mediation and Conflict Resolution Programs, 299

Discipline, 7, 24, 25, 110, 214; "assertive," 110, 119; cocurricular program, 336-37; consequences, 117-20, 124; "counting and charting," 124-25; hostile student, dealing with, 120-21; incentives, 127-28, 131; individual conference, 122-23; lack of, 50; parent involvement, 128-34, 411; personal student plans, 122-24; school-wide, 331-34; teacher burnout and, 110; time-out, 121-22. *See also* Cooperative learning; Moral discipline.

Discussion, leading a moral, 251-58; guidelines, 251-54; structured format for, 254-58

Divorce, 31-32, 96; Banana Splits program, 413-14; negative effects on child of, 32; sleeper effect, 32, 170. *See also* Family.

Dixon, Arne, 81

"Don't Be a Nerd" dilemma exercise, 255-58

Dove-Edwin, Horace, 19

Doyle, Peggy, 104

Drugs, 4, 18-19, 21, 45, 81-83, 212; abuse, 4, 13, 32, 43, 50, 60, 73, 375-77; combating drugs guidelines, 387; community schools, 385; "drug-free" schools, 384-85; effects of, 378-79; examples of abuse, 377-78; moral judgment about, 386; principles in establishing a drug-free environment, 381-84; school-community partnership to fight, 416-17; values education and, 27, 30, 81-83, 339; valuing personal health and, 385-86. *See also* Alcohol.

Dry Creek Elementary School, 81, 215, 326-28, 336-37

Dryden High School, 133

Dryden, New York, 96, 133, 182, 219

Dubel, Robert, 415

Dumas Elementary School, 330

Durkheim, Emile, 109, 110, 207

E

Eager, George, 365

East Harlem Maritime School, 164

Economic Policy Institute, 17

Edstene, Kay, 318

Educating for Citizen Action (Newman), 320

Educating for Citizenship, 262

Education: failure of, 90; goals of, 6, 67, 90. *See also* School; Teacher(s); Values education.

Educational Leadership magazine, 197, 237, 282, 316

Educational Testing Service, 183

Educators for Social Responsibility, 21, 183

Eger, Martin, 235-36

Ehrenreich, Barbara, 278-80

Eichmann, Adolph, 228

Eisenberg, Nancy, 55

Elasky, Bill, 161-62

Elementary schools: class meetings in, 145-47; community service programs, 317-18; computer software, 258; cooperative consequence setting, 118; drug/alcohol abuse, 377, 379-80, 388; moral culture, 324-25, 326-41, 343-47; published curricula, 181-83; puppets, 293; values education, 24-30. *See also* Curriculum; specific schools

Ellicott City, Maryland, 186

Elmira, New York, 114, 307, 313

Emily Carr Elementary School, 101, 186, 313-14, 331-32

Emotion: and character, 56-61; and reason, 52, 60; and will, 62. *See also* Moral feeling.

Empathy, 25, 52, 59, 61, 78, 96, 313

Endwell, New York, 116

Engel, Joan, 258-59
English, teaching values with, 174-77, 194
Enright, Robert, 297
Ensor, Sara, 311
"Environment of mediocrity," 210, 213
Environmental issues, 161-63, 179-80, 271, 273-75, 282-84, 317
EPIC (Effective Parenting Information for Children), 403
Ethical Culture Schools, 163, 173, 217, 261
"Ethical Person, The" exercise, 258
"Ethical Values in American History" (Nylen), 167-68
Ethics, 10-14, 22, 259, 261; programs for, 22, 166-67, 173–77; journal, 56, 265; literacy, 43, 55; self-control and, 60; in subject areas, 167-83, 262–63, 274–75
"Ethics in Action" project, 258-59, 265
"Ethics in the Boesky Era," 12
Ethics in Education, 168
"Ethics in the World" activity, 259
Ethics of American Youth, The: A Warning Call to Action, 14
"Ethics plays," 261
Exercises and activities, classroom: affirmation of self and others, 99-102; animal rights/respect, 163-65; anti-drug, 81-83; behavior improvement, 122-25, 132; communication, 154-57; conflict resolution, 296-97; controversial issues, 270-71, 272-75, 278-84; cooperative learning, 186, 189-97, 199-206; ethical issues in academic areas, 170-81; identity and group cohesion, 102-03; improving group interaction, 95-96; moral reflection (Kohlberg moral dilemmas), 239-48, 249, 252, 255-67; parental/family involvement, 402; rule-making, 112-15; sex education, 358; social awareness/social activism, 306-08, 309-11, 313-15, 317-18; for student input, 147-50; students getting to know each other, 91-94, 112-13; television viewing reduction, 408-09; values clarification, 236-39; valuing by group, 103-04. *See also* Class meeting; Curriculum; Programs; specific activities and exercises

Expectations, importance of high, 214-16; behavioral, 332-34
Expertise, developing, 216-17
Extracurricular activities, 336-40

F

Facing History and Ourselves, 26, 28-29, 182, 320, 321; "Choosing to Participate" minicourse, 320-21
Fagal, Janet, 94
Fairness, teaching as a moral value, 46
"Fallout Shelter, The" exercise, 236
Family, 4, 9, 31; abuse, 32, 75; breakdown/ changes, 19, 23, 31-33, 34, 109, 114, 395-98, 419; class as, 137; fathers in, 30-31, 109, 396, 397; home-school communication, 398, 403-06; role in values education, 20, 30-31, 34-36, 396-97; and schools, 24, 34-36, 71; The Year of the Family in Education, 398. *See also* Parents
Family Guides, 404-06
Family Science Fair, 402
Farmingham, Connecticut, TV Turn-Off Kit project, 408
Fast for World Harvest Day, 306-07
Feedback form for course, 148-49
Fellowship of Reconciliation, 299
Females, 5; behavior problem, example of, 126-27; cheating in marriage, 13; rape, attitudes on, 5, 55; self-destructive behavior, 19; sexuality, 16-17, 349-50, 359, 365-66, 368; suicide rate, 19; violent crime and, 4, 13-14
Ferrell, Trevor, 311-12
Field, Kristen, 91, 148, 197-98
Fields, W. C., 81
Fieldstone Lower School, 163, 173-80, 217, 261
Fifteen Thousand Hours (Rutter), 331
Fighting, dealing with, 289-91, 295, 296-99
Fighting Drinking and Driving: Tips from America's High School Students, 392
Finch, James, 26

Finkelhor, David, 351-52
Flach, Patricia, 181
Fleming, Bill, 331-32
Flint, Mark, 334
For Character, 24, 28, 330
Fordham University, 319
Fort Washington, Pennsylvania, 72
Fospero, Carl, 135-36
Frames of Mind (Gardner), 222
Frankfort, New York, 118
Fresno State University, 81
Frey, Gloria, 177-78
Friends' Council of Schools, 318
Friends: For Teens (Joyce), 359
Fulghum, Robert, 89
Fuller, Ron, 155
Fullilove, Robert, 376-77

G

Gallup Polls: on drug use, 377; on moral education, 21; on self-centeredness, 17
Garcia, Sheila, 404
Gardner, Howard, 222
Garrod, Andrew, 174
Gathercoal, Forrest, 113
Gefell, Catherine, 273-75
Generator, The: National Journal of Service Leadership, 318
Gilligan, Carol, 55
Ginott, Haim, 71
Ginsberg, Elliot, 400
Giraffe Gazette, 309-10
Giraffe Project, 309-12
Glasser, William, 208
Glendale Elementary School, 330
Goals, 215; academic, 214; group, 104-05, 197-98; I CAN COURSE, 218; life, 17-18; long-range, 212; school, 24, 326, 374, 402
God: human rights and, 40; moral decision making and, 41-42; and public schools, 37, 40; and television, 407
Golden Rule, 5, 43, 44, 235
Goldstein, Arnold, 292
Goller, Claudine, 409

Gompers Vocational-Technical High School, 381-82
"Good deeds tree" activity, 99
"Good ethics"/"bad ethics" drawings activity, 262-63
"Good feelings/bad feelings" exercise, 95
Good Samaritan/good citizenship awards, 312
Goodlad, John, 226
Gore, Tipper, 410
Gracemor Elementary School, 285
Grade 8 ethics course, 182-83, 258
Graham, John, 309
Grandparents' Day activity, 402
Grant, Pat, 133
Graves, Nancy and Ted, 299
Gray, Loretta, 165-66
Great Expectations program, 412
Green, Thomas, 213
Greenberg, Harvey, 83
Greenwich, Connecticut, 186, 303
Griffen, William L., 271
Groton Elementary School, 104
Groton, New York, 104
Group: appreciation, 195-96; development of, 194-95; feeling of membership, 102-08; incentives, 128, 225; interaction, 95-96, 155; interdependence in, 105-08; resistance to, 98; responsibility, 104-08; goals and rules for, 104-05; seat lottery, 94; valued by, 103-04, 335, 336-37. *See also* Class meetings; Cooperative learning; Exercises and activities, classroom.
Growing Up Together, 403
Guerrero, Bill, 383-84
Guest speakers, 179-80, 259, 374
Gula, Fred, 32, 330
Gulbin, Richard, 248, 249-50
Gyant, Lazett, 186

H

Habits of the Heart (Bellah), 107
Halpern, Ann, 221
Hamilton, Ohio, 411
Hamilton, Ontario, 25, 290-91, 293, 338

Handicapped/physically challenged persons, 182, 236, 292, 318; *Amigo* Program, 328

Hansgate, John, 395

Harding Elementary School, 136

Harmin, Merrill, 237

Harris, David, 170-72

Hartshorne, Hugh, 7-8

Harvard Medical School Health Letter Book, 388

Harvard University, 57, 79, 222, 303; Graduate School of Education, 23; study of violence in schools, 16

Hayward, California, 30, 185

Hearts of Men, The (Ehrenreich), 278

Heartwood, 181-82

Heath Elementary School, 155, 412

Helbig, Marcia, 146

Helene Dyer Elementary School, 417

Helpfulness, teaching, 46, 294, 313, 386-97. *See also* Social awareness/activism.

Hempfield Area High School, 285

Hentoff, Nat, 172, 310

Heraclitus, 49

Herbert, Victor, 382

"Here's Looking at You," 389

Heritage Heights Elementary School, 26-27, 317

Herron, Elaine, 219-21

Hewlett Foundation, 25, 28

Higgins, Ann, 324

High school. *See* Secondary school.

History curriculum, 167-72; Middle Ages, 177-78

"Hobby time" activity, 199

Hogan, Mary, 199

"Holiday for Heroes, A," 310

Holmes, Virginia, 91, 148, 197-98

Holocaust/Holocaust studies, 25-26, 28-29, 62, 182, 303, 310, 320

Holy Family Primary School, 307

Homer Elementary School, 156

Homework: importance of, 214; strategies for, 223-26; work ethic and, 222-25; values education (parent-child), 403-06

Homosexuality, 20, 363, 369-71

"Honest Boy and the Thief, The," 233-34

Honesty, 7, 20, 21, 54, 59; academic, 57-58, 76-78, 79; teaching, 45-46, 80, 147, 233-34, 252, 327, 402. *See also* Kohlberg.

Honig, Bill, 3

Horace Mann Elementary School, 412

Hostility: cooperative learning and, 185-86; interpersonal, 16, 94-95, 136; racial, 15-16

How Babies Are Made (Andry & Schepp), 372

How to Say No Without Losing His/Her Love, 359

Howard County, Maryland, 275

Huebner, Elaine, 190

"Hugs for health" exercise, 102

Human Life Center, 359

Hunt, Richard M., 303

I

I Hate Mathematics! Book, The (Burns), 190

"I'm important" activity, 103

I'm Not Alone (Limbacher), 263-64

In Good Conscience: Reason and Emotion in Moral Decision Making (Callahan), 52

Ina E. Driscoll School, 193

Incentives, 127-28, 131; guidelines for using, 128; group, 128, 225

Indiana, community service programs, 316

Individualistic learning, 189

Individuality, 9-10, 321-22

Institute for the Advancement of Philosophy for Children, 183

"Integrating Ethics into History" (Nylen), 168

Intellectual freedom, 276-78

Interdependence, 100, 105-08

Interest-centered teaching, 221-22

Intermediate schools. *See* Middle schools.

International Association for the Study of Cooperation in Education, 186

Interviews, student, 199

Investing in Our Children: Business and the Public Schools, 209
Irons, Peter, 172
Ispell, Olan, 385
Ithaca, New York, 75, 125, 145, 153, 221, 259, 292; Ithaca College, 126
"It's Up to Us" (video), 309

J

Japan: competition vs. cooperation, 188-89, 199; conference on moral education, 19; kindness, 396; violence/vandalism in, 13
Jefferson, Thomas, 6
Jellison, Jerald, 12
Jeremiah E. Burke High School, 298
Jewish Foundation for Christian Rescuers, 310
Jeys, Fay, 197
Jigsaw Classroom, The (Aronson), 193
Jigsaw learning, 192-93
Jobs, school, 339-40
Johns Hopkins University, 191
Johnson, Ben, 19
Johnson, David and Roger, 202, 282-84
Johnson Foundation, The, 318
Johnson City, New York, 99
Johnson City, Tennessee, 270
Jones, Barbara, 79
Jones County, Mississippi, 382
Joseph P. Kennedy, Jr., Foundation, 355-56
Josephson Institute of Ethics, 14
Journal of the American Medical Association: school-community anti-drug program, 416-17; on steroids, 377
Journal of Studies on Alcohol, 389
Journals, student, 80, 86-87, 260; ethics journals, 265
Joyce, Mary Roscoe, 359
Judgment, moral, 5, 8, 47, 52, 54, 61, 263-64
Judicious Discipline (Gathercoal), 113
"Just community" school program, 341-42
Justice, 42-45; teaching, 42-43
JustLife, 278

K

Kaminsky, Marty, 292-93
Kansas City, Kansas, 417
Kansas City, Missouri, 71, 417
Kaufman, Samuel, 368
Keeping Track: How Schools Structure Inequality (Oakes), 188
Kellog, Ruth, 405
Kelly, Molly, 374
Kenney, Lorraine, 163
Kent, Tim, 81-83, 272
Kilpatrick, Kirk, 60
Kindness, 54, 59, 396
King Ferry, New York, 179
Kingdom of Darkness (Brennan), 14
Kittle, Kathy, 105, 246-48
Kobrin, Barbara, 344
Kohlberg, Lawrence, 12, 55, 324; dilemma discussion in the classroom, 242-48; "just community" school project, 341-42; moral dilemma, 239-42; stages of moral reasoning, 240-48; "Sharon's dilemma," 243; teacher role and, 245-46
Kramer, Herbert, 79
KTV, Philadelphia, 375
Kuhmerker, Lisa, 174
Kur, Judith, 194-95
Kuralt, Charles, 310

L

La Cueva High School, 285
Ladenburg, Tom, 172
Lakeland Elementary School, 148
Lansing, New York, 90, 145, 204, 308; Elementary School, 148; Middle School, 204
Lauricella, Richard, 148
Lawrence Kohlberg's Approach to Moral Education (Power, Higgins, & Kohlberg), 324, 341
Law, rule of, 92, 114, 230
Law in a Free Society Project, 24-25, 182
Lawrence Elementary School, 92

Lazares, John, 411
Leadership, 24, 28, 214; parents' role, 401-02. *See also* Principal
Learning: difficulties, 34-35; disabilities, 96-97, 218-19, 313-14; partners (paired learning), 189-90; styles, 219-21
Learning About Parenting Program, 403
Lebo, Justin, 311
Lee, Bill, 194
Leman, Kevin, 366
Leong, Mike, 24-25
"Lessons of the Vietnam War, The," 270
"Let's Be Courteous, Let's Be Caring Project," 28
Lewis, C. S., 61
Lewis, Catherine, 199
Life skills, 187
Lilly Endowment, 316
Limbacher, Walter, 263
Lindsley, Ogden, 124
Lions Club International, 204
Lisa (Philosophy for Children), 183
Literature, teaching values and, 60, 174-77
Liverpool, New York, 129, 383
"Living the Constitution," 183
Lockwood, Alan, 170-72
Logical positivism, 8, 230
London, Perry, 23
Long, Kathy, 118
LoParco, Laura, 97-98
Los Angeles, California, 344; CICC parent training services, 403; DARE, 383-84
Lott, Joanne, 209, 215-16
Lotz, Louise, 85, 313
Love, 30-31, 72-80, 102, 368; teaching, 81. *See also* Sex education.
Love, Dating, and Sex (Eager), 365-66
Love Waits, 359
Lying, 5, 13, 47, 77, 252, 375
Lyman, Frank, 190
Lynch, Carol, 254-58, 261

M

Magnetti, Sister Joan, 303, 320
Mahoney, Tracy, 74

Maine-Endwell High School, 116
"Making Ethical Choices," 12-13
Males: behavior problems, 126; cheating in marriage, 13; rape, attitudes on, 5, 55; self-destructive behavior, 19; sexual behavior, 16-17, 349-50, 358, 359-60, 365-66; suicide rate, 19; violence and, 4, 13-14
Mallan, Joline, 102-03
Manring, Peggy, 291
Marblehead High School, 315
Marciano, John, 271
"Mark and the Movies" exercise, 246-48
Marsee, Betty, 82; Sean, 81-82
Martin, Maureen, 164
"Mary's Dilemma" exercise, 248
Mast, Colleen Kelly, 357
Materialism, 5, 17, 19, 21, 50
Matthewson, Donna, 146-47
May, Mark, 7-8
Maynard, Susan, 315
McConnell, Kim, 75, 112-13, 313
McCool, Maggie, 165
McEwan, Barbara, 113
McGinnis, Ellen, 292
McGonagle, Elizabeth, 413-14
McGuffey Reader, 7, 233-35
McPhail, Peter, 72
Media, 5, 12, 49. *See also* Television.
Medlock, Ann, 309
Megan, Colleen, 127-28
Melton, Frank, 310
Memphis, Tennessee, parent training, 402-03
Mentors, teachers as, 72, 84-86, 88
Mercovitch, Cathy, 190
Mercy College, 52
Meredith Magnet Elementary School, 214
Middle schools: class meetings, 144-45; community service programs, 317-18; computer software, 258; debating in, 272; mentoring in, 88; values education, 24, 263-64. *See also* Curriculum; specific schools.
Miller, Gayla, 113
Miller, Harry, 277
Miller, Michael, 321

Missouri/Parents as Teachers Program, 398-99

Mnoonkin, Robert, 359

Modesto, California, 296, 328

Mok, Paul, 63

Moline, Jon, xiii, 44, 263

Mondchein, Eric, 384

Montague, Ashley, 185

Montreal, Canada, 144-45, 185

Moral action, 51, 52-53, 61-62, 68. *See also* Responsibility

Moral authority, 111-12

Moral, Character, and Civic Education in the Elementary School, 347

Moral community. *See* Classroom; Community; Exercises and activities, classroom.

"Moral Crisis, The" (Nicgorski), 49

Moral culture. *See* School.

"Moral Development and Literature" (Garrod & Bramble), 174

Moral dilemma, 238-48

Moral discipline, 68, 110-11; cooperative rule-setting, 112-17; consequences, establishing/enforcing, 117-20; elements of, 131; examples, 126, 127; exercising moral authority, 111-12; goal of, 110; hostile student, 120-21; individual conference, 122-23; involving parents, 128-34; positive incentives, 127-28; profile of teacher, 133; self-control, 124-25; situational supports, 123-24; time-out, 121-22. *See also* Kohlberg.

Moral Education Forum, 174

Moral feeling (emotional side of character), 51, 56-57, 68; conscience, 57-58; empathy, 59; humility, 61; loving the good, 59-60; self-control, 60; self-esteem, 58-59

Moral life/living, 79, 51, 52, 57, 58, 62

Moral knowing (cognitive side of character), 51-53, 68, 229-30; decision-making, 55-56, 230; Kohlberg's moral dilemma/ stages of moral reasoning, 239-48; knowing moral values, 54-55, 56, 229; moral awareness, 53-54, 56, 229; moral reasoning, 55, 56, 229; moral reflection, 70, 201-02, 228-38, 266; perspective-taking,

55, 56, 229; self-knowledge, 56, 230, 264-65

"A Moral Obligation" (Callahan), 278, 280-81

Moral of the Story, The (Parr), 174

Moral relativism, 10-12, 230-31, 235-37, 250, 251-52, 267; classroom case study, 231-32; sex education, 353-54, 362-65, 373

Moral (obligatory) values, 38, 39; ethical tests for, 231; natural moral law, 41-43; respect/responsibility as, 43-45, 230; rights/obligations of, 232; time for, in classroom, 343-47; universal (shared), 38, 231, 236; work ethic, 211-12. *See also* Moral relativism; Values clarification.

Morality, 8, 14, 58; of desire, 60; learning, 10-12, 76-79, 90; new/modern views, 13, 45; prohibitive, 44-45; religion and, 39-43; relationships and, 71; rights and, 45; teaching about, 38, 41, 80, 174-81. *See also* Curriculum; School; Teacher(s); Values education.

Moral Judgment of the Child, The (Piaget), 55

Morals, decline in, 4-5, 8-19, 49, 68, 79

Moravia, New York, 44

Morris, Katy, 385

Morris, Lois, 163, 271-72

Morrow, Lance, 226

Mother Teresa, 18, 306; video, 310-11

Mothers, working, 31, 397-400

Mount Hebron High School, 186

Mountville Elementary School, 317

Movies: parental guidance, 409-10; R-rated, 16, 409-10; resources for supervision, 410

Multicultural education, 180-81

Murder, 4, 13-14, 44

N

Name-calling, 89-90, 100

Narcotics Anonymous, 386

Nathan Clifford Elementary School, 167

National Assessment of Educational Progress, 210

National Association for Mediation in Education, 299

National Association of Secondary School Principals, 392

National Center for Juvenile Justice, 14

National Coalition for the Homeless, 305

National Committee for the Prevention of Child Abuse, 381

National Council for the Social Studies, 25

National Crime Prevention Council, 316

National Institute Against Alcohol Abuse and Alcoholism, 15

National Institute Against Prejudice and Hostility, 15

National Institute on Drug Abuse, 18, 417

National Organization to Prevent Shoplifting, 14

National Peer Helpers Association, 383

National Research Council, 359

National School Boards Association, 25

Nelson, California, 215

Newman, Fred, 320

Newton, Massachusetts, 182, 298

New York City, mayoral commission on drugs, 385

New York State: Bar Association's Law, Youth, and Citizenship program, 384; Board of Regents, AIDS education mandate, 363

New York Times: -CBS poll on abortion, 277-78; Gompers High School article, 382; on moral relativism, 231-32; on Persian Gulf War, discussion in classrooms, 285; on right and wrong, 57; sex education manual article, 369-70; SPCA school programs, 164

New York University, 40

New Yorker, The, 250

Newsweek, 4, 7, 79, 310-11, 363

Nicgorski, Walter, 49, 60

Nickels, Linda, 75, 125-26, 145

1984 and Beyond: A Reaffirmation of Values, 424

No Is a Love Word, 359

"No TV for a Week" activity, 408

Nocula, Josine, 332-33

Noonan, John, 276

Noonewaug High School, 307

North Kansas, Missouri, 285

Notre Dame High School for Girls, 307

Novak, Michael, 50

Nozick, Robert, 57

Nucci, Larry, 41-42

Nuts and Bolts: A Survival Guide for Teachers (Christopher), 216

Nylen, Carol, 167-70, 417-18

O

Oakes, Jeanie, 188

Office of Adolescent Pregnancy Programs, 357

Ohio University, Institute for Democracy in Education, 161

Olbrycht, Lincoln, 196

Older Friends for Younger Children, 315

Olean, New York, 396

On the Road with Charles Kuralt (Kuralt), 310

One is One (Picard), 177-78

One on One: A Middle School Advisory System, 88

Ontario, 324-25; children and alcohol, 19; Ministry of Education *Personal and Societal Values* guide, 47, 252; PREPARE, 25, 182, 289, 338

Oral history project, 178-79

Oxfam America, 202, 306-07, 313, 397

P

Page, Jan, 296

Pardo, Winnie, 318

Pardoen, Alan, 37

Parents/parenting, 14, 20, 21, 23, 30, 50; community and, 70; drug/alcohol abuse, 380-81, 390; education, 390, 391, 402-03; guidelines for school partnership, 418; inadequate, 4, 24, 32-35, 209, 396; lack of supervision, 33-34; leadership role, 401-02; national campaign for parental involvement, 396-97; networking, 413; parent/child relationship, 33-34, 78; permissive, 30, 395, 410; program for, 25; as role model, 20-21, 30-31, 33, 70; Safe Homes program, 391; and schools, 26-27, 34-36, 37, 47, 128-34, 395, 398-99, 411; sex education and, 358, 360, 362, 371-72; support groups, 36, 413-14; and teachers, 75, 170; as teachers, 30, 47, 398-99, 400-13; value conflict with school, 34-35, 417-18; volunteers in schools, 182

Parents as Teachers Program (PAT), 398-99

Parr, Susan Resneck, 174

"Partner buzz" exercise, 156

"Partners" exercise, 91, 92

Pascal, Blaise, 61

Passalugo, Mr., 76

Patience, as target value, 47

Patriotism, 7; as target value, 46-47

Peace, 21, 43; as target value, 47

Peck, Scott, 61

Peer: abuse, 90, 96-99; acceptance, 94-95, 99-102; anti-work ethic of, 209-10, 212-13; counseling, 382-83; cruelty, 15, 55-56, 89-91, 96-99; drug use/drug prevention, 380, 382-83, 385, 387-89; helpfulness, 106; hostility among, 94-96, 99-101; ostracism/rejection, 90, 96-99, 291; pressure, 25, 33, 59, 83, 109, 261-62; support, 219, 263; tutoring, 60, 314-15. *See also* Cooperative learning.

People for the American Way, 40

"People hunt" exercise, 91-92

People of the Lie: The Hope for Healing Human Evil (Peck), 61

Peredo, Christine, 122-23

Perricone, John, 116-17

Persian Gulf War, 285

Personal and Societal Values guide, 252

Personalism, 9-12, 230, 235

Perspective-taking, 55, 56, 229

Peters, Sylvia, 330

Philosophy for Children program, 183

Phoenix, Arizona, 306

Piaget, Jean, 55, 135

Picard, Barbara Leonie, 177

Pierce Elementary School, 91

Pikesville High School, 401-02

Pittsburgh, Pennsylvania, 182, 285, 374

Place Called School, A (Goodlad), 226

Plagiarism, 79. *See also* Cheating.

Playground behavior/programs, 29, 333

Plato, 6

Pledge of Allegiance, 208

Plug-Lok, 408

Pontiac, Michigan, 170

Portland, Maine, 166-67

Positive Bus Program, 26-27

"Positive word power" exercise, 99-101

Postponing Sexual Involvement Program, 355

Power, Clark, 324, 342

Practicing Judicious Discipline: An Educator's Guide to a Democratic Classroom (McEwan), 113

Pregnancy, teenage, 16, 18, 19, 349-50, 364-65; boys and, 359-60; values education for, 27, 30, 356-59, 373-74. *See also* Sex education.

Prejudice, 15-16, 26, 60, 96, 180

PREPARE, 25, 182, 289, 338

Preparing Adolescents for Tomorrow, 25

PREVIEW: Movie Morality Guide, 410

Princeton, New Jersey, 320

Principal: discipline and, 331-32; leadership of, 325-26, 335, 345; power of personal example, 328-30; profile of, 325-28; staff relationships and, 342-43; television viewing and, 408; visibility of, 330-31

Probe questions, 245-48, 252-53

Problem-solving: class meetings and, 143-47, 288, 289, 292-94; in classroom, 85-86, 123, 289-91, 295, 296-99; skills, 29, 105-07, 288, 291-92. *See also* Conflict resolution.

"Profile of High School Community Service Programs, A" (Newman & Rutter), 316

Programs for values education, 24-30; *Amigo* Program, 328; Child Development Project (CDP), 25-26, 28-30, 112, 206,

Programs for values education (*continued*)
314-15, 400-401, 402; Community of
Caring programs, 355-56; community
service programs, 24, 28, 60, 70, 312-18;
DARE (Drug Abuse Resistance Education), 383-84; Decision-Making: Keys to
Total Success, 356-57; Facing History
and Ourselves, 26, 28-29, 182, 320, 321;
Great Expectations, 412; "Let's Be Cour-
teous, Let's Be Caring Project," 28; needs
of, 226-27; for parental separation or
loss, 413-14; Parents as Teachers Pro-
gram (PAT), 398-99; Positive Bus Pro-
gram, 26-27; Postponing Sexual
Involvement, 355; PREPARE, 25, 182,
289, 338; Preparing Adolescents for To-
morrow, 25; Project Respect, 356; SEX
RESPECT, 357-59'; Teen-Aid, 357; Teen
Fathers Program, 359-60; Value of the
Month program, 327-28
Project Respect, 356
Prothrow-Stith, Deborah, 298
Public Interest, The, 235
Purnell, Dick, 365, 366
Purpel, David, 342
Purpose for Living, 311
Psychology Today, 12-13

Q

"Quality School, The" (Glasser), 208
Quebec, 312; teacher/parent involvement,
129
Quest International, 204
"Quest" program, 204
Questionnaires: on Academic Attitudes and
Behavior, 57-58; "Making Ethical
Choices," 12-13; parents on curriculum,
405-06

R

Race issues/racism, 14, 15-16, 180, 185,
192-93, 209, 320
Rainbows for All God's Children, Inc., 414

Raising Good Children (Lickona), 241
Raising PG Kids in an X-Rated Society
(Gore), 410
Ramona the Pest (Cleary), 175-77
Rancho Romero Elementary School, 91,
123, 206, 402
Rapport, building, 75
Raths, Louis, 10
Reader's Digest, 81, 83
Reading partners, 186
Reading, Massachusetts, 24, 84, 140, 266,
419
Reason/Reasoning skills, 12, 25, 28, 30-31,
55-56, 62, 76, 79, 98, 118; Kohlberg's
stages, 239-48; and natural moral law,
42; religious beliefs and, 41; *See also*
Moral knowing.
*Reasoning with Democratic Values: Ethical
Problems in United States History* (Lock-
wood & Harris), 170
Recommended Movies on Video, 410
Reece, Colleen, 393
Reflection, moral, 201-02, 228-29; guidelines for teaching, 266; Kohlberg's moral
dilemma/stages of moral reasoning, 239-
48, 250-51; need for, 229-230; vs. moral
relativism, 23-32, 267; teaching of, 70,
253, 249-267; values clarification and,
235-39; values, obligatory, and, 232-35
Reilly Elementary School, 218, 265, 328-30,
332-33
Reitman, Jade, 339
Relationships, 15, 25, 43-45, 55, 71; family, 33-34; helping, 25; one-to-one, to
promote caring, 313-15, 317; parent-
child, 30-31, 33-34, 78; student-teacher,
71-76, 79, 83-86, 90. *See also* Family;
Peers.
Religion, 13, 20; American culture and, 39-
40; exclusion from schools/texts, 40-41;
and morality, 39-43, 50, 397; sex education and, 368-69
"Remembering" exercise, 155
*Rescuers of Jews During the Holocaust:
Programs and Resources*, 310
Research and Forecasts, Inc., 79

Respect, 26-27; for animals, 163-66; for children, 74-75; defined, 41, 67; in relationships, 43-45, 90-91, 97; teaching, 41-42, 47, 49, 67, 96, 162

Responsibility, 9, 24, 25, 26, 30, 33, 43-45, 54, 59; for animals, 163-66; civic, 17-18; classroom, 95-96, 104-08, 110; conflict resolution, 289, 286-97; defined, 44, 68; social activism, 312-22; teaching, 44-45, 47, 49, 67-68, 162

Rest, James, 55

R. H. Watkins High School, 382-83

Rhode Island, 163; Rape Crisis Center, 5

Rights, 9, 45, 92; animal, 165-66; civil, 15, 176; human, 13, 39, 90

Rippowam-Cisqua School, 93, 197, 337-38, 247

Ritter, Anna, 214

Riverdale, New York, 163, 173, 217, 261

Roberts Street Elementary School, 254

Robinson, Gary, 120-21

Role models, moral, 308-12

Role-playing: conflict resolution, 292-93; critical thinking, 270; developing competence, 62; moral decision making, 261-62; with puppets, 293

Roosevelt, Theodore, 3

Rose, Bill, 72-73

Rossi, Muriel, 159-60

Roubos, Anne, 156

Rules, 5, 25, 104-05, 237; classroom, 112, 151-52, 215; cooperative approach to making, 112-15, 137; for cooperative attitudes and skills, 284; drug/alcohol use in school, 381; establishing/enforcing consequences, 117-34, 153, 331-34; moral discipline, 110; in secondary-level classrooms, 115-17

Rutter, Michael, 331

Ryan, Kevin, 22, 59-60

S

Saenger, Elizabeth, 174-77, 261, 262-63, 265, 272-73

Salem-Marblehead, Massachusetts, 315

Sample, Steven, 396

San Marcos Junior High School, 27, 58, 356-57

San Ramon, California, 25, 28-30, 75, 83, 91, 112, 123, 145, 196, 202, 206, 313, 336, 400

Sarnecki, James, 5

Satanism, 14

Saterlie, Mary Ellen, 414, 415-16

Saunders, Stacey, 135

Scarborough Village Public School, 27-28, 338-39

Scarborough, Ontario, 27-28, 74, 101, 186, 313, 331; Board of Education, 201

Schaps, Eric, 400-01

Schepp, Steven, 372

Schickel, Trina, 182

School, 23-24; academic expectations, 212-16; assemblies, 338-39; community service in, 313, 316-18; concept of character, 49-51; drop-outs, 212; drug/alcohol prevention, 381-85, 387, 389-91; effective, characteristics of, 214; examples/successful values education programs, 24-27; family involvement in, 35-36, 395-98; as family resource center, 399-400; "four and fifth R," teaching of respect/responsibility, 43-45, 67-68; guidelines for parent-community-school cooperation, 418; guidelines (schoolwide) for teaching controversial issues, 276, 277; lack of parental support for, 34-35; moral community, 22, 63, 89-108, 334-36, 342-43; moral culture, 323-25, 346-47; religion excluded from, 40-41; spirit, 24, 94, 102-03, 197; TV viewing/critical watching, 408-09; value conflict with parents, 34-35, 417-18; values, teaching of, 3, 20, 21, 22, 37-38, 43-48, 63, 67-68. *See also* Classroom; Curriculum; Discipline; Principal; School government; Teacher(s); Values education.

School bus, morality on, 333-34; bus buddies, 334; Positive Bus Program, 26-27

School government/student council, 329, 332, 340-42; resource materials, 347
"School of the Twenty-first Century," 399-400
Schools Without Drugs, 381
Schuck, Ron, 179-80
Schuster, Charles, 417
Science: controversial issues in, 273-75; curriculum pressure, 344; "Ethical Issues for Debate in Science Education," 274-75; ethical issues in teaching, 161-66; Family Science Fair, 402
Science Hill School, 270
Scotia, New York, 330, 404
Scotia-Glenville Central Schools, 404-06
"Seat lottery" activity, 94
Second Chances: Men and Women, and Children a Decade After Divorce (Wallerstein), 32
Second Thoughts (film), 358
Secondary schools: academic achievement, 210; class meetings, 143-44; computer software, 258; conflict resolution and, 298-99; debate, 272-73; discussion leading, 251-54; ethics course, 82-83, 258; expectations of students, 215; feedback form, 148-49; guest speakers, 179-80; Learning About Parenting Program, 403; moral community, 94-96, 103, 135-36; moral culture, 323-24, 341-42; published curricula, 182-83; rule-setting, 113-17; social activism/community service, 306-07, 313, 315, 316, 319-20, 321; student input, 148-50; values education, 24, 27-29. *See also* Curriculum; Sex education; specific schools.
Secondary Virginity: A New Beginning, 359
Self-awareness, developing, 124-25
Self-centeredness/selfishness, 9-10, 12, 17-18, 19, 50, 322
Self-control, 25, 50, 60, 61, 121-25, 176, 265, 392-93
Self-discipline: character and, 54, 211-12; teaching as moral value, 46; *See also* Conscience of craft
Self-esteem, 25, 58-59, 61, 72, 74, 85, 109, 127, 139, 163, 187, 206, 211, 216, 222, 290, 318, 383-84, 401
Self-evaluation, 212; skills of, 216
Self-indulgence, 60, 237
Self-knowledge, 56, 229, 264-66
Self-respect, 43-44, 46, 59, 77
"Sentence starters," 155-56
Serrio, Dee, 26-27
"Sex and School Reform" (Cuban), 353
Sex education, 348-49; marriage approach, 360-61; contraception issue, 362-65; emotional risks of sex, 364, 365-68; guidelines, 367; homosexuality, 369-71; masturbation, 369; materials/pamphlets, 357, 359, 365, 371, 372; pro-abstinence approach, 354-59; programs, 353-60; religion and, 368-69; teaching sexual responsibility, 352; what hasn't worked, 353-54
SEX RESPECT, 357-59
Sexual behavior, 5, 10, 13, 16-17, 18, 19, 41, 60; abuse, 16-17, 75, 350-52, 381; contraception, 349; current patterns of, 349-50; flashbacks, 366, 368; movies, 409-10; pornography, 350, 409; precocity/premature, 16-17, 18, 349-50; promiscuity, 32, 366; roots of the problem, 350-52; television and, 407
Sexually Transmitted Disease (STD), 18, 349-50, 354; drug use and, 377
Shaheen, JoAnne, 296-97, 340-41
"Sharon's Dilemma," 242-45
Shoplifting, 11, 25, 76, 183, 242-45, 339
Shoreham, New York, 88, 317-18
Shoreham-Wading River Middle School, 88, 318
Short, Joseph, 307
Shriver, Eunice Kennedy, 348
"Silver Sisters, The" exercise, 264
Singer, Isaac Beshevis, 40
Single-parent families, 31, 32-33, 349-50, 402
Situation specific: behavior, 8, 58, 63; morality, 250
Six Pack and a Fake I.D., A (Cohen & Cohen), 392

Skaneateles, New York, 94, 120, 135, 291
Skillstreaming the Elementary School Child (McGinnis & Goldstein), 292
Skill training, structured, 288, 291-92; "moral coaching," 291
Skills for Working Together checklist, 199
Skon, Linda, 203
Slavin, Robert, 191
Small-group projects, 194, 341
S.M.A.R.T., 258
Smith, Karen, 186
Smith-Hansen, Phyllis, 90, 145, 204-06, 308-09
Smoking, 4, 50, 82
"Snapshot" activity, 92
Snuff, 81-83
"So Much Unfairness of Things" (Bryan), 250
Social awareness/activism: academic credit for, 316; activities, 306-08, 309-11, 313-15, 317-18; class buddies, 313-14; community service, 312-13, 315-18; cross-age tutoring, 314-15; developing in students, 304-05; guidelines, 319; older friends for younger children, 315; resources, 307, 308, 309-11, 316, 318, 321; role models for, 308-12; social justice, 318-22
Socratic teaching style, 245-48, 251-58, 267
"So Long Wonder Years," 4
Social studies curriculum, 25-26, 28-29, 40, 170-72
"Socially Responsible Science Education" (Gefell), 273-75
Society for the Prevention of Cruelty to Animals (SPCA), 164
Sojourner, 163
Sojourners, 278
Solway, New York, 148
Sommer, Peter, 178-79
Songs to foster community, 102, 150
South Bronx, New York, 341-42, 381-82
South Portland, Maine, 417
South School, 317, 339
Southern Teacher Education Center, 190
Special education, 292, 336-37
Spelling test activity, 193

Spencer, New York, 190
Sports/sportsmanship, 237-38; rating sheet, 338; steroid use, 377, 394
St. Cloud, Minnesota, 317
St. Louis, 419; high school student service, 24, 316; Teen Outreach program, 373-74
St. Patrick's Elementary School, 102
St. Paul, Minnesota, 412
Stanford University, 353
Stanley Foundation, 310
Starr, Jerold, 268, 270
Starratt, Robert, 319-20
STASIS Conflict Management Consultants, 295
Staub, Ervin, 62
State Street Elementary School, 94, 135
State University College at Buffalo, 403
State University of New York: Cortland, 133; Potsdam, 37
Stealing, 4, 41-42, 90, 76, 146-47, 153, 323
Stein, Benjamin, 407
Stenson, James, 50
Stevenson, Harold, 210
Stinson, Kathy, 208-09
Stoddart, Marion, 310
Storytelling, as moral teaching, 79-83
"Structured academic controversy" approach, 282-84; benefits of, 284; rules for, 284
Stuart Country Day School, 320
Student Council, 329, 332, 340-42
"Student of the week" activity, 104
Success: activities, 73; programs to foster, 218-19; self-esteem and, 59, 72, 137, 218-19
Suffering: desire to alleviate, 45; detachment from, 59
Suggestion box, 142, 147-48
Suicide, 19, 25, 188, 378, 388
Sullivan Elementary School, 419
Summit School, 413
Sweet Home Middle School, 26
Sweet Home School District, 26, 317, 393
Syracuse, New York, 105, 146, 377
Syracuse University, 213

T

Taffs, Audrey, 218-19
Talking Part, 183
"Talk ticket," 154
Target values, list, 47-48
"Teachable Moments," 310
Teacher(s): as caregiver, 68, 72-75, 152-55; -child conference, 80, 166; corrective feedback by, 85-86; discipline and, 331-32; as discussion leader, 245-48, 250-54, 271-72; drug use, 380; ethical thinking, 230-33; expectations, 214-16; guidelines for, 80; handling "wrong" answers, 73-74; impartiality vs. position-taking, 271-72; interventions, 104, 295; limits of, 87-88; love and respect for students, 72-75, 102, 111; as mentor, 68, 72, 80, 84-86, 88; as moral authority, 111-12; moral education and, 21-22, 23, 41, 47; parents, involving, 128-34, 271-72; pedagogy of, 226-27; rapport building, 75; relativistic approach, 232-33, 235-37; respect, teaching, 44, 67-68, 72-75, 96; responsibility, teaching, 44-45, 67-68; right and wrong, teaching, 60, 76-77; roles, 10-11, 67-70, 162, 201, 285; role model, 7, 68, 72, 76, 80, 117; in sex education, 372-73; staff/principal relationships, 342-43; stopping cruelty to "different" child, 96-99; -student relationships, 72, 77, 79, 83-86, 90; student self-esteem/success, 59, 72, 137, 218-19; tasks for, in conflict resolution, 294–95. *See also* Cheating; Conflict resolution; Cooperative learning; Curriculum; Discipline; Homework; Moral discipline; Moral knowing; Rules; School; Teaching strategies; Values clarification; Values education.
Teacher Magazine, 165
Teaching Morality to Kids, 204
Teaching strategies, 172-81; conflict resolution, 288-89, 297; guidelines, 180; learning styles, 219-221; students' interests and, 221-222

Teaching the Vietnam War (Griffen & Marciano), 271
Team: competition, 196; learning, 191-92; testing, 193-94
Teen-Aid program, 357
Teen Fathers Program, 359-60
Television, 19; guidelines for parents, 408-09; hours of viewing, 5, 406; Plug-Lok, 408; schools and critical viewing, 408-09; sex and violence on, 5, 16, 372, 407, 409; TV Turn-Off Kit, 408
Telling Right from Wrong, 57
Tellsworth, Ruby, 91, 123, 206-07
Temple, Texas, 214
Testing: homework-based quizzes, 223-24; standardized, 344-45; Team, 193-94
Texas A&M study of inhalent abuse, 377
Textbooks, ethical policies and, 163
Thain, Richard, 227
Tharpe, Peggy, 419
Theodore Roosevelt High School, 341-42
"Things I Love to Do" (values clarification exercise), 236-37
"Thinking chair," 146
Thinking magazine, 183
"Think-pair-share" activity, 190
"This was the week when . . ." chart, 145
Thomas Jefferson Research Center, 183
Thoreau, Henry David, 227
Thornley, Joel, 185
Thunder Bay, Ontario, 84, 216
Tilkin, Ro, 97
T.I.M.E. (Tots' Intensive Multidisciplinary Environment), 218-19
Time magazine, 15, 410
Time-out, 121-22
To Tell the Truth (film), 259-60
Tocqueville, Alexis de, 321-22
Together We Learn (Clarke), 201
Tom Snyder Productions, 258
Tracking, 188
"Training Children as Conflict Managers," 296
Transou, Carol, 270-71
"Treasure bag" activity, 93

Trowbridge, Ronald, 60
Trumansburg Middle School, New York, 113
Truxton Elementary School, 215
Tully Elementary School, 216
Tutoring, 60; cross-age, 314-15
TV Turn-Off Kit, 408

U

Understanding Handicaps program, 182
United Nations: report on premature sexuality, 18; Universal Declaration of Human Rights, 38
United States: academic achievement, 210; character and society, 49-50; citizenship, declining interest, 303-04; democratic process, 140; federal support of values education, 21, 397-98; impact of moral decline, 5, 12-19, 49, 68; poverty in, 305
U.S. Bureau of Labor Statistics, 399
U.S. Census, 303
U.S. Constitution, 39, 40, 41, 73, 113, 114, 171-72, 173, 251-52, 368; "Living the Constitution," 183
U.S. Department of Education, 25, 210, 330, 355, 371, 376, 381
U.S. Department of Health and Human Services, 18, 19, 358
"Use of Stories in Moral Development, The" (Vitz), 81
University of California: at Berkeley, 31; at Los Angeles, Higher Education Research Institute, 17; at San Francisco, 377
University of Chicago Graduate School, 227
University of Illinois, 41; at Chicago, 215
University of Miami (Ohio), 368; Medical School, 363
University of Michigan, 170, 210; cocaine use study, 18
University of Minnesota Cooperative Learning Center, 202
University of New Hampshire, 351
University of Notre Dame, 60
University of Southern California, 12, 396

University of Steubenville, 359
University of Texas at Austin, 326
University of Wisconsin, 297, 320
Upper Dublin High School, 72-73

V

Valentine, Bill, 263-64
Valentine, Mary, 219
"Value Clarity, High Morality; Let's Go for Both" (Harmin), 237
Value-free education, 20-21
Values education, 3-5, 10, 15, 19; action plan to start/maintain, 421-24; case for, 12-22; history of, 6-12; impact of, in schools implementing, 27-30, 182, 195; moral community and, 77, 89-108; challenges of, 58; goals of, 6-7, 55, 59, 67; government support needed, 397-98; parents as partners in, 400-13; in religiously diverse society, 39-43; school programs using, 24-27, 101, 166-67, 173-80, 182, 275, 326-28, 330; specific values to teach, 37-38, 43-48, 63; success story (Baltimore County), 415-16; support for, 21, 37, 345, 395; time for, in classrooms, 343-47; textbook policies and, 163. *See also* Class meeting; Conscience of craft; Curriculum; Moral discipline; Moral value; School; Sex education; Teachers.
Values and Teaching (Raths), 10, 235, 237
Values Education Centre, 27
Values clarification, 10-12, 96, 235-39; bad values of students, how to handle, 250-51; "value sheets," 238-39
Values Clarification: A Handbook of Practical Strategies for Teachers and Students (Simon et al), 10
Values Education Centre, 27
Values Education Council, 26
Values Tales, 235
Van Slyke, Bill, 259-61
Varenne, Herve, 102
Vatnick, Itzick, 102

Vietnam, 9; "Lessons of the Vietnam War, The," 270; teaching about, 269-71; *Teaching the Vietnam War* (Griffen & Marciano), 271

Violence, 4, 5, 13-16, 90, 96, 287; conflict resolution and, 287; lack of empathy, 59; prevention program, 298

Virginia sex education mandate, 360-61

Vitz, Paul, 40, 81

W

Wade, Richard, 337-38

"Walk a Mile" (songs), 102

Wallerstein, Judith, 31-32

Walt Disney Elementary School, 75, 85, 112, 202, 313

Walters, Karen, 103-04

Walzer, Michael, 107

Warwick, Rhode Island, 163

Washington, D.C., 165

Washington, George, 40

Watergate, 9, 228

Watson, Marilyn, 187

"We Are the World" assembly project, 181

Weedsport Elementary School, 103

Weekly Reader: drug/alcohol surveys, 377, 379-80; television viewing surveys, 406

West Frankfort Elementary School, 118

Westport, Connecticut, 253

Westwood Elementary School, 317

"Why Johnny Can't Abstain" (Bennett), 348

Why Wait? (Video), 357

Wilcox, Debbie, 99, 136-38

Wilson, Cathy, 193

Wilson, Christie, 385

Wilson High School, 358

Wilson Junior High School, 411

Wilson, Woodrow, 170-72

Wilton, Connecticut, 193

Window to the Womb (Video), 357

Wingspread: Principles of Good Practice for Combining Service and Learning, 318

Winkelman Elementary School, 28, 127, 134-36

Winkelgrams, 335-36

"Winning" curriculum unit, 338

Winston Education Center, 165-66

Winston-Salem, North Carolina, 413

Wisconsin, Department of Public Instruction, 398

"Woman Behind the Fetus, The" (Ehrenreich), 278-80

Womanity, 359

Woodbury, Connecticut, 307

Woodmancy, Neil, 105, 150-51

Woods, Ron, 266-67, 419

Woodstown High School, 165

Work ethic, 208; anti-work peer pressure, 209-10; goal-setting, 211-12; homework, 222-25; moral importance of, 8, 211; objectives, 213; teaching, 226-27

Workaholism, 227

Writing: behavior improvement plan, 122-23, 124; classroom behavior and, 136; conflict resolution activity, 296-97; debate follow-up, 273; in values curriculum, 86-87; questions for student, on abortion, 281; social activism activity, 312

Wynne, Ed, 215

Y

Yale Alumni Magazine, 12

Yale University: Center in Child Development and Social Policy, 399-400; Family Television Research Center, 406; Hartshorne and May study, 7-8; racism at, 15

Year of the Family in Education, The, 398

Z

Zigler, Edward, 399-400

Zimmerman, Mary, 26

Zoo, classroom, 162-63

About the Author

Dr. Thomas Lickona, a developmental psychologist and educator, is an internationally respected authority on moral development and values education. He is Professor of Education at the State University of New York at Cortland, where he has done award-winning work in teacher education and currently chairs the Teachers for the 21st Century project. A past president of the Association for Moral Education, he has also held teaching appointments at Boston and Harvard Universities and is a frequent speaker at conferences and workshops for teachers, parents, religious educators, and other groups concerned about the values and character of young people. He has lectured in the United States, Canada, Japan, Ireland, Switzerland, and Latin America.

Dr. Lickona's twenty years of work in teacher and parent education include consultation to schools across the country on the implementation of values and character education. He holds a Ph.D. in psychology from the State University of New York at Albany and has done research on the growth of children's moral understanding. His text *Moral Development and Behavior* is widely used in graduate study and his book *Raising Good Children* (with more than 150,000 copies in print) has been praised for translating the research on moral development into the language and experience of parents. He has been a guest on numerous radio and television talk shows, including *Good Morning America*, *Larry King Live*, and *Latenight America*. In 1984 he was named a State University of New York Exchange Scholar.

Dr. Lickona and his wife have two sons, one in graduate school and another in college, and live in Cortland, New York.